MW01055964

HOLLYWOOD ITALIANS

ALSO BY PETER BONDANELLA

Italian Cinema: From Neorealism to the Present

Machiavelli and the Art of Renaissance History

Francesco Guicciardini

Federico Fellini: Essays and Criticism

The Macmillan Dictionary of Italian Literature

The Eternal City: Roman Images in the Modern World

The Cinema of Federico Fellini

The Films of Roberto Rossellini

The Cassell Dictionary of Italian Literature

Umberto Eco and the Open Text: Semiotics, Fiction, Popular Culture

The Films of Federico Fellini

The Cambridge Companion to the Italian Novel

HOLLYWOOD ITALIANS

Dagos, Palookas, Romeos, Wise Guys, and Sopranos

Peter Bondanella

continuum
NEW YORK • LONDON

FORDHAM
UNIVERSITY
LIBRARY

MARYMOUNT
CAMPUS

2004

The Continuum International Publishing Group Inc
15 East 26 Street, New York NY 10010

The Continuum International Publishing Group Ltd
The Tower Building, 11 York Road, London SE1 7NX

Copyright © 2004 by Peter Bondanella

All rights reserved. No part of this book may be reproduced, stored in a
retrieval system, or transmitted, in any form or by any means, electronic,
mechanical, photocopying, recording, or otherwise, without the written
permission of the publishers.

Printed in the United States of America

Library of Congress Cataloging in Publication Data

Bondanella, Peter E., 1943–
   Hollywood Italians : dagos, palookas, romeos, wise guys, and Sopranos /
Peter Bondanella.
        p.   cm.
   Includes bibliographical references and index.
   ISBN 0-8264-1544-X (alk. paper)
   1. Italian Americans in motion pictures.   2. Italian Americans in the
motion picture industry.   I. Title.
PN1995.9.I73B66 2004
791.43'089'51073—dc22
                                                           2003020663

Unless otherwise indicated, all photographs and stills are courtesy the
British Film Institute Film Stills Archive (London).

Dedication

For Murray Abraham, Frank Adonis, Danny Aiello, Alan Alda, Don Ameche, Armand Assante, Frankie Avalon, Michael Badalucco, Ann Bancroft, Jon Bon Jovi, Ernest Borgnine, Elizabeth Bracco, Lorraine Bracco, Steve Buscemi, Nicolas Cage, Pasquale Caiano, Joseph Calleia, Frank Capra, Edward Carfagno, David Caruso, Richard Castellano, Federico Casteluccio, John Cazale, Feodor Chaliapin, David Chase, Eduardo Ciannelli, Michael Cimino, Nicholas Colasanto, Richard Conte, Francis Ford Coppola, Lou Costello, Richard Crena, Vincent Curatola, Bobby Darin, Cesare Danova, Joe Dante, Dom Deluise, Drea de Matteo, Robert De Niro, Brian De Palma, Danny De-Vito, Leonardo Di Caprio, Frank DiLeo, Vincent D'Onofrio, Jimmy Durante, Giancarlo Esposito, Jennifer Esposito, Edie Falco, Abel Ferrara, John Fiore, Anthony Franciosa, Connie Francis, Annette Funicello, James Gandolfini, Vincent Gardenia, Ben Gazzara, Michael Gazzo, Harry Guardino, Michael Imperioli, Gregory La Cava, Frank Langella, Anthony La Paglia, John Leguizamo, Tea Leoni, Ray Liotta, Robert Loggia, John Luisi, Ralph Macchio, Madonna Louise Veronica Ciccone, Henry Mancini, Frank Mancuso, Joe Mantegna, Gerry Marshall, Penny Marshall, Dean Martin, Al Martino, Mary Elizabeth Mastrantonio, Gina Mastrogiacomo, Victor Mature, Sal Mineo, Lisa Minnelli, Vincent Minnelli, Tony Musante, Katherine Narducci, Fred Niblo, Al Pacino, Chazz Palminteri, Joe Pantoliano, Vincent Pastore, Joe Pesci, Nicholas Pileggi, Joe Piscopo, Paula Prentiss, Louis Prima, Mario Puzo, George Raft, Aldo Ray, Michael Rispoli, Richard Romanus, Michael Santoro, Al Sapienza, Nancy Savoca, John Saxon, Stephen Schirripa, Annabella Sciorra, Catherine Scorsese, Martin Scorsese, Steven Seagal, Talia Shire, Tony Sirico, Frank Sinatra, Frank Sivero, Mira Sorvino, Vincent Spano, Joe Spinell, Sylvester Stallone, Connie Stevens, Quentin Tarantino, Marisa Tomei, John Travolta, Stanley Tucci, Aida Turturro, John Turturro, Nicholas Turturro, Brenda Vaccaro, Jack Valenti, Rudolph Valentino, Steven Van Zandt, Vinny Velca, John Ventimiglia, Frank Vincent, and Burt Young. My apologies to any other Hollywood Italians I might have omitted.

Contents

Introduction

"E pluribus unum"

        Latin motto on the Great Seal of the United States

"I am not Italian. I was born in Brooklyn."

        Statement attributed to Al Capone[1]

"Everyone is Italian!"

        Television advertisement for Fazoli's,
the fast-food chain serving "Italian" food

For the better part of four decades, I have dedicated my professional life to the study of issues associated with the highbrow culture of medieval, Renaissance, and contemporary Italy. Boccaccio, Machiavelli, Guicciardini, Cellini, Titian, Rossellini, Fellini are the names associated with my scholarship or my translations, and even though I have strayed from my original training in literature and political thought by devoting a good deal of time to Italian cinema, I have always been committed to figures and topics that are far removed from ethnic studies. My interest in Italian culture, however, has never been motivated by any desire to recover an Italian heritage lost through emigration to America. Although I have a vaguely Italian name (one that may have been spelled differently when my paternal grandfather arrived in this country from Sicily) and now teach in a graduate doctoral program offering advanced university degrees in Italian, my early ethnic, religious, and regional background was resolutely Scottish, Presbyterian, and Southern. When I attended what was then a staunchly Calvinist institution, Davidson College offered only one year of Italian upon demand when a professor of Spanish, Donald Tucker, could free himself to teach the course. From that wonderful language instructor, I was able to take only an intensive Spanish course the summer before I spent my junior year abroad in France, not Italy. Almost as an afterthought, I spent my second European summer living for several months with an Italian family in Rome and trying to teach myself Italian grammar with no more than a tattered copy of Speroni and Golino's *Basic Italian* as my guide. I lived in a Liberty building on the Tiber River, about as far from the Sicilian countryside of my father's ancestors as one could get. Only at the University of Oregon in a Comparative Literature Program did I begin the serious study of Italian language and literature, inspired not by my ethnic background but by my interest in political theory, Machiavelli, and the Renaissance. My efforts to do so were encouraged by two generous and humane professors, Chandler Beall and Emmanuel Hatzantonis, both of whom provided models of Italianate erudition that have always remained to inspire me. When I am asked by Italians in Italy where my grandfather lived in Sicily, I always reply "Corleone" in order to watch the momentary and embarrassed astonishment on their faces. Thus, what ethnic roots I profess from Sicily are those I learned about from the movies—strictly Hollywood Italian origins, not authentically Italian American ones.

I outline my background to emphasize that *Hollywood Italians* can make no experiential claims to a personal knowledge of the Italian American experience. And, as I said earlier, it is not motivated by a search for my ethnic "roots," but rather by my work—a number of books and articles on Italian cinema—the cinema shot at Cinecittà in Rome rather than on the lots and studios of Hollywood. After years of examining how Italians represented themselves in their own national cinema, it seemed logical and appropriate to take a look at how Americans, some of them Italian Americans, represent the same group of people after they are transported to another culture and another country or, subsequently, after they grow up in that other culture and country. Curiosity and an admiration for a variety of these films motivated this choice, not a search for personal identity.

The subtitle of the book (*Dagos, Palookas, Romeos, Wise Guys, and Sopranos*) makes it obvious that some of the images discussed are ethnic or racial stereotypes. The high-water mark of Italian emigration to America coincides roughly with the rise of the cinema industry in America, and the evolution of Hollywood Italian images reflects, to some extent, the ethnic prejudice against this particular ethnic or minority group. As many historians and sociologists have noted, Italians in this country were not initially considered Caucasian and were despised as even lower forms of humanity than their ill-treated black compatriots. Nonetheless, as true as such historical facts may be, they are insufficient grounds, in my opinion, to justify a serious examination of Hollywood Italians in the American cinema. Only Hollywood's interesting and cinematically significant representations of Italians throughout the history of American film art can do that.

The history of Hollywood Italians seems to follow a course all its own. Although regrettable examples of ethnic prejudice may still occur at the expense of individual Americans of Italian descent, America has fallen in love with all things Italian. No longer the country where starving civilians pleaded for surplus Hershey bars from victorious American liberators, Americans now identify Italy with high-fashion products delivered by Armani, Ferragamo, Missoni, Prada, Zegna, and many other recognizably peninsular brand names, not with the scrubby, dirty, and illiterate day laborers, organ grinders, and shoeblacks of the beginning of the last century who were once so frequently depicted and disparaged in the popular imagination. People who once laughed at my father's family as "spaghetti benders" now argue about the merits of Super Tuscan vintages, balsamic vinegar from Modena, and make their own *pesto* or *pasta fresca*. Nothing is more chic than renting a villa in Tuscany. While almost all foreign languages except Spanish are in decline, Italian enrollments in American institutions of higher learning have remained remarkably stable and no longer depend upon students with names ending in a vowel. The number of Italian Americans who have become heads of corporations, important government officials, writers, and professionals is enormous and still growing, and many (but not all) of the "Little Italies" of the past century have long ago been transformed by moves to upscale suburbs and other dramatic demographic shifts. In many cases, they remain vividly recollected only in photographs, movies, and memory.

Italian Americans have, by and large, assimilated into the American mainstream as much or even more than many other ethnic groups. And they have almost always done so not by claiming the status of victim, all too popular a means of gaining the attention of the press or the government in the facile multicultural politics of today, but by believing in the American dream: that hard work and education would ultimately result in progress, and economic betterment, and a place at the table, so to speak. The contemporary politics of multiculturalism disparages the myth of the "melting pot," a term invented by Israel Zangwill—a member of another once despised minority—a Jew who was not even an American citizen. The phrase *E pluribus unum* means "one out of many," a phrase that comes from one of a group of some ten pseudo-Vergilian poems in the Alexandrian style called the *Appendix Vergiliana*. One of these poems is called *Moretum* (meaning a kind of salad or hash). America's Founding Fathers probably mistakenly identified this Latin text as Vergilian, since as gentlemen farmers, they were so fond of Vergil's *Georgics*. The original line that suggested the motto on our Great Seal is actually *color est e pluribus unus* ("many colors blend into one") and refers to the making of a salad with various ingredients and a pestle.[2] Perhaps rather than focusing upon the metaphor of the "melting pot"—an image suggesting that the individual identity of the various components being blended together is basically obliterated—we should return to the original Vergilian context of the term, which is more like the making of a stew, soup, or a salad than an alloy.

In any good stew, soup, or salad, the different ingredients can always be identified; even while taken together, they create a unique taste different from that of any single ingredient. Moreover, taken together, the mixture produces something different from and better than the sum of the individual parts that go into the final dish.

Today, Italian Americans certainly belong in the mainstream, but Hollywood Italians continue to stand out as a group in the Hollywood pantheon, remaining far more "ethnic" than their real counterparts. Most of the "Little Italies"[3] on the silver screen have resisted the temptation to retire to the suburbs with greater tenacity than those actually in the metropolitan areas of the United States. Yet the currently most famous Hollywood Italians of the suburbs, the members of the New Jersey Soprano family, share all the common preoccupations of the suburban soccer moms and businessmen commuters with whom they live, including sessions with a psychiatrist to cure their "*agita.*"

Thus, the focus of this book is not upon the flesh-and-blood Italian Americans that one may encounter everywhere, but their surrogates, far fewer in number and more vivid in our collective imagination, that we encounter in the movies. In the movies, to a far greater extent than in our daily lives, these characters remain identifiable by their Hollywood representations not as Italian Americans but as "Hollywood Italians." Here, they are predominantly but not exclusively from New York, and here they are frequently presented as gangsters, prizefighters, Latin lovers, and poor emigrants—not corporation presidents, mayors, or college professors. In their worst moments, they become identified with stereotypes based upon ethnic, religious, or racial prejudice. In their most sublime artistic representations, as in *The Godfather* trilogy or *The Sopranos*, they have captured the popular imagination and even the admiration of generations of Americans while providing Hollywood with some of its greatest folklore, its most moving narratives, as well as some of its most original personalities.

Al Capone thought of himself as an American, not an Italian, and so, by the way, did Frank Capra, even though he, unlike the Chicago gangster, was born in Sicily. But Italian stereotypes have an interesting history. During the years immediately preceding World War II and while the conflict was being waged by the Fascist regime, Benito Mussolini used to disparage the United States as a mongrel nation populated by gangsters and Negro jazz musicians, both stereotyped images derived primarily from the movies. Yet, most Italians had relatives in the United States and no doubt took his statements with a large grain of salt. Mussolini's son Romano eventually became an accomplished jazz pianist despite his father's views, although he himself was probably not aware of the enormous contribution to the development of this "black" form of American music by musicians of Italian descent. The point is simple: people are generally more sophisticated about dealing with stereotypes in their cultures than is generally assumed or acknowledged.

Although the Hollywood movies portraying Hollywood Italians may often be based on stereotypes, similar cultural depictions throughout history have likewise produced outstanding works of art. The best example in the English-speaking world is that of Elizabethan England and its love-hate relationship with the Italy of the Renaissance and the Reformation.[4] Hollywood cinema may fruitfully be compared to the Elizabethan theater and English culture generally in the way they regarded Italians of the Renaissance. During the fifteenth and sixteenth centuries in Europe, Italy represented a school for all sorts of new ideas, values, and artistic forms. Her universities were the envy of every other civilized country. Her art and literature flourished under the influence of humanistic encounters with a revived Classical tradition. Her political thought was the most original and energetic of any, especially that of Machiavelli, whose realistic and often shocking views on necessity and pragmatism in governmental affairs disturbed Northern European sensibilities, if not their political practice. It is not by accident that Shakespeare and other Elizabethan dramatists located so many of their works in the Italy of their day, since Italy represented the place where the intellectual and artistic action was, just as Paris was the focal point for European culture in the nineteenth century and Germany became the capital for European science shortly thereafter. Italy was also home to the Roman Catholic Church, engaged in territorial disputes within the peninsula and in a heated religious battle with dissenters and heretics of all kinds throughout Europe. Despite their pan-European connections, the dominant personalities managing the Vatican were almost always Italians. Arguably no political or dynastic history is bloodier than that of England, yet Elizabethans enjoyed placing perfidious counselors and courtiers, poisoners, and murderous adulterers in an Italian context, perhaps understanding that any direct criticism could be life threatening. "Old Nick"—a preexisting nickname for the devil—became that of Machiavelli, who was incorrectly identified with the unchristian notion that any means are justified by any ruler's ends. Scandalous rumors about the incestuous relationships within the Borgia family—a pope, Alexander VI; his son, Cesare, Machiavelli's ideal prince; and his daughter, Lucrezia—were circulated by anti-Catholic and anti-Italian polemicists in both Huguenot France and then Protestant England. All this culminated in a portrait of a nation whose culture embraced godless materialism, corruption in the church, unscrupulous and treacherous dealing wherein one's word could be broken without prejudice and cruelty devised and carried out by sadistic rulers.

Obviously, a nation ruled by such figures as Mary Queen of Scots, Henry VIII, Elizabeth I, and Oliver Cromwell needed no lessons in double-dealing or violence from their Mediterranean counterparts. Yet, besides becoming the School of Europe in the fine arts, literature, education, and general good manners during the Renaissance, an aspect of Italian culture that caused the peninsula to be the envy of the nation, Elizabethan and Renaissance England also regarded Italy with fear, suspicion, and prejudice inspired by religious, philosophical, and essentially racial differences. Italy became, in short, what is called in the academic world the "Other" for many writers and thinkers of the period—a fascinating world that drew people to it but also a siren's song that could easily destroy true religion and moral behavior. In many cases, the Italian characters that populated the Elizabethan imagination—Shakespeare's Iago or Shylock, Jonson's Volpone, and so many lesser figures—represented clearly stereotypical characters. Many of the most interesting characters created by such dramatists had Italian sources in Bandello, Boccaccio, Ariosto, or Cinthio. Yet, who would reject Shakespeare's *Othello* or *The Merchant of Venice* solely because the protagonists reflect difference?

Hollywood Italians play a similar role in the American cinema. Produced by an industry that was shaped substantially by recent emigrants from the non-Mediterranean cultures of Central Europe, as Neal Gabler and others have shown,[5] cinematic representations of Hollywood Italians quite naturally embodied the ambivalent views of Italians that Americans of recent and much earlier vintage held of these new and colorful arrivals—they were different. Not surprisingly, they became in the American imagination a reflection of the Other. Yet, when these representations are examined carefully, they reveal a great deal of begrudging admiration, interest, and envy. Representations of Hollywood Italians are, in short, as complex as the new art form that depicted them and as multifaceted and fascinating as the very real flesh-and-blood emigrants who would, over several decades, become mayors of New York City (Fiorello La Guardia, Rudy Giuliani), idolized pop singers (Frank Sinatra, Dean Martin), Hall of Fame baseball players (Joe DiMaggio), as well as famous Wise Guys (Al

Capone, Lucky Luciano), fearless Palookas (Jake La Motta, Rocky Marciano), and seductive Romeos (Rudolph Valentino, Frank Sinatra, John Travolta).

I have organized *Hollywood Italians* out of chronological or historical order. Since Hollywood films with Hollywood Italians have largely been genre pictures, the most obvious subcategories being that of Wise Guys, Romeos, and Palookas, the interesting developments in such representations often take place more within a genre than across generic or chronological boundaries. That is to say, one gangster film featuring protagonists of Italian descent may have far more to do with another similar gangster movie of an earlier era, to which it is artistically indebted, than with a film about a Hollywood Italian prizefighter or Latin lover that is its contemporary. And the history of that generic development through time may be more important to the history of the cinema than the interrelationships between different genres. This is most obviously true in the case of *The Sopranos*, a work best considered not as a television series but, rather, as a collection of films created by an auteur with complex scripts and production values that few television series have ever even attempted to equal. Moreover, *The Sopranos* reflects a postmodern fascination with its gangster-film ancestors and of Hollywood Italian Wise Guys that could only emerge from a very sure grasp of film history on the part of its creators.

It is often said that the American cinema represents a fascinating chronicle of American history.[6] Hence, it should be revealing to explore how American films have portrayed the basic experience of coming to America and living in an ethnic area, and how they have expressed the essential values nearly all commentators on Italian American life define as most important: those surrounding *la famiglia*.[7] With that foundation, it is then possible to appreciate such figures as Palookas, Romeos, and Wise Guys (funny or not), and Sopranos that populate the Hollywood Italian universe.

Acknowledgements

I am grateful to Gian Piero Brunetta of the University of Padua for asking me to write an essay on Italian Americans in the Hollywood cinema that was the inspiration for this book. My thanks also go to Tulane University and my students in a seminar there on Hollywood Italians I offered at that institution as the Mellon Visiting Professor in the spring of 2000. A grant from the Department of French & Italian and from the Institute for the Arts and Humanities at Indiana University helped me procure photographic illustrations for this work. My manuscript has profited from a close and sympathetic reading by my old friend Harry Geduld, who has forgotten more about the Hollywood cinema than I shall ever learn. My wife Julia also read the manuscript carefully and, once again, saved me from any number of stylistic blunders. Finally, I owe a huge debt of gratitude to my peerless editor, Evander Lomke, who knows every line of the *Godfather* trilogy by heart.

1

Dagos: Hollywood Histories of Immigration, *La famiglia,* and Little Italies

from the Silent Era to the Present

"Ain't nothing but trash, every one of them . . . dago . . . greasy wop . . . we don't need your kind . . ."

> The citizens of New Orleans (voice-over opening of *Vendetta*)[1]

"Common labor, white $1.30 to $1.50. Common labor, colored, 1.25 to $1.40. Common labor, Italian $1.15 to $1.25"

> Public Notice of daily wages for workers on New York City's Croton Reservoir in 1895[2]

"America is God's Crucible, the great Melting Pot, where all races in Europe are melting and reforming . . . The real American has not yet arrived. . . . he will be the fusion of all races, perhaps the coming superman."

> Israel Zangwill, *The Melting Pot* (1908)[3]

"I'd love to go in *Italia* again before I die. Now I speak English good like an American I could go anywhere—where millionaires go and high people. I would look the high people in the face and ask them what questions I'd like to know. I wouldn't be afraid now . . . Me, that's why I love America. That's what I learned in America: not to be afraid."

> Rosa Cavalleri (1866–1943)[4]

"Only my friends call me wop!"

> Angelo Maggio (Frank Sinatra) in *From Here to Eternity* (1953)

Vendetta (1999): Hollywood Looks Back at a Defining Moment in the Representation of the Hollywood Italian

As the best account of Italian American history points out, even before the massive migrations from Italy, Italians had the reputation of being a people so attached to the soil of their native provinces that they avoided emigration abroad. In fact, the early emigrants to America from Italy had been primarily political refugees and middle-class professionals, who experienced little ethnic prejudice. Yet, in only a few decades after the opening of Ellis Island in the harbor of New York City on January 1, 1892, millions of Italians, mostly from the Mezzogiorno—the South of Italy—had crossed the Atlantic and come to the United States to begin a new life. And, of course, faced with the personal, cultural, political, and economic characteristics of this very different group of Italians, American attitudes toward them changed drastically. The volume of the traffic was intense, but not everyone discovered his or her fortune in America. In fact, between 1880 and 1924, fewer than half of the 4.5 million Italians who came to America remained.[5] Italian emigration has always been identified with New York, Chicago, Philadelphia, San Francisco, Boston, and other predominantly eastern cities, but there were substantial populations of Italians who came to the South, particularly through the thriving port city of New Orleans. In Louisiana after the departure of many ex-slaves to the North had created a labor shortage, Louisiana began to encourage the arrival of Italian workers, even employing advertisements bragging about the Mediterranean quality of life in the region. In almost no time, the farming knowledge and the entrepreneurial skills of the Italian emigrants led them to successful ventures in the vegetable and fruit markets of the city. The famous French Market that is today the Mecca of tourists actually became an Italian market, and much of the French Quarter, particularly around Decatur Street, became a Little Italy. Italians found work on the docks of the booming harbor, while other farm laborers worked in strawberry fields in the countryside or the sugarcane fields.[6] Visitors to the city and state today are often surprised both by the number of Italian names on New Orleans stores, shops, and businesses, and by the large number of Italian names encountered, now primarily in the suburbs around Metairie, that only serve to emphasize the early massive presence of this group of emigrants, most of whom were Sicilians.

New Orleans is the setting for the film *Vendetta* (1999), a relatively high-budget film shot for Home Box Office, which has also produced *The Sopranos*. This accurate and compelling adaptation of Richard Gambino's book, entitled *Vendetta*, narrates the chilling account of America's largest lynching as it took place in New Orleans on March 14, 1891. Its victims were not African Americans, as most might expect, but, rather, eleven Italian Americans who had just been acquitted of the crime of murder or who would soon be tried for the same crime but would undoubtedly have been found innocent of the crime for which their compatriots had just been acquitted. The event sparked a wave of anti-Italian emotions all over America, which provoked a grave political crisis between the United States and Italy, and the prejudice that emerged from the lynching, which was widely discussed in American papers and magazines for some time after the event, was to a great extent responsible for the ongoing identification of Italian American emigrants with lawlessness and the Mafia.[7]

Vendetta treats the problems associated with Italian emigration to the South in the late nineteenth century, and although films about Italian gangsters are treated in another chapter, the connection between Italians and the Mafia so indelibly etched in the American imagination was born in the aftermath of the event dramatized in this film. When the American cinema soon afterward began to portray various kinds of emigrants arriving in the urban centers of the North in numerous brief films dating from as early as the first decade of the twentieth century, the association of Italian emigrants with the Mafia had already been made and was assumed to be true. Hollywood merely looked to the popular press for its subject matter.

Nicolas Meyer's direction of *Vendetta* creates a well-crafted film with seamless editing, numerous establishing shots, a Hollywood love interest between a young emigrant who is arrested but escapes lynching (Gaspare Marchesi, the son of Antonio Marchesi who was lynched) and an Irish girl named Meagan. Grainy photographs of impoverished and emaciated Italian emigrants arriving at the port of New Orleans open the film and an intertitle warns us that the film is a faithful recording of history. BASED ON A TRUE STORY is the film's first frame. The cast is excellent. Christopher Walken plays James Houston, the villainous Southern racist whose plot to take over the docks and the fruit trade from an Italian businessman, Joseph Macheca (Joaquim de Almeida), leads to the assassination of the local sheriff, Chief Hennesy (Clancy Brown), who has refused to use the law against the Italians unless there is some proof of their criminal activity. Four men murder Hennesy at night in the Italian section of town, and rumor spreads that his last words were: "The dagos did it." Houston, the mayor of the city, and a group of prominent businessmen associated with the power elite of the old South called the Committee of Fifty, chaired at one time by Edgar H. Farrar of the Board of Trustees of Tulane University, all apparently conspired to rid the city of the rising economic power of the Italians,[8] who had by the time of the lynching gained control of most of the docks and most of the vegetable and fruit trade in the city. Subsequent to the lynching, the New Orleans City Council passed an ordinance on April 25, 1892, that was aimed at destroying any Italian commercial presence on the docks, giving control of them to the new Louisiana Construction and Improvement Corporation, one of whose principals was none other than James Houston, who engineered the lynching. Moreover, another ordinance attempted to block Italian longshoremen from further work on the docks by giving that privilege to a union made up of white and black men but excluding Italians. When Italian longshoremen and prominent Italian businessmen protested, Mayor Shakspeare addressed them on May 16, 1891—only four months after the lynchings—in the following tone:

> I and every other decent citizen am disgusted with the Dago distur-
> bances and determined that they shall end immediately. . . . You have
> not learned the lesson taught your race by the people of New-Orleans,
> it seems, and I want you when you leave here to go home and tell your
> friends that if you make any more trouble, the police and Mayor of
> this city will not consider themselves responsible for the loss of you
> and yours. . . . I intend to put an end to these infernal Dago distur-
> bances, even if it proves necessary to wipe every one of you from the
> face of the earth.[9]

The shockingly racist tone of the speech perfectly reflects the attitude of the power elite of New Orleans who felt threatened by the rising economic importance of a group they despised not just as a different ethnic group but also as a different race. *Vendetta* is most persuasive as a historical re-construction of this pivotal event in Italian American history when it re-produces, often verbatim, the statements of the historical characters involved in the script. Moreover, the relaxed norms against the graphic de-piction of violence on the screen in the particular case of this film allow the shocking nature of the lynchings and the merciless racial killings of the Italian American victims to be vividly portrayed. The irony of the film, of course, is that Joseph Macheca—the most prominent and wealthy of the Italian American businessmen—was born in America and fought in the Civil War on the Union side to prevent just such racist treatment of African-American slaves. Like Al Capone, Macheca was a domestic Italian, not an imported one.

Vendetta will never rank at the top of anyone's list of memorable repre-sentations of Italian Americans. But like so many Hollywood films about the plight of blacks in a racist society, *Vendetta* reminds America of the kind of obstacles Italian Americans had to overcome in order to be considered "white" and worthy of being assimilated into the American dream. The Hollywood Italians depicted in it are unique: they are almost the contempo-raries of the figures depicted in the early era of the silent cinema, the poor emigrants in the urban ghettos of the North who were soon to be the focus of a number of popular movies. Unlike the Hollywood Italians of the early silent cinema, however, their representations are refracted through an entire century of social change in America. The purpose behind the style of their representation is to redress a wrong committed a century ago, something very far from the minds of early directors of silent cinema. In *Vendetta*, Mayor Shakspeare and James Houston frequently pronounce the word "Mafia" incorrectly—placing the stress on the last syllable rather than the first, as everyone has since learned to do. The nefarious association between poor Italian American emigrants and organized crime the New Orleans lynching did so much to effect would continue long after Americans learned to pronounce the word correctly. *Vendetta* is an important movie because it sets out to reverse a century of negative images.

The Silent Cinema Depicts the New Arrivals

The mass arrival of Italians to American shores coincided almost exactly with the invention and growth of the cinema. An impressive number of works treating Hollywood Italians appeared during the early days of the silent cinema.[10] Unfortunately, few of these films are on video or DVD formats. Without access to archives or research libraries, the movie-going public is largely cut off from access to these fascinating documents of the ways of visualizing early Hollywood Italians. D. W. Griffith (1875–1948), perhaps the greatest of all American directors in this period, did a number of Biograph pictures between 1907 and 1913 with Italian stories, including *The Greaser's Gauntlet* (1908), *In Little Italy* (1909), *The Violin Maker of Cremona* (1909), and *Pippa Passes* (1909)—a transposition of the Browning poem of the same name to the United States. His *Italian Blood* (1911) portrays a hot-blooded and jealous husband who is almost driven by his wife to murder his own children. Although *The Musketeers of Pig Alley* (1912), Griffith's film about gangsters in the cities, does not identify the criminals with any specific ethnic group, it helped to establish the popularity of a genre that had already been linked to Hollywood Italians even before Griffith. Griffith's *At the Altar* (1909) employs another Hollywood Italian stereotype—the jealous, irrational, and vindictive Italian lover who attempts to get revenge upon another man who is successful in love. Another of his works, *In Life's Cycle* (1910), focuses on a brother and sister: the man becomes a priest, while the woman is seduced and abandoned by a fickle lover, resulting in an illegitimate child.

Even when sympathetic to Hollywood Italian subjects, these early films embrace a stereotype of the Italian as a creature controlled by emotions and passions, a stereotype obviously indebted to Elizabethan drama, grand opera, and the sentimental theater of the nineteenth century. Still, a number of these films shed some light on the problems Italian emigrants encountered when they reached America. Works such as *Pasquale* (1916; William D. Taylor, director); *A Roadside Impresario* (1917; Donald Crisp, director); *The Ordeal of Rosetta* (1918; Emile Chautard, director); *Tony America* (1918; Thomas N. Heffron, director); *Society Snobs* (1921; Hobart Henley, director); *Puppets of Fate* (1921; Dallas M. Fitzgerald, director); *Little Italy* (1921; George Terwillinger, director); and *The Man in Blue* (1925; Edward Laemmle, director) depict the conflict that may arise when members of different ethnic groups fall in love or marry. Many of these films employ scenes set in Italy itself and often depict the immigration of the principal characters to New York City or other urban centers in the East. The most common connections between ethnic groups are, not surprisingly, given their common religion, between Italians and the Irish. *Head Over Heels* (1922, Victor Schertzinger, director), for example, examines the trials and tribulations of an Italian girl as she tries to assimilate into New York's WASP culture. *Rose of the Tenements* (1926; Phil Rosen, director), produced by Joseph Kennedy, Sr., the father of the future president, presents three different ethnic groups. Rose, an Italian flower girl, is the orphan of a deceased Italian gangster (again the Mafia raises its ugly role in stories about immigration). She is reared by a Jewish couple along with an Irish-American boy named Danny, with whom she falls in love and eventually marries after he has a brief encounter with political activism, during which he is falsely accused of being a bomb-throwing Bolshevik.[11] After the development of the early star system in the silent cinema, several Hollywood films cast popular leading actors as Italians in Italy (not Little Italy). Ronald Colman and Lillian Gish starred in *The White Sister* (1923; Henry King, director), a melodramatic account of an Italian noblewoman who is defrauded of her inheritance and becomes a nun. Victor Fleming remade it in 1933 with Clark Gable and Helen Hayes. In *The Wages of Virtue* (1924), Gloria Swanson must choose between the Italian who has saved her from drowning and an American. She prefers the latter. Regardless of the locale of such films, they associate Italy itself—like Little Italy—with passion, romance, and potential violence.

The Italian *(1915) and the Hollywood Italian Immigrant Experience*

Historians are unanimous in praising *The Italian* (1915; Reginald Barker, director) for its complex portrayal of the Italian immigrant. The well-known dramatic actor George Beban stars as Beppo Donnetti, who comes to New York to seek his fortune and make a new life for his wife and child. The legendary Thomas Ince (1882–1924) produced the film. Ince's work is renowned for careful construction, well-crafted scripts, and sophisticated production values. Originally entitled *The Dago*, its title was apparently changed at Beban's request: his career reflects a sincere interest in immigrants, and in their representation in theater and film. Only a few years later, he played the lead in another immigrant film about Italians, *One More American* (1918; William De Mille, director), the story of the conflict between an Italian and an Irish ward boss who attempts to keep the Italian's family from entering Ellis Island but who is eventually foiled at the last minute.[12]

A number of aesthetic elements sets *The Italian* apart from the other films treating the Italian immigrant experience. In the first place, this is a feature film (six reels), not a one- or two-reeler. Its melodramatic plot reflects a serious sense of artistic construction, aimed at milking the last bit of emotion out of the audience. George Beban's outstanding performance shows his roots in the dramatic theater. The settings are also interesting, even if not realistic by today's standards. Finally, the depiction of the tragic story of Beppo shows a certain sympathy for the character of the poor Italian bootblack but also includes a callous disregard for depicting Italian immigrants in a stereotypical manner, an attitude that no doubt reflected the opinions of the majority of Americans at the time.

Its plot is simple and compelling. Beppo Donnetti is a Venetian gondolier who falls in love with Annette Ancello, goes to New York to make their fortune, and brings her to marry him when he has earned enough money as a bootblack. While in New York, he encounters an Irish ward boss, Big Bill Corrigan, who pays him the money he needs to send for Annette if he will help garner the Italian vote for his candidate, Alderman John H. Casey. As the intertitle puts it, Corrigan says: HERE'S A LITTLE PRESENT FOR YOU. HAVE YOUR WOP FRIENDS VOTE FOR THIS GUY. Annette arrives, and they soon have a son named Tony, but a heat wave causes their son to contract an illness (probably yellow fever or cholera, a typical disease of the urban ghettos), and the doctor sends Beppo for pasteurized milk, without which the baby will die. On his way to buy the milk, two non-Italians rob Beppo, and when he sees them later and attacks them, he ends up in jail after Corrigan refuses to help him. We can only imagine what the Irishman said about lawless Italians, since there is, of course, no sound track, but the impressive action shot depicting Beppo dragged along by Corrigan's car represents one of the high points of the film with the complexity of its photography. While he is in jail, his son dies, and Beppo plans a vendetta against Corrigan, whose daughter is also ill. But when he sees the little girl in her crib and recognizes, as the sentimental intertitle puts it, THE GESTURE THAT WAS LITTLE TONY'S is the same as that of Corrigan's daughter, his anger subsides, and later he is seen mourning over the grave of his lost son.

The Italian *(1915; Reginald Barker, director). Beppo, a Venetian gondolier (George Beban), before his immigration to America. From Library of Congress Film Stills Archive.* Reproduced from the Collections of the Library of Congress.

The viewer is struck by a number of interesting features in this film. It opens and closes with George Beban wearing a smoking jacket and holding a pipe, in what is obviously an upper-class living room. He picks up a book that is entitled "*The Italian* by Thomas H. Ince and C. G. Sullivan" and begins to read it, as the film fades to the monastery mentioned in the first paragraph of the book. At the close of the film, when Beppo is placing flowers on his son's grave, we return to Beban closing his book, obviously moved by the story he has read, while curtains are drawn over the last frame in imitation of the closure of a play, thus reminding us that Beban is a dramatic actor. Why employ such a strange parenthesis to enclose the narrative? One obvious explanation is to convey that Beban is a legitimate theatrical performer. According to accounts of the making of this movie, Beban had to be practically coerced into taking the part and demanded a salary for his work quite out of line with payments for film actors. Clearly he wanted to protect his reputation. Since we know that Beban insisted on changing the title of the film from *The Dago* to *The Italian* and also acted in the previously mentioned *One More American*, another major film on

The Italian *(1915; Reginald Barker, director). Beppo (George Beban) as a bootblack in New York City. From Library of Congress Film Stills Archive.* Reproduced from the Collections of the Library of Congress.

Italian immigration, it is also likely that he felt sympathy for oppressed immigrants. By showing that a blue-blooded aristocrat in a silken smoking jacket could be moved by Beppo's story, Beban clearly takes the side of the unfortunate Italian gondolier.

Other aspects of the film are worth noting. The Venice scene was shot in Venice, California (and therefore was relatively convincing), while the New York City scenes are shot in San Francisco. There are, however, the peddlers, the open fire hydrants during the heat wave, and the urban bustle we have come to associate with New York scenes at the turn of the century. Some of the Italian features of the film are less persuasive. Beppo may be a gondolier, but his costume, and those of the peasants shown in the opening scenes of the film, clearly come from Southern Italy. Beban supposedly bought his costume from a Sicilian immigrant, so this may not be surprising. Certainly Ince and his director could tell little difference between a Venetian and a Sicilian. Nonetheless, the intertitles reflecting conversations spoken by Beppo actually mimic the kind of Pidgin English that would have been spoken by Italian immigrants. When he sees his son for the first

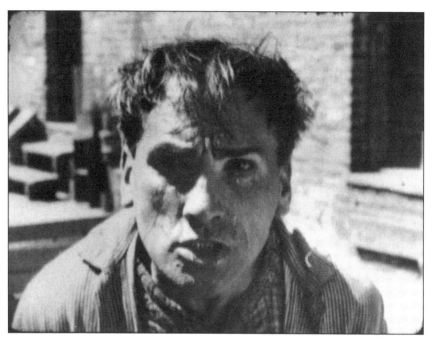

The Italian *(1915; Reginald Barker, director). The Italian as a creature of emotions—Beppo (George Beban) pictured in close-up as a wild animal over the injustice of his daughter's death. From Library of Congress Film Stills Archive.* Reproduced from the Collections of the Library of Congress.

time, the intertitle reads: SANTA MARIA! HE IS SLEEPA JUST-A-LIKE-A-ME, HIS HAND STUCK UNDER HIS-A-CHIN. When he tries to save his son, he is made to say: I MUST GET-A-DE-MILK OR MY BABEE IS DIE. I prefer to believe that this kind of language is employed in a search for linguistic realism, not to belittle the character. Moreover, a letter written to Annette to bring her to America displays perfectly correct Italian (for a man who is not university educated) before the audience sees the English translation, thereby emphasizing the production's desire for accuracy. Despite making obvious mistakes, Beppo clearly represents a character worthy of pity and respect. The melodramatic plot obviously aims at moving the audience's emotions, not unlike the many other tearjerkers of the silent cinema. Silent films are notoriously difficult to present to modern audiences, but even the most cynical spectators may be moved by Beppo's plight. This is one silent movie with real staying power.

Beppo's portrayal in *The Italian* certainly contains many of the elements that characterized the superstition, prejudice, ignorance, and lack of empathy on the part of Americans of the period who viewed the great Italian

The Italian. *Beppo dragged by a car, one of the most complex sequences in the film. From Library of Congress Film Stills Archive.* Reproduced from the Collections of the Library of Congress.

influx into the United States with a jaundiced eye. After all, even Ince, who produced the film, originally called it *The Dago*, and the Irish ward boss's attitude in the film denigrating Italians as *wops* is far from unusual. Unlike *Vendetta*, which has a century of social change behind it, including the contemporary multicultural attitude that all ethnic groups are victims, and which clearly sides with the embattled Italian immigrants in New Orleans, *The Italian* pictures the plight of Beppo from the outside—with compassion and pity but from a slightly patronizing position that is clearly superior to its subject matter. Like so many of his compatriots, Beppo embodies the perceived Italian penchant for the *vendetta*, and no amount of Americanization—symbolized in the film by the shaving of the omnipresent Italian American black mustache after Beppo arrives in New York City—seems to diminish this almost universal stereotype. But the figure is represented with great dignity and even comic twists, making Beppo a far more lovable figure than we might expect. So much in love with his future wife that he daydreams while poling his gondola in Venice, he runs into a bridge, knocking himself into the canal. Later in New York, when his son is born, he is so excited that he runs into a peddler, who seems to be a Jewish merchant of

Eastern European origin, creating a chaotic scene outside his tenement. When the angry peddler and the crowd that has gathered to support him learn that Beppo has become a father, they all become friendly, and Beppo stands them all to drinks at the local bar.

In short, what emerges from *The Italian* is an unusually complex view of tenement life and multiethnic immigration in America, and the film consequently retains its value not only as social history but also as a work of art.

Animal Crackers *(1930) and Ethnic Humor*

In fashioning a history of Italian immigration in America through the cinema, the amusing contribution of Chico Marx and the Marx Brothers' films cannot be ignored, even though they are in no way intended to be realistic. Leonardo "Chico" Marx (1887–1961) made a career out of imitating Italian American accents in his comic films. His screen name Chico seems vaguely Italian but apparently derived from the result of a typo in the spelling of his real nickname "Chicko," referring to his passion for beautiful women ("chicks"). The error was never corrected after the actor realized that the new spelling was most appropriate to his screen persona. The characters Chico portrayed in a series of zany comedies—Chico in *Monkey Business* (1931), Baravelli in *Horse Feathers* (1932), Chicolini in *Duck Soup* (1933), and Fiorello in *A Night at the Opera* (1935)—all have in common representations of Italian ethnicity, but the classic example of this type of ethnic-comic character may be seen in *Animal Crackers* (1930; Victor Heerman, director), with Chico playing the role of Signor Emanuel Ravelli, a musician hired to perform at a reception given by a wealthy socialite, Mrs. Rittenhouse (Margaret Dumont), for an African explorer named Captain Jeffrey T. Spaulding (Groucho Marx). A rich art dealer, Roscoe Chandler (Louis Sorin), brings an expensive painting to present to the party, Beaugard's *After the Hunt.*

During the party, Ravelli performs a number of comic routines involving linguistic mistakes, malapropisms, and generally off-the-wall one-liners, his Italian accent appearing when most useful comically and then disappearing whenever not needed. First-generation Jews and Italians, not to mention other linguistic and ethnic groups, grew up alongside each other in New York's Lower East Side tenements, and as Charles Musser has rightly noted, living there was a constant struggle to understand different accents, languages, pronunciations: first-generation immigrants might never get the hang of it, but their children's ears would be more attuned to the meanings, and therefore the comic possibilities, of such wordplay in dramatic or film dialogue.[13] In *Animal Crackers,* the comic force of the film comes not just from Chico's pseudo-Italian American dialogue but also from the fact that characters such as Spaulding and Ravelli are obviously Jews pretending to be something else—in Spaulding's case, a WASP explorer, in Ravelli's case an Italian musician whose name recalls that of the French composer Ravel and which Mrs. Rittenhouse confuses with ravioli. This role playing lies at the core of the film. Suspecting that Mr. Chandler, the art collector, is a fake, Ravelli recognizes him from a birthmark on the arm as Abe Cabibble, a fish seller from Prague, who is obviously yet another Jew passing himself off as a WASP in high society. When Ravelli asks how Chandler managed to transform himself from Cabibble to Chandler ("How did you get to be Roscoe W. Chandler?"), Chandler/Cabibble replies: "Say, how did you get to be an Italian?" Not only for Chandler but for the audience as well, Ravelli deflects the pertinent question with the remark: "Never mind. Whose confession is this?"

The characters in *Animal Crackers*, not just the Jewish-Italian Ravelli but each of the other Marx Brothers, parody stereotypes associated with ethnic groups—the dominant WASP culture, the Jewish culture producing the anarchic humor of the film, and the Italian immigrant whose linguistic routines pay homage to their common origins in the tenements of the Lower East Side. Nothing about these images pretends to be even remotely associated with a realistic portrayal of life in the urban ghettos from which they originate, but their comic send-ups of social role playing surely indicate the heightened awareness members of ethnic groups had about the role language and stereotypes may play. *Animal Crackers*, in particular, embodies a democratic comic spirit in its undermining of society's barrier between different ethnic groups. After all, if three Jews can pretend to be African explorers, WASP art collectors, and Italian musicians, just how meaningful is ethnic identity? If ethnic identity can be assumed and put on or taken off like a dinner jacket, perhaps much of society's preoccupation with social rankings and appearances matters very little in the long run.

The Great Depression and Hollywood Italian Laborers: Christ in Concrete *(1949)*

Christ in Concrete, a novel by Italian American bricklayer and writer Pietro Di Donato (1911–92), remains for many historians of the Italian American experience the "prototypical 'ethnic' novel."[14] Relegated to the category of proletarian novel, ethnic novel, or even Italian American novel, Di Donato's masterpiece bested John Steinbeck's *The Grapes of Wrath* in a selection by the Book-of-the-Month Club in 1939, when both novels appeared. *Christ in Concrete* began as a prize-winning short story, a narrative that eventually became the first chapter of the novel. Its adaptation by director

Edward Dmytryk may arguably be an improvement on what is a fine novel, although it languished for many years in storage without being distributed.[15] A masterpiece, *Christ in Concrete* is also one of the few Hollywood films treating the subject of the Italian American worker with dignity, infusing its protagonist with a tragic grandeur and complexity worthy of great drama. It also depicts quite believably the difficulties Italian workers faced in the building trades, one of the major occupations in which they made important and lasting contributions to the building of the urban spaces they inhabited.

One of the few American films to depict people at work, *Christ in Concrete* also offers one of the first Hollywood representations of Italian Americans that reflect the influence of Italian cinema—specifically, the postwar neorealist film. It was produced as a B movie with a brief shooting schedule (60 days) and a low budget ($500,000). Its producer, Ron Geiger, had been responsible for the distribution of Roberto Rossellini's *Open City* (1945) and *Paisan* (1946). Most likely, Geiger envisioned Dmytryk's film as a means of cashing in on what he perceived to be a relatively small but profitable market for starkly realistic films with ethnic Italian themes in the wake of the popular works of Rossellini, De Sica, and other Italian directors. Initially, Geiger may have considered Rossellini to direct the adaptation of Di Donato's novel. Dmytryk cast an Italian actress, Lea Padovani, as Annunziata, the wife of the Italian mason and construction worker Geremio (Sam Wanamaker), who is the film's protagonist. Although always notoriously unwilling to acknowledge any influence on his work from other directors or films, Dmytryk admits in his memoir: "I had seen a young player perform exceptionally well in an obscure Italian film. Her name was Lea Padovani."[16] It is virtually certain that the film Dmytryk mentions is *Il sole sorge ancora* (1946, released as *Outcry*) by Aldo Vergano (1891–1957). It would have been almost impossible for Dmytryk, one of Hollywood's most talented B-film directors, to ignore Italian neorealism or German Expressionism, each of which influences certain aspects of the cinematic style of the film.

Born of emigrant parents from the Ukraine, Dmytryk himself ranked among the Hollywood leftists eventually cited for contempt by the House Committee on Un-American Activities. At the very time *Christ in Concrete* received the Premio Pasinetti at the ninth Venice Biennale Film Festival, Dmytryk was serving a prison sentence as one of the Hollywood Ten. Because he eventually "named names" and was removed from the blacklist, he was, like director Elia Kazan, never forgiven by many Hollywood activists and fellow travelers. During the production in England, both lead actor Sam Wanamaker and scriptwriter Ben Barzman were essentially in exile from America as a result of their leftist or Communist affiliations, and subsequent

Christ in Concrete *(1949; Edward Dmytryk, director). Geremio (Sam Wanamaker) and Annunziata (Lea Padovani) celebrate their wedding day as the Italian immigrants assemble for a traditional Italian festival together.*

investigation by the House committee. These key individuals, all of whom had obvious ideological pretensions in their art, shared a great many general political and social beliefs with many of the leftist directors in Italy, such as Vergano or Visconti, who played an important part in the neorealist movement. *Christ in Concrete* was distributed in Italy after the Venice festival as *Cristo fra i muratori* (literally "Christ among the brickmasons"), and the Italian print suppressed the initial opening scenes of the work, transforming the picture into a more clearly chronological movie rather than emphasizing its flashback—all more typical of American *film noir* under the influence of German Expressionism. The Italian print was thus closer in spirit to neorealist narrative than the original American version, and it is no surprise that contemporary critics such as Guido Aristarco, Alberto Moravia, Henri Agel, Giorgio Moscon, and Amedée Ayfré,[17] all of whom contributed in significant ways to reviewing and popularizing neorealist films in Italy, praised Dmytryk's work.

Christ in Concrete adapts only "Geremio," the first of five sections that make up the original novel. Its ideological message clearly reflects the leftist leanings of its makers, and in no other American film of the period is the dignity of manual labor so strongly championed. A belief in the dignity and nobility of manual labor, one of the principal characteristics of Italian American men, has been so integral a part of the Italian American experience that it has often been blamed for the failure of Italian Americans, especially in the first half of the twentieth century, to take full advantage of higher education as a means for rising into the middle class, as other ethnics, the Jews in particular, have done so successfully.

Geremio's story unfolds in a long flashback that takes up most of the screen time. The film opens, however, with a brilliant sequence that is almost a classic textbook demonstration of *film noir* style: the steaming manhole covers so familiar to viewers of films set in New York City are faithfully reproduced in the English studio, not on location; the strange and threatening angles of the tall buildings symbolize Geremio's drunkenness; the flashback that follows the opening sequence structures the entire film and undercuts the strictly chronological order of the narrative favored by Italian neorealists but popularized by the inheritors of German Expressionist style who produced Hollywood's B movies. Before we learn of Geremio's story in the flashback, Dmytryk uses Kathleen (a figure not found in the original novel) to juxtapose Geremio's Italian American ethnic heritage to his desire to achieve assimilation as an American ethnic. Kathleen is played by Kathleen Ryan, a member of Ireland's Abbey Theatre, whose brogue is unmistakable in *Christ in Concrete*. Kathleen represents the ever-present temptation to assimilate, to purchase the American Dream at the price of losing one's ethnic identity. Viewing manual labor as less than "respectable," she would obviously rather have a husband or a lover who clerks in a grocery store or sells shoes—a white-collar occupation at all costs, even at lower wages. Geremio's wife Annunziata remains fanatically attached to the idea of buying her own house much as Beppo's wife in *The Italian*, who would not permit herself to be brought to America until Beppo had a place of his own in which to welcome her. Her fanatic need for this home drives Geremio to overwork and eventually, although indirectly, causes his death and the death of all his comrades. Besides the clash of cultures revealed in the juxtaposition of the Irish American Kathleen and the very Italian Annunziata who, unlike Geremio, seems to have no desire to become Americanized, a second and even more important confrontation in the film departs drastically from the novel. Geremio's eventual death, buried in the wet concrete of a construction project that is flawed by too little protection for the workers he supervises, seems to be determined less by blind fate or an inscrutable divine plan than as political retribution for his ultimate betrayal, not so much of his wife and family but his proletarian comrades at the infamous "job."

Dmytryk's ideological message derives from his portrayal of Geremio's relations to the other Italian workers on the construction site. After the supervisor Murdin offers $100 to the fastest bricklayer, Geremio must choose between the temptation to take all of the money as a single, individual worker (the path of bourgeois individualism) and the ideal of proletarian solidarity, working as a team and dividing the prize money between the five comrades who function, as the men describe it, as five sticks in a bundle. In this instance, Geremio stifles his baser capitalist instincts and works for the common good. When the Great Depression of 1929 destroys the prosperity of the construction industry, Geremio begins to change. In addition, we see some disastrous consequences of the failure of American capitalism, the driving force behind the Italian dream of paved streets of gold in America. A pathetic scene, not unlike a later equally moving scene in De Sica's neorealist classic *Umberto D* (*Umberto D.,* 1951), shows Geremio in an encounter with a friend begging outside a shop window. To emphasize the destructive force of purchasing the house, Dmytryk invents another ethnic character not found in the novel, an older Slavic immigrant named Jaroslav, who agrees to let Geremio and Annunziata pay for the house on long-term credit when he could more easily sell it to someone with the cash to purchase it immediately.

Geremio's greatest sin is his entrance into the higher echelons of the construction industry. Joining the ranks of the *padroni,* he becomes foreman of Murdin's dangerous demolition project, ultimately sacrificing the safety of his friends. Now he is even forced to eat alone, setting himself off physically as well as ideologically from his former comrades. In the movie, unlike the novel, Geremio first breaks faith with his fellow workers; later he betrays his marriage as well. But both his affair with Kathleen and his work as a foreman reflect his refusal of proletarian solidarity with his friends. Geremio is allowed the opportunity to confess his sins to his comrades on Good Friday (an appropriate day for contrition), and the moving speech he delivers to his fellow workers causes them to accept him back into their company with the simple humanity of the Italian working class. Turning his back on the *padroni* comes too late, however, and he dies as a working-class figure of Christ, or as one perceptive critic noted, as a modern Job, whose destiny remains tragic but as obscure as that of the biblical patriarch. His horrible death, drowned in a set of wet concrete with his arms outstretched reminiscent of Jesus on the cross, emphasizes the bittersweet reality of the American Dream for so many of his compatriots.

Christ in Concrete *(1949; Edward Dmytryk, director). After becoming a foreman, Geremio (Sam Wanamaker) dies in a horrible accident at his workplace.*

Few films before or since *Christ in Concrete* have managed to depict the harsh struggle of Italian American immigrants for success in America with such tragic emotion and dramatic force, while avoiding the usual stereo- typical depiction of the Italian American male or the family he heads. Geremio is a figure worthy of comparison to Arthur Miller's Willy Loman, and his death, like Loman's, represents a modern American capitalist version of a classical tragic hero.

From Here to Eternity *(1953): Hollywood Italians on the Eve of the Attack on Pearl Harbor*

Director Fred Zinnemann's adaptation of James Jones's best-selling novel *From Here to Eternity* (1951) received thirteen Oscar nominations, won eight awards, and relaunched the entertainment career of Frank Sinatra (1915–98), whose popularity as a singer had begun to wane before he reinvented himself as a Vegas entertainer in the 1960s. Rumored maneuvers necessary for Sinatra to land the role produced another great episode in Italian American cinema: the character of Johnny Fontane (Al Martino) in *The Godfather* (1972), an Italian American singer and godson of the Mafia boss who lands a similarly coveted role in a film and salvages his career through the famous expedient of the bloody horse's head under the producer's silk sheets. *From Here to Eternity*, Jones's *Thin Red Line* (1961), Norman Mailer's *Naked and the Dead* (1948), and Joseph Heller's *Catch-22* (1961)—among the best known of the American novels treating World War II to have been written by authors who actually served in the conflict—are all characterized by a visceral distaste for the regimentation, erasure of individuality, and mindlessness the authors perceived in military life. The title of Heller's book has itself become a proverbial shorthand expression for absurd situations with no solution.

From Here to Eternity contains so many controversial topics (prostitution, illicit sexual encounters, cruelty and sadism in the armed forces) that many American filmmakers at the time felt it would be difficult to adapt the novel for the screen without running afoul of the censors. A second-rate company commander, Captain Dana Holmes (Philip Ober), seems more interested in winning the regimental boxing championship than in being a good soldier, and the individual actually leading his company is a thirty-year non-commissioned officer, First Sergeant Milton Warden (Burt Lancaster). Warden ends up carrying on an illicit affair with Holmes's lonely wife Karen (Deborah Kerr). The plot revolves around Holmes's attempt to force a bugler, Private Robert E. Lee Prewitt (Montgomery Clift) to fight as a middleweight in the regimental competition; Prewitt's friendship with his Italian American buddy, Private Angelo Maggio (Sinatra); and the parallel affairs involving Warden and Karen Holmes, on the one hand, and Prewitt's infatuation with a prostitute who calls herself Lorene (Donna Reed), on the other.

The film adaptation of Jones's novel continues its attack upon the brutality of Army life and its destruction of individuality. While Sergeant Warden admires Prewitt's abilities as a bugler and as a soldier, he thinks his stubborn refusal to give in to Holmes represents a stupid personal decision. Prewitt remarks: "A man don't go his own way, he's nothing." Warden's response juxtaposes the philosophy of rugged individualism espoused by Prewitt with the motto of the organization man that will be so important in the 1950s: "Maybe back in the days of the pioneers, a man could go his own way. But today, you gotta play ball." As Maggio tells the boxers who threaten Prewitt as he is playing pool, "the guy don't have to fight if he don't want to without gettin' kicked around."

From Here to Eternity also presents an ugly form of ethnic prejudice aimed at Italian Americans in the person of Maggio. In the New Congress Club, a bordello masquerading as a social club, Maggio runs afoul of the Sergeant of the Guard at the stockade of the Schofield Army Barracks. "Fatso" Judson—played by Ernest Borgnine—who was of Italian American descent and soon to win an Oscar for his altogether different role as the mild, soft-spoken Italian American butcher of *Marty* (1955)—insults Maggio's sister while the soldier is showing the friends in his outfit a picture of his family of fifteen people. At various times in the film, Judson calls Maggio a "little Mussolini," a "tough monkey," but mostly a "wop." At one point, Maggio provides his famous response—"Only my friends call me wop"—and begins a brawl that requires Warden's intervention to prevent Judson from attacking Maggio with a switchblade knife. Later, it is significant that Maggio addresses Prewitt with a term made famous by Roberto Rossellini in his epic neorealist film *Paisan* (1946, *Paisà*) only a few years earlier: "Enjoy yourself, paisan. . . ." The English term *paisan* derives from the Italian word *paisano*, itself derived from the word *paese*, meaning town or village: a *paisano* is therefore someone from one's hometown, a countryman, a close friend. This is the word that American servicemen learned in Sicily when they landed on the island to liberate it in 1943, a term of friendship and community that was used by both the Italian natives and their GI liberators. And it is a word employed by Italian Americans as well. Still more significant is that Prewitt begins to call Maggio *paisan* thereafter in the film and eventually kills Judson in a knife fight to avenge Maggio's death in the stockade due to Judson's brutality and torture.

From Here to Eternity presents a masculine world where soldiers such as Prewitt, Warden, and Maggio are married to their respective careers in the military, not their female objects of desire. The most significant element in the representation of this particular Hollywood Italian, Angelo Maggio, is that Maggio becomes, along with Robert E. Lee Prewitt, the embodiment of the American belief in rugged individualism and rejection of conform-

From Here to Eternity *(1953; Fred Zinnemann, director). Angelo Maggio (Frank Sinatra) is overmatched when he tries to tangle with "Fatso" Judson (Ernest Borgnine) and is restrained by Robert E. Lee Prewitt (Montgomery Clift).*

ity, an ideal not previously associated with Italian Americans. Part of Hollywood's stereotypical Italian image continues—Maggio drinks, loves to carouse, and basically allows his instincts to rule his reason. But fundamentally, this "typically Italian" emotionalism seen in the silent cinema's Hollywood Italians does not alter the fact that now an ethnic, a representative of the "Other," stands for values as American as apple pie, while the more recognizably WASP or Anglo figures, such as Captain Holmes, embody an ethnic of conformity that the film critiques as basically un-American. Unlike the novel's relentless dissection of Army ethnic prejudice, conformity, and anti-individualism, the film mutes these themes in comparison to Jones's original narrative. In the novel, Holmes's treatment of Prewitt passes unnoticed, whereas in the film he is forced to resign in disgrace, guaranteeing a happy ending of sorts. Prewitt, a poor Kentucky kid named after a Confederate general who defended the institution of slavery, and Maggio, a Hollywood Italian, paradoxically stand for the freedom of the individual to follow his or her own path. Tragically, they both die for their troubles—Maggio tortured in the stockade, Prewitt shot when trying to return to his unit after the Japanese attack on Pearl Harbor.

The Rose Tattoo *(1955): Generational Conflict and Ethnic Community*

Tennessee Williams's play *The Rose Tattoo* (written in 1948, produced in 1950, and published in 1951) reflects a happy period in the playwright's life: the time spent in New Orleans where Williams fell in love with his longtime companion, Frank Merlo, a member of the large Sicilian community in the Louisiana area. Although Daniel Mann's film adaptation of the play was shot in Key West (another favorite Williams haunt, along with Rome), a screenplay written by Williams himself depicts life in an Italian American community in Louisiana, where most of the adults, including the priest, still speak Italian while their children are bilingual. Despite the film's emphasis upon the link between being Sicilian and being emotional, a universal Hollywood stereotype, its convincing portrait of an ethnic community owes much to Williams's own observations of Louisiana's Italian Americans in the late 1940s.

The rose has always been a popular symbol for passion and love, but Williams gives this shopworn image a new twist. His play and the film for which he wrote the script revolve around a rose tattoo first associated with a very WASP platinum blond named Estelle (Virginia Grey), who enters the opening sequence by leaving a Bourbon Street tattoo parlor and announcing to some inquisitive children that she has just had a rose tattooed over her heart. She then goes to the home of Serafina Delle Rose (Anna Magnani), a seamstress living in a small fishing town on the outskirts of New Orleans, to ask her to make a shirt out of rose-colored silk cloth for her lover, who, she says, is as "wild as a Gypsy." Estelle goes off to the Mardi Gras Club in New Orleans where she is a blackjack dealer, while Serafina speaks to her sleeping husband, who is a truck driver/smuggler and informs him that she is pregnant. After suddenly leaving the house abruptly without even saying goodbye or remarking on his forthcoming child, he is killed during a police ambush in the countryside. Subsequently Estelle turns up at Serafina's home dressed in mourning, and we discover that her lover was Serafina's husband Rosario—something apparently everyone in the tightly knit Sicilian community knew except Serafina and her daughter—and her neighbors attack Estelle, shouting "assassina" in Italian until she is rescued by the parish priest.

The film then cuts to a period three years later (no dates are given but judging from the cars in the film, the time frame is more or less contemporary). Although Serafina sews all the prom dresses for the entire Italian community, she refuses to allow her daughter Rosa (Marisa Pavan) to dress up for the prom and graduation from high school. Rosa wants to be an American girl, free to follow her fancies, whereas Serafina expects her to accept the sick and self-indulgent life of mourning that she believes she must embrace for the rest of her life. Rosa meets a young sailor named Jack Hunter and stays out with him late, telling her mother she has been studying civics with him. When her mother refuses to believe this obvious excuse, Rosa's parody of her mother's Sicilian-accented English reflects the conflict of two generations:

> "You don't study no civics tonight." Why do you talk like you just came over in steerage. This isn't Sicily and you're not a baronessa. You do sewing. Daddy . . . Daddy hauled bananas, he hauled bananas and something under the bananas. . . .

"The Sheik of Araby" resounds on the player piano. This musical motif was originally inspired by one of Rudolph Valentino's most famous movie performances, and it continues to play throughout *The Rose Tatoo* to emphasize the power of love that eventually triumphs. Rosa feels ashamed of her mother's Sicilian attachment to her dead father, based on self-delusion. The rest of the film progressively destroys Serafina's illusions about her husband Rosario and offers a parallel between the passion Rosa feels for Jack and what Serafina begins to feel for a happy-go-lucky Sicilian named Alvaro Mangiacavallo (Burt Lancaster).

Serafina learns of her husband's unfaithfulness from two loose women eager to encounter men attending a political convention in New Orleans: one of them has asked Serafina to sew a blouse for the occasion. They, too, know about Estelle's affair with Rosario, eventually reacting to Serafina's puritanical attitudes by telling her that Estelle not only had an affair with him but that she, too, bought "a rose tattoo on her chest . . . same as the macaroni's. . . ."

Serafina's passion for her errant husband had always been expressed within the bounds of holy matrimony, but now Rosa's budding sexuality becomes almost aggressive. She tells Jack that you learn to dance with a man by feeling his moves with your body and that he has made her feel like a woman for the first time in her life. Serafina's sexuality lies dormant underneath her surface morality like a volcano, while she sees Rosa as "a wild thing" and even forces Jack to promise in front of a statue of the Madonna that he will respect Rosa's "innocence." Of course, she has made sure that Jack is Catholic as well. Their exchange also demonstrates their conflicting cultures, Sicilian and American:

> JACK: I guess Sicilians are very emotional people.
> SERAFINA: I want nobody to take advantage of that.

JACK: You got the wrong idea about me, Mrs. Delle Rose.

SERAFINA: Hummm. . . . I know what men want . . . not to eat ice cream or dance on the floor. . . . no. . . . and boys are the same, only younger.

Alvaro Mangiacavallo appears after almost half the film has run: he is slightly crazy, unmarried, and *simpatico* in the extreme. Moreover, when Serafina offers to darn his shirt, his muscular body arouses her sexual interest: "Madonna Santa, my husband's body with the head of a clown! A clown that smells like a goat!" She offers him the silk shirt she has sewn after he announces that he is an eligible bachelor and has nothing more than "love and affection in a world that's lonely and cold" to offer. Now Alvaro starts up the player piano, and "The Sheik of Araby" theme song takes on renewed meaning.

Serafina's iron resolve to honor her husband begins to melt. Alvaro shows her a rose tattoo he has had placed on his chest to show her how much he loves her, but this only inspires her to force Alvaro to take her to the Mardi Gras Club to confront Estelle, still hoping to learn that her husband was always faithful. In an emotional scene near her blackjack table, Estelle actually bares her breasts to show Serafina her tattoo—discreetly turned away from the camera's eye! Serafina's response is to return home, smash the urn containing her husband's ashes, eventually accepting Alvaro's comic but authentic suit for her affections. The final scene shows Alvaro singing a comic song in Italian ("rondinella felice" or "happy little swallow") with the approval of the entire neighborhood. Serafina is also reconciled with her daughter, approves of her marriage to Jack, and once again she starts the player piano with its theme song of "The Sheik of Araby" as she invites Alvaro into her home with the beguiling remark: "Now we can go on with our conversation." A crazy neighbor that according to Serafina has the evil eye (the *mal'occhio*) closes the film with a cackle and a final judgment: "Them Italians is at it again . . . and a truck driver in the household."

Tennessee Williams knew the Sicilian community of New Orleans quite well, thanks to his partner Frank Merlo. He lived in the French Quarter, at the time populated primarily by Italian immigrants. Moreover, he apparently wrote *The Rose Tattoo* for Anna Magnani, an actress he met and admired in Rome during the years immediately following the American occupation of Rome and whose voluptuous earthiness he had obviously admired in such neorealist classics as *Open City* and *The Miracle* (1948) by Roberto Rossellini, who had also been her lover at one time. What is striking about this film is the stellar performance that earned Anna Magnani an unheard-of honor, the Oscar for Best Actress, a prize never before bestowed on an Italian actress and one that would not be repeated until Sophia Loren won the same award for Vittorio De Sica's *Two Women* (1959, *La ciociara*). Her performance strikes a believable although highly emotional note, one that seems not so much a stereotypical portrait of a Sicilian woman as a replay of the unforgettable role she fulfilled in Rossellini's *Open City:* earthy, voluptuous, passionate, and comic in the most serious and humane sense of this term. The film portrays in a memorable way two generations in conflict within a vibrant ethnic community that offers emotional support for both the traditional Sicilian values of the old country—what many scholars of the Italian American experience have labeled *la via vecchia*[18]—and the new and more open values of the New World in which she now lives with her daughter, who must negotiate a safe passage between these two sometimes mutually exclusive systems of morality. As a historical document, *The Rose Tattoo* depicts an ethnic community that has not been solely reconstructed by the nostalgic power of memory, unlike many of the films explored later on in this chapter.

The Hollywood Italians of both the play and its film adaptation belong to an ethnic world that was, at the time the play and film were presented, still very much alive in Southern Louisiana. The film also embraces the new ways of loving in America: Serafina's arranged marriage as a young bride from Sicily ended in death and betrayal because of a blond WASP hussy, but the marriage of Jack and Rosa and the love affair between Serafina and Alvaro promise to end happily (a completely unusual conclusion for a Tennessee Williams play or film adaptation) precisely because these new passions are founded upon a typically American openness to a freer and more honest expression of basic human emotions.

Marty *(1955): Fatso Judson Falls in Love*

Ernest Borgnine (1917–) was frequently typecast as a heavy in numerous supporting roles, such as that of Fatso Judson in *From Here to Eternity*, not to mention similar parts in *Bad Day at Black Rock* (1955), *The Dirty Dozen* (1967), and especially *The Wild Bunch* (1969). Subsequently, on the popular television series *McHale's Navy* (1962–66), he demonstrated a range of acting talents that included comedy. His performance in *Marty* earned him an Oscar for Best Actor, as well as acting awards from the New York Film Critics, the Golden Globes, and the British Academy of Film and Television Arts, while Delbert Mann received an Oscar for Best Director, and the film won an Oscar as the year's Best Picture. Some of the most interesting films of the 1950s were in contention for awards that year (*East of Eden, The Rose Tattoo, Picnic, Rebel without a Cause, Bad Day at Black Rock*), and the actors

The Rose Tattoo *(1955; Daniel Mann, director). After years of acting like a traditional southern Italian widow, Serafina (Anna Magnani) finally succeeds in laughing and having fun with a happy-go-lucky Sicilian bachelor named Alvaro (Burt Lancaster).*

competing for recognition included Sal Mineo, James Dean, Frank Sinatra, and Anna Magnani, to mention only the most famous. Yet, *Marty*'s simple story line and its moving account of a timid Italian American butcher working in an Italian American neighborhood in the Bronx was the surprise winner of most of the attention during that year's ceremonies. The film was produced by an independent company set up by Burt Lancaster and Harold Hecht, and was developed from a television play written by Paddy Chayefsky (who received the Oscar for Best Screenplay). Burt Lancaster, fresh from the triumph of *From Here to Eternity*, provided the narration for the film's trailer, in which he describes (self-interestedly, of course, as its producer) the film as "the most beautiful love story I've ever seen in a movie" and notes that the film's location, East 187th Street and Arthur Avenue in the Bronx, was near where he was born. He also emphasizes the fact that the neighborhood was characterized by "many racial strains" and that New York was "just a huge collection of neighborhoods." Essentially, he is arguing that they intended to make an ethnic picture, and indeed, *Marty* provides a fascinating portrait of the different attitudes toward love between generations in a manner that recalls *The Rose Tattoo*. *Marty*, of courses, focuses upon the male Italian American, not the female.

Marty Piletti is an overweight and awkward butcher, who has graduated from high school, served in the Army until the age of twenty-four, and returned home to a household of six siblings, all of whom are married except him. As a student, he was no intellectual but did well in high school, excelling in tough subjects (German, math). The obligations he felt to help his family and his five other brothers and sisters kept him from taking advantage of the GI Bill, and he, therefore, never attended the university. Now aged thirty-four, all his siblings are married and some already have families, but Marty remains stuck at home with his mother Theresa (Esther Minciotti) who constantly nags him about finding a wife. Frustrated by his failure to find love, he has practically given up because underneath his burly exterior, Marty possesses a sensitive soul that completely negates the stereotypical macho, Latin Lover image of the Italian American male. At the local bar where other single bachelors of the neighborhood hang out, Angie (Joe Mantell) and Marty exchange the film's memorably sad but funny lines:

ANGIE: What do you feel like doing tonight?
MARTY: I dunno, Angie. What do you feel like doing?

These two sentences become the film's mantra. At home, Marty finally explodes at his mother's nagging insistence upon marriage and reveals his inferiority complex:

Whatever it is that women like, I ain't got it. I chased after enough girls in my life. I . . . I went to enough dances. I got hurt enough. I don't wanna get hurt no more. I just called up a girl this afternoon, and I got a real brush-off, boy! . . . I'm just a fat, little man. A fat ugly man. . . . Ma, whaddaya want from me? Whaddaya want from me? I'm miserable enough as it is.

Finally driven to distraction, Marty and Angie go to the Stardust Ballroom, a local dance hall, where the miracle occurs: he meets a high-school chemistry teacher named Clara Snyder (Betsy Blair) who is being dumped by her blind date, and Marty's compassion for the girl kindles an immediate attraction between the two lonely hearts. Marty dries her tears, confesses that he, too, cries a lot, and explains his good-natured character by the pain he has suffered: "You don't get to be good-hearted by accident. You get kicked around long enough, you get to be a . . . a real professor of pain. I know exactly how you feel."

This Cinderella story pairing the traditional ugly duckling with the antithesis of the ethnic Latin Lover becomes more complicated with a sub-

Marty *(1955; Delbert Mann, director). A lonely bachelor named Marty Piletti (Ernest Borgnine) tries to change his habitual bad luck with women after he meets a high-school chemistry teacher named Clara Snyder (Betsy Blair).*

plot involving Marty's mother Theresa and her sister Caterina (Augusta Ciolli). The two Italian women, immigrants who still speak their native language, are obsessed by a paradoxical but natural obsession for Italian or Italian American mothers: while they want their sons and daughters to marry and have children, they also fear they will be forced to live alone once they have no husband for whom to cook and clean. Thus, sons become surrogates for departed husbands.

When confronted with Clara in her home, dread of abandonment quickly strikes Theresa, and when Clara volunteers the opinion that she feels young married couples should have their privacy, Theresa Piletti begins to echo her sister's paranoid fears, declaring:

> It's a curse to be a mother, I tell you. . . . Itsa very sad thing whena you son hasa no place for you in his house . . . you gotta have a housa to clean. You gotta have children to cooka for. Dese are the terrible years for a mother.

Clara's innocent remark that mothers need more to give their lives meaning than their children receives the sarcastic reply: "Well, thatsa whata they teach you ina New York University? Inna real life, it no work out like this. You wait until you are a mother." Once Clara has left the house, Theresa declares that college girls are only one step removed from hookers and orders Marty not to bring her back because she is not Italian. One point in her favor, Clara's Catholicism, does not emerge at this point.

Traditional mythology maintains that when an Italian American male has a choice to make between his mother and his wife or girlfriend, the mother always wins. And indeed, this seems to be the direction the film is heading as Marty fails to call Clara at the appointed time for a second date and heads off to the bar with his bachelor friends. At the bar, three of them carry on a completely chauvinist discussion about how Mickey Spillane's Mike Hammer novels demonstrate the proper attitude toward women. Angie and Marty's other friends criticize Clara (they classify women they don't like as "dogs"). Suddenly Marty hears the film's famous refrain, only now spoken by others ("What do you feel like doing, Angie?" "I dunno. What do you feel like doing?" "I dunno."). In a moment of courage, he tells his friends that they are wasting their time, that he had a wonderful time with the woman they dismissed as a "dog," and rushes to a public phone booth to call her. The film ends with Marty talking to Clara.

The simple, uncomplicated narrative line of *Marty*, not unlike equally simple yet eloquent storylines of Italian neorealist classics from only a few years earlier, struck a chord in audiences all over the world. Who has not had fears and disappointments when attempting to meet the other sex?

Who but the most disagreeable, egomaniacal Latin Lovers? Part of the power of *Marty* is that it succeeds in treating such a theme with an Italian American lead. Rather than a modern Romeo, Marty lacks even the modicum of those social graces usually associated with Italian men, who are supposed to sweep women off their feet with their good looks, their charm, and their animal sex appeal. Ernest Borgnine plays against his usual role, and the film undercuts the ethnic stereotypes we frequently associate with Italian lovers. In spite of the memorable performances of both Borgnine and Betsy Blair, however, perhaps the most memorable sequences of the film involve the two Italian widows: Esther Miniciotti and Augusta Ciolli provide completely authentic characterizations of an earlier generation of female immigrants who came to America, like Serafina Delle Rose in *The Rose Tattoo*, committed to a life given over completely to the care of their husbands, husbands who frequently disregarded their self-sacrificial definition of the tasks of motherhood. Marty's attachment to a strong, independent American (but Catholic!) woman such as Clara holds out the promise that the third generation of Italian American sons and daughters may well adopt a very different cultural model than that of the self-effacing and sacrificial—yet controlling—wife and mother who gives her husband and family everything, leaving no meaning in her life when her family leaves home.

Little Italy as Paradise Lost in Postwar America: Hollywood Italians in Mac *(1992),* Big Night *(1996),* A Bronx Tale *(1993),* Household Saints *(1993),* Love with The Proper Stranger *(1963),* ItalianAmerican *(1974),* Moonstruck *(1987),* True Love *(1989), and* My Cousin Vinny *(1992)*

It is a commonplace that Italian American immigrants took longer to emerge from the laboring classes to reach the middle and upper-middle classes in America than other groups who arrived in America at approximately the same time. In this regard, Jewish immigrants are most frequently cited, and indeed, the canonical novel of the Italian American experience, *Christ in Concrete*, even contains a Russian Jewish character named Louis Molov, the friend of Geremio's son Paul, who realizes (unlike Geremio, whose culture stresses the nobility of manual labor, not book learning) that education and books are the ticket out of the ghetto where immigrants were condemned to physically demanding, low-paying, low-prestige jobs. Louis's book of choice is, ironically, Thorstein Veblen's *Theory of the Leisure Class*, and to the contemporary reader, Louis seems destined to make a career as a professional or even a university professor unlike his Italian American neighbors who will spend an additional generation in their rise out from the depths of the working class. Even as late as the mid-1950s in *Marty*, the timid butcher admits that his trade has low social status and regrets not receiving proper university training, especially since (as noted) he was very good in tough subjects in high school. The immigrants who settled in America by 1920 had children like Marty who later served in the American armed forces during World War II and were subsequently eligible for the GI Bill, the ticket to advanced education for many. Their children, a third generation of people of Italian descent, found it much easier to move on to higher education and to climb the ladder of success in America. Today, during the first decade of the twenty-first century, chief-executive officers of major corporations, university presidents, and high-ranking politicians and professional people with Italian names or Italian origins are so numerous that they need not be listed. And in the Hollywood cinema, as the dedication to this book suggests, Italian Americans have recently played a significant role in shaping the image of Hollywood Italians in the mass media. As America has transformed itself into a homogenized land of shopping malls and suburbs rather than a collection of individual urban ghetto villages in metropolitan centers that initially welcomed foreign immigrants, the present generation of filmmakers has looked back on the past of their childhood and the world their fathers and mothers made with understandable nostalgia for the family, community, religious values, and the memories of that period.

Mac, a film directed by actor John Turturro and dedicated at its conclusion to the memory of his father Nicholas R. Turturro, celebrates the same working-class values of dedication to a high tradition of craftsmanship that has characterized Italian builders since the cathedrals of the Middle Ages and Renaissance were constructed in the Old Country. Set in the Italian section of Queens in 1954 (exactly the same period depicted in *Marty* with far less nostalgia), this interesting film traces the conflicts between the three Vitelli brothers: Mac (John Turturro), Vico (Michael Badalucco), and Bruno (Carlo Capotorto). *Mac* also continues a practice common since the 1970s, from Scorsese and Coppola to *The Sopranos*—that of casting large numbers of authentic Italian Americans as Hollywood Italians, giving the film a truer ethnic flavor. As the credits roll, its powerful opening image of booted feet striding through mud and wet concrete on a construction site visualizes its major theme of the nobility of manual labor that *Christ in Concrete* celebrated in a more obviously ideological manner. A number of musical pieces, such as Italian folk songs carried over from the Old Country, Enrico Caruso, and music from Verdi's opera *Il trovatore*, provide nostalgic ethnic commentary, and unlike the sound tracks of other films in this period depicting Hollywood Italians, the music here looks primarily toward the past rather than toward contemporary songs by popular groups, as is so typical of the films by Scorsese and others of his generation.

As each of the three brothers approaches their father's coffin at a wake, the director constructs a spooky scene in which the dead father inspires a personal memory in the life of each brother as a boy. In three flashbacks, Mac learns honesty by being sent to one of his father's customers who tries to avoid paying his father for the work he has done for him; Vico learns to urinate on his soft hands to avoid the blisters that construction work causes; and Bruno watches as his father paints a fresco-like narrative painting on their staircase. Then, this stern first-generation patriarch reminds his three offspring of the simple values that he has inculcated in them:

> By the work one knows the workman. . . . Rome wasn't built in a day. You remember . . . there's only two ways to do something . . . my way and the right way, and they are both the same.

The archaic wailing of Italian-speaking women dressed in the traditional black widow's weeds of the Mezzogiorno at the funeral drives the point home that these values are both ancient and foreign—imported into the New World. Mac accepts his father's advice as the golden rule. As he puts it, happiness is "loving your job . . . every job is like a . . . first love." Nonetheless, Bruno is really more interested in painting and Vico likes a good party more than construction and carpentry. Unlike his brothers, Mac is obsessed with placing studs in the proper place to make a sound wall, not the cheaper, sleazier method of spacing studs further apart to save a few cents, as his Polish boss forces him to do. He convinces his two brothers to go into construction on their own, building four houses on spec near an insane asylum and a cow pasture that reeks of manure, land they can afford to purchase with the meager funds at their disposal. The shrieks of the inmates and the stench of the fields almost destroy any chance of finding customers for the homes, but Mac's manic drive to complete four well-built houses that are the antithesis of the contemporary Levittown mass-produced domiciles prevails. His single-minded determination finally alienates his brothers so that they abandon him just as he is about to launch a second and much more ambitious project. In the process, Vico and Bruno also reject the traditional values of their father and their heritage. In effect, they have been Americanized in the sense that they adopt the values of the dominant culture, not those of the patriarch or his son Mac.

In a moving conclusion, Mac brings his young son to see the four beautiful homes he and his brothers built and tells him that in his grandfather's

Mac (1992; John Turturro, director). The three Vitelli brothers—Bruno (Carlo Capotorto), Mac (John Turturro), and Vico (Michael Badalucco)—bid on a lot, gambling that they can make a profit from building a house on spec.

day, people still cared about craftsmanship and the necessity of doing honest, competent work with their hands. In what would have constituted a rebuttal to the image of success offered by *The Man in the Gray Flannel Suit* (1955), Sloan Wilson's best-seller that depicted an entirely different set of 1950s values, Mac warns his son: "Not today. Today, it's the man who can talk who's respected. Before it was the man who could do . . . they were ones looked up to . . . to reach the goals it's nice, it's pleasant . . . it's the doing that's the thing."[19]

Most likely Turturro was inspired to make this film by an understandable desire to honor his father and his Italian American cult of craftsmanship and perhaps to pay homage to an Italian film made only a few years earlier by Paolo and Vittorio Taviani, *Good Morning Babylon* (1989). In that work, the Tavianis depicted a pair of Italian immigrants who learn the craft of building from their father who has worked on Italian cathedrals and later share their construction skills in Hollywood with D. W. Griffith, employing the detail of an elephant from the façade of the cathedral in Pisa as the basis for the design of an elephant that plays a crucial role in the

Babylonian set of *Intolerance* and makes their fortunes in America as set designers. At the close of the film, Griffith makes a speech that implicitly embraces the idea of filmmaking as a craft not unlike the building of the great medieval and Renaissance cathedrals in Italy.[20]

Like *Mac,* which was Turturro's directorial debut, *Big Night* is actor Stanley Tucci's first effort as a director, with the assistance of Campbell Scott. This film, too, is set in an Italian American community in the 1950s but in New Jersey, not New York City. This light-handed and well-directed comedy also casts doubt not only on American values but on Italian American culture as well, identifying it with the new consumer society of the 1950s through the metaphor of cooking rather than carpentry. On a single street are two Italian restaurants. One, the Italian Grotto, is operated by a successful Italian immigrant named Pascal (Ian Holm) who caters to the worst excesses of bad Italian American cooking and to the ignorant expectations of unsophisticated clients who identify Italian cuisine with red sauce and pizza—live performances of mediocre singers wailing the usual songs foreigners always identify with Italy after a week's tour of Rome, Florence, and Venice ("O sole mio" and so forth); pasta as a side dish rather than as an independent first course; everything drenched in tomato sauce without any particular taste; flaming desserts; and huge quantities of everything, all cooked with no particular

Big Night *(1996; Stanley Tucci and Campbell Scott, directors). The talented but temperamental chef Primo Pilaggi (Tony Shalhoub) and his maitre d' partner, his brother Secondo Pilaggi (Stanley Tucci), discuss the ingredients of a meal.*

skill but with panache and salesmanship. While the Italian Grotto is predictably packed with Anglo clients, across the street the smaller and less pretentious restaurant called the Paradise is run by two brothers, the talented chef Primo Pilaggi (Tony Shalhoub) and his maitre d' brother Secondo (Stanley Tucci). There, as Primo declares in his broken Italian that sometimes requires English subtitles, the dominant atmosphere must be one of tradition and reverence for the genius of Italian cuisine, combined with the individual chef's creativity. "To eat good food is to be close to God," Primo says, and he is enraged when one of his few customers complains about the delay required when dishes are made specifically to order and demands pasta as a side dish with risotto. Secondo attempts to reason with and instruct the customers, remarking that "sometimes spaghetti likes to be alone," but Primo is enraged when he must cook pasta as a side dish with rice, declaring that the woman is a "criminal" and shouting angrily: "If you give people time, they learn." Secondo, who must pay the bills with very little income from so few customers, replies: "I don't have time for them to learn. This is a restaurant, not a fucking school!" While Primo describes the kind of cuisine that Pascal offers as "rape" and says that the man should be imprisoned for what he serves, Pascal has clearly adopted American culinary values along with American business sense. Central to being successful in America, described by Pascal as "the land of fucking opportunity," is marketing: "Give to people what *they* want. Later you can give them what *you* want!"

Secondo enjoys a secret affair with Pascal's mistress Gabriella (Isabella Rossellini), but Pascal focuses only on the genius of Primo's cooking and devises a scheme to ruin the brothers, thereby forcing Primo to work for him. He proposes that with their last funds, the brothers invite Louis Prima, the famous Italian American jazz musician, to an extraordinary dinner that reporters will write up in the papers, thereby attracting customers. His plan is never actually to invite his friend Prima, and the sumptuous meal lovingly prepared by Primo lacks its main guest.

Much of the film's narrative concerns the preparation of the meal, done with the tender care that Mac required of his workmen on his houses. When Secondo finally realizes that Prima is not coming, he announces: "Let's eat!" And what follows is a triumph of conviviality and culinary genius introduced by Rosemary Clooney's classic rendition of Prima's "Mambo Italiano." Pascal provides lavish praise for the meal, employing his favorite American swear word when he informs Primo "this is so fucking good I could kill you!"

After Secondo discovers Pascal's real intentions are to take over Primo's skills as a chef (and not to take revenge for Secondo's affair with his mistress), Secondo tells Pascal that Primo's kind of talent and love for his art is "rare" but that "you are nothing." Pascal's reply ("I am a businessman. . . . Tell me, what exactly are you?") underlines perfectly the clash of two very different mentalities—one associated with craft and tradition from Italy, and another, the diametrically opposed American values of fast and flashy cuisine drenched in tomato and garlic sauce with no perceptible art.

Unlike *Mac*, where the brothers clash and two of the three reject their traditional belief in craftsmanship, Primo and Secondo fight but they are reconciled in an empty kitchen, where they share a simple omelet prepared and consumed in a single long shot reminiscent of similar scenes, some also in kitchens, in the best neorealist films of Roberto Rossellini, Luchino Visconti, and Vittorio De Sica, or other films treating the ritual of eating Italian food made by Ettore Scola that are indebted to the neorealist model of De Sica.[21] The impact of Italian cinema upon Italian American directors of Tucci's generation cannot be ignored. Martin Scorsese, for instance, has documented the ways in which Italian neorealism and the great post-neorealist art films by Fellini, Visconti, and Rossellini have shaped his cinematic vision in a documentary entitled *Il mio viaggio in Italia* (*My Voyage in Italy*, 2002), a companion piece to his documentary on American films. Scorsese was, of course, once married to Roberto Rossellini's daughter Isabella, whose presence in *Big Night*'s cast immediately brings to mind the question of influence.

What makes *Big Night* unusual in the context of depictions of Hollywood Italians is that Tucci's critique aims not just at the juxtaposition of Italian cuisine, symbolizing Italian values and culture—on the one hand—and American culinary ignorance, symbolizing American values and culture—on the other. Less obvious but no less important is the fact that *Big Night* also shows us a certain kind of Italian American cuisine—and by extension, Italian American culture and values—to be as shallow as those of the America that has apparently corrupted them. Pascal's customers have no understanding of authentic Italian food, but there is no long line of sophisticated Italian American immigrants outside the door of the Paradise either, even in a New Jersey filled with immigrants from Italy. The Italian Americans of New Jersey flock to Pascal's Italian Grotto. In other words, Tucci's film implicitly contains criticism of the ethnic culture it describes as well as the dominant culture that surrounds it.

A Bronx Tale shares a number of similarities with *Mac* and *Big Night*. It is the first directorial outing by accomplished actor Robert De Niro. It is important to note that in these three movies about Hollywood Italians, three important Italian American actors have attempted to rediscover their ethnic roots in different ways through a nostalgic look back in time to their

A Bronx Tale *(1993; Robert De Niro, director). A young Calogero (Francis Capra)
refuses to identify the local Mafia boss, Sonny (Chazz Palminteri), remaining true
to the code of* omertà.

parents' generation. Like Turturro's *Mac*, *A Bronx Tale* contains a dedication at the end of the film to the director's father, Robert De Niro, Sr.

De Niro's coming-of-age film covers the years between 1960 and 1968 in
the Fordham section of the Bronx (East 187th Street), an Italian American
neighborhood at that time not far from the setting of *Marty*. The picture develops through a voice-over narration by the protagonist, a young Italian
American boy named Calogero (played at age nine by Francis Capra and by
Lillo Brancato at age seventeen). Sonny is played by Chazz Palminteri, who is
also the author of the original play upon which the movie is based. He is the
local Mafia boss who hangs out in a bar called Chez Bippy and who takes
Calogero under his wing when the boy refuses to tell the police it was Sonny
who killed a man in front of his eyes. The entire film juxtaposes the values of
Calogero's father Lorenzo (Robert De Niro) with those of the mobster.[22]
Calogero must choose between his father's work ethic and honesty, on the
one hand, and the cynical, violent lifestyle espoused by Sonny, based upon a
philosophy that "nobody cares or gives a damn" and justified intellectually by
quotations taken out of context from Machiavelli's *The Prince*. At one point
in the film, Sonny declares that he has learned about the importance of
"availability" from Machiavelli—Sonny could live anywhere he liked but he

stays in the neighborhood and hangs around Chez Bippy to keep his eyes on things just as the model prince must go to his provinces personally to live with his subjects so that he may spot trouble when it is brewing and not after it has developed into a crisis. Even more importantly, Sonny warns Calogero that it is much better to be feared than to be loved, but he claims that even when feared, he works hard to avoid being hated (the advice Machiavelli offers in the famous chapter 17 of *The Prince*).

Although exotic nicknames are certainly not a particularly Italian custom (judging from my time in Italy), it seems that Hollywood Italian gangsters cannot avoid having them. In fact, Sonny's "crew" at Chez Bippy all have the usual nicknames we have come to identify with Italian American gangsters: Jimmy "Whispers," Sonny's main man, never speaks loudly; Giorgio "the Whale" is obese (Calogero says his shadow once killed a dog); Eddie "Mush" is a loser with no luck, and anything he does turns to mush; and so forth. Sonny therefore gives Calogero a nickname: "C." This act of naming reflects the Mafia boss's power over his subordinates as well as the set of values that tempts Calogero into following a violent lifestyle that will undoubtedly end in prison and trouble. Lorenzo takes offense at the nickname, since Italian American tradition gives the son the grandfather's name, and Calogero's father thinks using a nickname shows disrespect for his roots as well as respect for a gangster mentality. Lorenzo is an honest man who drives a bus and refuses to have anything to do with Sonny and his crew. When Calogero refuses to identify Sonny for a murder he commits (something that Lorenzo realizes is morally wrong but necessary to save his son's life), Sonny offers him a job delivering numbers for $150 a week from his bus (a fortune in those days) which he indignantly refuses. If Sonny's creed is "nobody gives a damn" and "it is better to be feared than to be loved," Lorenzo argues for the courage and dignity of the working man, telling his son that the real heroes of the neighborhood are the working stiffs who get up every morning to support their wives and children, and that people feel no love for Sonny—only fear. Lorenzo repeats over and over again that the saddest thing in the world is wasted talent, that Calogero must learn how Sonny squanders his abilities and future by choosing the path of least resistance toward quick gains and dangerous choices. After discovering the $600 Calogero has earned by carrying drinks to the floating craps game in the back of Chez Bippy (once shooting the dice for Sonny, he made eleven passes in a row!), Lorenzo goes to the bar and confronts Sonny in front of his men, showing him disrespect but also forcing him to admit that interfering with a man's children is off limits, even for a Mafioso. Although Sonny gives Lorenzo a tongue-lashing, the fact that he avoids harming him physically even though he has been challenged in public shows that Sonny realizes he is wrong. According to a code as ancient in Italian culture as the Mafia code of *omertà* (the code Sonny serves), a man's family is also sacred and off limits to others.

The film then flashes forward eight years to 1968, where Calogero is hanging out with his own group of potential juvenile delinquents and petty criminals at their own social club, The Deuces Are Wild, an obvious imitation of Sonny's hangout at Chez Bippy. Sonny has now become an important boss, but the neighborhood has begun to change: blacks drive through the area from time to time, causing consternation among Calogero's friends. De Niro introduces the question of racial prejudice into the plot in this fashion and even has Calogero fall for a black girl named Jane who enrolls at his high school. Nonetheless, Calogero's friends are determined to get into trouble: they beat up some blacks riding bicycles near The Deuces Are Wild and subsequently go to the black area of town to intimidate the residents with Molotov cocktails. When one of the cocktails tossed into a store is tossed back into their car by one of the blacks, the car explodes, killing all of Calogero's friends. Calogero has been saved by a miracle, because Sonny has warned him that all of his friends are "jerkoffs," not real tough guys. He even drags

A Bronx Tale *(1993; Robert De Niro, director). An older Calogero (Lillo Brancato on the far left) hangs out with his adolescent friends at their social club, The Deuces Are Wild, an institution they have formed in imitation of Sonny's social club, Chez Bippy, where the local Mafiosi congregate.*

Calogero out of the car physically just a short time before their ill-fated mission to the black ghetto ends in death.

Much popular culture "wisdom" has of late identified Italian Americans with racial prejudice toward blacks, and De Niro addresses this issue directly but with an entirely different focus from that of Spike Lee, the black director well known for his negative portrayal of Italian Americans as racist bigots. Little Italies represent communities forged by bonds connecting people of like origin, religion, and culture. When outsiders enter such communities, their inhabitants sometimes feel threatened. De Niro shows that this kind of suspicion of outsiders characterizes not only the Little Italy of the Bronx but also the black section where Jane lives. Calogero is chased out of that area after he walks her home, in much the same way (although less violently) as his friends threatened blacks in the Italian community. When the white boys die in the exploding car, an angry black crowd gathers that is as menacing as any ever seen in any Italian community.

De Niro has cleverly contrasted two sets of values, one the traditional Italian sense of honor and dignity connected with a job well done, and the other an equally traditional Italian code of honor connected with organized crime. A father and a foster father embody these ideals. Calogero learns something from both figures. The director brings the three characters together at the funeral for Sonny, who was murdered without warning at a party by the son of the man he killed eight years ago as Calogero looked on. The scene has the usual mobster pomp: enormous wreaths of flowers, apparently grief-stricken henchmen, and an open coffin. By the time the commotion ends, only one person remains at the funeral home. We see Calogero telling the dead Sonny that he was right: "Nobody cares." Then Lorenzo amazes his son by showing up at the coffin out of respect for Sonny and because he saved his son's life. Calogero finally learns the lesson that his father had been trying to teach him for eight years and makes the crucial choice between the values Sonny represents and those his father has inculcated in him: "Nobody cares, huh? You were wrong about that one . . . wasted talent." If Calogero finally accepts the fact that his father's mantra about wasted talent was correct and that Sonny, for all his charm, was the prime example of a wasted life, Lorenzo has also changed in relation to his son. He understands that his son needed to make the choice between Sonny's values and his own by himself without pressure from his father. He seems to recognize that his son has come of age when he employs Calogero's nickname "C" in addressing him as they leave the funeral home. Once thought of as disrespect to their forebears, now Lorenzo accepts this change of name because his son has shown the maturity to select his own path in life.

No doubt influenced by Martin Scorsese's typical use of contemporary sound tracks, De Niro's sound track boasts a number of songs identified with the 1960s, including a number of doo-wop numbers: "Streets of the Bronx" by Cool Change; "Baby, I Need Your Loving" by the Four Tops, and "I Wonder Why" by Dion and the Belmonts, to name only the most famous. He is also not afraid to make fun of the Italian Americans he pictures. At one point the refrain of one of the doo-wop numbers repeats the term "wop" numerous times at the opening of the film, warning the viewer in an intentionally provocative fashion, that this film will be about Italian Americans. He even pictures fat Italians in T-shirts sitting on street corners, never avoiding the entire idea of ethnic identity. As the film opens, Calogero's voice-over announces pompously that around the neighborhood in the evening, one could hear "the sound of young Italian men romancing their women." This remark is juxtaposed to an image of a neighborhood male driving a car and following a girl who is obviously furious with him, as he exclaims: "Hey, Marie . . . get in the fucking car . . . come on, baby, you know I love you." In short, De Niro is comfortable depicting his Hollywood Italian characters in stereotypical fashion, because the direction of the whole film cuts against such stereotypical ideas about Italian Americans and about stereotypes in general. Calogero rejects the Mafia and ultimately grows up, preferring his father's values to those he admired as an immature youth. But whereas Lorenzo was a bit edgy about Calogero dating a black girl, the gangster Sonny advised his protégé that there were only three great women in a man's life and that if he thought he loved her, he should disregard the social pressure in the neighborhood that argued for racial prejudice against blacks. Calogero begins the film as a potential "Guido," the kind of shallow person represented by Tony Manero (John Travolta) in *Saturday Night Fever* (a film discussed in the section devoted to Hollywood Italian Romeos). Although he even has the obvious desire to imitate the neighborhood gangsters, both his father and the mobster he admires push him to get an education and to avoid the kind of life Sonny lives. In the final analysis, Calogero understands that they have both offered sound counsel.

Most representations of Hollywood Italians embody a male viewpoint, but two films directed by an Italian American woman, Nancy Savoca (1960–   )—*True Love* (1989) and *Household Saints* (1993)—offer decidedly feminist perspectives on Italian American values relating to marriage and the family. The second of the two films, *Household Saints*—like *A Bronx Tale*—traces an Italian American family over several decades beginning in 1948 and continuing to the first years of the 1970s. It is an adaptation from the novel of the same name by Francine Prose. Savoca opens and closes her adaptation with an important narrative frame presumably taking place in 1989, a few years before the film was made. Three generations of a single family gather for a picnic meal under a trellis in what appears to be the suburbs, not a Little Italy in Manhattan, Queens, the Bronx, or Staten Island. Eating a plate of sausage, the grandfather tells the assembled group that this dish is nothing like the "miracle sausage" you used to buy in the old neighborhood at the Santangelo Butcher Shop. His wife then says that the butcher's daughter Theresa was a saint, and that Joseph the butcher won his wife in a pinochle game. At that point, Savoca cuts to a flashback in 1949 and the San Gennaro Festival where people in the neighborhood of Little Italy in Manhattan watch the celebration from the fire escapes of their tenements as the credits roll. Four men, all Italian American workers in T-shirts, meet for their regular pinochle game: Joseph Santangelo (Vincent D'Onofrio), Lino Falconetti (Victor Argo), Nicky Falconetti, Lino's son (Michael Rispoli), and another neighbor. On this scorching summer day without air-conditioning, Lino, in a fit of heat prostration and alcoholic stupor, bets his daughter Catherine (Tracey Ullman) in marriage against the cold air from Joseph's butcher-shop freezer. Naturally, Lino loses, and he orders his daughter to get sausage from Joseph's shop to feed the Santangelo family a meal in the Falconetti home.

Catherine's supper is a genuine meal from hell, thanks to her complete incompetence in the kitchen and the cruel and insensitively supercritical remarks made by Joseph's mother (co-founder of The Living Theatre, Judith Malina). This kind of disastrous repast is one of the recurrent motifs in representations of Hollywood Italians, precisely because mealtime, so important an aspect of Italian or Italian American culture, presents a perfect occasion for depicting clashes of values and generational conflict. Here, Joseph's mother describes how another son married a woman who named their children Stacey and Scott. Who is going to protect these children, she asks, since there are obviously no saints named Stacey and Scott in any Catholic pantheon with which she is familiar. Then she mutters in Italian "women today are ignorant," knowing that Catherine understands Italian. Choosing a name in Italian culture represents an important moment in a child's life, since good Catholics of the period believed that their namesake protected them. Anglo names simply would not do. After the meal, Lino slaps Catherine for serving what he calls "crap" and orders her to marry Joseph as if he were in Italy:

> LINO: You're marrying that guy . . . it's settled . . . I've given my word.
> CATHERINE: What? Your word? What do you think this is, the old country? This is America.
> LINO (screaming): This is my house!

Catherine obeys but because Joseph really cares for her, the arrangement works. Although Catherine has to endure a honeymoon night with mother Santangelo in the same apartment, Joseph's sexual prowess causes passion to bloom between them, and she is soon pregnant. Her mother-in-law continues to torture Catherine, telling her that she has "marked" their child because she was present in the butcher shop when Joseph killed a live turkey. According to Mrs. Santangelo, Catherine must pray before a picture of the mother of the Blessed Virgin, Saint Anne, if she is to avoid having a child shaped like a turkey! Innocent of any real knowledge about childbirth and forced to listen to these old Italian-wives' tales, Catherine is terrified and her first child miscarries. She goes to bed for eight months in mourning, during which time all the house-plants she has lovingly tended wither and die. One Sunday, she awakens and feels better, while in the house, all the dead plants have apparently flowered. Flowers blooming at unusual times or in unusual places have traditionally symbolized sainthood in the Catholic Church, and Savoca employs this bit of folklore to raise one of the themes of the movie: the nature of sainthood. Joseph declares that this flowering is no miracle, because he has watered the plants, but it is Easter Sunday and her husband has actually bought new plants.

The real miracle is Catherine's psychological rebirth. While the couple set about making another baby, the mother finally passes away in her kitchen. Now Catherine makes the sausage for the butcher shop with the mother's recipe, but things have entirely changed. Catherine gets a new, contemporary hairstyle, she paints the walls bright colors, throws or packs away all the mother's votive statues and her junk, and changes her life. In the process of her rebirth, her daughter Theresa is born.

At this point, the film changes directions, for its focus shifts from Catherine and Joseph to Theresa's childhood and youth. We shift to 1968, where Theresa is a young girl yearning to become first a nun and then, when this is not possible, a follower of Saint Thérèse of Lisieux (1873–97), called the Little Flower. Saint Thérèse's philosophy of life proclaimed that even the most humble chores could be a vehicle for spiritual holiness and service to God: "To ecstasy I prefer the monotony of daily toil," as the saint put it and as the young Santangelo daughter writes in her diary. Theresa therefore devotes her life to the saint's "little way," as it was called.

Italian American males traditionally have less attachment to the Church than their female counterparts, and Joseph explodes when Theresa announces she is not going to college and wants to join the Carmelites, declaring that he does not want a daughter of his "to line the pope's pockets" and that nuns "are sick women and my daughter isn't sick."

Savoca's portrait of the role of religion and superstition in an Italian American household in the first half of the film, juxtaposing Mother Santangelo's Old World wives' tales with Catherine's ignorance, then her liberation, follows the kind of trajectory that a contemporary American feminist would applaud. Savoca's originality, however, lies in her courageous choice to give Theresa's religious search for holiness equal time. Besides denigrating motherhood, many contemporary feminists have cast aspersions upon female chastity and the vocation of a nun, rejecting not only motherhood but also saintliness. As Savoca reminds us, however, Italian culture has always had a particular fascination with sainthood. Even Mussolini, in a famous speech immortalized by an inscription on the Palazzo della Civiltà Italiana (now called the Palazzo della Civiltà del Lavoro) in the EUR district of Rome, had described Italy as a nation of poets, artists, heroes, thinkers, scientists, navigators, immigrants, and saints. Catholics all over the world revere such pivotal figures of Catholic devotion as Saint Francis of Assisi and Saint Catherine of Siena (Italy's patron saint), not to mention a host of others.

Savoca first juxtaposes the superstitions and wives' tales of the first generation of Italian immigrants (Joseph's mother) with the growing Americanization of a second generation (Catherine and Joseph). In the second half of the film, she goes even further to set up comparisons not only between the second and third generations but within the third generation as well. Finally enrolled in a local college, Theresa meets Leonard Villanova (Michael Imperioli), who explains what he calls the Villanova Life Plan to her: "First, I get the St. John's law degree. Then I want a Lincoln Continental. I want a family and a townhouse on the Upper East Side, and I want membership in all those clubs that always turned up their noses to the Italians." When he says he plans a career in television law, Theresa asks: "You mean like Perry Mason?"

Moving in with Leonard, Theresa follows the "little way" of the Little Flower before she experiences what seems to others as madness but which she declares is a miracle: Jesus appears to her, and he multiplies the red plaid shirts Leonard wears by the hundreds (a parody of the miracle of the loaves and the fishes in the New Testament). She is taken away to the mental institution, where she eventually dies. On the day she passes away, the dead flowers in the courtyard bloom much as Catherine thought her houseplants had flowered years earlier just before Theresa was born. Savoca wants her audience to ask themselves about the meaning of sainthood in the modern world. First-generation immigrant Italians believe in miracles and pray to votive statues of saints for their every need. Second-generation Italian Americans are more skeptical, navigating between the old ways and the new. The third generation, typified by Leonard's desire to get rich and get even, appears mystified by Theresa's more ancient desire to attain sainthood. Is Theresa, as a nun declares, suffering from "acute hallucinatory psychoses brought on by a particularly difficult and prolonged adolescent psycho-sexual adjustment" or is sainthood possible in twentieth-century Little Italy? The fact that it is a nun who delivers the diagnosis underscores just how far contemporary Italian and Italian American values have moved away from traditional ones, including fervent belief in the supernatural and a religious impulse, toward a contemporary interest in the materialism typical of the rest of American society.

The opening frame narrative of the film returns in its conclusion as the grandparents of the group—Mary (Irma St. Paul) and Mario (Leonardo Cimino)—bring their long story to a conclusion, noting that people believed the Santangelo sausages cured people of illnesses in the old neighborhood and that after Theresa's death, everyone at the hospital was cured. Mary asks her incredulous daughter and grandchildren: "She saw God in her work—how many of us can say that?" Her question is surely difficult to answer for most of us. The fact that the entire account of the "miracle sausages" exists within an Italian American family narrative frame also emphasizes one other important trait of the ethnic group to which the characters belong: a talent for storytelling with vivid images that Savoca celebrates and continues herself.

Put this way, we can see a continuity of values between such films as *Mac, Big Night, A Bronx Tale,* and *Household Saints*—the idea that God is present in a job well done, the same belief that inspired the workmen on the medieval cathedrals to fashion perfectly even the parts of the structure that could not be seen, since God could see all. Savoca's original consideration of the nature of sainthood also has important links to earlier treatments of sainthood in the Italian cinema associated with Roberto Rossellini and Federico Fellini. In particular, *Il miracolo* (1948; *The Miracle*)—part of a double bill entitled *L'amore* (*The Ways of Love*), scripted by Fellini and directed by Rossellini—portrayed a peasant girl (Anna Magnani) who believes a wandering man played by Fellini is actually Saint Joseph, who leaves her pregnant. Like Theresa, who is convinced that she has a calling blessed by Christ, she is convinced that her pregnancy is a miracle. Cardinal Spellman and other important Catholic clerics, however, thought differently about Rossellini's film, deemed it blasphemous, and arranged to have it censored. Nonetheless, in a historic decision delivered on May 26, 1952, the United States Supreme Court in *Burstyn v. Wilson* overruled a 1915 decision and declared that cinema as an art form was included under the free-speech protections guaranteed by the Constitution and affirmed that censorship on religious grounds was not permitted.[23] Another Rossellini film, *Europa '51 (1951, Europe '51)*, seems even closer to Savoca's evocation of saintliness misunderstood in a secular world. In this film—also scripted in part by Fellini without credit—Rossellini depicts a rich woman named Irene (Ingrid Bergman) who reacts to the mysterious death of her son by turning to works of saintly charity. Her saintliness causes her to be rejected by her family, condemned to a mental institution by the courts, and even criticized by unsympathetic representatives of the Catholic Church, who paradoxically are usually the first to reject claims of sainthood advanced for people by the faithful in the modern world. And of course, three important Fellini films of the 1950s constituting studies in spiritual poverty and representing what I have called elsewhere a "trilogy of grace and salvation"—*La strada (La Strada,* 1954); *Il bidone (Il Bidone* aka *The Swindle,* 1955), and *Le notti di Cabiria (The Nights of Cabiria,* 1956)— all explore the dimensions of spirituality and sainthood in a materialistic and uncomprehending world. It would be almost impossible for contemporary Italian American filmmakers of Savoca's generation not to have learned something from such Italian models.

The focus upon fathers and sons in *A Bronx Tale* or *Mac* may be contrasted with Robert Mulligan's *Love with the Proper Stranger.* This highly successful film won Natalie Wood an Oscar nomination as Best Actress for her outstanding performance as Angie Rossini, the Macy's clerk who has a one-night stand with a jazz musician named Rocky Papasano (Steve McQueen) and must later contact him to arrange for an abortion. At the time the film was made, the sexual revolution that began with the birth-control pill and culminated in making abortions legal in the United States had just begun to permeate society at large, and as the film demonstrates, many of these then-radical ideas had not yet been accepted by many staunchly Catholic Italian Americans. Like *Marty, Love with the Proper Stranger* is an unpretentious black-and-white film with affinities to the classics of Italian neorealism in its simple plot, its engaging dialogue, and its attempts at offering its protagonists as emblematic of humanity in general. This last characteristic of the film is best captured in the opening and closing shots. The first sequence of the film shows an empty union hall that slowly fills up until it is crowded, the credits begin to run, and Rocky emerges from the crowd. He is hailed by Angie, who informs him that she is pregnant, but he is unable to remember her name or who she is when they first meet. The film concludes with a populist finale as the camera pulls back on a shot of Rocky and Angie, to reveal a large crowd outside Macy's department store. After they have decided to marry and save the baby, they thus become part of a larger group and have presumably become "typical" of others in the

Love with the Proper Stranger *(1963; Robert Mulligan, director). Jazz musician Rocky Papasano (Steve McQueen) meets Angie Rossini (Natalie Wood) to arrange her abortion, breaking all the unwritten rules of their ethnic culture.*

crowd. De Sica used this kind of opening and closing in such neorealist classics as *Ladri di biciclette* (1948; *The Bicycle Thief*) and *Umberto D* (1951; *Umberto D.*) to great effect, pulling emblematic figures out of a group and then reintegrating them at the film's conclusion. As the release date of Mulligan's film occurs during the time of the Italian cinema's greatest popularity in America, a link between De Sica's well-known films and *Love with the Proper Stranger* is not unthinkable, even if the ending of the American film seems directly to contradict the Italian neorealist tendency to reject "Hollywood" endings.

Perhaps some viewers of this interesting film will find the casting of Natalie Wood and Steve McQueen as second-generation Italian Americans an obstacle to analyzing it. Except for the fact that Natalie Wood is a brunette, neither actor shares the now recognizably Hollywood Italian physical features we have come to associate with Italian Americans after several decades of films by Martin Scorsese and Francis Ford Coppola, or by the television series *The Sopranos*. Neither Rocky nor Angie is especially Catholic. Statues of the Virgin Mary, San Gennaro, or votive candles do not surround them. Both dress in an understated fashion—no enormous gold chains or big hair. Both lack the usual overemotional tics that point to Hollywood Italian identity. In fact, they seem more like WASPs than an authentic member of a Mediterranean ethnic group. Their "Italian-ness" is barely discernible.

Still, this lack of immediate ethnic details linked to these characters plays a positive role in the film. Angie and Rocky are second-generation Italian Americans with parents and siblings who are, in many respects, firmly rooted in American culture linguistically even though they still share some of the Old World attitudes about love and marriage that Rocky and Angie have obviously abandoned if they are considering an abortion. Rocky's parents still speak Italian to their sons, who understand it but rarely use the parent's language, but they can also speak English well with only a slight accent. They may eat bread and salami in the playground where they relax, but they have been Americanized to an extent far greater than, for example, the Italians in *Christ in Concrete*. Angie's brothers speak a working-class brand of New Yorkese, not Italian, but they have continued the Italian macho attitude about an unmarried sister, following her around in their fruit truck, constantly trying to make dates for her with Italian American bachelors (the fact that they must be Catholic is assumed), and interfering in her life without realizing that an American woman, unlike the traditional Italian woman, prizes independence over family ties. When Angie threatens to leave the house to be free, her mother begins the typical martyr act of a parent abandoned by her children; her brother Dominick (Hershel Bernardi) concurs, telling Angie to go if she prefers to live "with strangers." Faced with this kind of opposition, Angie stays home and cries herself to sleep.

The sequence where Angie and Rocky go to have the abortion is one of the most successful moments of the film. Although Rocky has obviously lived his life up until the moment Angie told him he was the father of her child as a carefree musician living with a likable striptease dancer named Barbie aka Barbara of Seville on stage (Edie Adams), the news begins to force him into accepting responsibility for his thoughtless actions. Although Rocky and Angie are not fervent Catholics, their upbringing has obviously not prepared them for the squalor of the back-room abortion that would enable them to avoid marriage. It is to take place in a semi-abandoned and unheated tenement building on a dirty blanket. The old woman who is to perform the abortion would frighten anyone, as would her accomplice who is only interested in grabbing all the cash he can extort. The location of the site where the abortion is to be performed, as well as his understandable remorse, move Rocky to stop the abortion and embrace Angie on the floor, as the frightened abortionists rush out of the room with the money.

Rocky is willing to "do the right thing," as he puts it and marry Angie, and eventually he finds Angie's brother Dominick, receiving a black eye in the process after revealing that Angie is pregnant. Dominick declares to his sister: "We had a long talk, and the thing is, he came to me like a man, and he's willing to marry you." When Angie asks why Rocky has now decided to do this, Rocky says: "I'm willing to take my medicine." Rocky's answer presupposes the Old Country values—that unwanted pregnancies and forced marriages concern the men of the family, who must uphold the family honor by forcing women in the family to obey their rules. "Taking his medicine," however, is exactly the opposite of what the Americanized Angie desires: if marriage represents no more than a form of imprisonment for Rocky, she prefers not to marry him. To reinforce this conflict between different value systems, we are also shown Angie's mother crying and muttering in Italian "vergogna, vergogna" ("shame, shame") and their priest, who seems amazed by the fact that Rocky is willing to get married while Angie refuses marriage unless it is of his free will.

Angie's desire to have a husband who wants to be her husband pushes her into accepting the generous offer of marriage from Tony Colombo (Tom Bosley's first important film role), who also offers to recognize the baby as his own. Angie considers this solution and even comes to a sit-down dinner where she is to be introduced to Tony's Italian mother, who puts on the usual ethnic performance that emphasizes the cultural and moral gulf between two generations, dramatizing the differences between the parents from the Old Country and their younger, partially Americanized children. The couple wants candles to make the dinner more romantic, but Mother Colombo squelches this bit of emotion with the remark that "it's romantic enough" and she wants to see what she is eating. Tony's sister eats with them, revealing that she has assimilated the most pretentious airs of a university intellectual that could be imagined. She is apparently taking a course on love at the university and declares that "Love, as such, is definitely a middle-class idea and it's on the way out." This line of conversation is hardly the one the couple needs to hear just before announcing their wedding. The combination of the overcritical Italian mother and the pretentious university student provides not only comic relief after the emotionally compelling abortion scene but also interrupts the announcement of their engagement.

Rocky has afterthoughts and begins to court Angie, who skillfully employs his sense of jealousy to entice him to fall in love with her. Rocky has moved beyond the "taking my medicine stage" but still feels uncomfortable with the idea of overtly romantic love, love as he puts it with all the "bells and banjos." But eventually, love conquers all, and Rocky stations himself outside Macy's entrance playing a banjo with bells, carrying a sign reading BETTER WED THAN DEAD. Angie has finally won Rocky on her own terms, and their embrace concludes the film.

That the two principal actors playing Rocky and Angie lack immediately and easily identifiable Italian American physical characteristics or mannerisms in *Love with the Proper Stranger* paradoxically increases the appeal of the movie. This fact serves to emphasize the entirely different sets of values and expectations of two different generations, as well as their sharply differing views of marriage and the family on the part of Italian American women and men. Rather than constituting a saccharin-sweet Hollywood ending, Angie's decision to marry Rocky at the conclusion of the film demonstrates her determination to have love on her own terms as an independent American woman, rejecting the arrangement of a shotgun marriage that traditional Italian American culture saw as the only alternative to an unacceptable and sinful abortion. It could well be said that *Love with the Proper Stranger* is chronologically the first representation of a Hollywood Italian that takes the woman's point of view and critiques the traditional Italian American male reaction to love, marriage, and family.

Martin Scorsese made *ItalianAmerican* for the American Bicentennial celebration in a series of films on ethnic groups sponsored in part by the National Endowment for the Humanities.[24] It is a documentary about Scorsese's parents, Charles and Catherine Scorsese, who discuss their Sicilian ancestry and their lives in Little Italy on Elizabeth Street in Manhattan. The film seems more like a home movie than a professional documentary, because its camera work, lighting, and editing remind the viewer of a student production rather than the work of an accomplished filmmaker, which Scorsese was at the time, having just shot *Mean Streets* the year before. His goal is to depict the importance of *la famiglia* (the family) in the culture of Little Italy and in his own background. Catherine proves to be a natural comic, and since this documentary she has appeared in a number of films with Hollywood Italian characters, not only those by her son but also in *Moonstruck*, for example, where she plays a customer in an Italian American grocery store, and in *The Godfather Part III*. The Italian home revolved around the kitchen more than any other room in the house, and naturally the director asks his mother to explain how she made tomato sauce for pasta. Running after the ending credits of the film, her recipe was greeted by a standing ovation when the film was shown at the New York Film Festival in 1974.

More than just a paean to the Italian American family, however, Scorsese's other important theme of this work is the narrative tradition of Italian

American culture. The stories told by Charles and Catherine are larger than life. Impoverished as a boy, Charles earned money by lighting candles for the Orthodox Jews who were not permitted to do so on the Sabbath; Catherine recounts a romantic story about how back in the Old Country, her mother fell in love with her father at first sight because of his handsome soldier's uniform. During their childhood, between seven and fourteen people were living in their crowded apartments, including not only family members but also boarders. Bathrooms were sometimes only "backhouses" or outside latrines ("backhousa," as the immigrants pronounced the American word), and they had little furniture; they scrubbed wooden floors with wire brushes and had so much work to do that there was never time to be tired. Charles offers the explanation that since they had no radio or television and little money to go to the movies when they were young, people naturally turned to storytelling. The stories told by these first-generation Italian Americans, born in Little Italy of Sicilian immigrants, obviously furnish the director with raw material for his later films. As any good Italian boy should, Scorsese concludes his documentary when his mother tells him: "Now that's enough for today, Martie."

The primacy of the family in the representation of Hollywood Italians also finds one of its most felicitous expressions in the very successful romantic comedy by Norman Jewison, *Moonstruck*. The film garnered six Oscar nominations. Cher won Best Actress for her performance as Loretta Castorini, a thirty-seven-year-old widow who has agreed to marry a mamma's boy, Johnny Cammareri (Danny Aiello), but who falls passionately head over heels for Johnny's brother Ronny (Nicolas Cage), a baker who has refused to speak to his brother for half a decade; he blames Johnny for distracting him in the bakery, causing Ronny to cut off his hand, now replaced by a prosthetic device. Ronny loves grand opera and his declarations about how the loss of the hand has ruined his life—his fiancée abandoned him immediately after the accident—seem taken right off the stage of Lincoln Center. Johnny leaves for Sicily after asking Loretta to marry him, but it is clear he is completely dominated by his mother, who makes a profession out of controlling her son.

Jewison's film paints a very appealing portrait of the interrelations of the Italian Americans who have lived for decades in the boroughs of New York City outside the island of Manhattan. A philandering NYU professor of communications—who dates his students and regularly receives a glass of water in the face from them when they break up with him in the Grand Ticino Restaurant near the Castorini home—walks Loretta's mother, Rose (Olympia Dukakis), home one night and is amazed at the Castorini home. To him, it is a mansion worth about five million dollars at current real-estate prices (he lives in a one-room apartment in Manhattan). Yet for Rose, her home is just where she has always lived while real-estate prices rose, since Italian Americans living there preferred not moving outside the old neighborhood if at all possible. Rose and her husband Cosmo (Vincent Gardenia) are going through a rough time in their marriage, since Rose realizes that Cosmo has a mistress. Asking the professor why men chase women, Rose receives the answer that recurs over and over again in the film: because they are afraid of death. In fact, the film opens with the credits rolling over a corpse in the Nucciarone Funeral Home, evoking the theme that choosing a safe, conventional, and secure life cannot replace one filled with passion and risk taking.

All of the characters manage to carry off the most romantic and even pretentious lines of the script with skill. This is due in large measure to the Oscar-winning screenplay of John Patrick Shanley, his first film script but informed by his considerable experience writing for the theater. For example, although highly improbable, Ronny and Loretta should be "moonstruck" and fall in love as though they were living in the world of *La Bohème*, the Puccini masterpiece they attend at the Met, where they run into Loretta's father who has brought along his "bimbo" mistress. Ronny believes in following one's heart, not one's head. As he says to Loretta,

> Playing it safe is about the most dangerous thing a woman like you can do. . . . Loretta, I love you. Not like they told you love is . . . and I didn't know this. But love don't make things nice. It ruins everything. It makes things a mess. We aren't here to make things perfect . . . we are here to ruin ourselves and to break our hearts and love the wrong people and . . . die . . . Now would you come upstairs with me and get in my bed?

Miraculously, and with the assistance of the beautiful harvest moon that shines on all the residents of Little Italy, Ronny's request works. It is significant that Loretta takes his gloved hand, the one that he lost in the accident, when she agrees to his request.

Moonstruck does not end on this note, for as in any good comedy, marriage must conclude the action and all the loose ends must be straightened out. In this case, these loose ends threaten the family, not only the relationship between two brothers (Johnny and Ronny) and Loretta, but also the marriage of Rose and Cosmo Castorini, as well as the relationship of Cosmo's father, known as the Old Man (Feodor Chaliapin) to his relatives and his five dogs that he walks religiously throughout the film. This is an extended family, and the upheavals around the breakfast table must also

Moonstruck *(1987; Norman Jewison, director). Breakfast at the Castorini family kitchen table: Cosmo Castorini (Vincent Gardenia) sits stunned across from his wife Rose (Olympia Dukakis), since she has just ordered him to give up his mistress; in the background his daughter Loretta (Cher) has just accepted a proposal of marriage from Ronny Cammareri (Nicholas Cage), and the two embrace. Rose's sister Rita (Julie Bovasso) and her husband Raymond (Louis Guss) watch on the right as mamma's-boy Johnny Cammareri (Danny Aiello) stares at the bride he has suddenly lost in his brother Ronny's arms.*

include the Cappomaggi family—Rose's sister Rita (Julie Bovasso) and her husband Raymond (Louis Guss)—who run an Italian grocery store in the neighborhood. Upon his return from Palermo, Johnny announces that his mother has miraculously recovered and that he cannot marry Loretta—to do so would be to risk killing his mother. Like so many Italian or Italian American men, Johnny is a mamma's boy to the end. Ronny asks him for his pinky ring, proposes to Loretta at the breakfast table (a site where a moment before Rose has just demanded that Cosmo stop seeing his girlfriend), and the Old Man orders his son to pay for the wedding. With all the threats to the family removed and with the triumph of passionate, operatic-style romantic love over every obstacle, Jewison's beautiful film concludes with a rousing toast by all to "the family, *la famiglia*," and the camera moves around the rooms of the first floor until it focuses upon an old photograph of the original immigrants from Italy, one of those ancient family pictures that always seems to decorate the homes of both Italian Americans and Hollywood Italians.

Jewison manages to create a light comedy out of this operatic situation without the slightest bit of condescension. Far from creating patronizing stereotypes of working-class Italian Americans, with a great script he manages to persuade his audience for a brief two-hour period that romantic love provides solid foundations for Hollywood Italian households. Every one of the performances in the film, both the stars and the character actors, is perfect. No other film has yet to offer such a positive and nostalgic view of Little Italy as a Paradise Lost where men and women love each other, live in tightly knit families in an ethnic neighborhood, and follow their hearts rather than their heads. The old stereotype of the passionate, emotional Italian here receives a positive coloring.

Made only a year after *Moonstruck*, Nancy Savoca's *True Love* provides a far less appealing picture of romance in Little Italy. It narrates the story of the preparations for and the conclusion to a marriage taking place in June 1988. Donna (Annabella Sciorra) and Michael (Ron Eldard) appear to be the ideal Italian American couple, but as the preparations for the wedding cause tension between them, we see the marriage seemingly pushed along more by a kind of inertia and peer pressure than by real passion and commitment. As she did in *Household Saints*, Savoca immerses us in a working-class section of a Little Italy, this time in the Bronx. The characters she portrays are young adults, slightly classier and slightly older than the characters of *Saturday Night Fever*, the classic film that popularized what has been termed the "Guido" and the "Guidette" figure in Italian American culture, and in the representations of Hollywood Italians in the American cinema:

> *Guido* is a pejorative term applied to lower-class, macho, gold-amulet-wearing, self-displaying neighborhood boys, supposedly derived either from the typical Italian first name ("Guido") or from the Italian *guidare* (to drive), a reference to their penchant for cruising in hot cars, those "id-mobiles" that serve as the Guido's boudoir. *Guidette* is their gum-chewing, big-haired, air-headed female counterpart.[25]

Michael is good at what he does, working in a butcher shop, but he is uncomfortable with the responsibilities that will come with matrimony. One of his male customers tells him ominously a few days before the wedding that he should look at Donna now, because after her first child, "she'll blow up like a balloon." His peers, macho Italian American males, constantly try to divert his attentions away from Donna, complaining that she is "leading him around by the nose." During a quiet evening of babysitting when they are about to make love before the wedding, Michael allows his loser friends Kevin and Don to lure him away from even the promise of steamy sex. Michael goes as far as to tell Donna he wants to go out with the boys for several hours after their wedding party just before their first night of wedded life. He is completely impervious to the thought that this moment would be special in Donna's life. Quite naturally, she rushes into the ladies' room to cry in the toilet stall, surrounded by her bridesmaids. Given a number of important tasks to perform for the wedding (buying the ushers' gifts, paying the priest at the wedding rehearsal, arranging for a ride to the airport for the honeymoon vacation), Michael fails to accomplish any of them.

Donna clearly has second thoughts about this marriage. Although she is sexually attracted to Michael, they probably have very little in common except for their sex drives, their common Italian American heritage, their interlocked friends and relatives, and their neighborhood and its culture and mores. The only example holding out hope for the future of their relationship is an entirely different couple, Donna's mother and father. They eloped, avoided an extravagantly lavish and garish Italian American wedding (for Donna's wedding the planner suggests that the mashed potatoes be dyed blue to match the wedding colors!), and they are obviously still in love and still sexually attracted to each other as much, if not more so, than they were when they were first married. Perhaps Savoca suggests by this contrasting pair of young and older lovers that something in the Italian American experience over the past several decades has changed the way Italian American men and women are romantically connected. If *la famiglia* triumphs in *Moonstruck* and smoothes out any potential for future mischief, in *True Love* its restorative power seems far less promising or effective.

Jonathan Lynn's *My Cousin Vinny* shows us a classic Guido and Guidette couple, somewhat older than is the norm: Vincent La Guardia Gambini (Joe Pesci) and his fiancée Mona Lisa "Lise" Vito (Marisa Tomei who received an Oscar for Best Supporting Actress in the film). Two New York boys—Bill Gambini (Ralph Macchio) and Stan Rothenstein (Mitchell Whitfield)—drive to the West Coast through Wazoo, Alabama, where they are mistaken for a pair of robbers who have murdered the clerk at the convenience store, the Sac-o-Suds. Slapped in prison by Southern police officers who serve in a thoroughly integrated police force and who are exactly the opposite of the ignorant, racist redneck, the lyncher of blacks, Jews, and other ethnics (including Italians) that is so unfortunate and frequent a stereotype in the Hollywood cinema, Bill and Stan are nevertheless persuaded by prejudice and, no doubt, by films depicting the South in a highly negative fashion, that law enforcement in Wazoo is corrupt, that Southerners all sleep with their close kin, and that they are all members of the Klan. They expect a Bubba to show up in their cells and to transform them into his sex slaves. Since Stan's parents are on a cruise and cannot be reached, Bill calls his mother, who sends their cousin Vinny, a recent law-school graduate, to the rescue.

Vinny arrives in Wazoo in a huge red Cadillac convertible accompanied by his gum-chewing, wise-cracking, high-heel-and-hot-pants-wearing Guidette, Mona Lisa. His attire is no less flamboyant: black sweater under a black leather jacket with silver-tipped cowboy boots, and the inevitable metal chain around his neck and dark sunglasses. While the Southerners do not really live up to the stereotypes the New York City folks have of them, Vinny and Mona Lisa appear to embody everything ever said about the bad taste and low-brow culture of Italian Americans, and everything uncouth and coarse represented in many images of Hollywood Italians in the American cinema.

My Cousin Vinny nevertheless confounds our initial expectations, and the viewer quickly understands that the characters are far more complex than the customary stereotypes of Southerners and New York Italian Americans would suggest. Much of the hilarious comedy in the film derives from confusion over regional accents. The Southerners and New Yorkers both stumble over the different pronunciations of various common words. When Vinny refers to the "two youths" accused of committing the crime, he pronounces the word as "two yutes," an expression that the intelligent and cultured Judge Chamberlain Haller (Fred Gwynne) finds completely incomprehensible. On the other hand, Vinny and Mona Lisa are puzzled by grits and especially shocked by the fact that a local black café owner cooks them with a breakfast fried in lard. The linguistic comedies of errors abound in the film, the result of a very strong script.

Initially, *My Cousin Vinny* also seems to continue the usual stereotyping of the Italian American from New York as an uneducated slob. Vinny requires six years to pass the bar exam, and his lawyer's degree comes from an non-prestigious institution which contrasts with the Duke University law degree of the imperious judge. Mona Lisa appears to be an airhead. Yet their natural intelligence, although not honed to smoothness by an Ivy League education and a proper upbringing, triumphs as Vinny reveals himself to be a natural trial lawyer and Mona Lisa shows she knows a great deal more about automobiles than the state's expert witness.

First, Vinny destroys the credibility of a number of eyewitnesses who claim to have seen Bill and Stan leave the Sac-o-Suds immediately after the clerk was killed: an elderly and sweet black woman needs glasses; another witness could not possibly have seen through his dirty windows; and a third witness who claimed that he was cooking his grits and was away from the window for only five minutes is confounded when Vinny declares, to the nodding approval of all the grit-eating population of Wazoo, that everyone knows it takes at least 15-to-20 minutes to cook non-instant grits, a fact Vinny learned at breakfast earlier when he tried his first taste of this Southern delicacy. All seems lost, however, when the state's expert witness declares that the tire tracks outside the convenience store are positively a match with the 1964 Buick Skylark convertible the boys were driving. Suddenly, during a lunch break, Vinny scrutinizes the photo of the tracks Mona Lisa took earlier and sees the truth. Calling her to the stand as a hostile witness (they are having a serious lovers' quarrel because Mona Lisa is offended by the fact that Vinny does not want her assistance), she astounds the court with her technical knowledge of automobiles.

It seems that three generations of Vitos have been automobile mechanics on both sides of the family, and Mona Lisa points out that the car tracks were made by a car with Posi-Traction and an independent rear suspension. Only the 1963 Pontiac Tempest had these two characteristics, and the particular kind of tracks left by the criminals could not, therefore, have been made by the boys' automobile. Her expert testimony moves the judge to dismiss all charges: the Guido lawyer has outwitted the well-educated district attorney and astounded the erudite judge. The film further breaks down the borders between North and South when this Hollywood Italian couple is assisted by

My Cousin Vinny *(1992; Jonathan Lynn, director). The perfect Guido, Vincent La Guardia Gambini (Joe Pesci) thanks his fiancée Mona Lisa "Lise" Vito (Marisa Tomei) for testimony that allows him to win his difficult murder trial in the deep South.*

a sympathetic Southern sheriff who is no racist Bubba. He helps the pair run down the essential information crucial to winning the case.

My Cousin Vinny confronts two very different kinds of stereotypes, both of which can regularly be found in American films: on the one hand, the Guido and Guidette, Italian Americans with vulgar, working-class tastes, who speak English in what only a New Yorker can describe as a normal accent, and who are not known for their brain power; and on the other, the racist-redneck-yahoo Southerner characterized by prejudice, ignorance, and violence. Both stereotypes are deconstructed, shown to be superficial cultural assumptions.

Little Italy Heats Up: Hollywood Italians Misbehave in The Wanderers *(1979),* Mean Streets *(1973),* Do the Right Thing *(1989), and* Jungle Fever *(1991)*

In the films treating Little Italy and the *famiglia* considered to this point, the negative characteristics of Hollywood Italians have been limited to minor peccadilloes—adultery primarily, but also vulgarity, bad grammar, bad pronunciation, and bad manners. Of course, the worst example of Hollywood Italians behaving badly will be found in the gangster films (examined in a later chapter of this book). A smaller number of important movies are on the borderline in this regard, depicting Hollywood Italians as street-gang members, engaged in petty crimes (numbers running, small scams) that nevertheless threaten to produce dire consequences or to lead to ruin, and as members of an ethnic group especially prone to racial prejudice against African Americans.

The most entertaining and least disturbing of this group of four films is Philip Kaufman's *The Wanderers*, a bit of period nostalgia made under the obvious influence of Scorsese's *Mean Streets* (1973) but set in the Bronx of 1963 just before the Kennedy assassination. It might well be described as a Hollywood Italian version of the Puerto Rican *West Side Story* that substitutes classic rock 'n' roll of the pre-Beatles era for the Broadway musical numbers of that more famous film. The title of the picture shares its title with a famous song by Dion ("The Wanderer") that provides the theme for a group of Italian American high-school students in the Bronx who have formed a gang called the Wanderers. The world pictured in the film is a world of ethnic gangs, not only Italian Americans but also blacks, Latinos, Asians, Irish, and so forth: the Wanderers, the Pharaohs, the Wongs, the Del Bombers, the Fordham Baldies, and the Ducky Boys. Each gang has a distinctive jacket and hairstyle as well as an ethnic identity, but their behavior reflects gang behavior in a kinder, gentler ghetto world. All but the

Ducky Boys engage in essentially harmless "rumbles" that follow strict guidelines of no guns, no knives, and no drugs. The Ducky Boys, on the other hand, are essentially violent psychopaths-in-the-making. Although there is absolutely no evidence of drug use, abuse of alcohol is considered normal, and there is the classic high-school party in the home of one of the Italian American girls named Despie Galasso (Toni Kalem), a perfect Guidette for the perfect Guido, Richie (Ken Wahl in his debut). This party naturally takes place when the father and mother are away at a social event, but the parents, in this case, are people with whom Richie should not trifle: Chubby Galasso (Dolph Sweet) is one of six enormously overweight brothers who control the Mafia in the area. Just as gang behavior in *The Wanderers* harkens back to an era before drive-by assassinations with automatic weapons, the Galasso brothers describe themselves as "sportsmen" and employ the same term for their black criminal counterparts when they place wagers on the climactic football game between the Italian American gang and the black gang. Football and not zip guns settle disputes in this age of innocence.

In spite of its gently homogenized character, *The Wanderers* serves as a very good barometer of the behavior of Italian American youth in the early 1960s, with its wonderful musical score, its preoccupation with sex, its profanity, its period muscle cars covered with chrome, its gum-chewing student misfits, and its racial conflicts. It is impossible to doubt what is on the minds of the high-school boys in the film: sex and male bonding in the gangs. Actually, the second urge may be stronger than the first. We see this in the hilarious opening sequence of the film where Richie finally "goes all the way" with Despie in front of a television set, but only after he tells Despie he loves her. At the moment Richie achieves climax, he hears one of the Wanderers whistling for help and he rushes off to his male buddies. One of the gang, a likable but naïve kid named Joey (John Friedrich), has angered the Baldies by comparing their shaved heads to penises. Moments later, the overconfident Wanderers are cornered by the much larger Fordham Baldies, led by Terror (Erland van Lidth) and egged on by his pint-sized girlfriend Peewee (Linda Manz). Just when it seems that the Wanderers are going to be beaten to a collective bloody pulp, an unnamed but very athletic boy chewing a matchstick—a Super Guido—appears and gives the order: "Leave the kid alone." This "Man With No Name" engages in a series of hard stares at the Baldies in what is clearly a parody of the popular gunfights in Sergio Leone's spaghetti westerns, the films that made Clint Eastwood an international star and were so integral a feature of the cinema in the decade leading up to the shooting of *The Wanderers*. The close-ups of the faces of the gang members staring each other down show the obvious

The Wanderers (1979; Philip Kaufman, director). Members of the Italian American gang the Wanderers show us what they have on their minds as they drag Main Street in the Bronx.

influence of Sergio Leone. This powerful unnamed figure appears and then disappears as if by magic, just like the Eastwood character, the Man With No Name. Only later do we learn that his name is Perry, that he is a nineteen-year-old Italian American student large for his age because he has been held back in school, and that he has moved into the apartment building in which Joey lives.

Even though the film's protagonists are gang members and their gum-chewing, big-hair girlfriends, the tone of *The Wanderers* remains surprisingly comic and innocent. Although a Marine recruiter who tricks the Fordham Baldies into enlisting offers a hint of a very different world, 1963 represents a time before the Vietnam War heated up, before drugs had destroyed the inner-city ghetto life of the various ethnic groups pictured in the film, and before gang violence turned truly lethal. The mob, too, has a benign character. All of this will change, the film seems to suggest, after the assassination of President Kennedy—sometimes mythologized as the end of Camelot, a kind of American Golden Age—an event that shakes the film's characters like no other in the film. And at the close of the movie, some of the characters (Perry and Joey) leave their comfortable and familiar ethnic neighborhood and drive to California to seek a new and different fortune.

A number of elements in the film point to the seminal impact of Scorsese's *Mean Streets:* the profane language, the sound track of contemporary pop music, the gritty feel of the urban landscape that projects an image of New York copied countless times since 1973. Some characters are permitted to flee this ethnic island that seems frozen in time; others are condemned to remain there. Richie's hormones and his failure to use birth control trap him in the neighborhood. Despie becomes pregnant, tells her gangster father, and he confronts Richie, ordering him to marry his daughter and join the family business:

> Look, I ain't no hard guy. I was your age once and I used to put 'em away like there was no tomorrow. . . . I never did it with nobody's daughter! Not only did you do it with my daughter but you knocked her up, you dumb wop! You ain't got nothin' up here, it's all down here [he grabs Richie in the crotch] . . . The thing is . . . you knocked her up and now you gotta pay the price and do the right thing. It's the sportsman's way . . . Now you're scared [he pauses to pour two drinks]. Get up! [he proposes a toast] To my new son-in-law!

There is plenty in *The Wanderers* to preoccupy any sociologist or psychologist. Gang behavior certainly reflects a lack of moral education and support at home, and the role of *la famiglia* in the film is far from edifying. Joey's Italian American father Emilio (William Andrews) is a shallow weightlifter with an anger-management problem. In this respect, Emilio represents an anticipation of the Hollywood Italian male with a similar defect—Jake La Motta in Scorsese's *Raging Bull* (1980), a film discussed in another chapter. Emilio sneaks into Perry's mother's apartment for sexual gratification, rather than going home to the vanished charms of his harried and chain-smoking wife (Olympia Dukakis).

Racial prejudice characterizes all the gang members, both black and white. One of the most successful scenes takes place in the civics course of Mr. Sharp (Val Avery), a chaotic classroom filled almost equally with Italian American and black males, each in different and rival gangs. The teacher writes on the board that ALL MEN ARE CREATED EQUAL and asks the class who wrote it. The Smart Alecks respond in unison: "You did!" This is exactly the kind of humor audiences would come to expect from the television series *Welcome Back, Kotter,* a popular show that aired between 1975 and 1979. In it, John Travolta played the quintessential Guido, Vinnie Barbarino, a role that seems close to the Richie character of *The Wanderers.*

That program launched Travolta to international fame along with *Saturday Night Fever* in 1977.

At this response from his class, the ever-optimistic Mr. Sharp takes a count of the different ethnic groups represented in the class, revealing eighteen Italians, fifteen blacks, and one Jew (in addition, one of the blacks claims he is an Eskimo!). Then the blacks and the Italians are asked to list all the derogatory racial slurs that they know about each other. The resulting two lists (nigger, jungle bunny, boogie, coon, bobo, spear chucker, jig, spook, spade versus grease ball, guinea, wop, dago, swamp guinea, mountain wop) lead to a scuffle and eventually to the football game called to settle their disputes. In *Do the Right Thing*, Spike Lee employs an even greater number of racial slurs in a similar fashion. The use of these ethnic and racial slurs is reminiscent of the comedian George Carlin's famous lists of dirty words and points to a loosening of the restrictions on such coarse language that for many decades characterized Hollywood scripts. This kind of linguistic honesty may well be, in this context, another aspect of the influence of Scorsese's *Mean Streets*.

Much of the emotional power generated by today's so-called "cult" movies derives from their music. Many of the films depicting the ethnic experience in New York City employ sound tracks composed of dozens of pop songs from the past. In *The Wanderers*, the pre-Beatles music of Dion— ("The Wanderer," "Runaround Sue"), the Contours ("Do You Love Me?"), the Shirelles ("Soldier Boy," "Baby, It's You"), the Four Seasons ("Sherry," "Walk like a Man," "Big Girls Don't Cry"), Ben E. King ("Stand by Me"), Smokey Robinson ("You've Really Got a Hold on Me"), and the Isley Brothers ("Shout")—produce an audio vision of an imaginary Little Italy where social problems are not yet out of control and where racial strife ultimately leads to good clean fun on the football field.

One element that threatens the nostalgic view of life in the Bronx of 1963 is the Ducky Boys, a violent group of juvenile psychopaths who kill at least one of the Fordham Baldies and attack the black and Italian American gang members while they are playing football. Appearing several times in the film before this concluding melee, the Ducky Boys are always enveloped in a surrealistic lighting and misty fog that emphasize their menacing and intimidating behavior. Their presence and the death of President Kennedy warn the audience that "the times they are a-changin'," the title of the Bob Dylan folk song that plays toward the end of the film. The social pretensions of the Dylan music and its future-oriented target (the demonstrations for racial equality and to end the Vietnam War that will soon begin to tear America apart) stand in sharp contrast to the pop music associated with the Hollywood Italians of the Bronx neighborhood, concerned primarily with teenage sex, prom night, groping in the back of convertibles, and make-out parties in the home of parents who have gone out for the night.

In terms of production dates, Scorsese's breakthrough film *Mean Streets* comes before *The Wanderers*, although the period treated in Scorsese's film occurs after the early 1960s and takes place in Little Italy in Manhattan, not in the outer borough of the Bronx. Actually, due to budget problems, Scorsese filmed much of the work in Los Angeles during twenty-one days, with only six days of shooting in New York City, which included the San Gennaro Festival, Coney Island, the Empire State Building, the bar's alleyway, the cemetery, and the restaurant.[26] Nevertheless the "feel" of *Mean Streets*, due to Scorsese's skillful preparation of lighting, locations, and dialogue, is entirely that of New York City. The title of the film comes from an important essay on the detective novel by Raymond Chandler entitled "The Simple Art of Murder" (1944):

> But down these mean streets a man must go who is not himself mean, who is neither tarnished nor afraid. . . . He must be, to use a rather weathered phrase, a man of honor, by instinct, by inevitability, without thought of it, and certainly without saying it. . . . The story is his adventure in search of a hidden truth, and it would be no adventure if it did not happen to a man fit for adventure.[27]

The plot wanders around an essentially disconnected narrative about Charlie (Harvey Keitel), the nephew of an Italian gangster named Giovanni (Cesare Danova), and the group of Italian American males who live and hang out in Little Italy (Scorsese's childhood neighborhood in Manhattan). Charlie's Uncle Giovanni has promised him the management of a restaurant in the neighborhood, since Oscar, the owner, is about to go broke because of loans owed to the Mafia boss. But Giovanni wants Charlie to stay away from his girlfriend Teresa (Amy Robinson), whose epilepsy the gangster associates with insanity. Giovanni also demands that Charlie stay away from his best friend Johnny Boy (Robert De Niro), Teresa's brother, because he is also crazy and "honorable men go with honorable men." Johnny Boy has borrowed from every loan shark in Little Italy, including Michael (Richard Romanus), one of Charlie's close friends and a budding gangster himself. Tony (David Proval) completes this group of Hollywood Italian wastrels: he is the owner of the sleazy bar where the group of males drink, party, and bond; they also witness a shooting that kills one of Tony's customers.

By Scorsese's own testimony in his four-hour documentary *Il mio viaggio in Italia, Mean Streets* owes a great debt to the model of Federico

Fellini's *I vitelloni* (1953, *The Vitelloni*), a coming-of-age film that follows
five slackers around their provincial city on the Adriatic coast of Italy.
Fellini's adolescents growing up in the 1950s, however, lack the violent edge,
the profanity, the rage, the immorality, and the close association with the
underworld that characterize Scorsese's citizens of Little Italy. Fellini's nostalgic view of his youth also avoids the brand of Italian American Catholicism and the particular brand of Catholic guilt that marks Scorsese's film as
a work of art created by a man who once attended a seminary and considered becoming a priest. In addition, there is nothing of the film buff in
Fellini's work, which is less indebted to the history of the cinema than to
Italian popular culture (vaudeville variety theater, cartoons, and his own
fantasies and dreams). Both films, however, employ a voice-over commentary, and Scorsese undoubtedly learned the technique of mixing the voices
of the director and a character on the voice-over from Fellini's example.[28]
Scorsese's *Mean Streets* emphasizes its debt to the cinema by sending its protagonists, whenever they have free time on their hands, to exactly the kinds
of works film buffs preferred in that golden age of cinéaste culture—Roger
Corman horror pics starring Vincent Price, westerns, and old *films noir* starring Glenn Ford. He introduces the four friends in much the same fashion
Fellini presents his five likable loafers in *I vitelloni*. In successive vignettes after the opening voice-over and shots showing the annual Neapolitan Festival of San Gennaro in Little Italy, each individual is introduced quickly and
skillfully by a single action that defines his character (or lack of it): Tony
throws out a drug addict who has been shooting up in his bar's toilet;
Michael, always missing out on the big score, buys a load of Japanese lens
covers he takes for the far-more-expensive Zeiss camera lens made in Germany; Johnny Boy blows up a mailbox on the street for no apparent reason;
and Charlie confesses himself in church and then holds his hand over one
of the votive candles, an action he repeats several times in the film. Scorsese's characteristic use of a mobile and highly involved camera—often a
hand-held camera as opposed to a more traditional tracking shot closely
following a character through a location as if it were his point of view—may
be explained not only by his low budget but also by his identification of that
particular style with one of his favorite directors, Sam Fuller.[29]

Mean Street's copious use of popular music contemporary with the period of the action (as opposed to music composed especially for the film)
has since been imitated by every director making a gangster film or a work
situated in New York's ethnic communities. As he put it, he only used

> the music I grew up with ... In our neighborhood you'd hear rock 'n' roll
> playing in the little bars in the back of the tenement buildings at three in

the morning, so that was "Be My Baby," when Harvey's head hits the pillow. For me, the whole movie was "Jumpin' Jack Flash" and "Be My Baby."[30]

Perhaps the most impressive sequence is the celebrated first entrance into Tony's bar, a location in New York that has been lit in an eerie red light to render it a Dantesque, hellish location (a technique Spike Lee later employs in *Do the Right Thing*). First the camera follows Charlie as he enters the bar and seems to glide through the crowd, eventually dancing on the stage with a black topless dancer. A few minutes later, as Charlie speaks of doing penance—he frequently uses Catholic metaphors, blesses his friends, and speaks of sin, guilt, and sainthood—his earthly penance and cross to bear, as he puts it, arrive in the form of Johnny Boy, who enters the bar with two Jewish girls he has picked up in the Village. Arm and arm, Johnny Boy and the two women move down the bar toward Johnny in slow-frame motion as if time is about to stop in the bar. Scorsese's editing transitions are also notable. One of the opening sequences is what purports to be a home movie shot in a small box on the screen surrounded by black. The entire cast of characters, including the parish priest, is shown in this badly made work, but its use in the opening of the film establishes two

Mean Streets *(1973; Martin Scorsese, director). While heading toward a career working for his Mafioso Uncle Giovanni (Cesare Danova), Charlie (Harvey Keitel) retains a deep attachment to Catholic values, symbols, and rituals.*

things. The home movie seems to indicate that the fiction of the film is that it is really a true documentary, and framing the figures in the home movie inside a black and menacing border suggests that they are trapped in their environment (one of the main themes of the picture). The home movie then blends in seamlessly with footage shot at the San Gennaro Festival, continuing forward the suggestion that *Mean Streets* represents a realistic portrait of an ethnic neighborhood.

The very first sequence of the film, however, and the key words in the script, are spoken over a black screen just before the home movie: "You don't make up for your sins in church. You do it in the streets. You do it at home. The rest is bullshit and you know it." Martin Scorsese, not Harvey Keitel/Charlie, speaks these words and this Felliniesque technique of the director's direct intervention into the narration through the voice-over also encourages the viewer to see Charlie's story as a version of the director's autobiography. Later, Scorsese (not Keitel) says in voice-over: "Lord, I'm not worthy to eat your flesh, not worthy to drink your blood." Scorsese makes another and final appearance in the violent finale of the film, a role that anticipates a similar and more famous appearance in *Taxi Driver* (1976). Here, Scorsese can be seen sitting in the back of the car driven by Michael and shooting at the car in which Charlie, Johnny Boy, and Theresa are riding. *Mean Streets* ends violently and almost without any explanation of why Michael and his accomplice Scorsese would shoot not only at Johnny Boy but also at his other two friends.

Seeing *Mean Streets* some three decades after it first appeared uncovers some minor flaws, but the mature Scorsese style of such masterpieces as *Taxi Driver* and *Goodfellas* is already apparent. Although Scorsese's view of Italian American Little Italy and the Hollywood Italian characters he creates to populate this cityscape of the mind are deeply flawed, often negative, and even unlikable, they represent powerful images that come to influence the course of American cinema for years. Perhaps the most original aspect of Scorsese's cinematic style in *Mean Streets*, as least insofar as representations of Hollywood Italians are concerned, is the director's visualization of Catholic notions of sin, guilt, and expiation. In employing Roman Catholicism as a source for his cinematic imagery, Scorsese may well have been influenced again by Fellini, whose entire body of work reflects a deeply Catholic consciousness, if not the conscience of a practicing Catholic. In fact, the remarks Scorsese makes about Fellini's works in his recent documentary on Italian cinema would point to an important lesson he learned from such films as *La strada* or *Le notti di Cabiria*, where Fellini places Catholic religious concepts within a secular framework. Scorsese applies this lesson quite successfully in *Mean Streets*.[31]

Spike Lee also documents this special case of Hollywood Italian males behaving badly in Little Italy in two films—*Do the Right Thing* and *Jungle Fever*. Perhaps it is more accurate to say that in these two films, everyone behaves badly—white Hollywood Italians and black African Americans—but director Lee criticizes only the negative behavior of his Hollywood Italians. In each film, Lee explores the dynamics of the relationships between the Little Italies of New York City and the inhabitants of black communities.[32] To say that Lee's films are controversial would be an understatement. *Do the Right Thing* shows the racial relations between white Italian Americans and blacks of Bedford Stuyvesant in Brooklyn as abysmal and practically without hope of redemption. *Jungle Fever* explains a racial love affair between a married black professional from Harlem and a working-class Italian American Catholic girl from Bensonhurst as a throwback to racial attitudes toward blacks stemming from the plantation era. It, too, is doomed to failure. The most intriguing thing about both movies is that the representatives of these two ethnic groups come from strong neighborhood communities. The sense of community they both share, however, seems to have created as many problems in each ghetto as it has resolved.

In *Do the Right Thing*, Lee constructs an idealized black community in a single block of Stuyvesant Street between Quincy Street and Lexington Avenue. In it, he places a collection of colorful characters with close personal ties, the kinds of affective bonds commonly employed to demonstrate community in the Little Italies inhabited by Hollywood Italians. Mookie (Spike Lee) is a high-school graduate who delivers pizzas made by Sal's Famous Pizzeria. He ducks responsibility as often as possible (he already has a son out of wedlock). Few whites live on the block, but one white man named Clifton (John Savage), an urban homesteader, is a third-generation New Yorker who has bought a brownstone because of the high rents in Manhattan. The most important non-black presence in the neighborhood is the cruising police patrol and Sal's Famous Pizzeria, run for the last twenty-five years in the same location by Sal (Danny Aiello, who won an Oscar as Best Supporting Actor for his performance), and his two sons Pino (Richard Edson) and Vito (John Turturro). Radio Raheem (Bill Nunn) wanders around the neighborhood playing Public Enemy's "Fight the Power" on his enormous ghetto blaster without any visible means of support; his obnoxiously loud music triggers the race riot at the end of the film. Sal orders Raheem to turn his radio off in the pizzeria, and when Raheem refuses to do so, Sal smashes it with his baseball bat, touching off the violence. Buggin' Out (Giancarlo Esposito) plays a loudmouth would-be revolutionary who attempts to organize a boycott of Sal's Famous Pizzeria because Sal's Wall of Fame contains photographs of famous Italian Americans (Al Pacino,

Frank Sinatra, Robert De Niro among them) instead of "brothers." Other interesting figures include the local drunk-philosopher Da Mayor (Ossie Davis); an older black woman named Mother Sister (Ruby Dee) who looks out the window all day; an ultracool disk jockey (Samuel L. Jackson); and three unemployed black men who act as a kind of Greek chorus, providing commentary on the action. In addition, there are a few Latinos and a Korean family who operate the only grocery store in the area.

Lee's neighborhood thus represents an idealized black setting, far from the reality of the district during the time the film was filmed.[33] In the first place, it would be highly unlikely for a pizzeria run by Italian Americans to have remained in the district; rather it would most likely have moved years ago to the Italian American district of nearby Bensonhurst, as Vito recommends to his father Sal. Secondly, in spite of a number of racially charged incidents taking place around the time of the film's production, the New York Police Department had made giant strides toward integration by then, and it would be almost unthinkable for a police patrol in the area to be made up solely of white cops. At the time the film appeared, the ethnic conflict in Bed-Stuy, Spike Lee's neighborhood, "reflects the context of the late 1960s much more accurately than the present situation, in which Blacks are increasingly confronted in their neighborhoods by other American ethnic minorities as well as newly arrived immigrants."[34] Lee also taunts his audience by showing an inscription on a wall, TAWANA WAS RIGHT, even after it had been revealed that Tawana Brawley had lied to the police about being assaulted by several whites. Moreover, Bed-Stuy represents in the popular mind and in reality a place characterized by high unemployment, substandard housing, high dependency on government welfare, and omnipresent drug abuse. Yet, all of this is basically absent from Lee's vision. Brent Owens, the location manager of the film, reports in the script that without the policing of the set by Louis Farrakhan's Brothers of the Fruit of Islam, the film's shooting would have been interrupted by the presence of drug dealers and criminals nearby. Two crack houses adjacent to the location were shut down, and spent M-16 cartridges littered the abandoned buildings nearby, testimony to the armed presence of crack dealers.

Spike Lee is unafraid to show all the rough edges of racial relations, especially the hateful language. His attitude, however, reflects a particular pattern of racism of his own, especially his consistent depiction of Italian Americans as bigots in a number of his films. This attitude toward Italian Americans pervades not only *Do the Right Thing* and *Jungle Fever* but also *Summer of Sam* (1999), Lee's less successful interpretation of the 1977 Son of Sam murders that pictures an Italian American neighborhood in the Bronx (a similar neighborhood pictured in *The Wanderers*) as a paranoid group of individuals looking for a scapegoat. Basically, if we are to judge from the director's journal and production notes published with the script, Lee believes that victim status (a status he clearly attributes primarily to blacks and no other ethnic group) entitles members of that group to commit racist acts or speak racist thoughts blamelessly. Other groups who have suffered in the past (the Irish, the Jews, Italian Americans, etc.) do not seem to earn this privileged immunity.

Thus in Lee's film, the bigoted comments of Vito, Sal's son, embody an inherently racist strain in Italian American culture. When the pizzeria is destroyed by an angry crowd of blacks who have grown up on Sal's pizza, it is Mookie—played by the director himself—who starts the riot after Radio Raheem dies from a police choke hold after the fight between Sal and Radio Raheem over his ghetto blaster. Lee's black characters utter the same kinds of odious racial slurs that non-blacks use, but they are essentially immune from criticism. One of the most powerful scenes in the film occurs in a Brechtian moment when five members of five different ethnic groups (Italian American, African American, Puerto Rican, Irish or Anglo, and Korean) look directly into the camera and in a quick-cutting montage deliver the following insults to each other:

MOOKIE: Dago, wop, garlic-breath, guinea, pizza-slinging, spaghetti-bending, Vic Damone, Perry Como, Luciano Pavarotti, Sole Mio, nonsinging motherfucker.

PINO: You gold-teeth, gold-chain-wearing, fried-chicken-and-biscuit-eatin', monkey, ape, baboon, big thigh, fast-running, three-hundred-sixty-degree-basketball-dunking spade Moulan Yan.

STEVIE: You slant-eyed, me-no-speak-American, own every fruit and vegetable stand in New York, Reverend Moon, Summer Olympics '88, Korean kick-boxing bastard.

OFFICER LONG: Goya bean-eating, fifteen in a car, thirty in an apartment, pointed shoes, red wearing, Menudo, meda-meda Puerto Rican cocksucker.

KOREAN CLERK: It's cheap, I got a good price for you, Mayor Koch, "How I'm doing", chocolate-egg-cream-drinking, bagel and lox, B'nai B'rith asshole.[35]

Again, this dialogue has the flavor of a George Carlin list of dirty words that cannot be employed in public. Most of these racial slurs here will be painfully clear to everyone, but perhaps "Moulan Yan"—a particular Italian American derogatory term for blacks—deserves some glossing. Alternately spelled a number of ways (such as "mulignan"), the word derives from the standard Italian word for eggplant—*la melanzana*. Maria Laurino's book on being Italian American recounts an anecdote about an elderly Italian American gentleman who reported being assaulted and robbed by a big "mulignan." After asking what the word could possibly mean from a colleague, the incredulous desk officer at the police station wrote that the man had been assaulted by a huge eggplant![36]

There are, to be sure, moments of honesty in *Do the Right Thing*. ML, one of the three choral loafers, complains about the Koreans having a business after practically getting off the boat yesterday, while the brothers in the hood have no businesses at all: "Either dem Koreans are geniuses or we blacks are dumb." His colleague Coconut Sid responds with the predictable explanation that race is the answer, but then the third man, Sweet Dick Willie, comments "Old excuse." The obvious answer is the one most people in the area do not want to hear—long hours, the work ethic, and a family working together have produced both the Korean grocery and the Italian American pizzeria, whereas welfare, teen pregnancy, drug addiction, unemployment, and a sense of victimhood entitlement have produced less tangible economic

Do the Right Thing *(1989; Spike Lee, director). Vito (John Turturro) and his father Sal (Danny Aiello), proprietors of Sal's Famous Pizzeria, stand opposite the wall covered with Italian American cultural heroes and have an animated conversation with Buggin' Out (Giancarlo Esposito) and Mookie (Spike Lee) seated beneath the framed pictures.*

results for others. But Lee at least ventures the possibility that the answer to
the question ML poses may not be such a favorable one.

The precise moment that sparks the riot and the burning of the pizzeria—the source of most of the critical commentary about *Do the Right
Thing*—occurs during the confrontation between Radio Raheem and Sal
in the pizzeria and the destruction of the boom box by Sal's Mickey Mantle baseball bat. In Lee's script, the moment is described in this fashion:

> RADIO RAHEEM: "My music!" Radio Raheem picks Sal up from be-
> hind the counter and starts to choke his ass. Radio Raheem's prized
> possession—his box, the only thing he owned of value—his box,
> the one thing that gave him any sense of worth—has been smashed
> to bits. (Radio Raheem, like many Black youth, is the victim of ma-
> terialism and a misplaced sense of values). Now he doesn't give a
> fuck anymore. He's gonna make Sal pay with his life.[37]

Exhibiting the strength of a madman, Radio Raheem's choking attack
nearly kills Sal. It is justified in the script and in the film because Sal has attacked his manhood and the object that defines his personality. In Lee's
view, Sal's defense of his pizzeria, built by his own sweat and labor over
three decades, provides proof of the inherent racism of Italian Americans
as an ethnic group. Lee complains that the normal view of this sequence
equates Raheem's death with the destruction of Sal's property, but this is
not an accurate viewing of the ending of the film. Raheem resists arrest and
dies from a choke hold instigated by his stubborn refusal to stop fighting
and his superhuman strength that requires an entire squad of police to
subdue. His death is a tragic mistake but cannot be blamed on Sal's racism.
Elsewhere in the script and his journal, Lee's remarks indicate what
amounts to a personal score that he seems to want to settle with Italian
Americans. Once he gleefully comments that "I'm gonna have this Black-
Italian thing down to a T. Some Italians may say it's biased, but look at how
the Black characters were portrayed in Rocky films."[38] Another remark over
an Eddie Murphy skit about Italians in *Raw* underscores his belief that
blacks and Italian Americans are essentially alike and that Italian Americans even imitate blacks without realizing it: "Eddie had them down:
yelling MOULAN YAN [nigger] this, MOULAN YAN that. The most truthful
thing he said is that Italians act like niggers more than niggers do. It's true,
they certainly act Black but don't know it."[39]

One Marxist critic has noted that Lee's cinema suffers from a very thin
dividing line between Brechtian "typical" characters depicting "typical"
scenes and characters "a breath away from the stereotypical, archetypal,

conventional, representative, average, and so on" that lend themselves to "caricature and distortion" and "often embody gender or racial stereotypes."[40] Another student of the image has argued that Buggin' Out wants a brother's picture placed on Sal's Wall of Fame because the blacks demand not self-respect (something the critic claims they possess already in *Do the Right Thing*) but the respect and acknowledgment of whites and equal billing on the private spaces of Sal's business that defines who are Americans and who are not.[41] Lee's *Do the Right Thing* is as powerful a description of racial conflict as can be found in the Hollywood canon, but its premises often seem to be based on the same racial attitudes it condemns.

Jungle Fever reflects an equally troubling bias in Lee's outlook on racial relationships between black Americans and Italian Americans. In this disturbing film about the *inevitable* failure of an interracial love affair, Lee casts Wesley Snipes as Flipper Purify, the upper-middle-class successful black architect, who falls for Angie Tucci (Annabella Sciorra), an Italian American secretary from Bensonhurst with only a high-school education, betraying his upscale light-skinned black wife Drew (Lonette McKee), a buyer for Bloomingdale's. Flipper's father, a pious former preacher (Ossie Davis) eventually kills Flipper's crackhead brother Gator (Samuel L. Jackson) in a fit of insane self-righteousness. Unlike *Do the Right Thing*, the plague of drug addiction in the black community is so important a secondary theme in *Jungle Fever* that it almost interferes with Lee's primary interest, interracial marriage. "Jungle fever" is a derogatory term like "high yellow" or "octoroon" that, if employed by a white director or scriptwriter, would elicit charges of racism. But Lee employs it precisely because he knows it will set his white audiences on edge and on the defensive. At another ethnic dinner from hell—this time interracial in character—the Good Reverend Doctor Purify explains to Angie what this particular disease is all about. It all started when the white plantation owners put their lilywhite wives on moral pedestals, too pure to touch or to profane with sex. As a result they were forced to relieve their sexual drives with their black female slaves. The white women, frustrated by this position that effectively denied them sexual relief, thus desired the black bucks they spied on the plantation. The black "bucks" are supposedly so physically well endowed that no white woman can resist them or do without them once they have "gone black." Drawing the argument to a dramatic close, the reverend informs his son that he has desired to "fish in the white man's cesspool" and that "I don't eat with whoremongers."

This explanation of the origin of the urge to have interracial sexual relationships may be termed the "Mandingo" syndrome, after a similar argument advanced by a novel and film of the same title (1975) starring James

Mason as a crazy plantation owner whose daughter has a black slave lover (boxer Ken Norton), described by black film historian Donald Bogle as "part noble tom/part sexy buck."[42] By all indications, Spike Lee concurs with the Good Reverend Doctor and with the general drift of *Mandingo:* relationships between Italian Americans and African Americans can only be generated by sick curiosity about "doing it" with someone of another ethnic or racial group, not by friendship, affection, and love. Unlike *Do the Right Thing,* however, *Jungle Fever* depicts black bigotry in Harlem that is as cruel and irrational as the racial prejudice encountered in Little Italy. Behind this Mandingo mythology are certain implied ideas about racial affairs that seem to have been invented by grade-B scriptwriters of another generation: black men have prodigious sexual members and indefatigable stamina; white women yearn for the kind of sexual servicing white men cannot provide; white men, on the other hand, envy the black man's sexual prowess and at the same time want to taste the forbidden fruits of black love, and so forth. If it is true that blacks and whites (and more specifically Italian American whites) go to bed with each other in pursuit of strange, psychologically demeaning myths and stereotypes they hold about another race—that light skin attracts dark skin and the reverse, that breaking a racial taboo explains the sexual attraction of people from different cultures, neighborhoods, and ethnic groups—then Spike Lee's film provides a very bleak picture of race relations in America. Perhaps the only note of hope in the film comes from Paulie (John Turturro), Angie's jilted boyfriend who discovers that after she has rejected him in favor of a black man, he finds himself attracted to a personable black schoolteacher, who buys a paper each morning in his coffee shop. She agrees to go out with him, and even though his Italian American Guido friends actually beat him up since, in their eyes, he betrays the neighborhood values, he still shows up at her doorstep. In spite of the fact that his father Lou Carbone (Anthony Quinn) represents the quintessential racist, not unlike Angie's father and two brothers who beat her mercilessly when they learn of her affair with a black man, Paulie may actually be genuinely attracted to this woman and not just a victim of "jungle fever."

Hollywood Italians, La famiglia, *and Little Italies in the American Cinema*

An analysis of Hollywood's history of the Italian American immigrant experience, the Little Italies of the great urban centers, and the Italian American belief that *la famiglia* is a primary cultural value yields some interesting insights. Placing the twenty-some feature films discussed in some detail in this chapter in historical order based upon the eras they represent (rather than in chronological order by the year of their production) provides an impressive panorama of the Italian American experience represented by a number of Hollywood Italian film images. Limited attention has been paid by Hollywood to discrimination against Italian Americans: *Vendetta* and *From Here to Eternity* raise this theme, which has obviously been far less interesting to writers and studio owners than discrimination against other ethnic groups, such as Jews or blacks. Nevertheless, a significant number of Hollywood productions depict traditional Italian American working-class values—class consciousness in *Christ in Concrete*; the dignity of labor in *Mac, A Bronx Tale,* and *Big Night.* By far the most important representations of Hollywood Italians focus upon the neighborhood—the values of Little Italies and the role of the family in the urban communities. This is particularly true in *Moonstruck* but also in *Marty, The Rose Tattoo, Love with the Proper Stranger, Household Saints, True Love,* and *ItalianAmerican.* In almost all of the films about Italian Americans (with the exception of *Vendetta* and *The Rose Tattoo,* films that depict events taking place in the important Italian American communities in Louisiana), Little Italies are in Manhattan or in the New York City boroughs of the Bronx and Queens, or in nearby New Jersey, and the Hollywood Italians in these films are predominantly Sicilian in origin.

A number of these portraits of ethnic life define Little Italy as a setting of the mind that inspires nostalgia and the desire to return to the kind of community typified by such ethnic enclaves before changes in demography virtually destroyed most of these urban villages. Yet, a dark side of Little Italy also emerges in these films, a negative aspect of Italian American cultural and social values that depicts Hollywood Italians as the quintessential bigots and racists. Such closely knit communities may actually presuppose the exclusion of other ethnic or racial groups. Although some films view the working class as a potentially noble and dignified group, others see the working-class Italian American as a Guido or Guidette—part of a tasteless, uneducated, prejudiced group of characters with vulgar gold chains, big hair, and abrasive manners.

The Web site of the National Italian American Foundation claims that Italian Americans make up the fifth largest ethnic group in the United States. During the 2000 census, the American population totaled 281,421,906 people. Of that number, some 273,000,000 individuals reported a national origin in this descending order: English, German, Irish, American, and Italian. 15,942,683 individuals claimed Italian ancestry, but the total number of Italian Americans is no doubt higher since all people taking part in the census did not report a national origin, and some of those reporting their ethnic origin as "American" were doubtless of Italian origin as well. If this is the case, then the worst disservice Hollywood has done to Italian Americans is not to have portrayed them as Latin lovers, prizefighters, gangsters, or even racists but to have placed them in a ghetto based upon working-class occupations, closed cultural values, and geographical location predominantly in the New York area. Surely the over fifteen million Italian Americans do not all live in New York City, nor do they all work primarily as manual laborers, wear huge, vulgar gold chains, actively oppose integration, chew gum, or listen to doo-wop music. Many are certainly CEOs of large corporations (Lee Iacocca of Ford and Chrysler, and Carleton Fiorina of Hewlett-Packard), jurists (such as Anthony Scalia), writers (John Ciardi, Gay Talese), university presidents (A. Bartlett Giamatti), and professional people in many fields, including education, medicine, law, labor unions, and public service. Surely they deserve some attention in the American imagination that Hollywood controls. Yet the Hollywood Italians of the silver screen are crowded into a very tiny and limited spectrum of locations, occupations, and social values.

In spite of the limited scope of the representations of Hollywood Italians in American cinema, the impact of these films has been extensive. By my count, the major films discussed in this chapter have received nineteen Oscars in almost every conceivable category and twenty-three other unsuccessful nominations. They have been honored at Cannes and Venice with a number of key prizes and have received five signs of recognition from the New York Film Critics, as well as an additional seven prizes from the Golden Globes awards. Hollywood Italians in these films have had an important impact upon the myths created by American cinema even without regard to other categories (lovers, prizefighters, gangsters) in which they have also played crucial roles. Although much remains to be done if the reality of Italian Americans and the representations of Hollywood Italians are to move closer together in the American cinema, these measurements of progress stand as a recognition of the vital role Italian Americans have played in the creation of America's identity.

2

❧

Palookas: Hollywood Italian Prize Fighters

"I was wrong, Marie, about the Kid. I guess I've been wrong about a lot of things. You two go on being happy, being in love. Be careful about how to tell Mom about this."

The dying words of Nick Donati (Edward G. Robinson)
in *Kid Galahad* (1937)

"Millionaires no necessary . . . Joe lova music . . . Joe taka disa violin . . . piecea wood . . . and wita his two hands . . . handsa so beautiful . . . so fine . . . he makea music."

Mr. Bonaparte (Lee J. Cobb) describing his son's
musical talent in *Golden Boy* (1939)

"Well, there goes another little greaseball on his way. Ten years from now, the death house at Sing Sing!"

An Irish policeman's description of Rocky Graziano (Paul Newman)
as a young juvenile delinquent in *Somebody up There Likes Me* (1956)

"He's a nice, a nice kid. He's a pretty kid, too. I mean I don't know, I gotta problem if I should fuck him or fight him."

Jake La Motta (Robert De Niro) describing his upcoming opponent
Tony Janiro to the mobster Tommy Como in *Raging Bull* (1980)

"This is what I'm looking for. 'The Italian Stallion.' Look, it's the name, man. 'The Italian Stallion.' The media'll eat it up. Now who discovered America? An Italian, right? What would be better than to get it on with one of his descendants? Southpaw, nuthin.' I'll drop him in three. *APOLLO CREED MEETS THE ITALIAN STALLION.* Sounds like a monster movie."

Apollo Creed (Carl Weathers) decides to fight an unknown
Italian American fighter in *Rocky* (1976) for the ethnic publicity

GAZZO: "How about investing in condominiums?"
ROCKY: "Condominiums?"
GAZZO: "Yeah, condominiums."
ROCKY: "I never use them."

Palooka dialogue in *Rocky II* (1979): Gazzo (Joe Spinell), the Mafioso
loan shark, gives Rocky (Sylvester Stallone) some financial advice

Depictions of Italian Americans in Hollywood films, even when those featuring gangsters, boxers, or Latin lovers are excluded from consideration, focus upon characters of lower-class origins without much education. The fact that over fifteen million Americans of Italian origin do not fit neatly into this kind of cultural ghetto has had little impact upon such representations. Of course, other ethnic groups have suffered from the same kinds of distorted images: not all Irish men were policemen, even fewer blacks were Stepin Fetchits, and so forth. The role of Italian American prizefighters has certainly done little to change the stereotypes. Indeed, Italian American boxers such as Rocky Graziano and Jake La Motta, both of whom wrote autobiographies that furnished stories for successful and influential films, merely continue the identification of Italians with lower-class environments. Rather than being dagos, they become palookas, a word defined as an incompetent or easily defeated player, especially a prizefighter, that may have been coined by Jack Conway (1886–1928), a popular editor and writer for *Variety* magazine.[1] Another more complete definition glosses two meanings for the word: "one refers to an unsuccessful boxer, especially one who is both large and stupid, the other to any large and stupid or clumsy person, an oaf or lout."[2] This same source further adds that the word was first recorded in print in 1925, and the most important boxing periodical, *The Ring*, defined the word in 1926 as "a tenth rater, a boxer without ability, a nobody." Thus, the term pre-existed the popular comic strip *Joe Palooka*, created by Ham Fisher (1901–55) in 1927 that featured a somewhat inarticulate and simple boxer with fists of iron but a pure heart and high ideals. Joe Palooka became an extremely popular hero and was even employed by the government in wartime propaganda. This cartoon character may be taken as representative of a certain kind of boxer frequently associated with Italian American prizefighters and called by various names—*sluggers, brawlers, street fighters,* even *yokels.* Their violent style of boxing may be juxtaposed to the more "stylish" or "scientific" boxers. The first such "scientific" boxer was Gentleman Jim Corbett, whose life was depicted in *Gentleman Jim* (1942; director, Raoul Walsh), starring Errol Flynn in the title role. Many but not all of these "stylish" boxers have been black, such as Joe Louis, Sugar Ray Robinson, or Muhammad Ali. As Gerald Early puts it, "excepting Jack Dempsey and Gene Tunney, virtually every white champion has been, despite his style, a yokel."[3] Furthermore, Early argues that "the world's best boxer needn't fear the man who is almost his equal but rather the man who could not possibly match his skill.... Technique ... must always fear not other technique but the utter void of technique."[4] Early's observation about the clash of technique and the lack of technique in the ring goes a long way toward explaining some of the puzzling results in the history of prizefighting: how some fights end in almost no time at all, whereas other apparently mismatched fighters manage to do extremely well against superior opponents. It is also important to remember that prize-fighting was one of the few noncriminal ways that an uneducated person could become a wealthy celebrity.

This kind of Manichean struggle in the ring between different kinds of fighters also explains much of the appeal boxing has had to such writers as Ernest Hemingway, Norman Mailer, and Joyce Carol Oates, all of whom have written extensively on the subject. Along with boxing audiences, writers also seem to have a universal emotional preference for the "street fighter," the "puncher," the "mauler," over the "boxer" because they are by definition the underdogs in a fight with a man possessing superior boxing skills and similar weight. Norman Mailer has claimed that

> there are fighters who are men's men. Rocky Marciano was one of them. . . . They have a code—it is to fight until they are licked, and if they have to take a punch for every one they give, well, they figure they can win. Their ego and their body intelligence are both connected to the same source of juice—it is male pride. They are substances close to rock. They work on clumsy skills to hone them finer, knowing if they can obtain parity, blow for blow with any opponent, they will win. They have more guts. Up to a far-gone point, pain is their pleasure, for their character in combat is their strength to trade pain for pain, loss of faculty for loss of faculty.[5]

By definition, such fighters (as opposed to boxers) have "heart"—the favorite expression of boxing fans for bravery and courage in the ring, usually courage in the face of overwhelming talent. They become "crowd pleasers" since they are perceived as "game fighters," able to endure punishment. In the process, they also become interesting symbolic figures. Joyce Carol Oates suggests that such fighters seek physical pain:

> Brawling fighters—those with "heart" like Jake La Motta, Rocky Graziano, Ray Mancini—have little choice but to absorb terrible punishment in exchange for some advantage (which does not in any case always come). And surely it is true that some boxers (see Jake La Motta's autobiographical *Raging Bull)* invite injury as a means of assuaging guilt, in a Dostoyevskian exchange of physical well being for peace of mind. Boxing is about being hit more than it is about hitting, rather just as it is about feeling pain, if not devastating psychological paralysis, more than it is about winning.[6]

Italian American prizefighters materialize at a specific historical time and come, in general, from a very specific environment (urban ghettos in the North) and social class (the most disadvantaged people in these ghettos). An important study of the various ethnic groups prominent in boxing during certain key years studied (1909, 1916, 1928, 1936, and 1948) demonstrates conclusively from a large sampling of boxers analyzed that there is a direct correlation between waves of immigration and the predominance of different ethnic groups.[7] In 1909, for example, Irish fighters are most numerous, followed by German and English boxers. In 1916, the Irish and the Germans occupy the first two places but Italians move to third in number. In 1928, Jews were the most numerous boxers but Italians had moved up to second place ahead of the Irish. In 1936, the Italians finally reach first place, followed by the Irish and the Jews. But in 1948, black prizefighters outnumbered the second-place Italians, followed by another emerging ethnic group in third place, the Mexicans. Thus, Italians entered the profession of prizefighting in the 1920s and the 1930s after the waves of immigration in the United States peaked, but as they were assimilated into mainstream America, their numbers began to drop off slowly but surely in the 1940s and the 1950s, even though the most famous Italian American champions (Rocky Marciano, Jake La Motta, Rocky Graziano) emerge during this late period. The same study also underscored an important sociological characteristic of those who used boxing to escape from the conditions of poverty and lack of opportunity that ghetto living imposed upon them. Juveniles growing up in the lower socioeconomic levels, who saw gang fights as a normal condition of life, entertained fantasies about "easy money," lacked real vocational opportunities, and remained generally isolated from middle-class culture, were as likely to become criminals as boxers: the major difference resided in the role model available for the youngster, whether criminal or prizefighter. If a gangster lived in the neighborhood (as was the case in *A Bronx Tale*) rather than a boxer, the future of a young adolescent might well turn out totally differently.[8]

Writers and film directors also find boxing an appealing subject because of its intrinsic symbolic appeal. Prizefighting became one of America's national crazes in the late 1920s and the 1930s, as the sport moved from the smoky clubs and bars of the frontier or the inner city to arenas where the "swells" and the wealthy, their beautiful women clothed in furs, began to think of a boxing match as something of a social event. It rivaled baseball in importance and certainly outpaced professional football and basketball at that time. Radio broadcasts, a medium that seems perfectly suited to both boxing and baseball, also brought boxing into every living room without the necessity of entering a fight arena, a place that was not particularly attractive to families. A number of symbolic issues came to be expressed in the bouts of the period and continue, in some measure, to the present. One of the most important, of course, was the theme of the "great white hope," the search for a Caucasian heavyweight to oppose a black champion. This idea emerged during the time Jack Johnson, the black heavyweight champion between 1908 and 1915, scandalized America by engaging in sexual relationships with white women.[9] Thus, beneath the "sport" of boxing there was frequently a subtext of racism and ethnic hatred. But this conflict was perhaps natural in a sport that had Anglo-Saxon roots in eighteenth- and nineteenth-century English ideas about boxing, from the early bare-knuckle fights to the modified Marquess of Queensberry rules that largely govern the sport today (including the use of gloves, three-minute rounds, standardized judging and referees, and weight classes). Successive ethnic groups outside the WASP norm saw boxing as a means of joining mainstream culture as well as a way to proclaim their ethnic virility. Many of the most famous bouts of the 1930s were infused with political messages. The "foreign invasion" of European or South American champions or contenders during this period also forced a relaxation of the unwritten rule against white fighters contending with blacks, thus giving Joe Louis an opportunity he might have missed had he been born a decade earlier. Jewish-American champion Max Baer beat Max Schmeling of Germany, dealing a blow to Hitler's anti-Semitic propaganda. Schmeling's non-title defeat of Joe Louis in 1936 obviously made the German dictator happy until 1938, when Louis defeated the German ignominiously in just two minutes into the first round. Primo Carnera—the Italian giant whose boxing skills represented the classic example of the technique-less Palooka—eventually met Joe Louis in 1935 in Yankee Stadium. The fight was billed as Italy versus Abyssinia, and the American public as well as the sportswriters took the side of Abyssinia (as they did in the war between Italy's fascist dictatorship and the African country that it invaded). Louis pulverized Carnera in six rounds, just as he would do against Schmeling in New York City in 1938. In an ironic quirk of fate, Louis (a black American in a segregated society) managed to represent America symbolically not only against the German Nazis but also against the less-threatening Italian fascists in the ring.

Besides the intrinsic issue of male virility that rests at the heart of a violent sport like boxing and the various racial, ethnic, and political conflicts that can be superimposed upon the sport by the press and the entertainment industry for symbolic and economic purposes, there is also the important issue of boxing's link to organized crime. Just as it proved difficult to separate the Wise Guys from the Dagos in Little Italy, it is equally impossible to do so entirely with the Palookas of Little Italy. Since boxers and criminals came from virtually the same environment and social class, it is perhaps inevitable that they were linked together. The Antitrust and Monopoly Committee of the United States Senate undertook investigations in the 1960s that revealed a shocking degree of domination over professional boxing, especially in New York City during the 1940s and 1950s, by Italian Americans associated with the Mafia. Frankie Carbo and Blinky Palermo virtually controlled the assignment of important fights, particularly in the heavyweight division, most of which took place in New York, where organized crime was most powerful. Two famous Italian American fighters, Rocky Graziano and Jake La Motta, experienced difficulties in their career with Italian American mobsters. Graziano canceled a bout in 1947 three days before the fight because he had been offered $100,000 to "take a dive." As a result, he felt pretending to be injured was the only means he had to avoid breaking a law and offending the mobsters whom he refused to identify. As La Motta would testify in 1960, at almost the same time that Graziano was being pressured to throw fights, La Motta had been forced to throw a fight against Billy Fox in 1947 in order to obtain the promise for a title bout. Even though La Motta had defeated virtually every ranked fighter in his class, arriving at a title match was virtually impossible without the blessing of the Mob. La Motta made his loss to the inept Fox so obvious, however, that it was clear to anyone seeing the fight that he could have easily beaten his opponent. The deal had apparently been struck with Blinky Palermo (Fox's manager) and an associate of Carbo. Carbo eventually went to jail in 1959, pleading guilty to a number of racketeering charges, but even in jail, he continued to control Sonny Liston and the heavyweight championship bouts until Liston defeated Floyd Patterson in 1962 and took the title. Doubt has always surrounded the subsequent defeat of Liston by Cassius Clay in 1964, and mob interference with the outcome of that fight may well have been the reason why the future Muhammad Ali emerged victorious.[10] If a sporting event involves betting, organized crime will be interested in manipulating its outcomes. Boxing remains one of the sports in which betting is most popular, and the involvement of criminals would only surprise the most naïve.

Kid Galahad *(1937): Honest American Fighters and Crooked Italian Managers*

Michael Curtiz's *Kid Galahad* is a rather unbelievable story about a hayseed from the Midwest named Ward Guisenberry (Wayne Morris) who becomes a prizefighter working for an Italian American manager

named Nick Donati (Edward G. Robinson). He falls in love with his manager's sister Marie (Jane Bryan) while the manager's girl Fluff Phillips
(Bette Davis), falls in love with him. Donati's nemesis is a crooked manager who is also one of the town's top men in organized crime, Turkey
Morgan (Humphrey Bogart). As the film opens, Nick learns that his
fighter Jim Burke has taken a dive in a match with Chuck McGraw, Morgan's fighter, causing him to lose $17,000. He decides to spend his last cent
on a party, and during the celebration the hotel bellhop appears—the personification of provincial innocence. He neither drinks nor smokes and
comes from a farm town to which he hopes to return after making enough
money to buy some land. He is also sufficiently handsome to attract
Fluff's attentions. Although Guisenberry is unsophisticated, he has a heart
of gold and rushes to the defense of offended womanhood without hesi-
tation. In an argument with Chuck McGraw, who has crashed the party
with his boss Turkey Morgan, Fluff is shoved by the brutish fighter. The
bellhop responds by knocking him down with one powerful punch. Since
McGraw is the contender for the title, this incident naturally causes a great
deal of comment and interest in Guisenberry's potential as a boxer. Donati
both disapproves of Fluff's attraction to the handsome hotel employee and
wants to exploit the young man's boxing talent. By engineering a fight with
Chuck McGraw's brother, Donati thinks he is punishing Guisenberry for
his attraction to Fluff and mollifying Morton, who is embarassed by having his contender fighter flattened under his very eyes. Not surprisingly,
rather than suffering the beating both Turkey and Nick think Guisenberry
deserves for very different reasons, Guisenberry wins handily versus the
more experienced McGraw brother despite the odds. Immediately, Turkey
Morgan tries to sign up the bellhop as his fighter, but Guisenberry (unaware that Nick harbors deep resentment against him because of Fluff,
whose attentions he never returns) remains loyal to Nick, who has given
him his break to boxing. He even decks Morgan—a man known as a vicious murderer and the gang boss of the town. Needing to hide his protégé from the mob for fear of retribution, Nick takes the fighting bellhop
to his family's farm.

In the country, and away from the evil-and-corrupted city, the ethnic aspect of Nick's life comes out most clearly. The trip to the pure, simple, natural countryside from the city presents a major theme of the film.
Guisenberry comes from the farmland and retains his natural goodness
despite his contact with urban corruption. This theme has been a staple
Hollywood plot since the first talkie, *Lights of New York* (1928; Bryan Foy,
director), and a theme that remains pervasive in American literature and
culture. Nick's mother and sister, who remain in the country, exhibit the

same kinds of wholesome values, but Nick has left this pastoral oasis and has been tainted by his associations with criminals and boxers.

When Nick returns home to his mother and sister, he immediately reverts to speaking a respectable standard Italian with his mother. Indeed, this is the only means by which the audience may discern (other than his name, Donati) that Nick's ancestry is Italian. The use of standard Italian, and not a dialect from the South, is even more extraordinary because of the length of time it consumes during the film and also because no subtitles are provided. Even though the level of conversation may not be sophisticated, Robinson and the Latino actress playing his mother (Soledad Jiménez) do a creditable job of reproducing the Italian language that the film links to a pastoral oasis of innocence and goodness. Guisenberry has been given the fighting name of "Kid Galahad" because of his defense of women and his purity. While on the farm, he falls in love with Nick's sister Marie, who has been schooled in a convent to keep her away from temptation and to protect her from the moral corruption Nick feels will destroy her innocence in the city where he operates. Marie begins to follow the Kid's fights after he returns to the city, and at one point when he visits her on the farm, she is reading an article comparing him to a medieval knight and praising his monastic lifestyle.

The film's thematic axis thus revolves around a series of conceptual oppositions: the city/corruption/mobsters/fight-fixing versus the countryside/innocence/goodness/fair play. The Italian American ambience of Nick's country home stands in stark contrast to the American city where Turkey Morgan—an Irish criminal, not an Italian American one—calls the shots. Nick's move from his idyllic point of origin to the city also changes him for the worst. Driven by jealousy because of Fluff's love for Kid Galahad—a love never reciprocated by the boxer—Nick decides to double-cross the Kid. Nick bets $50,000 on Nick's opponent, Chuck McGraw, and Turkey Morgan adds another $150,000 to that bet. Needless to say, if the Kid does not lose the fight, Nick will be held responsible. Nick can justify his betrayal of the Kid by his own personal feelings of animosity, but he is also unaware that the Kid intends to quit the ring after this bout. So far as Nick is concerned, there are plenty of future chances to win a title and to make more money with Kid Galahad.

Nick's plan is to advise the Kid to follow an incorrect strategy against McGraw. Since McGraw is a brawler rather than a scientific boxer, Nick tells his fighter to slug it out with McGraw instead of tiring him out until the final rounds. This strategy has disastrous results until half the fight is over. As the match is obviously going badly for the Kid, Fluff goes to Nick and persuades him not to betray his protégé. Nick suddenly decides to change course—only one of the elements of the plot that make *Kid Galahad*'s script somewhat unbelievable: he decides to do the right thing and forget about his bet or about Turkey Morgan's warning that a double cross will mean his death. Once Nick changes strategies and tells the Kid to box, not to punch, the Kid eventually wins. Back in the dressing room, Turkey Morgan turns up with an accomplice, a paid assassin who poses as a fight photographer. In the ensuing shootout, Nick shoots Turkey. Where the pistol he is carrying comes from is unclear, but the gun is obviously necessary to end the film with a deathbed speech by Robinson, who receives a fatal wound. This soliloquy was almost obligatory for Robinson after the famous dying words of the gangster Rico in *Little Caesar* (1930; Mervyn LeRoy, director). Nick makes a final speech to his sister Marie, gives his blessing to the love affair between Marie and the Kid—thus reversing his patriarchal male Italian attempts to control her life—and dies after telling Fluff that "it took us a long time, me and you, but we did what we set out to do, we got us a champ."

Kid Galahad has numerous defects as a film. Nonetheless, the performances of Bette Davis and Humphrey Bogart (not yet megastars) and Edward G. Robinson are entertaining even if the twists and turns of a weak script detract from the overall impact. The movie is interesting for its juxtaposition of Italian American provincial innocence and American big-city corruption. It is unique in picturing an Italian American fight manager, whereas most Hollywood Italian Palookas are prizefighters. Nevertheless, as a reflection of Italian American involvement in the world of professional prizefighting, *Kid Galahad*'s portrait of mob corruption reflects a far more realistic picture of the actual state of affairs than its relatively sugar-coated re-creation of actual boxing in the ring, where almost nobody ever bleeds or seems to get his hair mussed. The shocking violence that characterizes many of the great fights in boxing history—or the great boxing matches in film history—is totally absent here, as it is in a more important work, *Golden Boy*, directed by Rouben Mamoulian with a script based on a highly successful three-act Broadway play of 1937, written by Clifford Odets. But Curtiz's film has far fewer defects than the 1962 remake starring Elvis Presley, also entitled *Kid Galahad* and directed by Paul Karlson. In this pale imitation of the original, the Italian American manager (Edward G. Robinson) is replaced by Gig Young's character named Willy Grogan; Charles Bronson plays the boxer's trainer. Basically, the ethnic presence in the original film is completely missing.[11]

Golden Boy *(1939): Italian Culture (Music) versus American Culture (Boxing)*

Golden Boy represents something of a remake and a correction of the worst structural defects of *Kid Galahad*. Its plot is far simpler and more persuasive. The hayseed farm boy named Ward Guisenberry is transformed into a first-generation Italian American named Joe Bonaparte, a starring role in which William Holden broke into the movies. Joe's manager is Tom Moody (Adolphe Menjou), whose girlfriend Lorna Moon (Barbara Stanwyck) actually falls in love with the boxer. Even the gangster who controls boxing and attempts to influence Joe Bonaparte's career, Eddie Fuseli (Joseph Calleia), is a stronger and more interesting figure than the one played by Humphrey Bogart in *Kid Galahad*. More importantly, Eddie Fuseli is an Italian American gangster. As Fuseli informs Joe, "I'm Italian too. Italian-born but an American citizen." Like the battling bellhop, Joe Bonaparte gets a lucky break in the gym when one of Moody's fighters breaks his hand training and Joe volunteers to take his place. This leads to the inevitable victory in the ring for Joe, achieved while his father (Lee J. Cobb) is waiting

Golden Boy (1939; Rouben Mamoulian, director). American-born Joe Bonaparte (William Holden) realizes his hands are too scarred from boxing as his immigrant father (Lee J. Cobb) holds the expensive violin he has purchased for his son's musical career.

at home to give him his twenty-first birthday gift: a rare Ruggieri violin, for which Joe's immigrant father, who runs a small Italian grocery store, has paid the then-enormous sum of $1,500. This unusual situation in which a talented prizefighter is also a talented violinist sets up the central theme— a conflict between Italian culture (represented by the ethereal world of highbrow music) and American culture (represented by the violent low-brow sport of boxing). Whereas Joe has been brought up to believe that music is more important than anything else in the world, he has also been reared in America and has absorbed some of America's drive for success: "Papa, I want to own things and to give things. Everything you want from breakfast until you turn out the light. I want you to go to concerts every night. Money's the answer. I can get it fighting. No other way. I won't get it playing the violin." His father counters with the argument against materi-alism: "Money, money . . . we gotta hearts . . . we gotta hands . . . we gotta take care of them, huh? You listen to me . . . do what is in your heart, not in your head . . . in there isa music, violin." Unlike *Kid Galahad* where at least two characters (including the star, Edward G. Robinson) speak a very re-spectable brand of standard Italian, in *Golden Boy* Lee J. Cobb's broken English represents more of a parody of the language spoken by the resi-dents of Little Italy than anything else, while William Holden never utters a word of Italian, dialect or otherwise, and from a physical point of view looks anything but Italian. His boxing style is that of the scientific boxer with technique, not the slugging, brawling style typical of other Hollywood Italian Palookas. Joe Bonaparte is, in fact, the only Hollywood Italian Palooka whose physical appearance, speech mannerisms, and body lan-guage mark him as a member of anything but the urban ghettos that pro-duced almost all Italian American prizefighters. His talent with the violin at least provides a believable reason why he fights in this manner rather than slugging his way to the top, for it is obvious in his early fights that he is trying to save his hands as much as possible.

Barbara Stanwyck delivers a great performance as Lorna Moon, playing the tough girl with a heart of gold to perfection. At first she is persuaded by Moody to talk Joe into fighting: "I like men who reach for a slice of fame" she tells him, and when he hesitates, she rebukes him: "See you in 1960— maybe you'll be somebody by then." That is all the provocation Joe needs to make his decision to set his music aside. When Lorna visits Joe's home and meets his father, she realizes that Joe should really be a musician, and she begins to fall in love with him. As she comes to see this other side of Joe, she has second thoughts about his career as a boxer: "Joe. . . . I was wrong about you. . . . I've seen you get hard shelled and tough . . . you belong in your home with your violin. . . . Joe, maybe you should give up fighting."

Golden Boy (1939; Rouben Mamoulian, director). Gangster and fight promoter Eddie Fuseli (Joseph Calleia) shows Joe Bonaparte's manager Tom Moody (Adolphe Menjou) how easily a good fight can be arranged with the right "connections" as Joe (William Holden) and Tom's girlfriend Lorna Moon (Barbara Stanwyck) look on.

By now Joe is linked to Eddie Fuseli, the shady Italian gangster who admires good prizefighters and forces Tom Moody (with Joe's consent) to sell him a piece of Joe's contract. The links of boxing to organized crime, implicit in *Kid Galahad*, are even more obvious in *Golden Boy*. Tom Moody may resent Joe Bonaparte because Lorna Moon falls in love with his fighter, but he is at least an honest manager. As such, he is unable to guarantee Joe really important bouts. In contrast, Eddie Fuseli gets Joe important matches with a single phone call in Tom's office because of his gangster connections.

As Joe becomes more and more successful in the ring, he becomes more and more an American. He cuts his Italian curls, he becomes obsessed with material things (a new car, silk shirts, dressing well, impressing Lorna), and he wears double-breasted pinstripe suits that make him appear to be a more handsome version of his eminence grise, Fuseli. Joe's big bout is with a black fighter, The Chocolate Drop, and before the contest begins, Joe's father comes to visit him for the first time in his entire boxing career. Earlier, Joe had asked for his father's blessing—what he calls "giving the word"—

for his vocational choice, and his father had refused. Now, when his father sees the world in which Joe lives, he believes that all is lost: "Now I know. Itsa too late for music. Now I see. I sorry for you. I give you the word to fight. . . . I hopea you win every fight Joe."

When compared to the horrifically violent and bloody sequences in *Raging Bull* or the Rocky series, the sequence of the match between Joe (NEW YORK'S FAVORITE SON) and The Chocolate Drop (THE PRIDE OF HARLEM) seems almost restrained. Nevertheless, Mamoulian shows us shots of the crowd screaming for blood that suggest Sergei Eisenstein's use of close-ups, which depict the animal lust for violence at the core of prize-fighting. And the end result of Joe's important bout is the accidental death of The Chocolate Drop. Joe visits the dead man's dressing room and speaks to a grieving family, who actually forgive him. This only increases his guilt, which pushes Joe to abandon boxing and all its American materialism: "I'm a cheap edition of you, Fuseli, but tonight's the end. I'm quitting . . . I'll never put on a glove again." Joe stands up to Fuseli's threats and leaves a deserted Madison Square Garden with Lorna, who delivers the central theme of the script: "Now you can go back to yourself, to your music. . . . Your hand will heal and you'll play again. You must. Nothing can stop you when you do what's in your heart. We have each other, Joe, we'll find a way." The film concludes with Joe's tearful return home to his father, who welcomes him with open arms as Brahms's "Cradle Song"—a piece Joe once mastered but was unable to play well after bruising his hands in the ring—resounds in the background.

Golden Boy stands apart, in some respects, from the rest of the important films featuring Italian Palookas. Its protagonist is anything but a Palooka, a street brawler in the ring who speaks broken English and comes from an urban ghetto. Although his father was born in the Old Country, Joe Bonaparte looks and dresses like a middle-class, All-American boy with no accent or trace of his ethnic origin. In the ring, he fights like a gentleman, not like the typical boxer with the killer instinct, even though the result of his most important bout is the death of his opponent. The drama of his life revolves around a contrast between two stereotypes: that American culture is violent and materialistic, symbolized by the physical body language of the boxing ring, while Italian American or Italian culture embraces the higher and more cultivated intellectual and emotional language of music and the violin. And American culture also seems to have produced Fuseli, the Italian gangster who is proud of his American citizenship and who has abandoned his Italian roots for the immediate materialistic goals of American life.

Somebody up There Likes Me *(1956): the American*
Dream Comes True

If the world of *Golden Boy* seems strangely unlike the atmosphere of Italian American urban life, it nevertheless shares a number of similar elements with the bio-picture about Rocky Graziano's life and boxing career, most particularly the link of boxing to organized crime. Robert Wise's film was based on a highly successful autobiography, also entitled *Somebody up There Likes Me*, which Graziano wrote with Roland Barber. *Golden Boy* begins in medias res: Joe Bonaparte appears and begins prizefighting as a mature young man without any explanation of urban-ghetto life. Except for Lee J. Cobb's bad imitation of an Italian American accent, the ethnic content of the film is limited to an abstract contrast between Yankee materialism and Italian musical culture. Both Graziano's autobiography and its cinematic adaptation have far more ambitious goals. Both present the story of how a bad kid turned good through the beneficial influence of prizefighting, while depicting how much of the negative influence upon the main character's life came out of the Italian American family structure, which is often praised as one of the stronger, more positive, features of this ethnic culture. Moreover, the book and the film offer a social and psychological explanation for why urban-ghetto children become fighters in the first place, one that many scholars and historians of the sport accept.

Graziano's autobiography presents a depressing portrait of his Lower East Side origins. Graziano's immigrant Italian father was also a boxer who gave up the sport at his wife's insistence. But his failure to make a success of his fighting career and his frequent unemployment turned him into a nasty drunk. One of the first sequences in the film shows Nick Barbella (the family's real Italian name) drinking with his friends and teasing Rocky by boxing with him and hurting him until he cries: when Rocky refuses to fight anymore, his father says "I don't like crybabies . . . get up . . . get up." Shortly thereafter, he tells his son: "I look at you and I see the devil. Get out of my sight." Living in a poor neighborhood where the most conspicuous success stories involve gangsters or prizefighters, where few of the inhabitants have any education beyond high school (or even grade school) in an era before the opportunity to go to college became a widespread phenomenon with the GI Bill after World War II, Rocky had an angry, unsuccessful role model in his father. Thus, it is not surprising that Rocky became a juvenile delinquent. Wise's film masterfully presents the transition from small child teased by a belligerent father to small-time criminal in a few brilliant sequences. He cuts from the opening sequence depicting the sadistic boxing

Somebody up There Likes Me
(1956; Robert Wise, director).
Nick Barbella (Harold Stone)
teases his son Rocky (Tony
Rangno) and calls him a
crybaby.

scene with his father to what might be described as a classic *film noir* sequence. As the young Graziano runs away from some Irish cops, who predict he will end his life in Sing Sing within ten years, modern jazz plays on the sound track, and we cut suddenly from the young boy to Paul Newman running from the police over the tenement roofs of his neighborhood. The strange angles and the overhead shots of fire escapes and city landscapes that audiences have come to identify with 1950s-crime films indicate the direction Rocky's life is going to take if nothing occurs to change it. *Somebody up There Likes Me* argues a thesis found in any number of recent books on the history of boxing: namely, from the Anglo-Saxon origins of prizefighting in the nineteenth century to the professional boxing matches of the twentieth century, urban poverty, racial or ethnic discrimination, and relative deprivation generate the "motivational impulse to enter the ring" and remain the "common denominators" of the professional boxer.[12] Graziano's autobiography, and the film upon which it is based, explain deviant behavior by environmental factors:

> It was like the whole gang of us started out together in 1932, and kept graduating together up through the years to the big top. Some of us even

made it all the way to the biggest top of all—the death house. Only somewhere along the way some screwball angel threw a wrench in the plan for me, and I wound up a legitimate guy.[13]

Although this "screwball angel" plus the love and support of his mother and wife are the only variables Graziano cites to explain why he did not end up in prison or the death house with the rest of his neighborhood friends, boxing (the natural extension of his propensity to fight in school and in the ghetto) also plays a large factor. After being sent to a reformatory, Rocky ends up on Riker's Island, a real prison, where he meets Frankie Peppo (a brilliant but uncredited appearance by Robert Loggia), who sees how handy Rocky is with his hands and proposes that he go into the fight game to make money. Peppo is an Italian American gangster who fixes fights and owns a piece of two different boxers. As he says: "Sometimes they win, sometimes they dive like swans. Either way, there's money in it." Peppo later appears when Graziano is the target of an investigation into alleged criminal associations and possible fight fixing at the pinnacle of his career just before he is to have a shot at the championship title against Tony Zale. After the reformatory and Riker's Island, Graziano is drafted into the Army in 1942 but slugs a captain, goes AWOL, and turns up at the famous Stillman's Gym in New York City, where he fills in for a missing sparring partner and nearly beats the poor man to a pulp. In the film, this unfortunate individual is described simply as a top light heavyweight, but in Graziano's autobiography he is identified as the former middleweight champion of Argentina.[14] Thus the serendipitous episodes in both *Kid Galahad* and *Golden Boy* that explain how the battling bellhop and Joe Bonaparte got their start in the fight game were not as unrealistic as they might have seemed.[15] Although Graziano had fought as an adolescent in New York City boxing matches for youngsters, his real training in the ring came from the boxing team at Leavenworth, where he was sentenced to a year for desertion before he was dishonorably discharged from the Army. In an important scene inside Leavenworth, Graziano beats a prison bully to a bloody pulp with his strong right hand and the boxing team coach sees his raw but undeveloped talent. His speech to Graziano represents an important theory of how boxers motivate themselves to take the terrible punishment in the ring:

I don't think you'll ever show any real style like some of my boys, but you'd like 'em all. You'd like 'em all because you've got something inside of you that a lot of fighters don't have, never will have, no matter how much I teach them—hate. I don't know why it's there, I only know that anybody that hits you, he better start ducking fast. Because that hate pours into that right hand of yours and makes it like a charge of dynamite.

One critic has rightly called boxing a "metasport" because it reveals the essence of the violence that lies at the core of many sports but that is controlled and channeled in other sports into more benign directions by rules, pads, and referees. Other sports "degenerate" into a brawl when the rules break down, but boxing "orders and preserves the energies released at such moments" and is "both the most primitive of contests and a match for any in the complexity of its strategies, counter-strategies, rituals, and traditions."[16] Joyce Carol Oates agrees with Graziano's explanation of his talent, for she believes that "boxing is fundamentally about anger ... [boxers] constitute the disenfranchised of our affluent society, they are the sons of impoverished ghetto neighborhoods in which anger, if not fury, is appropriate—rather more, perhaps, than Christian meekness and self-abnegation."[17]

Somebody up There Likes Me, as the title suggests, represents a kind of Italian American Horatio Alger story. As an analyst of the Graziano-La Motta legacy in boxing notes, Graziano's story in both his autobiography and the film represents a story of "human reclamation," the moral of which is that "we can learn to be somebody else"; it is "the American success story, structured rather like all American autobiographies of the bad youth who finds himself in young adulthood."[18]

Since the narrative treats the conversion, in a sense, of an evil man into a good one, Graziano's autobiography actually follows a time-honored tradition in Western literature that may be traced back to Saint Augustine's *Confessions*. Although Graziano's title and remarks in the film and the autobiography tend to suggest that the conversion from evil to good is the outcome of the beneficial effects of his "screwball angel," the narrative emphasizes that the love of Graziano's family—his long-suffering mother and his faithful wife Norma—is actually the fundamental reason behind his conversion. Only after he reconciles with his hated father can Graziano change and be awarded the championship title he has worked toward for so long. Just before his fight with Tony Zale in Chicago, during which Graziano takes the middleweight title by a knockout in the sixth round, Wise organizes a number of events in the film to lead toward this conversion. Graziano leaves his training camp and flies back to his ethnic origins, the Italian ghetto of Lower East Side New York City, where he meets a number of people from his past. From the ice-cream parlor owned by his philosopher friend Benny, Graziano calls Frankie Peppo but avoids being corrupted by his Mafia associates who would gladly fix the upcoming title bout. Outside the ice-cream parlor, he runs into his old childhood friend Romolo (Sal Mineo), who is running from the police and who is frantically looking for a gun to rob a nearby bookie joint. Romolo asks Graziano, "We ain't got a chance, guys like us . . . do we? . . . do we Rocky?" Outside, Graziano sees a Dantesque vision of criminality: prostitutes parade on the streets looking for clients, and young men who remind us of Graziano are being arrested by the police: "Get in there, you no good little grease ball," a cop remarks as he hauls one of them off to jail. Nothing seems to have changed since Graziano's childhood when another policeman predicted he would end his days in jail. Everywhere Graziano looks, he sees what seems to be a direct correlation between poverty and deprivation, on the one hand, and criminality, on the other. Benny tells Graziano how all of the old gang went to prison, some sentenced to the electric chair, and others killed during their lives of crime. Benny informs Graziano he has to begin to take responsibility, to "pay the check," as he puts it, and to stop blaming himself and his background for the bad things that happen in his life. Earlier in the film, the camera had focused on a razor advertisement in a shop window in which Gene Tunney was touted as a user of that particular brand of razor. Now, in the same window, Graziano sees himself featured in the same ad that had once featured the great heavyweight who bested Jack Dempsey and was one of his role models and idols as a young boy. Moved by these scenes that force him to make a momentous personal decision about the direction of his life, Graziano goes home and finds his father. As usual, they argue, but then Rocky reaches an understanding with his father and about himself, realizing that his father had not been as lucky as he has been and that he gave up his dream because he loved Rocky's mother. His father finally tells him, "Be the champ, like I never was." In effect, Graziano's father gives him "the word" (the traditional Italian paternal blessing) just as Joe Bonaparte's father finally does in *Golden Boy*.

Wise thus structures the crucial moments before Graziano's final triumph in such a manner that the sequences leading up to the epic Zale fight are actually stages on the road to self-knowledge, reconciliation, and understanding. In effect, Graziano's entire life was on a downward spiral until he began to box and began to learn about the power of love. Once those moral lessons have been learned, he is rewarded by success in the championship bout. Round one goes badly and Graziano is knocked down. The camera cuts to a view of the Lower East Side neighborhood, completely deserted as everyone there is huddled around the radio giving their favorite son their support. Eventually, however, virtue is rewarded, Graziano bests Zale, and he achieves his dream of the middleweight title.

Somebody up There Likes Me *(1956; Robert Wise, director). After winning the championship, Rocky Graziano (Paul Newman) parades through the neighborhood with his wife Norma (Pier Angeli) in a Cadillac convertible—proof that his life has been a success story.*

The camera immediately cuts to Graziano's old neighborhood in New York City through which Graziano and his wife parade in a Cadillac convertible: when Rocky remarks on how lucky he has been and that "somebody up there likes me," his wife replies, "somebody down here too." The film concludes on a heavily sentimental note with Perry Como singing the film's theme song, "Somebody up There Likes Me."

Graziano's autobiography and Wise's direction structure their narratives in such a way that we hardly notice how short Graziano's tenure as middleweight champion actually was or how, in reality, he lost two of the three bouts with Tony Zale and fell to ignominious defeat when he encountered the superior boxing skills of a Sugar Ray Robinson, Jake La Motta's nemesis. *Somebody up There Likes Me* offers the perfect model of the American-immigrant dream: in it, an Italian American "greaseball" manages to rise above his economic, social, and psychological disadvantages to make something of himself and, in the process, becomes a role model for other Italian Americans in his neighborhood.

Raging Bull *(1980): Jake La Motta and the Suffering Redemption of the Italian American Palooka*

As Gerald Early rightly notes, Graziano's autobiography stresses the idea that a bad youth may find himself and change his life; the moral of his life story is that "we can learn to be somebody else," while Jake La Motta's autobiography proclaims that "we must learn to live with ourselves" and is a tale of "utter absurdity."[19] Of all the films representing Hollywood Italian Palookas, Martin Scorsese's *Raging Bull* has received the most critical acclaim. Made on a relatively low budget ($18,000,000), it made a respectable but modest profit (gross receipts in the United States were $30,000,000),[20] but its appearance sparked a number of polemical reviews (both positive and negative),[21] and its reputation has grown as Scorsese's own position as one of America's most original auteurs has risen since its appearance. The film received seven Oscar nominations (Best Actor, Best Film Editing, Best Actor and Actress in Supporting Roles, Best Cinematography, Best Picture, and Best Sound). It won Oscars in the first two categories, Best Actor (Robert De Niro) and Editing (Thelma Schoonmaker), almost by acclamation, and Joe Pesci's supporting-role performance made him a star.

Mean Streets first thrust Scorsese into the critical limelight with a film about growing up Italian American in the urban ghetto of New York City's Little Italy. One of the best discussions of *Raging Bull* argues that

> the spine of Scorsese's work is a series of disturbing studies of young Italian manhood in America: films that are full blooded yet fragmentary in their quasi-documentary manner, elliptical in their narrative disjunctions, profoundly unsettling in their emotional and physical violence, focusing on self-destructive characters who virtually dare us to identify with them.[22]

Morris Dickstein's characterization of *Raging Bull* would fit *Mean Streets* and *Goodfellas* as well. This perceptive critic claims that "Scorsese the Italian Catholic turns a boxer's story into a stations-of-the-cross movie" and that boxing films, first popular during the period that also witnessed the flowering of *film noir,* were frequently really about "the dark night of the soul" rather than prizefighting, just as the adventures of the detectives in the *noir* tradition pointed to a metaphysical dimension not exhausted by their "whodunit" plots.[23] Critics who stress Scorsese's Catholicism and the macho mentality of his male protagonists are infinitely closer to what really makes Scorsese's films fascinating than another group of commentators, who focus

Raging Bull *(1980; Martin Scorsese, director). Jake La Motta (Robert De Niro) in the company of Tommy Como (Nicholas Colasanto), a Mafia boss who takes an interest in Jake's career.*

on the thesis that *Raging Bull*—and indeed, any boxing film—is primarily about homoeroticism.[24]

Although changed in important ways from the original autobiography of the same title, the story behind *Raging Bull* strikes the reader as superficially similar to Rocky Graziano's life story: both men go to the same reform school, where they even meet; both learn to box as a way out of the anger and economic deprivation typical of many inhabitants of New York City's Little Italies, although La Motta came from the Bronx rather than the Lower East Side; both became champions in their weight class but encounter Mafia corruption on their rise to the title; upon retirement, they became comedians of a sort in nightclubs or on television; and of course, both wrote or had ghost-written autobiographies made into important films.

Similarities between the two figures end there. *Somebody up There Likes Me* is, in most respects, a version of the stereotypical American Dream narrative so beloved of Hollywood. *Raging Bull,* on the other hand, is a nightmare vision of the dark underside of Jake La Motta's lifelong battle with anger and self-hatred. In the most interesting change from book to film (besides the fact that Scorsese basically attributes many events in the autobiography to La Motta's brother rather than to La Motta's friend Peter Savage, who is a co-author of the autobiography), Scorsese omits the event

Raging Bull *(1980; Martin Scorsese, director). Jake La Motta (Robert De Niro) in one of his golden moments—his victory over Tony Janiro (Kevin Mahon).*

that La Motta himself believes is the defining traumatic moment of his life. In the first chapter of the autobiography, La Motta explains how, as a young man, he believed he killed a bookmaker named Harry Gordon in a robbery since Gordon's death had been reported in the newspaper the day after the robbery. Years later, on the night that La Motta won the championship of the middleweight division from Marcel Cerdan of France (June 16, 1949), Harry Gordon turns up in his dressing room. He did not die but survived the robbery-assault and moved to Florida, where he began a legitimate and successful business. Ironically, Gordon never knew the identity of his attacker and became Jake La Motta's biggest fan, since La Motta was his last remaining tie to the old neighborhood:

> I now had the title and the knowledge that I was not the rotten, sneaky murderer I had thought I was. Gordon hadn't died. I hadn't killed a man. Something was still eating me, but at least I felt a whole lot cleaner than I had. But somehow, I also felt a lot less vicious as a fighter. I think that the moment I discovered I was not really a murderer, I also stopped being a killer in the ring. Something had gone out of me.[25]

Scorsese completely removes this explanatory motive from his film, and its removal makes La Motta's rage in the film extremely difficult to understand. Because his rage seems to have no apparent origin, critics have fixated on what they claim to see as a homoerotic relationship between Jake and his brother Joey (Joe Pesci), and between boxing in general and homoerotic behavior. Yet, they are incredibly selective about the aspects of the film that they pounce on to stress the homoerotic element in *Raging Bull.* Jake's description of his opponent Tony Janiro (cited at the beginning of this chapter) returns over and over as evidence of the alleged homoerotic motivation behind Jake La Motta's violence. Yet, when Jake fights Sugar Ray Robinson, the homoerotic element suddenly disappears from such critical interpretations. Given La Motta's fixation with Robinson throughout his life, such a series of grudge matches between a white Italian American slugger and a black technician known for his "scientific" boxing skills would presumably occasion some remark about a long, unrequited love affair!

The sad fact is that most contemporary movie critics simply find boxing distasteful. They cannot identify with ghetto dwellers like Jake La Motta who see boxing as another way to prove their masculinity through violence, and the only way critics can understand this anger or violence is to interpret it as a sign of something else more repressed and hidden in Jake's character. Scorsese removes the most obvious explanation for Jake's anger and his feeling of self-loathing (the murder of Henry Gordon) precisely because he wants a character who is pure anger, almost a monster—a figure who cannot be explained away by a simple incident years ago in his youth. Jake La Motta combats the demons within himself, and the Catholic Scorsese is more concerned with redeeming a sinner than in explaining the origin of the sin.

One thoughtful early reviewer, David Denby, stressed the fact that both Scorsese and De Niro did everything possible to prevent the audience from identifying with Jake La Motta in the film. As he puts it, "De Niro doesn't want us to identify. His furious, cold, brilliant performances are a way of saying, 'Don't try to understand me, because you can't. I'm not the same as you—I may be better or worse, but I'm not you.'"[26] La Motta's entire life may be summed up in a brilliant scene of De Niro alone in a ring, photographed with an eerie lighting that suggests the sequence is a dream. As the opening credits are presented, La Motta (dressed in his leopard-skin dressing gown and hood) shadowboxes around the ring while the Intermezzo from Mascagni's *Cavalleria Rusticana* plays on the sound track. Shadowboxing is something that all boxers do to train themselves for a fight, but the image of slow-motion shadowboxing lends itself perfectly to La Motta's psyche: he is punching against nothing, against shadows, inner demons haunting him that are never really explained. The choice of musical motif is also important, since Mascagni's opera, also chosen, as we shall see, for the resounding conclusion of Coppola's *The Godfather Part III*, is about the violence that plagues the primitive world of Southern Italy with its codes of honor and masculinity. Even the fight scenes in the film, when compared to the endless slugging matches typical of the *Rocky* series, show an artistic style that resembles a black-and-white dream, as old-fashioned flash cameras pop off and send jets of blinding light toward the ring and the screen; stylized, slow-motion shots of boxing gloves striking chins and faces produce slow-motion spurts of blood and saliva. Ultimately, Scorsese's camera makes an aesthetic experience out of the violence of boxing, but it also reveals that nowhere else but in the ring is Jake La Motta so much at home and so little bothered by complex psychological issues. There, as the pure animal, the archetypal brute, La Motta partakes of a physical and emotional experience that can only be suggested by Mascagni's beautiful music, a mystery based on violence and a willingness to suffer physical pain in order to inflict greater pain upon his opponent.

One of the most puzzling aspects of *Raging Bull* is its thoroughly unlikable protagonist portrayed by one of the most brilliant performances in postwar American film. In his Oscar-winning performance, Robert De Niro became so adept at boxing, sparring with the real Jake La Motta during training, that La Motta said he could easily be ranked as one of the country's top twenty middleweights.[27] Even more impressive is the physical transformation of De Niro's body throughout the film from extremely fit fighter in his prime to a bloated, out-of-shape boxer—a condition the actor produced by gaining between fifty and sixty pounds as he toured France and Italy for four months, literally stuffing himself, forcing Scorsese

Raging Bull *(1980; Martin Scorsese, director). Jake La Motta (Robert De Niro) in fight-ing trim and years later as an overweight, out-of-shape nightclub comedian.*

to pay the film crew as he gained weight and to postpone the "fat" scenes until the very end of production.[28]

It is interesting that Scorsese's film opens and concludes with sequences depicting La Motta not as a boxer as he is shown during the opening cred-its but as the comedian he finally became. At the beginning, a title card reads NEW YORK CITY 1964 and the camera shows a sign outside the Barbi-zon Plaza Theatre: AN EVENING WITH JAKE LA MOTTA TONIGHT 8:30. La Motta appears—fat, puffy, and out of shape—practicing his badly recited Shakespearian lines in front of his dressing room mirror. His monologue ends with the exclamation "That's entertainment!" And the camera cuts to another superimposed title card reading JAKE LA MOTTA 1941 and a close-up of La Motta receiving several murderous punches in the face in an en-tirely different kind of spectacle—prizefighting—specifically, a bout against Jimmy Reeves when La Motta was a leading contender for the title. What follows are the most violent scenes in the film: a woman in the audi-ence screams, fights break out among the spectators, and another woman in the audience is even trampled by the crowd. In effect, the entire narra-tive of *Raging Bull* is a flashback from 1964, as La Motta's biography un-folds backward.

At the conclusion, the narrative returns to the ex-boxer's dressing room. The comedy act is billed as an evening of La Motta's recitations of passages from Rod Serling, Budd Schulberg, Tennessee Williams, and Shakespeare. But it is Terry Malloy's famous "contender" scene from *On the Waterfront* (1954), as performed by Marlon Brando, which occupies La Motta's attention. In Elia Kazan's film, Malloy blames his brother for his failure to be a contender and for his permanent status as a Palookaville fighter (Malloy refers to his fate as having received "a one-way ticket to Palookaville"). Unlike La Motta, Malloy never becomes a champion. And Scorsese employs the imitation of Brando's famous "contender" scene to make a comment on the impact of La Motta's brother on the fighter's life and career, since La Motta's brother Joey was ultimately responsible for La Motta's relationship to the mob:

> I was never no good after that night, Charlie. It was like a peak you reach, and then it's downhill. It was you, Charlie. You was my brother. You should've looked out for me a little bit. You should've taken care of me just a little bit instead o' making me take them dives for the short-end money. You don't understand. I coulda had class. I coulda been a contender. I coulda been somebody instead of a bum, which is what I am. Let's face it. It was you, Charlie. It was you, Charlie.[29]

After the end of his boxing career, La Motta realizes in Scorsese's cinematic interpretation of his life (a far different conclusion from the one that can be drawn from the autobiography) that it was his relationship to his brother Joey that marked his personality and explained his behavior. As an inarticulate brute, the only means he has of expressing this realization is through the recitation by rote of lines from another film.

Critics have pointed to this sequence in the film as a metacinematic moment, where Scorsese foregrounds De Niro's remarkable acting performance by having him imitate one of the classic sequences of 1950s cinema as performed by one of the previous generation's defining acting styles (that of Marlon Brando). De Niro imitates La Motta imitating Brando. Yet, the relationship between the two films is even more complicated than that, for the major actors associated with a particular acting style of the 1950s—Marlon Brando, James Dean, Paul Newman—actually knew Rocky Graziano and Jake La Motta, who were celebrities in the New York City where they studied and worked. Brando and Newman in particular were well acquainted with the personalities and manner of speech characteristic of both Italian American boxers, and their personal knowledge of Graziano and La Motta contributed something of importance to their performances in *On the Waterfront* and *Somebody up There Likes Me*. In a sense, this scene represents more than De Niro imitating La Motta imitating Brando. More accurately, it is De Niro imitating La Motta imitating Brando imitating La Motta and Graziano! Scorsese himself seems to want the meaning of the sequence to re-main open ended. It took nineteen takes to complete De Niro's monologue,[30] and in an important interview on *Raging Bull*, Scorsese himself asks: "When he says in the mirror, 'It was you, Charlie,' is he playing his brother, or putting the blame on himself? It's certainly very disturbing for me."[31]

Obsessed as he is with Catholic notions of sin, guilt, and redemption—especially in the context of Italian American urban-ghetto culture, as we have seen from *Mean Streets*—Scorsese concludes *Raging Bull* not with De Niro's monologue but with a final title from the Bible (John 9:24–26, from the New English Bible):

> So, for the second time, [the Pharisees] summoned the man who had been blind and said: "Speak the truth before God. We know this fellow is a sinner." "Whether or not he is a sinner, I do not know," the man replied. "All I know is this: once I was blind and now I can see."[32]

In this way, Scorsese suggests that God's grace is mysterious, bestowed re-gardless of merit. Moreover, the fact that Jake La Motta is a sinner without any hope of redemption further glorifies the redemptive power of God's grace.[33] When scriptwriter Paul Schrader saw the completed film and the concluding citation from the Bible, he remained "absolutely baffled" and felt that such a conversion was unbelievable: "I don't think it's true of La Motta either in real life or in the movie; I think he's the same dumb lug at the end as he is at the beginning, and I think Marty is just imposing salva-tion on his subject by fiat."[34] But of course, much the same comment could be made of Scorsese's Catholic protagonist in *Mean Streets*.[35] Clearly, this imposition of Catholicism upon his plots is precisely one of the elements of Scorsese's cinema that can be traced back to his Italian American origins.

The Rocky Franchise: A Quintet of Films Chronicling the Ultimate Palooka

Few success stories in the history of Hollywood cinema are more striking than that meteoric rise to fame of the Italian American actor Sylvester Stal-lone (1946-) as a result of his screenplay for what became the surprise hit of 1976, *Rocky* (John Avildsen, director). After years of an unsuccessful search for financial backing, when Stallone finally persuaded a Hollywood studio not only to shoot his script but to place him in the starring role by ac-cepting a percentage of the profits rather than a large salary, he was virtually unknown as an actor. Nothing he had done to that point could be placed in the same class (either professionally or financially) as what was to become the *Rocky* franchise or his action film performances as John Rambo, whose name became a new term for American warriors—"Rambo." *Rocky* was followed in short measure by *Rocky II* (1979; Sylvester Stallone, director); *Rocky III* (1982; Sylvester Stallone, director); *Rocky IV* (1985; Sylvester Stallone, director); and *Rocky V* (1990; John Avildsen, director).

Stallone's creation of Rocky Balboa contains a number of elements drawn from earlier boxing films. The rags-to-riches story of a mediocre Italian club fighter with "heart" from Philadelphia who almost manages to beat the world's heavyweight champion, Apollo Creed (Carl Weathers), in a bout Creed has arranged for a publicity stunt, resembles the success stories behind the plots of *Kid Galahad* and *Golden Boy*, as well as *Somebody up There Likes Me*, where Rocky Graziano is discovered almost by accident in a gymnasium after successfully sparring with a professional boxer. Rocky Balboa worships the undefeated Italian American heavyweight champion, Rocky Marciano, and hangs a poster of his idol in his one-room apartment in one of the least economically fortunate neighborhoods of Philadelphia (albeit one neighborhood largely populated by Italian Americans). Rocky's real occupation, when he is not banging heads in the local fight clubs, is to collect overdue debts for a Mafia loan shark named Tom Gazzo (Joe Spinell). This aspect of the plot is also reminiscent of other Italian American Palooka films showing the close links between boxing and organized crime through the characters Turkey Morgan in *Kid Galahad*, Eddie Fuseli in *Golden Boy*, Frankie Peppo in *Somebody up There Likes Me*, and Tommy Como in *Raging Bull*. In the *Rocky* series, however, the Mafia and characters reflecting the fight-fixing talents of such real individuals as Frankie Carbo or Blinky Palermo are insignificant. Actually, in an interesting racial twist, the manipulators of boxing matches in the five *Rocky* films are either African Americans or Russians. Apollo Creed, for example, invents the gimmick that allows Rocky Balboa (descendant of the nation that produced Christopher Columbus) to be matched with the heavyweight champ in the first of the five films. Besides the publicity ploy that pits the champion against a descendant of the man whose discoveries created America, "land of opportunity," Apollo obviously wants to exploit the traditional quest for a "great white hope" by selecting someone he considers a hapless white Palooka as his target. In *Rocky IV*, a cold warrior from Russia named Nicoli Kiloff (Michael Pataki) persuades the now dethroned black champion Apollo Creed to meet his superhuman Ivan Drago (Dolph Lundgren), a fighter whose talents have been honed by the latest athletic technology and presumably the kinds of hormones, steroids, and sports drugs that made the Eastern bloc sports teams infamous. Finally, in *Rocky*

V, shady black promoter George Washington Duke (Richard Grant) maneuvers Rocky into fighting his protégé, Tommy "Machine" Gunn (Tommy
Morrison). To do so endangers Rocky's very life, since he has suffered life-
threatening brain damage while avenging the death of his friend Apollo
Creed at the hands of Drago in Russia. Mafia fight-fixers are absent from
Stallone's five films, but he still depicts unsporting and exploitive individuals eager to use the blood and tears shed in a boxing ring to make money
at the expense of a fighter's pride, health, or life.

Reportedly, Stallone was inspired to write the script of *Rocky* after wit-
nessing the famous boxing match in March of 1975 between Muhammad
Ali and a relatively unknown club boxer from New Jersey named Chuck
Wepner.[36] Wepner was known as "The Bayonne Bleeder," a nickname similar to the one invented by Stallone for his fictional creation Rocky Balboa,
"The Italian Stallion," and just as Wepner was one of the few boxers who
not only knocked Ali down in a fight but also went virtually the entire fifteen rounds with him before being defeated in the final round, so no one
before Rocky Balboa has ever survived more than twelve rounds with
Apollo Creed.

What makes *Rocky* a successful movie is not only its masterful training
and fight sequences but also the human interest stories concerning secondary characters around Rocky. Rocky falls in love with a shy girl named
Adrian (Talia Shire) who has been bullied by her Italian American brother
Paulie (Bert Young) into thinking that she is a "loser," just as Rocky is convinced that he is nothing but a "bum" as a fighter and as a human being.
This label is pinned on Rocky immediately in the film, even before the
opening credits have run, by a disgusted woman in the audience at a club
fight in which Rocky is facing Spider Rico.

Much of the force of the film arises from its ability to make us feel empathy for both Adrian and Rocky and to invest our emotions in their respective attempts to establish a positive self-image. Paulie, a disgruntled
and embittered man who sees Rocky's match with Apollo Creed as an opportunity to exploit his sister's relationship with Rocky, also displays a
rather heavy-handed Italian American view of his sister's relationship to
Rocky. He calls her a "loser" over and over again to Rocky, and when Rocky
rejects his nagging requests to find Paulie a job with Tommy Gazzo, his former gangster employer, Paulie attacks Adrian, insulting her with foul-
mouthed assertions about losing her virginity to Rocky and implying that
her relationship to the fighter represents an affront to Italian American
morality. Ultimately, however, Paulie serves Rocky as an assistant in the
ring, and he manages to obtain several thousand dollars by arranging with
a meat-packing company to give Rocky a satin boxing robe with their

Rocky *(1976; John Avildsen, director). The clumsy palooka Rocky Balboa (Sylvester Stal-lone) chats with his cynical manager Mickey Goldmill (Burgess Meredith) in the gym.*

name on the back. Finally, there is Rocky's manager Mickey Goldmill, a supporting role played brilliantly by Burgess Meredith, who sees in Rocky's bout with Apollo Creed his last chance to make an impact on the fight game and who says, when he sees the poster of Marciano hanging in Rocky's shabby apartment, that "ya kinda remind me of the Rock, ya know that? . . . Ya move like him, ya got heart like he did."

Once the improbable bout of a lifetime is established and the supporting cast of characters is introduced, *Rocky* turns to a cinematically impressive series of sequences detailing Rocky's five-week training for his match with the champion. Much of *Rocky* was shot on location in Philadelphia, and the hit theme song of the film (Bill Conti's "Gonna Fly") that accompanies the action at crucial moments of the film announces the developing near-triumph of the Palooka fighter over the complacent champ. In the early morning hours Rocky arises, drinks five raw eggs, and jogs through the deserted-city landscape. At the beginning of his five-week training period, he is out of shape (after all, he is a boxer who smokes cigarettes!), and the first time he climbs up the steep set of steps to the neoclassical Philadelphia Museum of Art at dawn, he wheezes from exhaustion. Mickey orders Rocky to stay away from Adrian, following the traditional superstition that sex before a fight weakens a fighter. Jake La Motta believed this as well, to the point of pouring ice water down his boxer shorts to chill his ardor. During an argument with Paulie, Rocky becomes so frustrated that he begins to punch with his bare fists the swinging frozen-beef carcasses where Paulie works. This colorful but savage exercise becomes Rocky's trademark (also providing a striking metaphor for boxing itself—pounding raw meat to a pulp), and the local television crews even interview him there, asking for a demonstration of his technique. As the training advances toward the final showdown, the montage of various sequences speeds up, always accompanied by the Conti theme song. Finally, as Rocky does one-armed push-ups, runs through the city's marketplaces and deserted streets, absorbs countless punches to his midsection, and pounds even more slabs of raw beef, he is in top condition, bouncing effortlessly up the stairs toward the Philadelphia Museum of Art as he turns and faces the panorama of the city, holding up his hands in triumph. Perhaps this single scene is the most memorable in the entire film, a perfect synthesis of sound and image.

The sequences depicting the epic match between Rocky and Apollo Creed are equally memorable. The editing maintains an extremely fast pace, the numerous camera angles are manipulated with expertise, and the result represents quite possibly the most dramatic boxing match ever filmed. Unlike Scorsese's *Raging Bull* (where the actual time spent on the matches La Motta fought is relatively very brief), the *Rocky* franchise lingers on the fights themselves in all of the films even though, as in the first *Rocky* film, the fights are carefully designed for maximum dramatic impact and gruesome realism. From the first round (when *Rocky* surprises Creed by flooring him) until the fifteenth, Rocky boxes like the proverbial Palooka: he absorbs massive punishment in order to inflict punishment on his opponent. Creed is obviously a better boxer and has more technical skill, but Rocky demonstrates by going the entire fifteen grueling rounds that he has more "heart." In fact, the conclusion of the fight has Creed on the ropes, obviously beaten but saved by the bell and pronounced the winner of the fight because of the points he piled up during the rounds that Rocky simply absorbed his punishment in order to get in close and pound the champion's body. The inevitable conclusion is the triumph of the Palooka who has demonstrated his "heart" in what is described as the greatest fight in the history of the ring. Rocky and Adrian embrace in a demonstration of mutual affection, and the film ends on a freeze-frame of their two faces together.

Everything about the first *Rocky* represents the accomplishment of an impossible dream. Outside the film, the circumstances of its production actually mirror the plot: a film costing about one million dollars grosses over one hundred million dollars and creates a superstar of its scriptwriter and protagonist. Rocky's performance in the ring seems to substantiate the proverbial American dream. Even though Apollo Creed exploits the idea that a man can achieve his dreams if he has enough courage to do so by dressing up as George Washington and Uncle Sam on different occasions to promote the match, Rocky's success in remaining in the ring, standing up to the heavyweight champion of the world and almost beating him by absorbing an amazing amount of physical punishment, demonstrates that "heart" remains the indefinable quality that creates winners.

Rocky won Oscars for Best Director, Best Film Editing, and Best Picture; it was nominated for six other Oscars (Best Actor in a Leading Role; Best Actress in a Leading Role; Best Actor in a Supporting Role; Best Music; Best Sound; and Best Screenplay). As Rocky says to his manager Mickey,

> It really don't matter if I lose this fight. It really don't matter if this guy opens my head, either. 'Cause all I wanna do is go the distance. Nobody's ever gone the distance with Creed, and if I can go that distance, you see, and that bell rings and I'm still standin', I'm gonna know for the first time in my life, see, that I weren't just another bum from the neighborhood.

More than boxing, *Rocky* is a film about self-respect, Italian American masculinity, and that archetypal Palooka virtue: "heart." Winning or losing is incidental.

Rocky II continues this central theme of "heart," while repeating the same cinematic style that made the original film so compelling. It opens with footage from the original story, reviewing the high points of the fight between Rocky and Apollo plus the romantic conclusion where Rocky and Adrian embrace. In the sequel, Rocky marries Adrian, buys a new car, and generally continues his uneventful life. Because of damage to his eye in the first fight, he has been warned not to continue boxing or risk losing his sight. In spite of this, the press and sports fans clamor for a rematch. Rocky attempts to exploit his new fame by working in commercials, but his inability to read the cue cards makes that impossible. His ninth-grade education makes it difficult for him to hold down a decent job, and eventually he is forced to work with Paulie at the meat-packing plant, carrying the same sides of beef he used to punch. Laid off from this job because he lacks seniority, Mickey takes Rocky on at his gym. But there, reduced to doing odd jobs, Rocky loses the respect of the fighters (in one scene people are reading a newspaper with the headline APOLLO CREED VERSUS THE ITALIAN CHICKEN). Rocky complains to Adrian that he has become a bum again, a nobody.

Meanwhile, Apollo Creed has gained little satisfaction from his victory. Creed receives numerous letters from fight fans, accusing him of faking the fight and basically impugning his manhood. His near loss of the heavyweight title to a club fighter, a Palooka, grates on the champion's self-respect. Unhappy and wanting to show that he really is the best fighter, he orders his publicity people to humiliate Rocky and to get him back into the ring. Eventually, the inevitable happens and Rocky decides to fight Apollo Creed, going back into training with Mickey.

A number of elements make this sequel different from *Rocky*. In training, Rocky is the toast of the town, especially the Italian American neighborhood: there is even an Italian-speaking priest who provides a blessing for his training (although Rocky never speaks a phrase of Italian). Now, Rocky seems to be defined by the press as an ethnic fighter (as the fight opens, an announcer declares: "I've never seen so many Italians in one place in my life"), whereas in the first fight, he was simply the embodiment of the American dream, the personification of the myth that in America, every man or woman has the chance to become rich and famous. Leading up to the concluding fight, the training styles of the two fighters stand in complete contrast: Rocky continues his jogging through the city, returning to the now-iconic stairs of the Philadelphia Museum of Art, while Apollo trains in sophisticated gyms like a man with something to prove.

The fight is also choreographed differently. Mickey has ordered Rocky to learn how to use his right hand (he is a southpaw, one of the reasons Apollo Creed had such difficulty fighting him). In training, the unorthodox punching meat carcasses of the first film now become the even more unorthodox racing around the yard after a chicken! During the fight, Rocky at first rejects Mickey's strategy and loses a number of rounds very badly, as Apollo taunts him in imitation of Muhammad Ali's method of taunting his adversaries. As the fight progresses, however, Rocky's heavy body punches wear the champion down, and the many slow-motion or point-of-view shots of boxing gloves slamming into Rocky's face offer once again an extremely violent re-creation of a boxing match. Naturally, for the purposes of dramatic effect, the fight must be decided in the last round, and Rocky finally switches from his right hand back to his left: both Rocky and Apollo slug it out and both fall down. When Rocky is the only one to arise, he is proclaimed champ. The film ends on a freeze frame of Rocky calling to Adrian: "Yo Adrian, I did it!"

After two films in a series focusing upon a character of Rocky's admittedly limited intellectual and emotion depth, it is not surprising that most film critics lost patience with the next three films. Unfortunately, each of these sequels employs exactly the same formulaic opening: footage from the previous film is used to give the viewer a quick review of the franchise history. *Rocky III*, however, is in many respects a slicker, more action-driven film than its two predecessors. Now Rocky is a rich champion who fights a number of less-than-sensational challengers while a real menace, Clubber Lang (Mr. T.), rises in the rankings and wants nothing else but a chance to fight Rocky. While Lang works and becomes stronger and stronger, murdering his opponents, Rocky enjoys a soft life, working for charity and living in a new environment of luxury. A statue of him with his hands raised in triumph now rests on the top of the steps at the Philadelphia Museum of Art. As Mickey tells him when Rocky stupidly accepts a challenge issued by Lang at the dedication of the statue, "The worst thing happened to you that could happen to any fighter, you got civilized." Subsequently, Rocky refuses to take his upcoming bout seriously, and his training is more a publicity event than a serious attempt to get in shape for what will be a dangerous fight. Rocky takes his opponents far too lightly just as Apollo Creed considered him an unlikely victor in his matches with Rocky.

The result is predictable. Before the fight, Clubber Lang insults and pushes Mickey around; Mickey has a heart attack and dies after the fight ends, but Rocky does not tell his faithful trainer the result. Lang nearly murders Rocky in the ring, knocking him out in the second round. (Rocky does not tell him he has lost.) Apollo Creed, now Rocky's close friend, volunteers to train Rocky for a rematch with Clubber Lang, telling Rocky that he needs to regain what Apollo calls "the eye of the tiger"—his killer instinct. Furthermore, Apollo has a surprise for Lang: he intends to train Rocky to box scientifically, not to brawl. To do this, he takes Rocky to Los Angeles, where he instructs Rocky in "rhythm" in the black ghetto of the city. Ultimately, Rocky improves his speed, mobility, and "rhythm" by adopting Apollo's methods, and once again *Rocky III* provides a series of training sequences, skillfully done, of swimming, jogging, and punching. Ultimately, Apollo's technique prevails, and in the climactic fight, Rocky manages to defeat Clubber with his newly acquired boxing skills, confounding his opponent who expected the usual brawler style of a Palooka.

Rocky IV is certainly the film of the quintet that was mercilessly (and justifiably) attacked by the critics as lacking inspiration. Now the competition between Rocky and a villainous opponent comes to exploit the cold war. This time, it is Ivan Drago (Dolph Lungren), a mechanical monster that kills Apollo Creed in an exhibition bout in Las Vegas and becomes Rocky's adversary. Here the competition is between a Russian robot and an Italian American Palooka with "heart." Much of the film provides a humorous representation of the kinds of slick media events that have changed the nature of boxing at Las Vegas venues, but Rocky eventually meets Drago in Russia. In the process of leading up to the inevitable showdown sequence at the conclusion of the film, Stallone as director uses footage from all of the previous *Rocky* films. Once again there are the for-mulaic training sequences, juxtaposing through montage Rocky's old-fashioned methods with Drago's "scientific" approach (including steroids and drugs). Naturally, the Communists cheat while Rocky, as the represen-tative of the All-American approach to boxing, plays it straight. As a Gor-bachev look-alike presides over the epic event, Rocky eventually wins in what seems to be an impossible struggle. Then, he addresses the Russian crowd and says to them: "If I can change, then you can change. Everybody can change." Although Stallone seems not to be embarrassed by the blatant appeals to patriotic ideology in the movie, most spectators by this point were. *Rocky IV* has virtually no redeeming features. It employs clichés, uses too much old footage because it has no imaginative sequences of its own, and is basically a very poor film. Almost everything about the *Rocky* series that had some links to Italian American culture—the Philadelphia neigh-borhood, the Italian-speaking priest, the Palooka who aspired to be like Rocky Marciano—has been abandoned in this dreary work.

A viewer screening the first four films in the quintet would expect *Rocky V* to be an even worse film. Surprisingly, *Rocky V* breathes a bit of life into the worn-out formulas by returning Rocky to his ethnic roots and values. Because of a crooked accountant who has made bad investments, Rocky has now lost his limo, his mansion, and most of his money. He can no longer box, since the fight with Drago left him with life-threatening brain damage.

In fact, Rocky now speaks with a slur like the punch-drunk Palooka he is. He returns to the old Italian American neighborhood, where he has in-herited Mickey's old gym. As his wife is forced to go back to work in the pet store nearby, Rocky now trains neighborhood fighters. *Rocky V* now fo-cuses upon Rocky's relationship with his son Rocky, Jr. Jealous of the atten-tion Rocky pays to his protégé, Tommy "Machine" Gunn, Rocky, Jr. seems on his way to becoming a juvenile delinquent like Rocky Graziano. The film departs from the combination of a montage of training sequences leading up to a final climactic prizefight precisely in order to chart the progress of Rocky's relationship with his son.

While one set of sequences traces Tommy Gunn's victories over a num-ber of opponents, another set of sequences juxtaposed to these bouts shows Rocky, Jr., training in order to defend himself at school and to make his father proud of him. When Gunn is just about to reach the level of ma-jor contender for the championship, the crooked black promoter George Washington Duke (a transparent parody of the contemporary fight pro-moter, Don King, who was once convicted of homicide) steals Gunn away from Rocky by promising him wealth and fame. Wounded by this experience, Rocky finally realizes that his real wealth is his family and his son, whose love he has alienated by paying too much attention to his protégé. In other words, *Rocky V* ultimately reasserts the dominant Italian American cultural value of the family. Although Rocky eventually defeats Gunn in a street fight and then punches out his manager as well, his real victory resides in the eventual realization that even without his wealth or his title, his true happiness lies in the love of his wife and son.

In a fitting and humorous conclusion to the quintet, Rocky and his son run up the steps leading to the Philadelphia Museum of Art, where the statue of Rocky stands. Rocky, Sr. gives his son his prized possession—a cuff link once belonging to the great Rocky Marciano, the only undefeated heavyweight champion in the history of boxing—and his son decides to use it as an earring. Rocky, Sr. replies: "You look like the daughter I always wanted" and then says: "I've been running up and down these stairs for twenty years and didn't know there were pictures inside!"

It is no accident that of the quintet of films that make up the *Rocky* franchise, the first and the last of them are the most interesting. The first *Rocky* film establishes a popular Italian American hero: a simple, unassuming Palooka who has so much heart that he wins a spot in boxing history. In it, the Italian American bum becomes the embodiment of the American Dream. In the last film, Rocky returns (albeit not voluntarily) to his origins and his roots in the Italian American community and discovers that family—*la famiglia*, not fame or fortune—constitutes the only true wealth.

A Comic Take on the Italian American Palooka:
Spike of Bensonhurst *(1988)*

Paul Morrissey's not-very-successful film seems to include all the worst elements of ethnic stereotyping, although it aims at the production of comic effects and not the denigration of the Italian Americans or the Puerto Ricans who are its protagonists. It seems to be a parody of Stallone's role as Rocky Balboa in the four *Rocky* films that enjoyed wide distribution before Morrissey shot this picture, and it has equally obvious links to the Tony Manero character that catapulted John Travolta to superstar status in John Badham's *Saturday Night Fever* (1977)—a film and a social phenomenon examined in the next chapter on Italian American Romeos. The Bensonhurst section of Brooklyn has long been an icon of stereotypical images of Italian Americans in the media even though at present its predominantly working-class Italian American population has been diluted by an influx of Russians and Asians. As Maria Laurino points out, Hollywood and the American mass media has endowed Bensonhurst with a predominantly

Rocky V *(1990; John Avildsen, director). After a long and stormy career, Rocky Balboa (Sylvester Stallone) discovers that the most important thing in life is family, as he spars with his son Rocky, Jr. (Sage Stallone), near the statue erected in his honor in front of the Philadelphia Museum of Art.*

working-class image that has extended from the enormously successful television series, *The Honeymooners*, starring Jackie Gleason as the irascible and often pig-headed bus driver Ralph Kramden, to the very popular television show *Welcome Back, Kotter*, where the high-school teacher Kotter (Gabriel Kaplan) attempts to instruct a predominantly Italian American classroom in Bensonhurst. This television series gave John Travolta his first wide exposure as actor in the role of Vinnie Barbarino, one of the "sweathogs" in Kotter's remedial classes whose official name was the Special Guidance Remedial Academics Group.[37]

Spike Fumo (Sasha Mitchell) of Bensonhurst follows both the acting style and the ethnic mannerisms of Vinnie Barbarino and those later to become famous with *Saturday Night Fever*'s Tony Manero—he is a "Guido" or a "Cugine," while Angel (Maria Pitillo), the daughter of the local Mafia boss, is a complete "Guidette" or "Bimbette." Outside the ring, Spike acts and speaks like both Tony Manero and Rocky Balboa. Inside the ring, however, unlike Rocky, he wants to protect his pretty-boy features and is perfectly happy to take part in the club fights organized and completely fixed in their outcomes by the local Wise Guys. Spike never raises any moral questions about the control of boxing by the Mafia, and he even seeks the support of Baldo Cacetti (Ernest Borgnine), his girlfriend's Mafia-boss father. He achieves this goal while at the same time making Angel pregnant, an incident reminiscent of the situation in *The Wanderers*. Because Baldo wants his daughter to marry someone with an education, and not a typical Bensonhurst Guido, he prefers the preppy Justin, the well-educated son of the Jewish congresswoman whom Baldo controls with bribes. To make the situation even more ridiculous, while Spike's father serves time in Sing Sing without betraying Baldo, Baldo provides an income for Spike's mother (Anne De Salvo), who has taken up with a lesbian lover!

Driven out of Bensonhurst by his desire to make Angel an honest Bimbette, Spike goes to live with a Puerto Rican boxer named Bandana (Rick Aviles), where we discover an even more absurd family than Spike's. Bandana's mother (Antonio Rey), who is a schoolteacher and should know better, greets Spike as if he were a celebrity: "The dream of my life—a Mafia connection! Someone that I can talk to, someone that will hear about our misery, and someone that will do something about it." Spike declares to Bandana that Italians would never allow their neighborhoods to be sewers run by crack dealers, and he even attacks the dealers on the porch steps and in nearby abandoned buildings. The irony, of course, is that the film shows Baldo as the ultimate source of the crack—drugs make a profit in the neighborhoods of other ethnic groups but are not permitted by the Italian Americans in their own backyards. Spike manages to impregnate Bandana's beautiful sister India (Talisa Soto) and has a dilemma on his hands—will he marry the Bimbette daughter of the Mafia boss or the Puerto Rican beauty? In the end, Baldo makes the choice for him, after breaking his hands and ending his unpromising boxing career. Baldo then marries Angel off to Justin, leaving Spike with India. The film ends with Baldo visiting Spike (now a policeman thanks to Baldo's connections with the police), who is the father of not one but two obviously non-Italian American children.

It is difficult to take *Spike of Bensonhurst* seriously. The acting is second-rate, the ethnic stereotypes of Italian Americans and Puerto Ricans would offend even a member of a right-wing supremacist group, and the film is both disorganized and incoherent. Yet, precisely because of its limited value as a work of art, the film reflects a number of characteristics of the Hollywood Italian Palooka and provides a bridge to the Hollywood Italian Romeo. Palookas, Romeos, and Wise Guys share many of the characteristics of the Hollywood Italian Dagos, a distinct ethnic group with its own specific and undesirable characteristics. Hollywood Italian dagos were predominantly working-class figures, and their class origins were often associated with tasteless behavior. To use the northern Italian term for them that is still applied by inhabitants of northern Italy to their southern cousins, they were by and large *cafoni*. Of course, they were not only working class in origin but also southern Italian in origin. And they came predominantly from the large Italian American ghettos in East Coast cities.

The Hollywood Italian Palooka hails from the same urban, working class, and East Coast background, and like his Dago counterpart, the Palooka shares a number of anti-intellectual traits and behavior patterns. Only the protagonist of *Golden Boy* runs counter to this kind of representation. The language spoken by Rocky Graziano, Jake La Motta, Rocky Balboa, and Spike Fumo instantly marks them as semi-literate, anti-intellectual Palookas whose brains are in their fists, not in their heads. Their chosen profession—prizefighting—has important implications for their relationships with the women to whom they are attracted. Indeed, boxing raises a number of important questions about the Italian American definition of masculinity—particularly in *Raging Bull*—and only in the *Rocky* series and in the infinitely less important *Spike of Bensonhurst* do the traditional values of the Italian American *famiglia* have any influence on their actions. Moreover, the presence of the Mafia creeps into all of the representations of the Hollywood Italian Palooka. It must be admitted that given the somewhat sordid history of prizefighting in America, this may be among the few elements of historical realism that representations of Hollywood Italian Palookas contain.

In any discussion of prizefighting films made in America, the Palooka would have to be given a very important place. Critically acclaimed works such as *Golden Boy, Somebody up There Likes Me,* and especially *Raging Bull* are landmarks not only in the history of the representation of Italian Americans by Hollywood but also in the development of American film as an art form. Although four out of five parts of the *Rocky* franchise may find few defenders of their artistic qualities, the first—and incredibly successful—film of the series created both a superstar and the reaffirmation of the American Dream. In a strange turn of events, Hollywood takes the downtrodden Dago and transforms him into the Hollywood Italian Palooka, an embodiment of the American Dream. In some of Hollywood's most interesting representations, however, the protagonists of these films may also reveal a dark underside of the optimistic dream that so seduced Italian American immigrants.

3

❧

Romeos: Hollywood Italian Lovers

"I'm the Sheik of Araby./Your heart belongs to me./ At night when you're asleep,/ Into your tent I'll creep./The stars that shine above/Will light our way to love./ You'll rule this land with me,/The Sheik of Araby."

"The Sheik of Araby," popular song by Harry B. Smith and Francis Wheeler (lyrics) and Music by Ted Synder (1921)[1]

"Lie still, you little fool."

Sheik Ahmed Ben Hasan (Rudolph Valentino) to Lady Diana Mayo (Agnes Ayres) in *The Sheik* (1921)

"I'd rather be a don of the Mafia than president of the United States."

Eddie Fisher quoting Frank Sinatra[2]

"I guess I like the guy. Shit, it's not his fault that the Kennedys are assholes. But if I didn't like him, you can be goddamed sure he'd be a dead man."

Sam Giancana, head of the Chicago Mafia, on Frank Sinatra[3]

"The dago's lousy, but the little Jew is great."

Frank Sinatra circa 1948 upon first seeing the Martin and Lewis comedy act[4]

"The guinea's not bad, but what do I do with the monkey?"

Louis B. Mayer on the Martin and Lewis comedy act before they became box office sensations in the cinema[5]

"We're not setting out to make *Hamlet* or *Gone With the Wind*. The idea is to hang out together, find fun with the broads, and have a great time. We gotta make pictures that people enjoy. Entertainment, period. We gotta have laughs."

Frank Sinatra to Sammy Davis on the making of *Ocean's Eleven*[6]

"I just talked to Jack, and he made me secretary of liquor."

Dean Martin's club act at the Sands in Las Vegas, the night after Kennedy's election as President[7]

TONY: "Oh, fuck the future."
MR. FUSCO: "No, Tony, you can't fuck the future. The future fucks you."

Tony Manero (John Travolta) and Mr. Fusco (Sam Coppola), his employer at the paint store, discuss Tony's future in *Saturday Night Fever*

TONY: "What are you anyway? Are you a nice girl or are you a cunt?"
ANNETTE: "I don't know. Both."
TONY: "You can't be both."

> Tony Manero (John Travolta) explains his views on women
> to his dancing partner Annette (Donna Pescow) in *Saturday Night Fever*

If there is any stereotypical image of Italians that has a longer history than the gangster, it is the "Latin Lover." Even the very names we employ in English to denote Romantic male figures, such as *Romeo* and *Casanova*, conjure up images of that mysterious, sensuous, and sinister Italy. The Italian libretto of Mozart's opera made even that Spanish synonym for great lover, Don Juan, more famous as the Italian Don Giovanni. To the names of Romeo, Casanova, and Don Giovanni, we must add an important fourth name that has become synonymous with romance and sex appeal in the movies: Rudolph Valentino (1895–1926). In the history of American movies, few other Italian Romeos—Frank Sinatra (1915–98), Dean Martin (1917–95), and John Travolta (1954–   )—may be said to have legitimate claims to rival the cinematic myth of the great lover created by Valentino.

Numerous Hollywood Italian actors have played leading male roles in a variety of dramatic films, but remarkably few of them have contributed to the myth of the "Latin Lover." We speak of the dramatic talents of Al Pacino and the intensity of Robert De Niro, but it is precisely the serious nature of the roles with which they are identified—not to mention the fact that their best-known performances belong to the gangster genre—which prevents identifying them as "Latin Lovers" or Hollywood Italian Romeos. Their relationships with women, their on-screen wives, often seem to be little more than calculated business arrangements necessitated by the Mafia code of family. Much the same identification with gangster films or *film noir* prevents us from identifying Hollywood Italians from another generation, such as Victor Mature or Richard Conte, as Romeos. Their films also largely emphasize family rather than romance. Hence, Hollywood Italian Romeos include only those actors who have established a mythic presence on the screen as romantic leads. Beyond a strict examination of the cinema, *understanding* the Romeo leads to broader questions of how such figures as Valentino, Sinatra, Martin, and Travolta have shaped popular culture and the entertainment business in general.

A cursory examination of men associated with the term "Latin Lover"[8] reveals that most Latin Lovers associated with the history of the cinema are from Latin or South America or Spain, not from Italy. Ramon Novarro (1899–1968), the star of such important swashbucklers or action films as

The Prisoner of Zenda (1922), *Scaramouche* (1923), *The Arab* (1924), *Ben-Hur* (1925), and *Mata Hari* (1932, with Greta Garbo) was born in Mexico. Very early in his career in the silent cinema, he was hailed as the "New Valentino." Antonio Moreno (1887–1967) made some ninety silent films and was perhaps Hollywood's best-known Latin lover in such films as *The Temptress* (1926) with Greta Garbo or *It* (1927) with Clara Bow. He also worked with Pola Negri and Gloria Swanson. Moreno was born in Spain. Gilbert Roland (1905–94), who helped Valentino dress as a bullfighter in *Blood and Sand* (1922) and dubbed for Novarro in one of his films,[9] made numerous films during a long career, including six Cisco Kid adventure films between 1946 and 1947. He was a Mexican. Other famous Latin Lovers were of Cuban descent (Cesar Romero, 1907–94; Ricardo Montalban, b. 1920), Mexican (Anthony Quinn, 1916–2001), or Argentinean (Fernando Lamas, 1915–82).

Rodolfo Alfonzo Raffaele Pierre Filibert Guglielmi di Valentino d'Antonguolla (aka Rudolph Valentino, The Sheik)

Hollywood Italian Romeos have had an impact on American-film culture far out of proportion to their relatively small number. The first and most important of them all, of course, is the legendary Valentino, born in Castellaneta in southern Italy (Puglia). He arrived in the United States in 1913 as part of the enormous wave of Italian immigration that came to American shores before the outbreak of the Great War, although he traveled in relative comfort. After a period of initial poverty in the New World, he became a taxi dancer, getting his big break when he replaced Clifton Webb as the partner of the popular dancer Bonnie Glass.[10] Not only did Valentino develop the image of the archetypal "Latin Lover," but his young death guaranteed his status as a mythic icon, much as James Dean's death while very young froze his screen image in time. Even his name conjured up images of valentines and romance, much as the same last name decades later encouraged wealthy American women to associate the designer Valentino's gowns with an exotic and romantic lifestyle.

Rudolph Valentino played many exotic roles, such as Julio Desnoyers, the playboy heir to an Argentinean cattle fortune who dies on the battlefield of World War I in *The Four Horsemen of the Apocalypse* (1921; Rex Ingram, director). In *The Conquering Power* (1921; Rex Ingram, director), Valentino is Charles Grandet in an adaptation of Balzac's classic novel *Eugénie Grandet*. In *The Sheik* (1921; George Melford, director), Valentino is Sheik Ahmed Ben Hasan, a pseudo-Arab of European background. In *Blood and Sand* (1922; Fred Niblo, director), Valentino portrays Juan Gallardo, a Spanish bullfighter. He was the title character in *Monsieur Beaucaire* (1924; Sidney Olcott, director). In *The Eagle* (1925; Clarence Brown, director), Valentino plays Vladimir, a Cossack who becomes a kind of Robin Hood in the Russia of Catherine the Great. Returning to his tremendously successful role as a desert Lothario, Valentino made *Son of the Sheik* in 1926 (George Fitzmaurice, director), a film released after his untimely death. In this very successful film, Valentino plays a double role: he returns as the protagonist of *The Sheik*, Ahmed Ben Hasan—now old enough to have a handsome son—and also plays the older man's son Ahmed. In only one of Valentino's major films, *Cobra* (1925; Joseph Henabery, director), does Valentino actually portray an Italian character—Count Rodrigo Torriani, a penniless playboy who comes to America (like Valentino himself) to make his fortune. The Latin Lover Rudolph Valentino was entirely a creation of the cinema, even though his talent as a tango dancer (a reflection of his work as a gigolo in New York before his move to Hollywood) explains part of his allure—the grace, elegance, and romance that he brought to the screen.

Sinatra, Martin, and Travolta were obliged to reinvent themselves over and over again to remain in the entertainment spotlight as Hollywood Italian Romeos. Because of his early death, Valentino never faced this situation after he became a star, although the birth of the talkies might have required some adjustments in his acting style. Yet, the few and influential silent films he left behind in his short career give every indication that he had the talent to evolve into a great comic actor during the sound era, as well as a romantic leading man, perhaps a figure rivaling Cary Grant in charm and poise. Even with the changes of style, taste, and fashion that have transpired since the appearance of his silent films, Valentino's presence on the screen is always mesmerizing. He has the poise of a panther but the physique of a man who diligently worked out, often with a personal trainer, long before bodybuilding became a fashion. In fact, a brief short film exists entitled *The Sheik's Physique*[11] that is devoted entirely to a few minutes of Valentino at the beach. It comes as a surprise to the viewer accustomed to the graceful movements of the actor while dressed to discover how muscular and athletic he actually was. In one famous scene from *Son of the Sheik*, Valentino (as the old sheik) bends an iron poker to show displeasure at his son's antics, and Valentino (as his son) bends it back to its former shape. With his muscular build, Valentino could effortlessly carry off such a scene. In those films in which he is called upon to ride a horse or perform physically demanding action, Valentino appears to be in complete control. He often does his own stunts. More than anything else, however, Valentino always seems to have an innate sense of the camera's presence

and position, and his charismatic personality communicates his magnetism and charm to a contemporary audience even after almost a century
has passed.

Valentino's road to stardom was rapid but not unmarked by both great
struggles and great strokes of fortune. Given his talents as a gigolo in the
New York City ballrooms and his handsome and photogenic but foreign
appearance, he was often first cast as a heavy in his early films, like *Eyes of
Youth* (1919; Albert Parker, director), where he plays Clarence Morgan, a
"cabaret parasite"—hired by a wealthy husband to place his wife in a com-
promising situation in a hotel room so that he can win a divorce without
being forced to pay alimony. In a brilliant but very brief sequence,
Valentino steals the scene in a bravura performance as an unscrupulous
cad who locks the hotel door behind an innocent woman who thinks she
has rushed to the scene of a serious accident that has befallen her corrupt
husband. The following year, in *The Wonderful Chance* (1920; George Ar-
chainbaud, director), Valentino portrays a similar kind of figure, a criminal
named Joe Klingsby who sports a mustache, straw hat, and the omnipresent cigarette that characterized many of Valentino's most famous future roles. Interestingly enough, these early criminal types Valentino plays
before he becomes a superstar are not Italian American gangsters.

The breakthrough film for Valentino was the first cinematic adaptation of
a hugely successful antiwar novel by Vicente Blasco Ibáñez, *The Four Horsemen of the Apocalypse* (1921). In this classic work, Valentino's dancing talent
provides one of the steamiest scenes in the film. As Julio Desnoyers, the
wastrel son of a rich landowner, Valentino dances a sexy tango with one of
the bar girls in a Buenos Aires tango parlor-brothel. The tango originated in
such brothels. By all accounts of audience reactions to this scene, Valentino's
tango was enough to make him a star. Later in the film, Desnoyers goes to
Paris where he teaches the Argentinean dance craze to the most beautiful
women of the city, carrying on an illicit affair with Marguerite Laurier, a
married woman. Much of Valentino's appeal in this film comes from his
masterful performance of this exotic Latin American dance, a sensual ballet
that mimics the sexual—the forbidden fruit. The character he plays considers adultery with beautiful women to be a normal course of events in a man's
life—a far cry from the straitlaced Puritan morality of other contemporary
Anglo-Saxon film stars. Yet, Valentino's seductive characters are never complete cads. At the close of *The Four Horsemen of the Apocalypse*, for example,
Julio heroically joins the French army and dies in the trenches defending his
adopted country.

This film made Valentino an overnight sensation. *The Conquering Power*
(1921) that followed showed Valentino's comic acting talents, but in this

case his character (Charles Grandet) shows a certain nobility, remaining true to Eugénie over the course of many years until the couple is finally romantically united at the conclusion of the film. As a true lover, he is anything but a seducer. Valentino's identification as a seducer, both charismatic and irresistible to the ladies, was confirmed, however, in a subsequent film, *The Sheik*, during the same year. Based upon a novel entitled *The Sheik* (1919) by Edith Maude, with a pornographic reputation that guaranteed over a million copies sold in the English-speaking world, the film played with the concept of racial miscegenation between white women and Arabs, who are defined in both the book and the film as nonwhites. When Diana Mayo (Agnes Ayres) and Sheik Ahmed (Valentino) meet, it is clear through the Sheik's appreciative glances that the Arab prince finds her physically attractive. The next day while she sleeps, he climbs up to her hotel balcony, unloading her pistol and replacing the cartridges with blanks, then from the courtyard below her window singing a serenade that obviously touches her heart. Later, he attacks her caravan in the desert while her attempts to shoot him with her pistol now loaded with blanks are ineffectual. He sweeps her into his arms and carries her off on his fine white stallion with the famous line, LIE STILL, YOU LITTLE FOOL! The Sheik seems torn between Oriental lust for a white woman, on the one hand, and his Parisian education, on the other, which urges him to exercise a more Western restraint. Later, a less-inhibited Arab bandit named Omair captures Diana and is about to ravish her when the Sheik comes to her rescue and is wounded in the process. While he recovers in her presence, one of the Sheik's European friends informs Diana that Ahmed is really not an Arab—his father was English and his mother was Spanish. With this racial impediment suddenly removed, their union is assured. Ahmed seems to revive precisely when he hears that Diana wants him to live and truly loves him.

The Sheik is a corny film, one that derives what little dramatic power it possesses from the fact that it concerns what was then considered to be an interracial affair. Valentino's close-ups in Oriental garb with his now-omnipresent cigarette in hand,[12] are, however, extremely effective. His Sheik is the archetype for those naughty, bodice-ripping lovers in Harlequin Romances that (mostly) women audiences, devour by the millions. The immediate postwar period in Europe and America was a time of sexual liberation. The tango-dance craze created a fascination with a dance form that, like the music of the jazz age, was born in a brothel. Jazz was often about sex, and the tango simulated acts of seduction and consummation. Wartime had loosened the bounds of traditional morality, as had the large-scale employment of women in factories and in positions unusual in that period for their gender. The flapper era following World War I produced a period of great upheaval in the customs and mores of Western civilization, and the appearance of a dark, handsome stranger with erotic and foreign overtones such as Valentino was exactly what the female population required to satiate its thirst for sexual liberation. Offering his audiences, in particular the women, a fantasy of being carried away against their will to a desert rendezvous with a handsome lover in the moonlight was an offer few of them could refuse. As one film historian of the silent cinema has so aptly put it, "The Valentino abduction . . . became the perfect liberation fantasy of an audience of women who know that they weren't going to get to go any other way."[13] It is not by accident that "The Sheik of Araby" became a popular song about naughty erotic adventures, or that a brand of American condoms would eventually be named "Sheiks" to profit from the commercial potential of the impact of the film on the popular imagination.

What is remarkable about Valentino's career is that this stereotypical seducer is not the kind of role he would always portray. In fact, his roles vary from films such as *The Sheik* or *Son of the Sheik*, where the protagonist is clearly identified as a romantic but predatory lover, to films such as *Blood and Sand*, *The Eagle*, and *Cobra*, in which Valentino plays a reluctant male trapped by the lustful designs of a female seductress, a situation completely reversing the expectations aroused by the two films in which Valentino plays a desert playboy.

Blood and Sand offers Valentino the opportunity to repeat his career-making tango as a successful toreador, but when his dance partner puts a rose in her mouth and kisses him after they dance, he is disgusted by her and announces: I HATE ALL WOMEN—BUT ONE. No doubt every swooning female in the audience imagined that one woman was she. *Blood and Sand* offers two kinds of women in bullfighter Juan Gallardo's life: his faithful and long-suffering wife Carmen (Lili Lee), on the one hand; and the scheming and immoral seductress Doña Sol, played to the hilt by Nita Naldi, on the other. Gallardo is lured to Doña Sol's home, which is furnished as an Oriental pleasure dome with a manservant dressed as an Arab who offers the bullfighter candy-striped cigarettes. Gallardo is surprised to discover that they will dine alone following Doña Sol's plan of seduction. As she plays the harp, Gallardo is tempted to make a pass at her but thinks of his faithful wife at home and decides to leave, shaking the woman's hand. But the temptation she presents is too great, and he finally gives in and embraces her. A subsequent intertitle announces in a moralistic tone: IMPURE LOVE IS LIKE A FLAME. WHEN IT IS BURNT OUT, THERE IS NOTHING LEFT BUT THE BLACKENED EMBERS OF DISGUST AND REGRET. Doña Sol's interest in Juan clearly derives from the pleasure she experiences in her efforts to corrupt his innocence. A strong sado-masochistic element in the film appears in a scene where he tries to reject her. She tantalizes him with her remark: SOME DAY YOU WILL BEAT ME WITH STRONG HANDS! I SHOULD LIKE TO KNOW WHAT IT FEELS LIKE! She bites him, and he pounces on her but finally succeeds in rejecting her advances, denouncing her as Eve, the biblical temptress in the Garden of Eden. But this only causes her to break out laughing.

Once Doña Sol has completely stolen Juan's innocence and senses his shame, she no longer has any real erotic interest in him, while dissipated and guilt-ridden, Gallardo goes into the ring unprepared, loses his nerve, and is fatally gored. On his deathbed, Doña Sol ignores his plight but his true-blue wife Carmen stays with him as he receives the last rites. Gallardo's dying act is to remove the ring—supposedly once worn by a Roman emperor who received it from an Egyptian princess—which Doña Sol gave him and to toss it on the floor, moving Carmen to smile, since she now knows he loves her alone. Carmen forgives Juan before he dies in her arms. In spite of the fact that Valentino's acting career is often linked to a new sexual awareness, such an ending affirms traditional morality just as some of Valentino's other performances may have played with or hinted at a more libertine approach to the subject.

Valentino as the target of female seduction continues in *The Eagle,* an adaptation of a story by Aleksandr Pushkin, in which Valentino plays a Cossack named Vladimir in the service of the Tsarina of Russia, Catherine the Great (Louise Dresser). Given the ruler's scandalous reputation for sexual insatiability (whether true or not historically), it is no surprise to discover early on in the film that the Tsarina takes on lovers and promotes them to generals if they please her in bed but has them executed if they do not measure up to her desires. She takes a fancy to Vladimir but he runs away, refusing to do his duty. He becomes The Black Eagle, a kind of Russian Robin Hood, robbing from the corrupt and the rich to give to the poor. He also falls in love with Mascha (Vilma Banky), the daughter of an evil landowner who has stolen his father's estate. The plot then imitates that of *The Sheik,* since The Black Eagle captures Mascha but announces grandly that THE BLACK EAGLE DOES NOT WAR AGAINST WOMEN and sets her free. Eventually, Vladimir and Mascha fall in love and even the Tsarina relents, giving them permission to leave the country and to live happily ever after.

In many respects, Valentino's performance in *The Eagle* represents his best acting. He is more than believable in action sequences and on horseback. His comic abilities come to the fore with a complex plot. And the women in this film (Vilma Banky and Louise Dresser) provide sterling acting performances that complement and highlight his own. The costumes are exquisite, and there is at least one stupendous backward-tracking shot over a banquet table loaded with foodstuffs that could serve as a guide to sophisticated camera movement.

The theme of Valentino as victim rather than seducer is even more accentuated in *Cobra*, the only one of all his major works in which he plays an Italian character. As Count Rodrigo Torriani, a titled aristocrat with little else but his palazzo, Valentino befriends an antiques dealer named Jack Dorning (Casson Ferguson). Dorning persuades Rodrigo to come to America to work with him because of his expertise in antiquities. The Count is a likable womanizer, a fact explained genetically by an amusing historical flashback to the original Count Torriani (Valentino with a beard) who entertains two women at the same time in his bedroom as an angry husband arrives in an effort to catch his wife in flagrante. Still, as the intertitle declares, TORRIANI SOON FOUND THAT NEW YORK WAS NO PLACE TO ESCAPE WOMEN, and he soon becomes the object of the attention of Elise van Zile (Nita Naldi), the niece of one of Jack's rich customers, Mrs. Huntington Palmer. One of the intertitles implicitly refers to Valentino's success in his first desert adventure film with the remark made by an indignant man who claims THAT INDOOR SHEIK has been flirting with Elise all night. When the man scuffles with Torriani in a nightclub, the Count decks him easily, no surprise to an audience aware of Valentino's well-publicized athleticism. As Torriani announces to his friend Jack, after Jack has bailed him out of yet another blackmail scheme by an unscrupulous woman, WOMEN FASCINATE ME—AS THAT COBRA DOES ITS VICTIM. As he says this, he points to a small bejeweled statue of a cobra hypnotizing a tiger (its decoration will later be recalled in a sleek black dress that Elise wears).

Perhaps more clearly than in any of his other films, *Cobra* emphasizes that the cobra is the woman, the femme fatale in wait for the Valentino protagonist and not Valentino himself. A few sequences later, the cobra statue fades into the image of a seductive woman as if to accentuate this point. The gold digger Elise succeeds in marrying Jack for his money, but as an emancipated woman (albeit an evil one), she has high demands for her own personal happiness, and certainly the wimpy figure of the American antiquarian arouses little sexual energy. Elise invites Torriani to a place where they can be alone—room 1002 of the Van Clive Hotel, a place she has obviously employed numerous times in the past for her sexual trysts. Elise dares him to hold and kiss her and then to deny her, and even though his refusal seems firm (YOU ARE INFAMOUS—YOU ARE POISONOUS—LIKE A COBRA!), he nevertheless agrees to go to the hotel. But once there, Torriani finds the strength to reject her advances with the memory of his good friend as his guide. Elise immediately calls an old flame to her room and subsequently we learn that

Cobra *(1925; Joseph Henabery, director). Count Rodrigo Torriani (Rudolph Valentino) attempts to fend off the predatory advances of Elise (Nita Naldi), his best friend's wife.*

they have both perished in a hotel fire. Eventually, Jack tells Torriani he has discovered the truth about Elise and about how he had refused her advances through reading her love letters, one of which Torriani had returned to her. Jack now falls in love with Mary, Jack's secretary (Gertrude Olmstead), the same faithful woman with whom Torriani has also fallen in love. In an act of gratitude and friendship, Torriani renounces his love and returns to Italy, leaving the field open for Jack. But first, he pretends to Mary that he is still the same inveterate womanizer that he was when he arrived in America in order to shift her affections from him to Jack. The last shot of the film shows his ocean liner passing the Statue of Liberty, but unlike so many other films about Hollywood Italians, this boat is heading back to Italy from the New World to the Old.

Son of the Sheik is surely the greatest of Valentino's performances, and yet its release was followed only a few months later by the actor's untimely death on August 23, 1926, at the age of thirty-one. The resulting free publicity from Valentino's demise guaranteed that the film made a fortune. By any standards of judgment, *Son of the Sheik* is a very good adventure romance. It has lots of real action, convincing combat scenes, beautiful costumes, exotic sets and locations, as well as numerous horses and extras. Its plot, enormously appealing, especially for Valentino's legions of female fans, involves the physical seduction of a beautiful dancing girl named Yasmin (Vilma Banky) by the young Sheik, the son of the protagonist of the earlier film, *The Sheik.* Valentino plays both the older man Ahmed Ben Hassan (now happily married to Diana Mayo, the woman he abducted years earlier) as well as his rakish son Ahmed. The love interest in this film, the beautiful Yasmin, is the daughter of a renegade Frenchman named André (George Fawcett). Young Ahmed falls in love with Yasmin, and the two arrange a romantic rendezvous in the ruins outside the city of Tauggourt, but her father and his gang of bandits capture Ahmed with the intention of holding him for ransom from his wealthy father. This allows the director the perfect opportunity to string Valentino up, tear off his shirt, and reveal an extremely well-developed torso and biceps for his eager female admirers.

Even though Yasmin has had nothing to do with this capture, Ahmed vows vengeance upon her after his escape, thinking she knowingly served as the bait to lure him into a trap. He abducts her violently from the Café Maure where she is dancing, rides off with her to his tent, carries her inside, and is about to ravish her when his father arrives and orders the girl's release. The sheik's servant gives the young man some humorous advice: WOMEN—BAH! HEED THEM NOT—FOR TODAY'S PEACH IS TOMORROW'S PRUNE! But a flashback to the famous scene in *The Sheik* in which the father tells Diana LIE STILL, YOU LITTLE FOOL reminds the audience that father and

Son of the Sheik *(1926; George Fitzmaurice, director). A publicity still of the type distributed by the film studio in response to fan mail: Amhed Ben Hassan, Jr. (Rudolph Valentino).*

son are very much alike—headstrong and romantic. Once he realizes his mistake, the son goes to rescue Yasmin from her father and his gang in town, and then his own father joins him for one of the great brawls in silent cinema. The film ends in a shot of Ahmed, Jr., embracing Yasmin on his horse as they ride into the desert dusk in silhouette.

Son of the Sheik *(1926; George Fitzmaurice, director). A period postcard depicting the dramatic scene between the young Amhed Ben Hassan (Rudolph Valentino) and the beautiful dancing girl, Yasmin (Vilma Banky).*

Son of the Sheik gave its audiences everything they could desire. Like its predecessor in the desert, the film plays around the edges of the touchy issue of miscegenation without actually violating any contemporary taboos. The affair between Diana (a white woman) and *The Sheik* of the first film ended as the audience learned that the Sheik was actually a European. In *Son of the Sheik*, the son of their union falls in love with an Arab woman whose father is actually French. In like manner, the rape in the desert is tantalizingly held out as a possibility to the audience even though, ultimately, the two Sheiks and their ladies finally fall in love with each other in a fashion that steps back from the brink of so strong a challenge to contemporary moral standards.

Valentino's appeal as the original Hollywood Italian Romeo was that of the outsider, the stranger, the foil to the American-movie heroes of the time who, like Torriani's friend Jack in *The Cobra*, were so honorable and such straight shooters that they become slightly boring. In contrast, Valentino projects an image of seductive charm, sexual prowess, and physical action—or at least the hint of it. The fact that he was not the rugged, All-American boy type who would kiss the horse rather than the girl, wore exquisite costumes beautifully, moved with the grace of a ballet dancer, but displayed a splendid physique and performed action sequences like a trained athlete, negated the male image of the Anglo-Saxon popular at the

time. He represented romance full of passionate embraces, elegant manners, and danger; an escape from the everyday, humdrum existence of so
many female spectators, who were enduring, not to mention being tortured by, their unhappy marriages and a very non-liberated lifestyle—
which many may well have seen negated in Valentino's charisma and the
alluring promise of his sex appeal. Despite the camp image of Valentino
contemporary popular culture has fabricated, his vast popularity was a response to the same popular impulse that continues to sell millions of romance novels every year. Valentino was the first cinematic superstar whose
female fans adored him. Unlike Sinatra's appeal years later, Valentino attracted adults rather than teenagers. Crowds attended his personal appearances, especially women, who mobbed him to take home the prize of a
piece of his clothing. If he seemed to promise sex, it was because the sex he
proffered was, in reality, another word for freedom and fantasy.

Dago Cool and the Rat Pack: Francis Albert Sinatra (aka The Voice, Ol' Blue Eyes, Swoonatra, and the Chairman of the Board) and Dino Crocetti (aka Kid Crochet, Dean Martin, and Dino)

Rudolph Valentino embodied all of the romance and the fascination of the
foreign and exotic qualities associated with a first generation of Italian immigrants in the United States. He was barely off the boat in New York City
before he was engaged in the entertainment business, first in dance halls
and then in the movies. As the archetypal Hollywood Italian Romeo, his
meteoric ascent to stardom embodied the kind of ethnic image still associated with Old World sophistication and European culture. Part of his appeal to his audiences of swooning women was that he represented the
epitome of the romantic, foreign-born Italian who was also strong and
dashing as juxtaposed to the dominant Anglo-Saxon culture and morality.
Regardless of what role he played, from a Cossack officer to an Arab prince,
Valentino was always recognizable as something essentially non-American,
and his appeal was always associated with a foreign image. This explains in
part why his performance in *Cobra* seems so credible, since the plot narrates a story that is very close in content to his own biography and career as
an immigrant in the United States.

In contrast to this first-generation image of the foreign Romeo, Frank
Sinatra and Dean Martin are clearly members of a second generation of
Italian Americans who were born in this country, grew up in ethnic neighborhoods in Eastern cities, and came to represent a greater degree of ethnic
assimilation into the mainstream of American popular culture than would

ever be possible for an individual like Rudolph Valentino. It would also be impossible to evaluate the impact of Sinatra or Martin upon Hollywood cinema without considering the mark their talents made in record production, nightclub acts, and television performances.[14] In many ways, the term "entertainer" suits each of them more perfectly than "actor" or "singer," because their work touched upon many kinds of popular spectacle. Each of these figures was a singer in the crooner tradition that began before World War II. With the exception of Rudy Vallee (the first singer to be called a crooner) and Bing Crosby, who was the most popular singer in the 1930s, the crooner epoch belonged to Italian American singers such as Sinatra, Martin, and a host of others: Perry Como, Carlo Buti, Phil Brito, Vic Damone, Julius La Rosa, Al Martino, Tony Bennett, Jerry Vale, Frankie Laine, Allen Dale, Don Cornell, and Johnny Desmond. In spite of the fact that some of these entertainers had anglicized their original Italian names (as did Dean Martin, originally baptized Dino Crocetti), they were immediately recognizable as Italian Americans and most music fans as well as music critics identified the crooner style with their ethnicity and with a jazz tradition to which many Italian Americans were closely related. What made crooner style possible was the invention of the microphone, which permitted a more intimate style of singing directly to an individual in an audience rather than being barely audible over an orchestra of the big-band era. Sinatra, in particular, learned how to exploit the microphone better than any other singer of the century, and when coupled with his unique phrasing and breath control that owed a great deal to the *bel canto* technique in Italian opera, Sinatra managed to enjoy a career that spanned many decades.

In his early days, Sinatra's music created the bobby-soxer craze during the World War II years and immediately afterward, causing thousands of girls and young women to swoon and shriek over his soulful singing with the bands of Harry James and Tommy Dorsey before he launched his career as a solo artist. Long before frenzied crowds of teenagers mobbed Elvis, the Beatles, the Rolling Stones, Michael Jackson, or Madonna, Frank Sinatra's singing career established the pattern of the singer as youth-culture superstar. At first, the frenzy was produced by clever public-relations gimmicks orchestrated by George Evans, Sinatra's press agent. Evans paid young women to scream and shout at his concerts and advertised in the papers that medical assistance was on hand for any in the audience who required it after hearing Sinatra sing. But in almost no time, the bobby-soxers (so called because they frequently wore short white socks with saddle shoes) arrived, swooned, and screamed, and were not being paid. Sinatra's early audiences thus became the prototype of the screaming mob of rock fans and rock groupies so familiar in contemporary popular culture.[15] Sinatra's career developed this public style of intense adulation that had a precedent in Valentino, and he was to enjoy probably more of it than any rock'n'roller.

As Jeanine Basinger has pointed out, Valentino and Sinatra had at least one trait in common: they both made women swoon and annoyed men.[16] Beginning his career singing in saloons, Sinatra first won first prize on a popular radio program that featured an amateur hour and then made the break into the big time as a vocalist with Harry James and Tommy Dorsey. After he left the Dorsey band in 1942—when he was exempted from the military draft because of a perforated eardrum—he became the single most popular male vocalist in America, driving his "bobby-soxer" audience of young girls and women crazy over his smooth ballads and romantic melodies. But as the distinguished biographer and former Marine William Manchester has noted, while causing the entire female population of the United States to faint over his crooning, some of the soldiers abroad resented the fact that Sinatra was classified as 4-F and had been deferred from the draft. More than that, they imagined that their wives, girlfriends, and sisters were in the audiences doing the swooning:

> Frank Sinatra was the most hated man of World War II, much more than Hitler. . . . Because we in the Pacific had seen no women at all for two years, and there were photographs of Sinatra being surrounded by all of those enthusiastic girls.[17]

It would take some time before the young and boyish crooner brought American men into his camp of admirers. Sinatra would finally do so after his career as a bobby-sox idol crashed in the early 1950s, when he was forced to reinvent himself with an entirely different and more adult (if sometimes negative) image of masculinity during his Rat Pack years.

By 1943, Sinatra was America's most popular vocalist. In 1945, columnist Westbrook Pegler reported that Sinatra had made more money than "any other individual in the world."[18] In 1946, he signed a five-year contract with MGM in Hollywood that would pay him $260,000 per year and would leave him free to retain the publishing rights to music in alternating films, the permission to make one film per year with another studio, and the liberty to make sixteen guest appearances on television per year. By this time, Sinatra was selling over ten million records per year.[19]

Suddenly, everything seemed to go sour. The fact that he had gone to Havana for a Mafia conclave honoring Lucky Luciano, a great fan of his singing, eventually became public when it was reported by columnist Robert Ruark. The Italian gangsters present at this event included all of the top names in organized crime: Albert Anastasia, Vito Genovese, Carlo Gambino, Joe Profaci,

Tony Accardo, Meyer Lansky, Sandro Trafficante, Carlos Marcello, Frank Costello, Joe Bonanno. Apparently, Sinatra also visited Luciano in exile in Naples before his death and even gave the gangster a gold lighter inscribed TO MY DEAR PAL, CHARLIE, FROM HIS FRIEND FRANK SINATRA.[20] Connections to gangsters would characterize his entire life, although Sinatra would always deny any wrongdoing, even to Congressional investigative committees.

At about the same time as this embarrassing bit of trivia from Mob history was becoming public knowledge, Sinatra had a scuffle (one of many during his long career) with an important Hearst journalist named Lee Mortimer, then entertainment editor of the powerful *New York Daily Mirror*. The fight sent Mortimer to the hospital. Subsequently, Sinatra claimed that Mortimer had called him either a "dago," a "dirty dago," or "a dago son of a bitch," but both Mortimer's denial and MGM's subsequent investigation of the incident indicated that this story was hatched to cover up Sinatra's bad temper. In 1950, George Evans, his public relations director, died suddenly, and as a result Sinatra lost the one man capable of protecting his reputation. Evans had, in fact, created a squeaky-clean image of Sinatra as a family man with no Mob connections, an image that Sinatra's temper tantrums and brushes with reporters—not to mention his amorous love life and frequent contacts with gangsters—constantly threatened.

The subsequent notoriety given to his divorce from his wife of many years and his torrid affair with Ava Gardner applied the coup de grace to the lily-white image bobby-soxers worshiped and Evans created. As if to make matters worse, Sinatra's voice failed, a result of hysterical aphonia that paralyzed his vocal cords. Even his 1950 television special was a bomb. Sinatra's bad luck and depression apparently produced one suicide attempt, the breakup of his relationship with Gardner, and Columbia Record's refusal to renew his recording contract. By the time he played Chicago's Chez Paree nightclub in 1952, a venue that held 1,200 seats, Sinatra was able to fill only 150 of them.

In 1951, Sinatra was summoned to a secret interview by the Kefauver Commission investigating organized crime in America. His well-known friendships with important Italian American gangsters would continue throughout his lifetime and would become particularly important during his Rat Pack years in the late 1950s and the 1960s. One of the most interesting legends about Sinatra's links to the Mob comes from Francis Ford Coppola's *Godfather* masterpiece. In that film, a crooner named Johnny Fontane (played by Al Martino, himself an Italian American crooner) seems modeled after Sinatra. According to Puzo's fiction and its adaptation by Coppola, Fontane was released from his big-band contract to sing solo, and therefore to become a star by an offer impossible to refuse from the Godfather. One of the most unforgettable scenes of *The Godfather* is the horse's head in the bed of Hollywood producer Woltz. Johnny Fontane—the Sinatra surrogate—supposedly won the role in an important war film, an obvious reference to Sinatra's casting in *From Here to Eternity* in 1953, a role that turned his failing career around, because the Godfather had Woltz's Arabian stallion killed to persuade him that Fontane was the best choice for the part. No Sinatra biographer substantiates either of these very colorful stories. Apparently, it was Ava Gardner who persuaded Harry Cohn to give Sinatra the Maggio role in *From Here to Eternity.*[21]

Despite a dark, even frightening side to Sinatra, another aspect of his complex personality demands appreciation and recognition. In 1946, he was awarded a special Oscar for a film advocating racial tolerance, *The House I Live In* (1945). It was precisely at this time that the FBI began keeping an eye on Sinatra for his left-wing associations. After the 1947 trip to Havana to meet Lucky Luciano and other members of the Mafia hierarchy, Sinatra's FBI file began to accumulate notations about organized-crime associations that the singer may have had. Sinatra was well known as a supporter of Roosevelt and the New Deal and for many years was a very vigorous backer of the liberal candidates of the Democratic Party, including Adlai Stevenson and John F. Kennedy. Only toward the end of his career did he begin supporting Republican candidates for office, including Spiro Agnew and Ronald Reagan, a man he had earlier professed to hate. He became one of the few entertainers to have organized the Hollywood stars taking part in presidential inauguration balls of entirely different parties— the Democratic inauguration of John F. Kennedy and the Republican inauguration of Ronald Reagan. The FBI files on Sinatra thus contain not only inquiries about his Mob connections but also his leftist proclivities and are sufficient to fill an entire book.[22]

Sinatra's generosity became legendary. He was capable of incredible acts of kindness to strangers or to ordinary people in need. Probably no single figure in all of show business did more to end racial segregation in the entertainment industry, both in Las Vegas and in Hollywood. In short, even before Frank Sinatra refashioned himself in the late 1950s to become the epitome of "dago cool," he had become a legendary character, a greater-than-life icon in American popular culture.

Dean Martin,[23] the other important player in what would become the Rat Pack, began his career in show business, like Sinatra, as a crooner. Born in an Italian American neighborhood of Steubenville, Ohio, a place resembling Sinatra's hometown of Hoboken, New Jersey, in its ties to corrupt politics and organized crime, Martin worked as both a casino dealer and as a boxer (winning eleven of his twelve fights) while trying his hand at singing in local clubs and dancehalls. Martin's singing model was Bing Crosby. In turn, Dean Martin became one of the models for Elvis Presley. Unlike Sinatra, whose music normally gave preference to the sophisticated type produced by Jerome Kern, Cole Porter, and other great American songwriters, Martin often sang Italian or Italian American lyrics. He was influenced by Phil Brito's renditions of Italian songs, particularly in an album cut in 1946 entitled *Phil Brito Sings Songs of Italy.*[24] During his many stints in various nightclubs, he met Jerry Lewis in 1946. By January 1947, their nightclub act had jelled, and their manager hired the same public-relations man, George Evans, who had created the bobby-soxer rage for Frank Sinatra and worked with other influential artists, such as Duke Ellington and Louis Prima. In almost no time, the unconventional combination of Martin as straight man/crooner and Lewis as zany adolescent—an act described by Lewis himself as "sex and slapstick"[25]—became the rage all over the country. People lined up to see them by the thousands at the most exclusive clubs in the major cities, including Frank Costello's Copacabana in New York, then considered the most sophisticated in the entire nation. The act juxtaposed Martin's cool, romantic character as a crooner and lady's man with Lewis's buffoonery. Their act led directly to a major film contract in Hollywood that produced an eleven-year partnership and sixteen pictures, including *My Friend Irma* (1949), *At War with the Army* (1951), *Sailor Beware* (1952), *Jumping Jacks* (1952), *The Stooge* (1953), *Scared Stiff* (1953), *The Caddy* (1953), and their last film together, *Hollywood or Bust* (1956).

Very few people except the French—who persist in believing Jerry Lewis is a comic genius—can bear to watch these films today. Yet it is impossible to underestimate their economic or social impact. Nick Tosches supplies one feasible explanation for their success, linking their popularity to America's desire to be deceived, to escape the horrible reality of the Cold War and its atomic menace, as well as to an increasingly coarse quality in American popular culture:

Martin and Lewis gave them that: not laughter in the dark, but a denial of darkness itself, a regression, a transporting of the preternatural bliss of infantile senselessness. It was a catharsis, a celebration of ignorance, absurdity, and stupidity, as meaningless, as primitive-seeming, and as droll today as the fallout shelters and beatnik posings which offered opposing sanctuary in those days so close in time but so distant in consciousness.[26]

Looking back on their early careers, it seems impossible that they were so famous and so fabulously rich from such a silly act. As Lewis himself admitted:

> Can you pay two men $9,000,000 to say "Did you take a bath this morning?" "Why, is there one missing?"—do you dare contemplate such a fuck-and-duck? Yet that's what we did. We did that onstage, and they paid us $9,000,000.[27]

As a result, even before Sinatra became a Vegas fixture, Martin and Lewis played for top dollar at The Sands and the Flamingo. Even Martin's records seemed to have a charmed life. His single "That's Amore" remained on the Top Ten charts at the number two position for five months. "Memories Are Made of This" stayed in the first position for six weeks and was on the pop charts for half a year. Everything the pair touched seemed to turn to gold, a parallel to Frank Sinatra's early singing career. Made for relatively very little money, their films grossed tens of millions of dollars each. *Sailor Beware*, for example, cost only $750,000 to make but earned $27,000,000 in worldwide box-office receipts during an era when tickets cost between twenty-five and fifty cents each in America. Martin and Lewis were far more important to Hollywood studios as moneymakers than the best films produced during this time, and they easily outdistanced the great classics of the time at the box office, including *Dial M for Murder, High Noon, Stalag 17, Singin' in the Rain, On the Waterfront,* and *The African Queen,* as difficult as this is to believe today.[28] Finally, in a well-publicized and very acrimonious breakup in 1956, Martin and Lewis severed their partnership and their friendship, and each struck out on his own.

Martin's first step seemed to have imitated Sinatra's sudden fall from grace. The first film he shot without Jerry Lewis, *Ten Thousand Bedrooms* (1957), was a disaster. Like Sinatra before his performance as Angelo Maggio in *From Here to Eternity*, Martin turned his career around with a similar act of professional courage, accepting a minuscule salary to play Michael Whiteacre, a would-be draft dodger caught up in World War II in an adaptation of Irwin Shaw's novel *The Young Lions* (1958). On this film, Martin worked with two of the greatest film actors of the period, Marlon Brando and Montgomery Clift. The picture was skillfully and professionally directed by the same Edward Dmytryk who had earlier created the fine adaptation of Pietro Di Donato's *Christ in Concrete.* Dino's performance amazed everyone but Brando and Clift, both of whom praised Martin's natural acting ability. After the critical success of *The Young Lions,* Martin made two films in 1959 that confirmed his acting talents: *Some*

Came Running, a movie in which Martin worked with Frank Sinatra and played an alcoholic Southern gambler; and *Rio Bravo*, a Western directed by the legendary Howard Hawks.

After these films, and until the demise of his long-running television show in the 1980s, Dean Martin never looked back at even the possibility of failure. Like Sinatra, his entertainment career on the stage, in the recording studio, on television, and in the movies consisted of an almost endless string of successes. Just as suddenly as Frank Sinatra turned around his fortunes, Dean Martin began a series of career moves that would put him, along with Sinatra, on top of the entertainment business for several decades until the end of his life. Perhaps the brief glimpse into the abyss of pop-culture failure that both Sinatra and Martin experienced at about the same time may explain, in some measure, their universally celebrated and widely imitated "dago cool" lifestyle.

The original Rat Pack was a group of friends who gathered at the home of Humphrey Bogart and Lauren Bacall, Sinatra being one of the group. After Bogart's death, Sinatra became titular leader of the group. It later changed from a strictly Hollywood social club to a small group of friends whose acts were identified with Las Vegas and included Sinatra, Martin, Joey Bishop, Peter Lawford, and Sammy Davis, Jr. Although Shirley MacLaine and Angie Dickinson were often associated with the group, the Rat Pack was essentially a male phenomenon, and the women with links to the men were often referred to as "mascots."

The culmination of the Rat Pack's popularity and power, in terms of influencing popular taste through the audiences that flocked to see their acts in Vegas-casino venues, took place around the time that the first Rat Pack film was shot at The Sands Casino in Las Vegas and then premiered in that same city. It was perhaps fitting that The Sands was the location for this pop-culture extravaganza, since Sinatra owned two points in the casino that were purchased in the legal manner and another seven points that had been given to him, it was rumored, by Vincent "Jimmy Blue Eyes" Alo, a mobster with connections to Meyer Lansky and the Genovese crime family.[29] After 1961, Martin also acquired a one-percent interest in the casino.[30] The obvious link of The Sands to the mob could be ascertained by anyone who cared to investigate, since its famous manager, Jack Entratter, had been brought to Las Vegas from New York City's Copacabana which was the property of mobster Frank Costello.[31] Its chief but unofficial operating officer was Joseph "Doc" Stacher, a shady figure with mob connections in New Jersey.[32]

Ocean's Eleven (1960) is not a great film; it is not even a very good film. But it reflects the Rat Pack phenomenon in a number of ways, especially in how it was shot. The Rat Packers seemed to do as little work as possible, in spite of the public relations releases that portrayed the event in Las Vegas as a "film-all-day, perform-all-evening, drink-all-night scene."[33] Veteran director Lewis Milestone (1895–1980), the maker of the classic *All Quiet on the Western Front* (1930), actually brought the film in under budget, even with all the distractions of Las Vegas and the antics of the Rat Packers. As the previously cited remark of Sinatra to Sammy Davis perfectly describes, the point of the film was not to make great art but to have fun—Rat Pack style. And this actually did mean filming during the day with only a few or even a single take, performing during the evening at the casino, and generally partying through the night. Even though Sinatra and Martin were highly talented actors, by the time *Ocean's Eleven* was being made, they were making so much money that they really did not want to be bothered with trying too hard. As Martin said, "They say this is hard work, this acting. What bullshit. Work? Work my ass."[34] The fact that their audiences were filled with people who were forced to work hard to make a living made them special, since they refused to make what they did look difficult.

Ocean's Eleven *(1960; Lewis Milestone, director). Danny Ocean (Frank Sinatra) and Sam Harmon (Dean Martin) plan the robbery of the century in their hotel room, surrounded by lots of liquor.*

Theirs was an attitude of nonchalance, of *sprezzatura*—the Renaissance Italian word coined by Balthesarre Castiglione, author of *The Book of the Courtier*. Martin's biographer Nick Tosches puts his finger upon another important aspect of Dean Martin's character that embodies a particularly Italian characteristic: *menefreghismo*, literally "I don't give a damnism."[35] The image of mature men acting like college-fraternity boys may seem boorish to some today, but their devil-may-care attitude about life was widely admired and imitated.

The other important aspect of *Ocean's Eleven* and the Rat Pack's impact upon popular culture at the time is that the Rat Packers blurred the distinction between show business or entertainment and their private lives. Particularly in their Vegas playpen, the work on the film spilled over into their activities on the stage and gambling in the casinos, not to mention their womanizing and their political activities. Just their presence in the casino, on the gaming floor, or in the lounge guaranteed a huge crowd; and when they were around, the casino took in record amounts of cash. Tosches writes:

> It was not just the dirty-rich *giovanostri* and *padroni* who were drawn to them, to their glamour, to the appeal of darkness made respectable. The world was full, it seemed, of would-be wops and woplets who lived vicariously through them, to whom the imitation of cool took on the religiosity of the Renaissance ideal of *imitatio Christi*.[36]

Their brand of "Dago cool" represented a refusal to follow the more staid morality of the Eisenhower years. They were unabashedly male chauvinists, boozers, inveterate smokers, practical jokesters, and mischief makers—the deluxe version of men behaving badly. In an age before political correctness, they violated almost every taboo imaginable. Playing on the summit meetings being planned at the time in Paris between Eisenhower, De Gaulle, and Khrushchev, Sinatra and his pals announced that they were holding a "summit conference of cool"[37] in Las Vegas during the shooting of *Ocean's Eleven*, and most Americans were far more interested in what the Rat Pack was doing in Vegas than what their political leaders might be planning for the future in Paris. Two biographers have summarized their image quite well:

> In 1960, Frank and the Rat Pack were the epitome of cool. Men wanted to be like them, live like them, make love like them; they wanted to stay out all night like they did, bed a different broad whenever they felt like it, and never fear any consequences. They wanted to smoke and drink until it made them sick, throw money around like it was meaningless, and feel

like irresponsible, irrepressible college boys again. In some ways the Rat Packers were the ultimate party boys. . . . To their fans, in fact to the entire public at large, Frank and his boys led the kind of lives other people only dreamt about. They got paid big bucks for doing what they loved instead of just having a "job" that merely paid the bills. They were adored and admired by millions of people, not just everyday folks but politicos and royalty and other movie and musical stars. They got instant attention, instant respect. They made hard work—filming all day, the show all night—look like fun.[38]

One of their famous visitors on the set of *Ocean's Eleven* was John Fitzgerald Kennedy, soon-to-be-elected President of the United States. The Rat Pack backed Kennedy's presidential nomination to the hilt, to the point that they were known in some circles as "the Jack Pack." Although entering the realm of gossip, hearsay, and legend, most biographers of either Sinatra or Martin agree on several points here. Kennedy's father, Joseph Kennedy, besides being something of a fascist sympathizer before World War II (when he served as Ambassador to the Court of St. James thanks to his financial support of Franklin D. Roosevelt) was deeply involved in illegal-liquor smuggling in Boston, probably working with Raymond Patriarca, then the head of the Mafia in that city. In some fashion or other, Frank Sinatra played the middleman with Kennedy and Sinatra's friend Sam Giancana, the head of the Chicago Mob, resulting in Mob support for Kennedy's successful primary victories in such unlikely states as Protestant West Virginia and later in the general election in Illinois. Sinatra even introduced one of his ex-mistresses, Judith Campbell Exner, to JFK when he visited the set of *Ocean's Eleven* in February of 1960. Subsequently, so the story goes, Exner also became the mistress of Sam Giancana. Thanks to Sinatra and his Rat Pack buddies, who had basically made John F. Kennedy an honorary member of their group, the President of the United States was sleeping with the mistress of the King of Gangland! The story becomes darker when John's brother, Robert, begins to share the favors of Marilyn Monroe (another ex-Sinatra and ex-JFK mistress) while he was also fanatically intent upon putting Mafia leaders like Sam Giancana into prison, regardless of their support for JFK during the election or any deals that had been made in recompense for their help. Las Vegas casino owners supplied Kennedy with over a million dollars in cash to finance his election campaign. The story becomes murkier still when these same Mafia leaders were implicated by some journalists in the (future) assassination of President Kennedy. Sam Giancana's contemptuous remarks about the Kennedys and their ties to Frank Sinatra (cited as one of the epigraphs to this chapter), apparently taken from FBI wiretaps, would suggest that there was some truth to such stories. At any rate, these narratives have now become the stuff of legend and are not only discussed as if true by numerous biographies of Rat Packers but also serve as the plot narrative for several crime novels by James Ellroy.[39]

Ocean's Eleven manages to capture, in some respects, the glamour and glitter of the Rat Pack era. It is essentially a combination of the buddy movie and the bank-caper genre. Although no masterpiece, the original stands far above Stephen Soderbergh's recent (2001) remake also entitled *Ocean's Eleven*, for the simple reason that the real Rat Packers possess more "cool," credibility (as they are essentially playing themselves), and more class than the likes of George Clooney, Brad Pitt, Matt Damon, and Julia Roberts. Indeed, the original film gained ninth place in box-office returns in the year it was released, outselling in America films of much greater historical significance, such as *Psycho, Exodus, Spartacus*, and *La Dolce Vita*.[40]

The plot of *Ocean's Eleven* focuses upon a group of twelve ex-paratroopers from the 82nd Airborne Division who liberated Europe and marched into Germany over the Rhine fifteen years earlier. Former sergeant Danny Ocean (Frank Sinatra) has assembled his former company commander, playboy lieutenant Jimmy Foster (Peter Lawford) and his ex-soldier buddies—a total of eleven men, partially explaining the eleven of the title, to rob five Vegas casinos on the famous Las Vegas strip. His GI pals include an unlikely cast of characters: a singing Sam Harmon (Dean Martin), a garbage-truck driving crooner named Josh Howard (Sammy Davis), an ex-con electrician named Tony Bergdorf (Richard Conte), and other minor figures. A mastermind criminal planner named Spyros Acebos, played for total comic effect by Akim Tamiroff, has figured out a foolproof plan to carry out this daring robbery. The men obviously agree to carry out the caper because they are nostalgic about their heroic days together fighting in Europe: a million-dollar split will solve most of their personal problems as well. As Danny Ocean says to Sam Harmon, "I think the only reason I got into this caper is to see you again." Male bonding and camaraderie are really the secret to the Rat Pack's values and also their appeal to audiences. In spite of feminist protests to the contrary, there were and still are many women attracted to masculinity of this sort even if it may appear to be a stage of arrested development.

Needless to say, the atmosphere of *Ocean's Eleven* is politically incorrect in the extreme. The women in the film are either bimbos who are picked up at the bar, such as the malevolent Adele Ekstrom (Patrice Wymore); mindless bubbleheads who stare adoringly at the Rat Packers when they sit at the bar or sing; or more intelligent women who nevertheless "stand by their men" in spite of their obvious defects, such as Danny Ocean's ex-wife Bea (Angie Dickinson). But they all dress with style and class, appearing at a bar or a restaurant, or a floor show, in high heels and elegant (for the period) evening garb. The stage is set for such an unabashedly sexist treatment of women with the first appearance of Ocean and Foster in the film: two obviously available blonds are giving Foster a massage. Sex for the Rat Packers is important but broads should not be treated as if they are too important. What really counts is what the men do together. When Ocean gets down to business (their caper), his dismissal of the blonds speaks volumes about the attitude of the film: "All right girls, time for your nap. Beat it!"

Nevertheless, the film provides material for a critique of Rat Pack morality. Bea may acquiesce in the sexual morality of her husband. Misunderstanding Sam Harmon's attitude toward her, she declares: "I'll consider mistress, play-thing, toy for a night, but I refuse to be your mother." Her marriage to Danny Ocean, she claims, has been "drowned in champagne" and seems to have been ruined by the penchant for danger Danny acquired during the war:

> He wants me back but not enough to give me what I want . . . I want a life that doesn't depend on the color of a card or the length of a horse's nose . . . We didn't have a home, we had a floating crap game.

From an examination of this quintessential Rat Pack film, it would be easy to draw the conclusion that sex actually takes third place to booze and tobacco. Everyone smokes and drinks all day, and everywhere. But it is all done with class. These bank robbers wear tuxedos and handmade-tailored suits, and they never go out without a perfectly folded foulard in the lapel pocket! From the standpoint of fashion and style, the Rat Packers have real elegance. Their manners, obviously, are another matter. Even their plan to rob the casinos represents a pre-High Tech world and relies more on cleverness and sleight of hand than gee-whiz gadgets that characterize today's action films. Essentially, they intend to blow up a power line and cross some wires in the casino's electric boxes, causing the cashier's safes to pop open. In his garbage truck, John Howard will pass by each casino and receive the cash in five handbags during the few minutes of darkness before auxiliary-power generators turn the electricity back on, and the money will pass through the police blockades as garbage.

Any tourist visiting Las Vegas today would not recognize the Vegas of the Rat Packers. During the heyday of Sinatra and company, Vegas catered more to gamblers than to tourists, and the Rat Packers attracted the wealthiest gamblers. The image of Las Vegas in the film reflects this attempt to associate gambling with style and glamour. Filmed in the major five casinos on the Las Vegas Strip at the time—The Sands, The Flamingo, The Riviera, The Sahara, and The Desert Inn—the Vegas of the Rat Packers represents exactly the opposite of today's gigantic theme park. The casinos were then smaller and more intimate, and the gamblers much better dressed. Rather than the tourists of today who think nothing of wearing gaudy shorts or cutoffs and halters during the evening in the casinos and who are generally shod in horrendously designed tennis shoes or tasteless sandals, the gamblers in the five clubs of the film are well-heeled, well-dressed and well-behaved. There are no fat or ugly people in the Rat Pack world. In truth, the atmosphere is more that of a sophisticated nightclub, like the Copacabana, than a garish tourist attraction.[41]

Of course, *Ocean's Eleven* is a film made to showcase the Rat Pack, not to make cinema history—an excuse for the Rat Pack to amuse themselves at the expense of the production company and to make money in the process, having a much better time than their counterparts on the screen. The ending of the film also represents a kind of *menefreghismo* that typifies their attitudes about life in general. When Tony Bergdorf dies after the robbery, the boys decide to get the hot bags of cash out of town by hiding them in his coffin. As they assemble in the chapel for the funeral services, anticipating the cash that they are about to receive in San Francisco, they suddenly realize that the noise they hear is from the crematorium as their stashed loot goes up in smoke. "Verily the Lord giveth and the Lord taketh away," the minister intones, and he knows not how true his remarks are. Such a disastrous result fails to discourage Ocean and his eleven henchmen. Perhaps their view of the universe may be summed up in the songs that are heard during the film: Dean Martin's "Ain't that a Kick in the Head?"[42] and Sammy Davis's "Yo Eleven." The first song embodies a *menefreghista* attitude about life: accept what comes and enjoy yourself at all costs. The second song refers to the game of craps and is an exclamation uttered by gamblers trying to throw an eleven—possible with only two combinations of the dice and therefore, a relatively difficult means of winning. "Yo Eleven" and "Ain't that a Kick in the Head?" might be the defining ideas in *Ocean's Eleven. Carpe diem*—seize the day—go for the difficult cast of the dice; and if you lose, wear a smile on your face, since hope, as the Italian saying goes, is always green.

This first Rat Pack film established the pattern for others to follow—that is, films that winked at the audience, acknowledging the Rat Packers' own awareness that they were putting the audience on, and that in some respects every film they made was a parody of a real film. The last shot of

Ocean's Eleven leaves one with the feeling that the entire work has simply been exactly the way Sinatra described the experience to Sammy Davis: "The idea is to hang out together, find fun with the broads, and have a great time. . . . Entertainment, period." This last shot is that of the marquee of The Sands with the name of the five Rat Packers (Sinatra, Martin, Davis, Lawford, and Bishop) featured in the casino lounge. It invites us to blur the distinction between their world and that of the movie we have just screened.

Other Rat Pack films followed in rapid succession and embodied the same devil-may-care attitude toward the production values of a normal picture, the same Rat Pack single-shot style, with similar social values in the scripts. *Sergeants 3* (1962; John Sturges, director) proposes a Western remake of *Gunga Din* (1939; George Stevens, director). Shot in the middle of nowhere in Kanab, Utah, a site containing stupendous Western locations, the Rat Packers were said to be bored with the only diversions in town, a Dairy Queen stand. As a result, they apparently imported hookers and sufficient booze to the small town to keep them amused playing cards when they were not on the set. More interesting was another Rat Pack Western made the following year, *4 for Texas* (1963), which opened with a bow to John Ford's classic *Stagecoach* (1939) before degenerating into an amusing contest between two operators—Zack Thomas (Frank Sinatra) and Joe Jarrett (Dean Martin), each of whom try to control gambling in Galveston, Texas, just after the Civil War. Much more entertaining than *Sergeants 3*, however, *4 for Texas* not only contains a wonderful cameo appearance by the Three Stooges but also leading ladies Ursula Andress and Anita Ekberg, the first coming off her rise to fame in *Dr. No* (1962; Terence Young, director) as Honeychile Ryder, James Bond's love interest, and the second celebrated all over the world for her wade in the Trevi Fountain in Rome with Marcello Mastroianni in Federico Fellini's *La Dolce Vita* (1959). The reasoning behind casting these two European bombshells was to afford the Rat Packers the opportunity to bed them, but just for back-up, many of the dance-hall girls in the saloons and riverboat actually were call girls recruited to keep up the spirits of the production company.[43] The dialogue here is even more sexist than in the first two Rat Pack films, and most of it is uttered with foreign accents by Ekberg and Andress, who do everything but drool over Sinatra and Martin until they eventually marry them at the close of the film. It is all in good fun, but Ekberg's remark that it all concerns "grown men acting like little schoolboys" reflects the tone of the film. Perhaps without realizing it, Ekberg had provided a working definition for the Rat Pack phenomenon.

The fourth and last Rat Pack film, *Robin and the 7 Hoods* (1964; Gordon Douglas, director) is possibly the most successful. It is an entertaining musical parody of a gangster film set in prohibition-era Chicago. Sinatra's signature song about Chicago, "My Kind of Town," was composed and first sung in the film. Sinatra and Martin play two gangsters named Robbo and Little John, Bing Crosby is Allen A. Dale, Sammy Davis is Will, and Barbara Rush is Marian Stevens. The conceit governing the entire movie is the parallel between Robin Hood and Robbo (hence all the other characters with names recalling the famous English medieval bandit who robbed from the rich to give to the poor). Edward G. Robinson opens the film with an address to an assembled mob of Chicago hoods right before he is murdered by an evil Guy Gisborne (Peter Falk). Thus, this opening sequence offers a perfect re-creation of the famous banquet scene of mobsters in *Little Caesar* in 1930, which launched the gangster film as one of the most popular genres in Hollywood history just as the opening sequence of *4 for Texas* recalls *Stagecoach*.

The improbable plot concerns the use by Robbo, Little John, Allen A. Dale, and Marian of soup kitchens for the poor that may also serve as fronts for other illegal activity. The three Rat Packers—Robbo, Little John,

Robin and the 7 Hoods *(1964; Gordon Douglas, director). Robbo (Frank Sinatra), Allan A. Dale (Bing Crosby), and Little John (Dean Martin) do an old vaudeville routine, tap dancing and singing about dressing well and having "style" or "class."*

and Will—are outsmarted by Allen A. Dale and Maid Marian, who take all the money, and they are left to conclude the film as three Salvation Army Santa Clauses begging for coins on the Chicago streets while the two more successful criminals pass them dressed in evening clothes as they step out of their elegant limo. Perhaps the most memorable gimmick in the film is a casino set that, at the touch of a button, converts into a mission serving the poor and the downtrodden when the law arrives to close the joint.

Both Sinatra and Martin made other significant films during the Rat Pack era that are far more serious works of art, such as Sinatra's *The Man with the Golden Arm* or *The Manchurian Candidate* and Martin's afore-mentioned *The Young Lions* or *Some Came Running*. But the Rat Pack films, beginning with the very profitable *Ocean's Eleven* and sputtering out with the other less memorable works, were made primarily to prove they could practically produce films in their sleep or while heading for the bar. It is no accident that each title contains a number associated with the game of craps. Rat Pack films embodied the essence of "dago cool." Yet, there is re-markably little reference to Italian Americana in any of these films. Danny Ocean and Sam Harmon evoke no ethnic origins. On two occasions in these films, the dialogue has ethnic overtones, but the references are to the actors themselves, not the characters they portray in the films. In *4 for Texas*, Martin as Joe Jarrett declares that "the blood of Christopher Colum-bus flows through my veins" in a comic moment when he falls into the river by the riverboat casino in the film. And in *Robin and the 7 Hoods*, Sinatra's character Robbo has a name that is probably Italian in origin, and at one point he tells Maid Marian that something he says to her is "an old Italian word."

The high-water mark of the Rat Pack can be dated from the time *Ocean's Eleven* was being made to the death of President Kennedy in No-vember 1963. These few short years saw a convergence of Rat Pack popu-larity in the entertainment world with the would-be playboy presidential candidate who, thanks to the Chairman of the Board, would share his bed with the mistress of a Chicago Mafia chieftain. Sinatra and his Rat Pack sang the national anthem at the Democratic Party convention that nomi-nated Kennedy and then organized the entertainment for Kennedy's inau-gural celebration in Washington after the election was over. But the links between Sinatra, his friends, and the Mob also came to the attention of the FBI and J. Edgar Hoover, who warned Attorney General Robert Kennedy about it. The result was that the Kennedy connection was abruptly sev-ered. While cuddling up to the Kennedys never appealed to Dean Martin, who was equally unimpressed by them or by mobster bosses, the effect upon Sinatra was devastating.[44] As Martin's biographer has put it, "Dean saw what Sinatra was too blind to see: there was no place in Camelot for wops."[45]

Besides the end of the Kennedy connection to the Rat Pack, other factors were changing the face of popular entertainment. New faces on the horizon—Elvis back from military service, the Beatles, a new generation of rock stars, and the entire counterculture to come—competed with their recordings and Vegas acts. As one of their historians has aptly described their era,

> they were the last redoubt of old-time showbiz against the hordes of teen culture; the acme of traditional performance based on vaudeville, burlesque, and Tin Pan Alley; the final moment during which adult entertainment could be said to have the undivided attention and undiluted respect of the world.[46]

Of course, their careers continued to flourish—for example, Dean Martin went on to star in a series of highly rated television shows for almost a decade—but never again did the essence of their entertainment style, Italian American males behaving badly, dominate show business as completely as it did for a period.[47]

Few people in the Rat Pack audience needed any reminder that Sinatra and Martin were Italian Americans, and there was never any question that their kind of style, glamour, and class (as well as their brand of boorishness and arrogance) had clear ethnic roots in the immigrant experience. Unlike Valentino, whose foreign origins were unmistakable and were exploited in making him an exotic and erotic representative of the Other, Sinatra and Martin remind us that the dagos and wops of Angelo Maggio's era could now "pass for white," in the vernacular of the period, and had now become naturalized sex symbols of a brand of gaudy glamour associated with Las Vegas that may well represent a unique moment in American popular culture.

Disco Dagos: John Travolta and the "Guido" as Superstar

The fourth figure worthy of consideration as an important Hollywood Italian Romeo—John Travolta—remains an important force in Hollywood today. Travolta hit the big time in Hollywood through films associated with music and dancing—a link to Valentino's rise to fame from being a gigolo, as well as the transition of Sinatra and Martin from crooner to actor and entertainer. *Saturday Night Fever* (1977; John Badham, director) and *Grease* (1978; Randal Kleiser, director) represent two of the most memorable and original films made during the 1970s. Together, they made John Travolta a superstar. Subsequently, Travolta's career went into a steep decline that was

marked by two horrendous remakes of the two signature musicals in a single
year (1983), both of which were embarrassments: *Staying Alive* (Sylvester
Stallone, director) and *Two of a Kind* (John Herzfeld, director). After these
career mishaps, not unlike the calamitous downfalls typical of both Sinatra
and Martin in the 1950s, Travolta's prestige and fame was revived with a brilliant performance in Quentin Tarantino's *Pulp Fiction* (1994), in which he
appears as Vincent Vega, an Italian American hit man who still knows how to
perform on the dance floor.

The ethnic stereotype of the Italian American "Guido" stands at the core
of such films as *My Cousin Vinny, The Wanderers*, or *Rocky*.[48] Travolta's status as the classic "Guido" begins with the television show *Welcome Back,
Kotter*, a situation comedy set in a Brooklyn high school that was tremendously popular between 1975 and 1979. Playing Vinnie Barbarino, the wise-
cracking "Guido" and leader of a group of misfits named the Sweathogs
who are always one step away from flunking out of school, Travolta became
a pop icon. He was one of the first television stars to make a successful transition to icon status in the movies. In both *Saturday Night Fever* and *Grease*,
Travolta portrays a working-class Italian American Guido who can dance.
In the process, he manages to create a romantic identification for the ethnic
character of the Guido, a stereotypical caricature of the working-class, blue-
collar, Italian American inner-city youth that had become identified only
with racism, stupidity, and bad taste.

Saturday Night Fever has become a mythic film. It embodied the essence
of the disco culture that swept over America in the late 1970s and the 1980s
in the same way that *Ocean's Eleven* reflected the ethos of the Rat Pack's
values from the late 1950s and early 1960s. The *Saturday Night Fever* sound
track was the most widely sold sound track ever. It contained a number of
the classic disco songs that were immensely popular as performed by the
Bee Gees: "Staying Alive," "More than a Woman," and "How Deep Is Your
Love, Night Fever." The film evolved from a trendy but influential article
published in *New York* magazine by Nik Cohn, a British rock journalist,[49]
an essay that was so widely publicized it came to be considered as a weighty
sociological statement about young men in Bay Ridge, Brooklyn. It described the tightly circumscribed lives of working-class Italian males who
had dead-end jobs during the week but who lived for the Saturday night
revels at the "in" disco, Odyssey 2001. Here is how Cohn described Vincent
(the focus of his essay) and his male friends:

> The basic commandments were simple. To qualify as an Odyssey Face, an
> aspirant need only be Italian, between the ages of eighteen and twenty-
> one, with a minimum stock of six floral shirts, four pairs of tight trousers,

Saturday Night Fever (1977; John Badham, director). A publicity still shows Tony Manero (John Travolta) in various dynamic dance poses from the film.

two pairs of Gucci-style loafers, two pairs of platforms, either a pendant or a ring, and one item in gold. In addition, he must know how to dance, how to drive, how to handle himself in a fight. He must have respect, even reverence, for Facehood, and contempt for everything else. He must also be fluent in obscenity, offhand in sex. Most important of all, he must play tough.[50]

The composite Guido called Vincent in Cohn's essay becomes the charismatic Tony Manero of the film. We are introduced to the character as the credits of the film are presented: Tony strolls cockily down a Bay Ridge street with a paint can in his hand, moving to the sound of "Staying Alive." He has the required ethnic swagger, wears the proper polyester clothes with wide collars and fancy imported Italian shoes, and he turns to look at either a new pair of loafers in the store windows or a beautiful woman nearby with equal attention. The camera work, cutting between his looks, what he sees, and his shoes strutting down the street, captures perfectly the actor's animal magnetism and sex appeal. In retrospect, it is impossible not to see that a star has been born even before the story begins, so perfectly

Saturday Night Fever *(1977; John Badham, director). The ultimate disco dago—John Travolta as Tony Manero in his famous three-piece polyester white suit with wide lapels and huge collar tabs. (This suit is now one of Hollywood's great memorabilia.)*

does Travolta's physical appearance embody the film's ethos. *Saturday Night Fever* attempts to do two, sometimes conflicting things: give an entertaining account of the dance craze of the disco era; and offer a sociological explanation for this cultural phenomenon in the Italian American community. The film succeeds spectacularly in its first goal although it fails, in many respects, as a true and realistic account of Italian American youth culture.

Ultimately, *Saturday Night Fever* is a coming-of-age film. Tony, at nineteen, faces the prospect of a dismal future if he continues working in the paint store. The bravado of his remarks about what he will do with his life ("Fuck the future," as he puts it) only hides his fears about being trapped in a dead-end job and in a depressing home with parents who can only nag him and praise their son Frank who is a priest. The scenes around the dinner table at the Manero household—the unemployed husband bickering with the domineering mother, the long-suffering grandmother remaining mute, Tony receiving the brunt of the hostility and frustration—represent a recognizable Hollywood stereotype: Italian American dinner Hell. They show an ethnic culture from which anyone with intelligence or ambition would take flight. The depiction of the Italian American family as an oppressive influence rather than a safe haven defines the story of Tony's brother Frank, who has entered the priesthood only to please his mother and whose decision to leave the priesthood produces a family crisis but also encourages Tony to strike out on his own.

In addition to the dramatic introduction of the protagonist to the tune of a disco classic as the credits unfold at the beginning of the film, two other sequences focused on Tony Manero stand out in *Saturday Night Fever*. The first is that in which Tony returns home from work and dresses to prepare for his Saturday night out. Here, the director treats Travolta's body from a voyeuristic point of view, making it the object of erotic glances in much the same manner as is traditionally done with the female body in the movies. Tony is first seen blow-drying his hair, then the camera cuts to an overhead shot of young people dancing in a disco club. It then cuts back to Tony and his hair, then to a Bruce Lee poster on the wall (only one of his behavioral models in the film). As Tony flexes his arms in a bodybuilding pose, the camera shifts to a low angle from the floor up, showing his athletic body dressed only in black briefs. Afterwards, the camera moves to several close-ups of a Farrah Fawcett poster (a popular female sex symbol of the period), suggesting that the audience should cast its gaze upon Travolta in much the same manner the viewer is traditionally cued to examine the female body. The shot of Tony's hand taking a gold chain (a clear Italian American symbol) from a jewelry box is followed by another shot of disco dancers, eventually ending in an extreme close-up of a gold cross and chain in his chest hair. Eventually, a very effective shot jumps from his disco shirt on the bed to Tony as he zips up his tight pants and moves his pelvis in a sexually suggestive fashion. Beefcake, bodybuilding, dancing, and jewelry all remind us of Valentino, the archetypal Italian American Romeo. The Bruce Lee poster relates to Tony's tough side (emphasized by the Cohn essay), but the shot of Farrah Fawcett seems to portray her as looking at Tony's body. The entire scene, consisting of many more shots than those mentioned here, establishes Tony Manero's body as a sexual object, identifying it with dancing (with the cuts to the disco) and as an Italian American body (with the particular style of dress and the gold jewelry) as well.

The second important sequence in the film develops the implications of the dressing sequence. At the Odyssey 2001 disco, Tony has met Stephanie Mangano (Karen Lynn Gorney), an Italian American girl who has ambitions of leaving Bay Ridge behind and moving to the more glamorous and more sophisticated borough of Manhattan. She basically defines sophistication as whatever contains less Italian American ethnic flavor. In the process, she makes Tony feel bad about his own situation, working in a dead-end job without any well-conceived ambitions for self-improvement:

> STEPHANIE: "You work in a paint store, right? You probably live wid your family, hang out wid your buddies, and on Saturday night you go and blow it all off at 2001, right? . . . You're a cliché, you're nowhere . . . on your way to no place!"
>
> TONY: "What'd you got? A fucking stairway to the stars or what?"

Her description of his situation is painfully accurate, even though her own Brooklyn accent and Italian American mannerisms, especially her gum chewing, would lead us to doubt the true depth of her own cultural sophistication. But at least she wants to improve herself. When she fails to show up at the disco the next week, Tony goes to the dance floor and dances completely by himself, producing the most famous sequence of the film, showing him in a wide variety of sexually suggestive poses and positions, and exploiting the raw energy of Travolta's great dancing talent.

Trapped as he is in what is presented as the classic Italian American Guido view of women, Tony is attracted to Stephanie because she refuses to sleep with him and is disgusted by Annette (Donna Pescow), who loves him so much that she offers herself to him without any reservation but, naturally, is quickly rejected when he discovers that she has taken no preventions against pregnancy. Attitudes about the other sex among these Italian American Guidos are completely hypocritical. As Tony puts it in the film, women are either "nice girls" or "cunts." This twentieth-century version of the Madonna–whore dichotomy rests upon a comic paradox. Men think of nothing else but whether or not a woman will "put out" for them, but when they do, the compliant women are treated with disrespect and contempt, and are rejected since they are the kind of women who sleep around. Of course, this attitude is completely counterproductive if the intended goal is to persuade young women to bed them, since the only intelligent response to it is the refusal to have sex before marriage.

The tragic consequences of Tony's sexist attitude toward women can be found in Annette's pathetic question to Tony: "Why do you hate me so much, when all I did was like you?" Later, in order to hurt Tony, she offers herself to his friends in the back of a car in which he is riding, but this only serves to drive him further toward Stephanie. But the death of one of Tony's Guido friends, Bobby C (Barry Miller), who falls off a bridge, apparently jolts Tony out of his inertia and drives him to Manhattan, where the film ends with his declaration that he agrees just to be friends with Stephanie. He, too, is moving to Manhattan.

When *Saturday Night Fever* focuses upon Tony's sex appeal and his talent as a disco dancer, the film achieves a rare synthesis of music and movement that ranks with many of the classic Hollywood musicals. When the film attempts to show some kind of character development in Tony or offers a broader, sociological analysis of Italian American youth and their dead-end pop culture, it simply fails. Equally puzzling, upon reflection, is the fact that the only memorable scenes in the film involve Tony shown by himself or dancing by himself. Far from representing an innovative or an original disco choreography, the concluding dance sequence with Stephanie is a much more sedate, even classical form of ballroom dancing that suggests Tony's disco days are over if he chooses Stephanie over Annette. Although Tony shocks Stephanie and his Guido friends by giving his first-prize check and trophy to the Puerto Rican couple who took second place, Tony's judgment is absolutely correct: they were far more charismatic dancers than he and Stephanie, and this fact promises little emotion for a future with her.

Nik Cohn's essay and the film it subsequently spawned have been taken as virtually scientific proof that Italian American popular culture resembles the world of Tony Manero. The working-class, undereducated Guido and his gold necklace, tight pants, gyrating pelvis, politically incorrect treatment of women, and sexy physique have become symbols virtually synonymous with Italian Americans in general in much the same manner that gangsters are matter-of-factly given Italian names in Hollywood. But as Cohn confessed on the twentieth anniversary of the film's opening, once more writing an essay in *New York* magazine, his essay was based upon a complete fabrication. Cohn knew absolutely nothing about New York, having recently arrived from Great Britain, and even less about Italian Americans. He had visited the disco for a brief moment with a black dancer named Tu Sweet. Tu Sweet told Cohn that disco culture originated in black–gay clubs and culture, and that its popularity among Italian Americans in Brooklyn was really not its best expression. Desperate for a story to give to his editor, Cohn simply concocted the story out of whole cloth after seeing a brief glance of a single figure who would become the Vincent of his essay and the Tony Manero of the film:

> One image stayed with me, though: a figure in flared crimson pants and a black body shirt, standing in the club doorway, directly under the neon light, and calmly watching the action. There was a certain style about him—an inner force, a hunger, a sense of his own specialness. He looked in short, like a star. . . . I didn't see the figure in the doorway again, and the others I tried talking to were unresponsive. Plus, I made a lousy interviewer. I knew nothing about this world, and it showed. Quite literally, I didn't speak the language. So I faked it. I conjured up the story of the figure in the doorway, and named him Vincent. . . . Then I went back to Bay Ridge in daylight and noted the major landmarks. I walked some streets, went into a couple of stores. Studied the clothes, the gestures, the walks. Imagined about how it would feel to burn up, all caged energies, with no outlet but the dance floor and the rituals of Saturday night. Finally, I wrote it all up. And presented it as fact. There was no excuse for it.[51]

Maria Laurino's discussion of her Italian American background notes that the images in both *The Godfather* and *Saturday Night Fever* have become so pervasively accepted as true to life in American popular culture that they have completely obscured any other image of Italian Americans but the Wise Guy or the Guido.[52] Nik Cohn's essay had a great deal to do with this negative stereotype, and even after confessing to his invention twenty years after the fact, he did not bother, as he admitted, to return any of the many checks the article earned him. As Laurino quite rightly puts it, these screen personas force Italian Americans into a "no-win position: choose to be a Bensonhurst Italian or an assimilated American, an ethnic champion waving a red, green, and white flag or a communal player hoping against hope to blend into Anglo-Saxon society."[53]

If *Saturday Night Fever* presented a false but charismatic portrait of Italian American life in Brooklyn, making Travolta a star in the process, his subsequent performance in *Grease* as Danny Zuko, a name with clear Italian roots as Zucco, was transported from the gritty streets of New York to the sunnier neighborhoods of Los Angeles. The portrayal of Rydell High School in a sunny California of the mind presents a nostalgic portrait of the 1950s, complete with hot rods, prom nights, malt shops, and music from the period plus new music to fit the story line. The film was a box-office smash, breaking all musical records for gross earnings before adjustments for inflation, and even though most of the actors appear far older than they should be to attend high school, the film cemented Travolta's reputation as a Hollywood Italian Romeo only a year following his rise to film stardom with *Saturday Night Fever*.

Unlike the first musical set in New York City, *Grease* reflects something of an ethnic cleansing of Italian American symbols. Stockard Channing's portrayal of Betty Rizzo offers one of the most complex images of an Italian American girl (albeit a Guidette) in the cinema of the period and actually steals the show from the stars, Travolta and Olivia Newton-John, who plays Sandy Olsson, the Australian sweetheart Danny Zuko meets at the beach one summer. Like *Saturday Night Fever*, *Grease* presents two different kinds of girls. Sandy is the nice girl, who refuses to have sex with our hero. Betty is obviously the other kind of girl and, having missed her period, she fears that she is pregnant. One of the musical's best numbers is a rejection of the virginal female icons of the 1950s—Sandra Dee, Doris Day, and Annette Funicello.

In sharp contrast to Betty's Italian American sensuality, Sandy is an Anglo-Saxon version of Stephanie Mangano, in some respects, just as Betty is a much more intelligent version of Annette. Thinking that she has been "knocked up," Betty sings a song about being "trashy and no good"—"There Are Worse Things that I Could Do," a lyric that concludes unhappily that "to cry in front of you, that's the worst thing I could do." The bad girl of the film is really a sensitive, brave individual. In contrast, before the conclusion, the goody two-shoes Sandy dons spandex pants, a leather jacket, takes up smoking cigarettes, sports a sexy hairdo, and sings "Goodbye to Sandra Dee." She has concluded that the only way she can win Danny is to be more sexually available. The film ends on a Hollywood happy note, with the entire cast dancing to celebrate the fact that Sandy gets Danny, while Betty, who has discovered that her missed period is a false alarm, gets the presumed father, Danny's friend Kenickie (Jeff Conaway). As entertaining as *Grease*'s production numbers are, its sanitized Broadway musical atmosphere with its happy ending is as unrealistic as is the fabricated story line of *Saturday Night Fever*. Even Travolta's dancing is less exciting. And his California-style Italian American Guido charm stumbles upon ethnic ambiguity, just as the Italian spelling of his name has been changed, and the ethnic origins of being a "greaser" are almost entirely hidden except for two off-color Italian phrases uttered by Rizzo and one of Danny's friends (respectively "fan culo" or "up yours"; and "puttana" or "whore"). That the last epithet is addressed to Eve Arden, the star of the famous radio and television program *Our Miss Brooks*, a 1950s icon almost as famous as *Ozzie and Harriet* and just as surely identified with straitlaced social behavior, certainly underlines the fact that the 1950s of *Grease* is a fanciful Hollywood invention.

Hollywood Italian Romeos had an enormous impact on American popular culture. Valentino, Sinatra, Martin, and Travolta have collectively shaped American ideas about what a romantic male leading actor might be in a film in important and original ways. If the silent-screen star helped establish a traditional American association of European actors with exotic and foreign romantic figures, Sinatra and Martin succeeded in presenting images of Hollywood Italian Romeos that transcended many of the conventional ethnic stereotypes. Their "dago cool" lay somewhere between the sophistication of a Cole Porter song in Frank Sinatra and the self-conscious parody of such a romantic image in Dean Martin. Only John Travolta's image in two key films of the 1970s depends upon a close identification with the same kind of lower-class Italian American stereotype already analyzed. Thus, the history of the Hollywood Italian Romeo figure covers a spectrum running from stereotypes we have already encountered in the figure of the inner-city immigrant or the palooka boxer to the more original contributions of Rudolph Valentino—the virtual inventor of the Hollywood Italian romantic lead—or those complex qualities we may identify with the "dago cool" of Frank Sinatra and Dean Martin.

4

Wise Guys:
Hollywood Italian Gangsters

"Arnie, you're through! . . . I'm taking over this territory. From now on, it's mine. Arnie, you'd better quit this racket. You can dish it out, but you've got so that you can't take it no more!"

> Rico Bandello (Edward G. Robinson) to Little Arnie Lorch
> (Maurice Black) in *Little Caesar* (1930)[1]

"L'il boy, in this business there's only one law you gotta follow to keep out of trouble. . . . Do it first, do it yourself, and keep on doing it."

> Tony Camonte (Paul Muni) to Guino Rinaldo
> (George Raft) in *Scarface* (1932)

"You know what I do to squealers? I let 'em have it in the belly, so they can roll along for a long time thinkin' it over."

> Tommy Udo (Richard Widmark) to Ma Rizzo
> (Mildred Dunnock) before he pushes her down a staircase
> in a wheelchair and kills her in *Kiss of Death* (1947)

MARTIN ROME: "How much money do you make a week?"
LT. CANDELLA: "$94.43."
MARTIN ROME: "Did you ever go to Florida a week, bet $200 on a horse?"
LT. CANDELLA: "No, but I sleep nights."
MARTIN ROME: "O.K. You played it your way, and I played it mine."

> Two Italian American childhood friends who took different paths:
> gangster Martin Rome (Richard Conte) and policeman Candella
> (Victor Mature) discuss their careers in *Cry of the City* (1948)

"After living in the USA for more than 30 years, they called me an undesirable alien. Me! Johnny Rocco. Like I was a dirty Red or something!"

> Johnny Rocco (Edward G. Robinson) to Frank McCloud
> (Humphrey Bogart) on the status of his citizenship in *Key Largo* (1948)

"Now you listen to me, you smooth talking son-of-a-bitch! Let me lay it on the line for you and your boss, whoever he is. Johnny Fontane will never get that movie! I don't care how many dago guinea wop greaseball goombahs come out of the woodwork!"

> Film producer Jack Woltz (John Morley) to Tom Hagen
> (Robert Duvall) before he receives an offer from Don Corleone
> that he cannot refuse in *The Godfather* (1972)

"Leave the gun. Take the cannoli."

Fat Clemenza (Richard Castellano) to hit-man Rocco Lampone
(Tom Rosqui) after he has murdered Paulie (John Martino) for his part in
the attempted assassination of Vito Corleone in *The Godfather* (1972)

SENATOR PAT GEARY: "I don't like your kind of people. I don't like to see you
come out to this clean country in oily hair and dressed up in those silk suits,
and try to pass yourselves off as decent Americans. I'll do business with you,
but the fact is that I despise your masquerade, the way you pose yourself. You
and your whole fucking family."

MICHAEL CORLEONE: "Senator, we are part of the same hypocrisy, but never
think it applies to my family."

Nevada's senator (G. D. Spradlin) denigrates the ethnic
background of Michael (Al Pacino) in *The Godfather Part II* (1974)

"Just when I thought that I was out, they pull me back in."

Michael Corleone (Al Pacino) on the difficulty of becoming
a legitimate businessman in *The Godfather Part III* (1990)

"Finance is a gun. Politics is knowing when to pull the trigger."

Don Lucchesi (Enzo Robutti) to Vincent Mancini (Andy Garcia)
on the relationship between money, violence, and
political power in *The Godfather Part III* (1990)

"As far back as I can remember I always wanted to be a gangster."

Henry Hill (Ray Liotta) in *Goodfellas* (1990)[2]

Hollywood Italians and the Gangster Genre

It seems clear that the linkage between criminality and Italian heritage was
established in America by the events that occurred in New Orleans at the
turn of the century, which are described in the made-for-television film
Vendetta, the first film discussed in this book. A series of crimes culminating in the largest lynching in American history (of Italian Americans, not
blacks) and the resulting possibility of warfare between the United States
and Italy could hardly fail to hold the public's attention. Careful observers
of the urban ghettos in which crime is rampant generally disregard any
ethnic explanation for crime, preferring instead to concentrate upon the
poverty of the ghetto inhabitants rather than their nationality. As Lincoln
Steffens once remarked in reply to a New Yorker who blamed Irish
Catholics for crime in the city, "The foreign element excuse is one of the
hypocritical lies that save us from the clear sight of ourselves."[3] Gang warfare in the mid-nineteenth century obviously had an ethnic element in the
great Northern cities, but gangs were generally associated with neighborhoods and were not strictly organized along ethnic lines. During the height
of Italian immigration in the United States and in New York City, gangs

flourished not only because of poverty but also because of political and social corruption. Policemen and politicians were often as crooked as the
gang leaders themselves.

   This gang world scrutinized and popularized by Martin Scorsese's *The
Gangs of New York* (2002), is based on Herbert Asbury's 1927 book of the
same name. Scorsese's film concentrates on the area south of Times Square
and in particular on the Five Points Gang that numbered some 1,000
members, and controlled territory between Broadway and the Bowery, and
Fourteenth Street and City Hall Park.[4] It is possible that Scorsese focused
on non-Italian criminals in these early New York gangs in part as a response to the repeated linkage between Italian Americans and gang violence to which, paradoxically, his own films have contributed. Italian
director Sergio Leone did much the same thing with his epic film on Jewish—not Italian American—gangsters in *Once upon a Time in America*
(1984). Scorsese's epic concentrates on the era in New York when gangs
were made up of recent immigrants (primarily the Irish) who found themselves in economic competition with the No-Nothings, self-proclaimed
"nativist" or "real" Americans—immigrants who had, ironically, arrived
only a few decades earlier. Had Scorsese placed his film in the New York
City of the late 1890s, he might well have been forced to give the narrative
something of an Italian American slant. By that time, the most important
criminal organization in the city, the Five Points Gang, was composed of
relatively recent Irish, Jewish, and Italian immigrants. Its leader was an enterprising Neapolitan named Paolo Antonio Vaccarelli who Americanized
(or more properly, "Irishized") his name to Paul Kelly. By all indications,
Kelly was a remarkable man who spoke three foreign languages (French,
Spanish, and Italian), dressed and acted like a member of fashionable and
educated society, and helped to organize the Longshoremen's Association
against other gangs hired by owners to intimidate the association's members. He ended his career quietly as a real-estate agent, remodeling the
older mansions of the rich into tenements that he rented to newly arrived
Italian immigrants.[5] At least one of Kelly's major henchmen was an Italian,
Louis Pioggi, known as "Louie the Lump." The Five Points Gang found itself in opposition to a gang led by Monk Eastman, a gang leader of Jewish
descent. Eastman eventually went to prison, was released, and served with
great distinction as a soldier in World War I. Something similar occurs in
an early John Ford film, *Born Reckless* (1930), where an Italian gangster
named Louis Beretti (Edmund Lowe) is sentenced to serve in the army
during World War I and does so heroically.

   Popular opinion could link Italian Americans to crime as a result of
historical memory of the notorious New Orleans lynchings. The fact that

Italian immigrants were deeply involved in the anarchist movement also helped to create a sense that Italian immigrants were lawless individuals. For example, Paterson, New Jersey, became famous as a textile town that numbered a great many anarchists of Italian descent. Italian-language newspapers devoted to anarchism were published in big-city ghettos as well. It is did not help the Italian American reputation for good citizenship that an anarchist named Gaetano Bresci from Paterson went to Monza, Italy, and assassinated King Umberto I on July 29, 1900.[6] After that assassination, Italians in Italy began to identify the United States as a breeding ground for anarchists and criminals, even though many of these anarchists had brought their political theory with them from Italy to Ellis Island, anticipating Benito Mussolini's frequent accusation after his rise to power in 1922 that America was a nation of gangsters. Mussolini's assertion avoided mentioning the fact that a number of American gangsters, and particularly those who were most famous, were of Italian ancestry. Mussolini came to this amusing conclusion after the enormous publicity American newspapers gave to Chicago gangland leader Al Capone, not to mention the fact that Mussolini (and virtually everyone else in Europe) eventually saw both *Little Caesar* and *Scarface,* movies based on Capone's life.

Prohibition produced the immense and previously unheard-of wealth that launched truly organized crime in America. And it is undeniable that Italian American criminals played a major role in the rise of this phenomenon in the 1920s and the 1930s. It is arguable, however, that some Italian Americans became criminals in America because of the prevailing lawlessness they encountered when they arrived here. In some ways, Al Capone's famous remark that he was born in Brooklyn and was therefore not an Italian underscores this primarily American explanation for the phenomenon of the American gangster and the rise of organized crime during the Prohibition era and afterward. One American historian, James Truslow Adams, would make a forceful case for this kind of sociological explanation in 1908, well before Prohibition created enormous wealth controlled by criminal bands who imported liquor and subsequently branched out into other profitable criminal activities, such as labor racketeering, numbers, prostitution, gambling, and drugs:

> It is impossible to blame the situation on the "foreigners." The overwhelming mass of them were law abiding in their own lands. If they became lawless here it must be largely due to the American atmosphere and conditions. There seems to be plenty of evidence to prove that the immigrants are made lawless by America rather than that America is made lawless by them.[7]

Italian American criminals before Prohibition certainly existed and generally practiced their trade primarily within the immigrant-ghetto communities, exploiting their weaker compatriots primarily by extortion and the protection racket. They may even have had some connection to the Sicilian Mafia or the Neapolitan Camorra. These small groups of ghetto criminals are usually known as the Black Hand or the *mano nera*, referring to the imprint of a coal-blackened hand that was often used to frighten Italian American immigrants in their homes. Black Hand extortion was almost always directed at wealthy immigrants who had the cash required to buy "protection" or to protect their family members from kidnapping. But the entire operation soon led to non-Italian imitators. The Black Hand became a kind of shorthand expression referring to such criminal gangs, just as Mafia has become a catchall term referring to all sorts of criminal gangs, those of Italian ancestry and those coming from very different ethnic backgrounds.[8] It is thus not surprising that the first silent films made in America about Italian American criminals focused upon this pre-Prohibition expression of Italian American lawlessness.

The Black Hand *(1906): Wise Guys in the Silent Era*

Early ethnic stereotypes branded Italian immigrants as highly emotional and sometimes prone to violence—the stereotyped image of the Mustache Pete, with his stiletto ready to take revenge for any perceived slight to his honor. This theme is central to Thomas Ince's *The Italian*, perhaps the most remarkable film made about foreign immigration in the silent era.[9] Even before Ince produced his 1915 classic, however, crime in Little Italy had attracted a good deal of attention. One of the earliest silent films that may be linked to the Italian American gangster genre is *The Black Hand: True Story of a Recent Occurrence in the Italian Quarter of New York* (1906; American Mutoscope and Biography Company). This is a film considered historically important enough to be one of the silent films recently restored by the Library of Congress. Basing its plot on the usual Black Hand extortion and kidnap schemes, the film opens with two Italians drinking wine and writing a letter in badly composed English to the prosperous owner of an Italian butcher store: BEWAR!! WE ARE DESPERUT! MISTER ANGELO WE MUST HAVE $1,000.00, GIVE IT TO US OR WE WILL TAKE YOUR MARIA AND BLOW UP YOUR SHOP. BLACK HAND. Lest the amused spectator of this film take the threat as a joke, employing bombs was apparently a weapon commonly used by the Black Hand.[10] Bombs were also the favorite weapon of the dreaded Anarchists of the period, many of whom, but certainly not all, were of Italian origin.

The Black Hand *(1906; Biograph Company). The illiterate ransom note: BEWAR!! WE ARE DESPERUT! MISTER ANGELO WE MUST HAVE $1000.00, GIVE IT TO US OR WE WILL TAKE YOUR MARIA AND BLOW UP YOUR SHOP. BLACK HAND. From Library of Congress Film Stills Archive.* Reproduced from the Collections of the Library of Congress.

This brief film (656 feet) then cuts to the butcher shop (a studio location) where the gang's extortion letter arrives by mail. Most viewers will be almost as interested in the incredibly low prices for meats (anywhere from ten to twenty cents per pound) as in the production values of the film. The butcher arms himself with a pistol. The camera then shifts outside to an authentic location—New York's Seventh Avenue—as an intertitle announces: THE THREAT CARRIED OUT. What follows is a very sophisticated use of a stationary camera to frame a number of important narrative details as people walk in and out of the camera's eye. During this very long shot down the street, one desperado walks toward the camera, while in the distance, little Maria walks down the sidewalk, perhaps to school. While one of the gang is giving Maria some candy, a carriage draws up to the curb, another man jumps out, Maria is scooped up, and the kidnapping is complete. The narrative then shifts to another studio location (the intertitle calls it THE GANG'S HEAD-QUARTERS), a junk shop. Maria attempts unsuccessfully to escape from an old woman taking care of her. Three Italian men, all with the inevitable mustaches, play cards and drink wine from the inevitable straw-covered bottle.

The action shifts back to the butcher shop, where the owner has called in the detectives, who examine the note. Note that in spite of the danger to himself and his family, this Italian American butcher has refused to follow the customs of the Old Country and the code of *omertà*. He has followed the American way, not what the Italians frequently call *la via vecchia* (the old ways) and has reported the crime to the police. Of course, the powerful opening sequence of Coppola's *The Godfather* recalls just such a situation: the undertaker Bonasera describes how he wanted to act like a good American and went to the local police when his daughter was molested, only to experience a complete disillusionment with the American justice system and to be forced to go, hat in hand, to Don Corleone for justice. In *The Black Hand*, the opposite occurs: the butcher's American response to his problem meets with success. First, in a note of comic relief, the detectives hide in the meat locker, nearly freezing to death in the process. They hop around because of the chill. When the kidnapper–extortionist arrives with a pistol to pick up his ransom, the two men literally pounce upon him as if he were a rabbit. In a concluding sequence, Maria is rescued from the kidnappers, two of whom are drunk when the police arrive.

The Black Hand *(1906; Biograph Company). The two enterprising detectives leap out and arrest the Black Hand gangsters in the Italian butcher shop. The butcher has acted as a good American citizen and has not followed the code of* omertà. *From Library of Congress Film Stills Archive.* Reproduced from the Collections of the Library of Congress.

This Black Hand theme was treated in a number of other silent films, most of which are inaccessible. As a result, we must be satisfied in most cases with reconstructed descriptions of them in several important scholarly sources or catalogues.[11] In *The Organ Grinder* (1909; Kalem Studios), an Italian organ-grinder provides information that succeeds in stopping a Black Hand kidnapping plot. It should not be overlooked that the Italian organ-grinder figure represented one of the most insulting and denigrating Italian American stereotypes of the period, since rather than identifying Italian musicians with the likes of Verdi and Puccini, it linked them to beggars and thieves. Making such a stereotype a hero took a pinch of courage. In *The Detectives of the Italian Bureau* (1909, Kalem Studios), another film about the kidnapping of a young girl by the Black Hand, the crime is thwarted because the Black Hand criminals are stopped by "courageous and honest men of Italian birth" who are "devoting their whole time to rounding up and punishing Italian criminals."[12] Such a plot provides some proof that not everyone in the film industry at the time automatically thought all Italian Americans were criminals and that some admired the courage of Italian Americans who fought crime rather than committed it. This silent film is probably the first example of what might be called the "bad-wop-and-good-wop-cop" theme, a practice of pairing a criminal ethnic character with an admirable ethnic character as the law-enforcement officer who hunts him down. This narrative twist will be particularly important in such films as *Scarface* and *Cry of the City* (1948), not to mention the more recent cop dramas *Serpico* (1973) and *Donnie Brasco* (1997), stories that stress the Italian American ethnic origins of the policemen who work undercover to destroy organized crime.

The theme of an "Italian squad" in the New York City police force reflects historical fact. At around the time *The Detectives of the Italian Bureau* was released, the New York Police Department appointed Lieutenant Joseph Petrosino to deal with Italian criminals and sent him to Italy to liaison with Italian authorities, where he was brutally murdered in Palermo in March 1909. His appointment had been based upon his ability to infiltrate Italian American gangs because of his ethnic background and his knowledge of the Italian language, not to mention his desire to disassociate his heritage from organized criminal activity. His brief but heroic career produced a four-reeler silent film entitled *The Adventures of Lieutenant Petrosino* (1912; Photoplay Company). His biography was picked up years later by Hollywood in several films devoted to Petrosino. The first film is entitled *The Black Hand* (1950; Richard Thorpe, director), in which J. Carrol Naish plays Louis Lorelli (the Petrosino figure) and Gene Kelly plays Johnny Columbo, an Italian who returns to New York to pursue a *vendetta* against the Black Hand who killed his father years earlier. The second such film is entitled *Pay or Die* (1960; Richard Wilson, director), with Ernest Borgnine cast as Lieutenant Petrosino.

Other silent films followed that focused attention upon Italian American criminals and the Black Hand or the Mafia. *The Criminals* (1913; Mecca Films) treats the kidnapping of a little Italian girl who is killed when her father refuses to pay the ransom. In *The Padrone's Ward* (1914; the Powers Company), an Italian American banker and guardian of a young girl refuses to be extorted. By accident, the Black Hand sends a man who is the girl's sweetheart to kill her, resulting in the failure of the plot and the capture of all the criminals. In *The Last of the Mafia* (1915; Sidney Goldin, director), an Italian detective is sent to New York to track Italian Mafia criminals who have come to America, and he is killed in a reversal of the events associated with Lt. Petrosino a few years earlier. An Italian American businessman is threatened by the Black Hand, his daughter is kidnapped, and a bomb explodes. The case is solved by Lieutenant Cavanaugh, an Irish Italian policeman, who rescues the girl and delivers the criminals to Italian authorities. This film points to another social phenomenon during the period, the intermarriages that frequently took place between Irish and Italian immigrants, such unions being facilitated by a common religion and close proximity in the urban ghettos that both groups inhabited.

Another interesting work produced during the same year (1915) is Thomas Ince's *The Alien*, an extremely complicated nine-reeler that presented an Italian falsely accused of a Black Hand kidnapping. It stars George Beban as Pietro Massena, the falsely accused Italian, an actor who portrayed the protagonist of *The Italian* (also produced by Ince). Beban apparently devoted a good deal of his professional life on the stage and in the movies to portraying Italian immigrants in a positive light. It should be remembered that it was Beban who persuaded Ince to call his film *The Italian* and not *The Dago*. The unusual circumstances of the release of *The Alien* in large urban areas should be mentioned here. In such venues as New York City and elsewhere with movie theaters that had large seating capacities, *The Alien* ended after its eighth reel with Pietro Massena (Beban) entering a flower shop and buying a rose for his daughter's coffin. The curtain then rose and Beban and the other actors in the film appeared onstage in person and brought the film to a close as a play. In fact, the film was itself based upon a play that Beban and Charles Dazey had written together in 1911, entitled *The Sign of the Rose*. After screenings in larger venues had taken place, a ninth reel was produced for screenings in smaller theaters in smaller cities, in which the conclusion of the play was filmed.

Poor Little Peppina (1916; Sidney Olcott, director), an important film starring Mary Pickford, presents a very complicated plot of kidnapping and intrigue that ends happily when the Mafia kidnappers of a young girl are apprehended. *The Criminal* (1916; Thomas Ince, director) is another film based upon a kidnapping of a young child, a plot so popular that it must have represented a real fear during the period. The children kidnapped are almost always female, and the rampant fear of such occurrences probably owes much to an equally common theme, that of white slavery. Most parents and law-enforcement officials apparently assumed that kidnappings were part of a larger white slavery trade. *Fair Lady* (1922; Kenneth Webb, director) treats the Mafia both in Sicily and in New Orleans in a complex tale of love and murder. Its New Orleans finale may remind us of how closely that city was tied to the Mafia of the popular imagination in the early decades of the twentieth century.

The silent cinema certainly did not depict all Italian Americans as criminals or members of criminal organizations, such as the Black Hand or the Mafia. Other ethnic groups were also linked to criminal activity, as Kevin Brownlow's *Behind the Mask of Innocence* demonstrates.[13] The definitive connection between Italian Americans and the gangster film would be established by two seminal works in 1930 and 1932: *Little Caesar* and *Scarface*. But a few key works between 1926 and 1930 set the stage for these two masterpieces by popularizing the gangster genre and, to some extent, by linking the genre to things Italian. Times were ripe for an explosion of interest in gangsters. The Eighteenth Amendment became law on January 1920, providing endless cash for gangster importers of illegal liquor for a thirsty nation whose taste for booze had not ended with the passage of Prohibition. Musicals from Broadway featured gangsters, such as the tremendous hit *Broadway*, created by George Abbott and Philip Dunning. It opened in 1926 and ran for seventy-three weeks before being sold to Hollywood for the incredible price of a quarter million dollars.[14] It probably inspired a number of films devoted to gangsters, including *Underworld* (1927; Josef von Sternberg, director); *The Racket* (1927; Lewis Milestone, director); *Chicago after Midnight* (1928, Ralph Ince, director); *The Heart of Broadway* (1928; Duke Worne, director); and *Dressed to Kill* (1928; Irving Cummings, director).

It was *Underworld* that first profited from the popularity of the gangster musical *Broadway* and helped to popularize the gangster genre in the cinema. The film was adapted from a treatment by Jewish writer Ben Hecht about Chicago and the Capone mob, but the possible Italian American content of such a narrative was changed by von Sternberg's stylish Art Deco rendering of a Chicago of his imagination, not the Chicago Hecht knew so well. Yet, audiences all over the world understood that Chicago stood for gangland crime, a fact underlined by the translation given to von Sternberg's film in France: *Les nuits de Chicago*. The completed film departs in many respects from Hecht's narrative about Al Capone. Indeed, one of the few references to Italians in it is a comic conversation between the two lead gangsters in the film, both of whom are obviously not Italian Americans. Rolls Royce, one of the protagonists, describes his gangster friend Bull Weed as "Like Attila at the gates of Rome," and Bull replies: "Who's Attila? The leader of some wop gang?"[15] *Underworld* was a very popular film, and Hecht won one of the first Academy Awards for Best Writing (Original Story) even though his original story had little to do with the film von Sternberg released. He would go on to write important scripts for gangster films with Italian American content, including *Scarface* and *Kiss of Death*.

The *Racket* represents another work that moved easily from the stage to the cinema. Originally created as a Broadway play, *The Racket* was produced by Howard Hughes, and written by Bartlett Cormack, a reporter for a Chicago paper and friend of Ben Hecht.[16] Its protagonist, an Italian American gangster in Chicago named Nick Scarsi, was portrayed by Edward G. Robinson, a Jewish-Rumanian immigrant well versed in dramatic roles from the theater who would be discovered for the title role of *Little Caesar* because of his successful portrayal of Scarsi on the stage. In the filmed version of *The Racket*, the role of Scarsi was given to another actor, Louis Wolheim. Both the play and its film adaptation were banned in Chicago (presumably the citizens of that city did not realize that criminals such as Al Capone and the corrupt policeman in his pay existed). Eight real Chicago hoodlums temporarily living in Los Angeles while things cooled down in their native city served as advisers on the film and were later quite upset with the completed work![17]

Another film that preceded *Little Caesar* and *Scarface*, *Doorway to Hell* (1930; Archie Mayo, director), appeared in the same year as the previously discussed *Born Reckless*. It actually opened one month before *Little Caesar* and chronicled the rise and fall of an Italian gangster named Lou "Legs" Ricarno (Lew Ayres). Ricarno was obviously modeled upon the Chicago gangster Johnny Torrio (1882–1957), the Italian American mobster who first organized and took control of the city's South Side and the man who brought Al Capone from Brooklyn to Chicago in 1919, handing over the city to Capone after he was wounded in an assassination attempt in 1925. *Doorway to Hell* was a smash hit, and when *Little Caesar* opened a month later, while *The Public Enemy* (1931; William Wellman, director) was rushed into production to take advantage of the growing popularity of the gangster film, the stage was set for the great surge of public interest in the genre.[18] Clarens also underscores the fact that James Cagney made his gangster debut as Ricarno's treacherous henchman in *Doorway to Hell*, probably setting him up for the selection as the protagonist of *The Public Enemy*. *Doorway to Hell* contained a number of scenes that later became familiar motifs in many other gangster pictures. One mobster flips a coin continuously (George Raft makes this tic famous in *Little Caesar*, but *Doorway to Hell* did not influence the other in this respect); a criminal goes to a plastic surgeon to make his dead brother look alive (a motif that *The Godfather* repeats with an undertaker); a tommy gun is hidden in a violin case for the first time in a Hollywood film; and speeding cars careen around street corners to the tune of gunshots. The popularity of the gangster genre in Hollywood can be measured by the fact that in 1931, the year after *Little Caesar*, twenty-five gangster films were made. The following year, in 1932, the year *Scarface* appeared, forty gangster films were produced, one-tenth of the entire industry's production.[19]

Little Caesar *and* Scarface: *the Classic Italian American Gangster*

The generic rules of the classic gangster film were formulated by the examples of three films that appeared in a brief period: *Little Caesar* (1930; Mervyn LeRoy, director); *Public Enemy* (1931; William Wellman, director); and *Scarface* (1932; Howard Hawks, director). Two of these three films present an Italian American model for the new urban, Prohibition-era gangster obviously modeled on Al Capone. In spite of the fact that Edward G. Robinson was a Rumanian Jew and Paul Muni an Austrian Jew, their interpretations of Rico Bandello and Tony Camonte—both stand-ins for Chicago's Big Al—were tremendously influential in shaping the cinematic image of the Italian American gangster. But just as quickly as this "classic" gangster formula was created, outside influences—the threat of censorship and boycotts, the rise of the Production Code in Hollywood, their controversial image of corrupt politicians and law-enforcement officials—forced the studios to modify this classic formula, and as film historian Thomas Schatz notes, this resulted in the strange fact that the gangster genre enjoyed the briefest classic period of any other genre, such as the musical, the Western, the hard-boiled detective story, the family melodrama, or the horror film.[20]

At the heart of the commercial cinema's desire to change the gangster film after the success of *Little Caesar* and *Scarface* was the very definition of what the gangster represented. During the height of the Great Depression when not only the American economy but America's faith in the dream of individual success was being threatened, depictions of outlaws who broke the rules and demanded power and respect did not fit the orthodox picture of the American dream. Because of Prohibition, the majority of Americans broke at least one law (that against drinking liquor) on a regular basis, and not a few of them had a grudging admiration for the gangster figure that seemed to rise above the economic despair of the times. Figures such as Baby Face Nelson, Bonnie and Clyde, and John Dillinger were often seen by the general population as Robin Hood figures during the Depression, although they rarely robbed the rich to give to the poor. Even more frightening to some who wished to censor or suppress such films was their depiction of the gangster, in the words of Robert Warshow, as a "tragic hero." Warshow's influential essay on "The Gangster as a Tragic Hero" (1948) and his comparison of the Western hero and the gangster figure in "Movie Chronicle: The Westerner" (1954) explore what disturbed many viewers of *Little Caesar* and *Scarface.* Warshow believed that the classic gangster film expressed "that part of the American psyche which rejects the qualities and the demands of modern life, which rejects 'Americanism' itself."[21] Its protagonist "is the 'no' to that great American 'yes' which is stamped so big over our official culture and yet has so little to do with the way we really feel about our lives."[22] In the case of both Rico Bandello and Tony Camonte, Warshow's formula for the modern American tragic hero fits each film exactly: "The typical gangster film presents a steady upward progress followed by a very precipitate fall."[23] It is because the classic gangster film focuses upon an energetic individual drive for personal success (the essence of the American cultural ideal) that it may also lend itself to metamorphic associations with larger ideas about social values. Warshow, who never lived long enough to see *The Godfather* trilogy, would nevertheless probably have agreed with one popular line of interpretation of the three films as gigantic Italian American metaphors for American culture in the broadest sense. This view is summarized in the famous exclamation of Hyman Roth (Lee Strasberg), Michael Corleone's Jewish gangster business partner, who informs his younger colleague: "We're bigger than U.S. Steel!" Implicit in that remark is the belief, or at least the assertion, that U.S. Steel and the mob really employ the same methods to reach success, the ultimate goal.

Rico Bandello presents a classic example of over-reaching ambition and hunger for raw power. He is first introduced to us in an extremely brief robbery he commits with his friend Joe Massara (Douglas Fairbanks, Jr.). For no reason whatsoever except to leave no witnesses, he murders the unfortunate gas station attendant he robs, then settles down with Joe to a meal of spaghetti and coffee. The moralistic outcome of his life is foreshadowed by an intertitle that opens the film, a biblical quotation from Matthew 26:52: FOR ALL THEY THAT TAKE THE SWORD SHALL PERISH WITH THE SWORD. Rico seems to come from nowhere. Unlike so many other Italian American gangsters in Hollywood films, he has no discernible family, no adoring mother, and no specific roots. During the opening sequences of the film, Rico's character is presented quite directly. He is uninterested in women or dancing or the normal kinds of good times most men pursue: "Dancin' ... women. And where do they get you? I don't want no dancin'. I figure on makin' other people dance." He does not drink. And it is not the money in crime that attracts him. What interests Rico is quite different: "Be somebody. Look hard at a bunch of guys and know that they'll do anything you tell 'em. Have your own way or nothin'. Be somebody." The only thing Rico seems to care about is his friendship with Joe, and this will eventually provide the "tragic flaw" in his character that destroys him. It is interesting that virtually every discussion of *Little Caesar* accepts the critical assertion that Rico's friendship for Joe has a homosexual basis when there is virtually no hint that this is the case in the film.[24] Male friendship and bonding are, of course, a very important Italian and Italian American trait and cultural theme. But unlike many Americans, Italian men do not consider physical contact—embraces, kisses on the cheek—as evidence of an effeminate or homoerotic side to their characters. That Rico places his hand on Joe's shoulder at one point in the film is very flimsy testimony to a homoerotic relationship.

Most of the Italian American symbols in the film come from the names of the characters or some of the locations. Diamond Pete Montana (Ralph Ince), one of the city's most important criminals (modeled on the actual Italian American criminal, Big Jim Colisimo, one of Capone's victims) has an obviously Italian name. Big Jim's second in command, Sam Vettori (Stanley Fields), as well as most of the members of his gang—Tommy Passa (William Collier), Otero (George Stone), and Killer Peppi (Noel Madison)—are clearly Italian Americans, and their ethnic origin is emphasized by the club out of which Vettori does business—the Club Palermo. The right-hand man of Vettori's non–Italian adversary, Little Arnie Lorch (Maurice Black) is also Italian—Ritz Colonna (Nick Bela). And the repulsive old hag who owns a fruit-and-vegetable store and who hides Rico when he is on the lam, Ma Magdalena (Lucille LaVerne), is clearly an older Italian immigrant.

The only real ethnic vignette in the film, apart from the fact that almost all the criminals in the narrative are Italian Americans, comes in a sequence featuring Tony Passa's guilt over his part in the robbery that resulted in the killing of McClure, the Police Commissioner, at the Bronze Peacock nightclub. Rico eventually kills Tony on the steps of the church as he goes to confess to Father McNeill, sent there by his honest and long-suffering immigrant mother. Here and in other films that present criminals of Italian American ancestry (such as *Scarface* or *Cry of the City*), their honest, law-abiding, and long-suffering mothers represent the best of their ethnic group's values:

You used to be a good boy, Antonio. Remember when you sing in the church, in the choir with Father McNeill. You in white. Remember? The church was beautiful. You a little boy with long hair. The tall big candles, flowers. Remember, Antonio?

The use of the virtuous mother to balance the sins of the sinful son may be compared to another popular means of presenting two sides of Italian Americans—the previously mentioned theme of "bad-wop-and-good-wop-cop" in such films as *Scarface* or *Cry of the City*. In both of these films, the nemesis of the Italian American gangster is the Italian American policeman. Having an Italian American policeman arrest an Italian American gangster represents Hollywood's idea of presenting both sides of an issue, and it was certainly a convenient means of denying that any ethnic stereotyping was involved in linking the mobsters in question to a particular ethnic group. Poor Rico has no family ties in the film. Ironically, his only "mother" in the film is the evil Ma Magdalena, who steals all his money and tosses him out into the street, telling him he will not even receive any of his money unless he is a "good boy."

The real power behind the mobsters of *Little Caesar*, known only as the Big Boy in the film (Sidney Blackmer), is clearly a member of the old WASP establishment who uses the gangsters to control the town. He was apparently modeled upon the historical figure of Chicago's corrupt mayor Big Bill Thompson. And the policeman who eventually kills Rico, Sergeant Tom Flaherty (Thomas Jackson), represents the usual stereotypical Irish cop. This points to one of the most important characteristics of Rico Bandello—his exaggerated sense of self-importance. The implication of the film is that the Rico Bandellos, Pete Montanas, Little Arnie Lorches, and Sam Vettoris are really only small cogs in a much larger criminal machine that includes the political leaders and the law-enforcement officials. Thus, Rico's nickname "Little Caesar" needs to be pronounced with the accent upon the adjective "Little." Director LeRoy undercuts Rico's megalomania in two important sequences of the film: during the testimonial dinner given to the gangster by his friends at the Palermo Club; and when Rico goes to the palatial mansion of the Big Boy to learn he has been promoted to take Pete Montana's place in the Mob hierarchy. In the first scene, Rico struts like a peacock but his coarse language and insecure personal body language underline his parvenu character. Even the gold watch he receives is stolen goods. His lack of class is confirmed immediately afterward at the Big Boy's mansion, where he gawks at the expensive furniture and thinks that the Old Master painting on the wall cost $15,000 because of its ornate frame, not its content! In real life, Robinson was a great connoisseur of modern art and, like actor Vincent Price, possessed an excellent painting collection.

Little Caesar *(1930; Mervyn LeRoy, director). Rico Bandello (Edward G. Robinson) addresses his gangster cronies at the Palermo Club.*

Rico's "tragic flaw" derives from his attachment to Joe. His meteoric rise
to power has been the result of his decisive ability to shoot first and ask
questions later, heedless of the consequences of his violent actions. Thus, he
murders the police commissioner in a robbery but manages to rise in the
criminal hierarchy, since this action inspires fear. Yet, his friend Joe knows
that he is the murderer of the commissioner, and when Joe distances himself from Rico and does not attend the testimonial at the Club Palermo, Rico
worries that Joe's desire to follow the wishes of his dance partner and sweetheart, Olga (Glenda Farrell), will lead him to betray the secret behind the
commissioner's murder. Accompanied by the sycophantic Otero, Rico confronts Joe but for the first time in his life, he cannot kill someone. As if to
underline the dramatic change in his character, Rico's face in close-up wears
a confused look and the frame goes out of focus for a moment. During the
entire film, Rico's motto has been what became a common expression in
American popular speech after the release of the film—"you can dish it out
but you can't take it." Now, Otero tells Rico "you're getting soft too" and
Otero tries to kill Joe. The result of this failure of nerve leads immediately to
his complete fall from power. Driven into hiding by what will certainly be the
testimony of Joe and Olga against him, Rico becomes a Great Depression-era

bum, first given shelter by the evil Ma Magdalena, the only mother Rico has ever known in the film. She steals all of the $10,000 he has hidden in her home, giving Rico only $150 when he leaves. Subsequently, like a skid-row derelict of the worst sort, Rico ends up in a fifteen-cents-a-night flophouse. His fall from power and grace is thus complete. One of the film's few intertitles, a legacy from the silent era, says it all: MONTHS PASSED—RICO'S CAREER HAD BEEN LIKE A SKYROCKET—STARTING FROM THE GUTTER AND RETURNING THERE.

Rico's demise comes from a clever ruse planted in the newspaper by his nemesis, Flaherty, a statement to the effect that Rico can dish it out but not take it himself. The policeman thus employs Rico's famous boast against him. This infuriates Rico, who calls Flaherty on the telephone, allowing the police to trace the call. Rico is reduced to a lonely, shadowy figure, reminiscent of so many other homeless, destitute people during the Great Depression. When Flaherty confronts him, he hides behind a billboard with a large poster advertising the musical show starring Joe and Olga at the Grand Theater: TIPSY, TOPSY, TURVY—A LAUGHING SINGING DANCING SUCCESS. Flaherty uses his tommy gun (the weapon of choice in the classic gangster film) and shoots Rico on the other side of the billboard. Rico dies as he lives—alone but defiant, his final words immortalizing Robinson's performance: "Mother of Mercy! Is this the end of Rico?" As Rico's dream of power and success is dashed, the film ends with the shot of the billboard that underlines an entirely different kind of dream world, one created by the Hollywood musicals of the period. But it, too, reminds us and the first viewers of this classic Italian American gangster film that Rico's life was also topsy-turvy, rising and falling in a meteoric manner that reminded contemporary viewers of the vagaries of their own precarious economic existence during the Great Depression. Rico dared to dream of rising above the situation imposed upon him by the difficult circumstance of the times, and even though his attempt fails, no doubt many viewers of the film when it first appeared could not but admire his refusal to accept the cards fate had dealt him.

The Tony Camonte/Capone figure in *Scarface* represents a far more complex version of the Italian American gangster. In the first place, the direction by Howard Hawks and the script upon which Ben Hecht worked make this film a far more complicated work. By virtue of its quality alone, the film challenged the norms for violence and taboo subjects subsequently associated with the infamous Production Code provided by the Motion Picture Producers and Directors Association (known as the MPAA) that really took effect in 1934, after the film's release. Indeed, a number of features of the film reflect opposition to its content. Its original title—*Scarface*—was changed to

Scarface, the Shame of the Nation—in an effort to demonstrate that its aim was to attack gangsterism, not to glorify it. Numerous cuts and minor changes in the dialogue were made to avoid offense, and even though the film is filled with violence, there is very little of it shown graphically on the screen. An alternate ending was shot in which Tony Camonte is executed by hanging, along with a very moralistic speech about how evil the gangster was and how richly he deserved to die on the gallows. This ending showed the execution by hanging rather than electrocution apparently because Hawks refused to film the alternate ending and Camonte's role was played by a stand-in, shot in such a manner that the audience is not aware that Paul Muni has been replaced. Because of the controversy over the film, its release was delayed; it was even banned in Chicago and other cities. When it finally appeared, its performance at the box office was less than expected. Hughes eventually withdrew the film from circulation, and it was very difficult even to see it until Universal Studios released it once again in 1979.[25]

Certain elements in this film make it of great interest to the history of Hollywood Italians. In the first place, it is a far more accurate portrait of the criminal (Al Capone) the film depicts, although by the time the film appeared, Al Capone was already serving time for income-tax evasion in Atlanta after being sentenced to an eleven-year term in 1931. In 1934, Capone was transferred to Alcatraz, and by 1939, his health was ruined by syphilis. He eventually died at his home in Florida in 1947.[26] Although a film tracing Capone's downfall and eventual miserable death would have satisfied the demands for a moralistic lesson in a gangster film quite admirably, Hawks and his scriptwriters were aiming at quite a different kind of image. Nevertheless, they filled the film with many of the factual incidents associated with Capone's rise and fall.

"Big Louis" Costillo (Harry J. Vejar), murdered at the opening of the film by Tony Camonte (Paul Muni), accurately reflects the old-fashioned, "Mustache Pete" approach to crime of "Big Jim" Colisimo, who was killed because he refused to move from prostitution to liquor smuggling when Prohibition began and forbade his subordinate Johnny Torrio to move into that field. In Hawks's film, "Big Louis" says: "A man-a always gotta know when he's gotta enough. I've gotta plenty. I gotta house, I gotta automobile, I gotta nicea car." Men like Rico Bandello and Tony Camonte in the movies, as well as Al Capone in real life, never had enough. Johnny Lovo (Osgood Perkins) who orders his subordinate Tony to murder Costillo in the opening of *Scarface* resembles, in some respects, the historical character Johnny Torrio, who brought Capone from New York to Chicago and who handed over control of the Chicago Mob in 1925 to Capone quite amicably (unlike what occurs in the film) after a failed assassination attempt. In *Scarface*, Johnny Lovo is executed by Tony's lieutenant Guino Rinaldo (George Raft) even though the models for these characters in the film, Torrio and Capone, were good friends and never experienced the kind of falling out among thieves that is so important to the plots of both *Little Caesar* and *Scarface*. Hawks also includes a filmed version of Capone's killing of his North Side rival, florist-shop owner Dion O'Bannion, in 1924. Capone brought in an East Coast hoodlum, Frankie Yale, to do the job. In *Scarface*, it is Tony's best friend, Guino, who takes care of this opposition to Tony's rise to power, and when he returns to report to Tony with a flower in his lapel, we know that the O'Bannion figure in the film—O'Hara—has been murdered. O'Bannion's funeral was one of the most colorful in mob history and was marked by exaggerated floral wreaths sent by his friends and enemies because of O'Bannion's love of flowers. Lavish displays of floral arrangements have become a traditional motif in gangster films, from *Little Caesar* (where Tony Passa's funeral seems taken from a contemporary newsreel documentary of a real gangland funeral) to *The Godfather* (where Don Corleone's funeral entourage contains a number of black Cadillacs filled with gigantic floral displays).

Perhaps the most famous episode in Capone's life reproduced in the film is a version of the St. Valentine's Day Massacre: the assassination of members of "Bugs" Moran's gang by Capone thugs is repeated in the film. Moran's character is called Gaffney (Boris Karloff) in the film and he, too, avoids an assassination just as Moran did by being late for his appointment. Tony's mob makes up for this oversight by murdering him later as he is bowling with friends. Tony Camonte's violent death, without ever seeing the inside of a jail cell, at the finale of *Scarface* marks a major difference between the film character and the historical Capone. Moreover, Tony's relationships to his sister Cesca (Ann Dvorak), his trusted lieutenant Guino Rinaldo, and his mother (Inez Palange) make of Camonte a far different kind of gangster than a true biography of Al Capone would have produced.

At about the same time as the production of *Scarface*, a New York theatrical agent announced that Capone would debut in his own film and would donate his two-hundred-thousand-dollar salary (a fraction of the estimated gross weekly income of some two million he was apparently making on illicit activities) to the unemployed. However, this project floundered on the Production Code's prohibition of films for charity or promotional purposes, and what would have been quite a remarkable film was never made, confining Capone's real image to the newsreels.[27]

As noted, compared to *Little Caesar*, *Scarface* presents a far more complex portrait of the Italian American aspect of a gangster boss with many additional details pointing to his ethnic origin or to stereotypes linked to Italians in general. Even before we see Tony's actual image on the screen as the film opens, a large black silhouette of his figure approaches "Big Louie" alone in the Costillo Café: the figure is whistling the sextet from Donizetti's Italian opera *Lucia di Lammermoor*. Tony's taste for Italian opera that he shares with the historical Al Capone was emphasized in the 1987 Brian De Palma film, *The Untouchables*. In one scene in that film, Capone (Robert De Niro) and the Federal agent Eliot Ness (Kevin Cosner) confront each other at the opera house. Like Capone, Tony has an X-shaped scar on his face, the explanation for the film's title. Again, just before Tony shoots his trusted lieutenant Rinaldo for what he believes is an offense to his honor—he has taken up residence with his sister Cesca during a month's vacation in Florida—Tony whistles the same Donizetti musical theme, announcing another killing. Only afterward does he discover to his horror that Rinaldo has actually married Cesca and has not besmirched the Camonte family honor.

Like Rico Bandello, many of the most important criminal associates Tony has are Italians (Costillo, Lovo, Rinaldo). In a switch from the Irish cop employed by LeRoy's earlier film, even the implacable policeman who pursues Tony to his eventual death in a hail of gunfire is an Italian named Inspector Ben Guarino (C. Henry Gordon). But in a note of realism, given the international reputation for corruption and crooked dealing that Chicago policemen had during the Capone era, Guarino wants to bring Tony down for personal reasons rather than for professional ones and would not hesitate to kill him in cold blood if he could find a means to do so without paying for it. At one point, the Chief of Detectives (Edwin Maxwell) reads Tony's rap sheet, and his description contains several details that link Tony to the historic Capone—that he was a former member of the infamous New York Five Points Gang, and that he came to Chicago from New York—both true of Al Capone himself.

The even more important Italian American character traits that delineate Tony's personality are associated with his family. Unlike Rico, who seems to have sprung from no discernible specific locale, who enters the film with no family or ties of affection outside his friendship for Joe Massara, and was interested in none of the traditional pastimes of gangsters, Tony has the kind of long-suffering Italian mother that reminds us of Tony Passa's mother in *Little Caesar*. But Mother Camonte not only serves Tony spaghetti and wine in her home. She also delivers passionate criticism of his profession and describes him as "a-no good," warning Cesca that "he don't give money to nobody for nothing." Both Tony's mother and Tony himself speak with a pronounced Italian accent, while Cesca speaks perfectly idiomatic American English. Although Tony retains many of the Old Country characteristics, especially an exaggerated and Southern Italian fixation with the sexual activities of his flapper sister, and a fear that the family honor may be sullied by her misbehavior at the tender age of eighteen, Hawks's clever presentation of him during the course of the film shows a kind of gradual Americanization of Tony. From the ugly, crude figure of the opening scenes, by the time of his demise, Tony barely speaks with an accent and has exchanged his bad taste in dress for expensive tuxedos in an attempt to cover up his ethnic background and his coarse origins.[28]

The most important aspect of the script that ties Tony to a tradition of infamous Italian behavior linked to the Borgias is the clear suggestion that Tony has an unnatural relationship with his sister Cesca that may go beyond the usual Italian obsession with family honor. In Tony's first argument with Cesca just before their mother denounces Tony as "a-no good," Cesca raises the issue of Tony's unnatural protectiveness: "You act more like . . . I don't know. Sometimes I think." Her remarks are interrupted (incest was not a theme commended by the censors or the Hollywood Production Code), but the obvious implication is that Cesca would have completed the sentence with the observation that Tony is acting more like a lover or husband than a brother. In a second confrontation that begins on a dance floor as Cesca dances much too closely to her partner, Tony becomes so angry that he rips Cesca's spaghetti strap on her evening dress, revealing a very sexy amount of skin, bra, and slip. At the film's conclusion after the police are assaulting Tony's fortified apartment, complete with steel shutters, to arrest him for the murder of Rinaldo, Cesca arrives to kill Tony out of revenge for killing her beloved husband. But in a sudden turn of events, she is unable to pull the trigger and decides to die with him. When Tony asks why she did not shoot him, before she embraces him she replies: "I don't know. Maybe it's because you're me and I'm you. It's always been that way."

This theme of incest derives from the initial suggestion of Hawks to Hecht that the Al Capone story should be told through the prism of the infamous legend of the Borgias. The role Renaissance Italy played in the Elizabethan imagination has been noted in the introduction: Marlowe, Shakespeare, and a host of other lesser lights portrayed Italy as a mysterious planet filled with papism, violence, poisonings, stilettos, Machiavellian politics, and incestuous relationships. "The ends justify the means" might be the motto for this imaginary world, and even if Machiavelli never said such a thing exactly, he was given credit for this amoral assessment of how life must be lived if men are to seize and hold power. Certainly "the ends justify the means" would be the perfect description of the moral universe of both Rico Bandello and Tony Camonte. The original screenplay of *Little Caesar* even begins with a spurious quotation from Machiavelli, making the linkage between Capone's Chicago and the Elizabethan figure of the Machiavelli villain quite clear.[29] This enormously simplified view of Renaissance Italy produced much great theater and rumormongering. The Borgia legend was born from the pages of the most important historical work written between Herodotus and Gibbon: *The History of Italy* (1561) by Francesco Guicciardini (1483–1540), a magnificent treatment of European history in the Italian peninsula between 1494 and 1534. Guicciardini was a very good friend of Machiavelli, whose name would eventually become synonymous with treachery and evildoing beyond the Alps despite his long employment in the republican government of Florence. Identifying Machiavelli with such evil behavior rather than reading more carefully both his treatise *The Prince* (1532) and his republican commentary, *Discourses on Livy* (1531) for their very complex discussion of morality and politics, became de rigeur beyond the Alps. And the identification of Machiavellian behavior with evildoing in politics seemed to be confirmed by one highly influential part of Guicciardini's history that treated the Borgia family: Pope Alexander VI (1431–1503); his sons Cesare, the duke of Valentinois (1475–1507), and Giovanni, the duke of Gandia (1486–97); and his daughter Lucrezia (1480–1519), who later married the lord of Pesaro and subsequently the duke of Ferrara. Guicciardini's narrative reports as rumor the following account of Borgia immorality: "It was equally rumored (if however it is possible to believe so great an enormity) that not only the two brothers, but the father himself, competed for the love of Madonna Lucrezia."[30]

Behind the classic American gangster film lurks the traditional stereotype of Renaissance Italy as the land of all possible evils that a misreading of both Machiavelli and Guicciardini did so much to create. But Hawks and Hecht were not the last American scriptwriters and novelists interested in gangsters who turned to the Borgia legend for inspiration. Although far less successful than *The Godfather*, Mario Puzo's posthumously published *The Family* presents a fictionalized account of the Borgia family in such a way that it obviously suggests the Mafia *famiglia* of Don Corleone or Tony Soprano.[31] A tune from Donizetti's opera *Lucia di Lammermoor* (1835) underlines Tony Camonte's worst crimes, but it must not have escaped Hawks or Hecht that just before writing that opera, Donizetti also created an equally famous opera about evildoing in the Italian Renaissance entitled *Lucrezia Borgia* (1833). *Scarface* thus manages to combine two sets of stereotypes, one as old as sixteenth-century England; and the other, more recent and associated in America with recent foreign immigration. Through the historical linkage to the Borgias, the first stereotype implicitly suggests that Tony's behavior may be explained by the Italian genetic code. The second and more recent stereotype explicitly suggests that gangsters arise from some intrinsic characteristic of Italian American culture.

Visually, *Scarface* is far superior to *Little Caesar* and shows the obvious influence of German Expressionism in its brilliantly done chiaroscuro lighting and its complex camera movements. In many respects, it provides inspiration for the rise of *film noir* in Hollywood cinema. *Scarface* also contains a visual leitmotif that is consistently developed throughout the film from the opening credits to Tony Camonte's violent death at its close. As Clarens summarizes it, the "suprarealistic" use of the *X*-motif "hovers over each impending victim" and emphasizes the "classic inevitability of tragedy," as Tony Camonte is destroyed by what Clarens correctly calls the "demons" in his own mind.[32] As the occurrences of this visual leitmotif become more frequent, part of the fascination is provided by the curious desire to locate them as the narrative unfolds. The first is a large *X* behind the opening credits. This is picked up by the X-shaped scar on Tony's face, uncovered when he is arrested in a barber shop and the towel taken off his face. Then, when Rinaldo first sees Cesca on her balcony, he is outside her window, flipping his habitual coin. She tosses him a coin, he gives the first coin to a nearby Italian organ-grinder with a monkey, and he continues flipping her coin. Part of the wrought iron balcony forms the figure of an *X*, not an auspicious sign for their future union. When the gang members murder a wounded rival in a hospital, there is an *X* on the curtain of the hospital room. During the ensuing gang war, several men are shot in public with X-figures either in the sidewalk or on traffic signs. The most obvious use of the motif is during the St. Valentine's Day Massacre, where seven X-figures are lined up on the ceiling above the dead victims. There is also a white *X* formed by the light on their bodies. When Gaffney hides out from Tony's vengeance, giving a reporter an interview, there is a white *X* behind him, and when he is finally cornered in a bowling alley, an *X* on his scorecard marks his demise. Perhaps most ominously, the X-shape of the spaghetti straps on the dress worn by Johnny Lovo's girlfriend, Poppy (Karen Morley), suggests that Johnny is not long for the world. Just before Tony shoots Rinaldo, there is a white *X* on Rinaldo's apartment door. When Cesca is killed by a ricochet just before Tony dies, there is a black shadow of a figure *X* behind the sofa. And finally, as we see "The End" on the screen, behind the letters there is another *X*. *X* indeed marks the spot in this classic film.

According to at least one account of the interrelationships between Hollywood and the Mob, Howard Hawks had contact with Al Capone during the making of *Scarface*. According to scriptwriter John Lee Mahin (who was eventually brought in to collaborate with Hecht on the screenplay), some of Capone's gang began to show up around the set. Hawks seemed to have contacts in Chicago, and the director eventually was confronted with three or four gangsters from Chicago who informed Hawks that "the boss" wanted to see the film. Capone apparently took some vacation time in California and Hawks invited him to see the rough cut of the film in a studio-preview theater. According to this report, Capone liked the film and even recognized George Raft as a member of Owney Madden's New York City gang (which he had been before he moved to Hollywood). Later, when Hawks himself went to Chicago, Capone offered him a cocktail party in his honor at the Hotel Lexington and presented him with a small machine gun as a gift. During Raft's publicity tour for the film, Capone called him in and asked him about the coin he flipped in the movie. Capone confirmed to Raft that he had, indeed, enjoyed the film and told Raft to tell his colleagues that if any of his gang had been tossing coins, it would have been a twenty-dollar gold piece, not a nickel.[33] Shortly thereafter, Capone was sentenced to eleven years in prison for tax evasion and failure to file tax returns.

As originally conceived, *Scarface* was a hard-hitting portrait of a man whose motto was "do it first, do it yourself, and keep on doing it." Even after many decades and the numerous compromises director Hawks and producer Hughes must have accepted to complete the film, *Scarface* represents the first true masterpiece in the gangster genre and, therefore, in the subcategory of those films that present Hollywood Italian Wise Guys. Neither Rico Bandello nor Tony Camonte is excused for their evildoing because of their unfortunate circumstances of birth or by the Great Depression. Instead, their will to power exposes them to character flaws that ultimately destroy

Scarface (1932; Howard Hawks, director). Tony Camonte (Paul Muni) prepares to shoot it out to the end in his home when surrounded and ordered to surrender.

them. In the case of Rico, it is his desire to be somebody and to rise above
the ignominious status of a nobody. His only flaw is friendship with Joe
Massera, a weakness that ultimately destroys him. In Tony's case, his overde-
veloped sense of Italian family honor forces him to commit a stupid crime
for which he and his sister alike pay. Machiavelli and the Borgias were in the
minds of their creators, and both Rico and Tony represent worthy Italian
American successors to the Italian Machiavels who so fascinated the English
popular imagination in the sixteenth century.

After Scarface: *The Production Code and the Erasure of Ethnic Identifiers for Hollywood Italians*

The violence and suggestive sexual themes in *Scarface* frightened many
moralists, and the depiction of Italian Americans offended the powerful
Order of the Sons of Italy, a large Italian American group that could play a
role in urban elections in the East Coast. *Little Caesar* and *Scarface* were released at the time that Hollywood was formulating the Production Code.[34]
The Motion Picture Producers and Distributors of America (MPPDA) was
formed in 1922 and became the Motion Picture Association of America
(MPAA) in 1945. It was first run by former Postmaster and Indiana political boss Will H. Hays and has always been identified with his name. By
1927, the group devised a list of topics that were entirely off-limits. These
themes included profanity, nudity, drugs, perversion, interracial marriage,
ridicule of religion, or offensive treatment of any nation, race, or creed.
Other topics, such as crime, brutality, seduction, and law enforcement,
could be treated with "special care." It should also be remembered that
films were not yet covered by the First Amendment guarantees of free expression. In 1915, in *Mutual v. Industrial Commission of Ohio*, on the contrary, the Supreme Court declared cinema to be a business, not a means of
expression, a decision that left the industry open to censorship at the local,
state, and national levels. It would not be until 1952, in *Burstyn v. Wilson*,
that the Supreme Court reversed this position and declared that the movies
were covered by First Amendment guarantees. Interestingly, this 1952 decision concerned not an American movie but Roberto Rosellini's *Il miracolo* (1948, *The Miracle*), a film scripted in part by Federico Fellini.[35]

The real threat to such self-regulation came with the advent of the talkies,
since speaking of taboo subjects opened up an entirely different range of
possibilities of offending traditional morality in the cinema. Initially, re-
garding the gangster film, the Production Code was really not seriously enforced against gangster films. But such pressure groups as the Catholic
Church, with its influential Legion of Decency, persuaded the studios that

real teeth should be put in the requirements. This resulted in the Production Code Administration (PCA) directed by Joseph Breen, and this office not only evaluated all films produced but had the ability to fine studios if they strayed from the Production Code guidelines. Now known as the Hays-Breen Office, the regulatory agency took aim at the gangster genre because it generally made the criminal the hero and did not cast either the cities of America or their law-enforcement agencies in a very positive light. The Production Code stipulated that films should not teach how to commit crimes, must not inspire any desire to imitate criminals, and could not under any circumstances make criminals heroic or justified. Criminals had also gained the sympathy of the public during the Great Depression, in part because they were initially identified with providing liquor to millions of Americans who hated the Volstead Act of 1920 and the Eighteenth Amendment of the Constitution that prevented them from drinking. When the Volstead Act was repealed after the election of Franklin D. Roosevelt in 1932, gangsters returned to more objectionable means of making money than gambling and bootlegging—extortion, prostitution, numbers, labor racketeering, drugs—which made it much more difficult to make heroes or unfortunate victims out of them in a film narrative.

The circumstances that existed when *Little Caesar* or *Scarface* were produced and those immediately afterward were quite different. Not only had Prohibition been ended but the Production Code, if adhered to in a strict manner—something that neither *Little Caesar* nor *Scarface* could be said to have done—would virtually eliminate any linkage in the cinema between ethnic groups and crime. Section 10 of the Code ("National Feelings"), in fact, required that "no picture shall be produced that tends to incite bigotry or hatred among peoples of differing races, religions, or national origins."[36] Some years after the Code went into effect, Breen's office refused their seal of approval to a project involving a biography of Al Capone in 1947 and then added a thirteenth section to the twelve other sections of the Code that prohibited any film dealing with the life of a notorious criminal using his name, nickname, or alias, and no picture based upon the specific life of any criminal would be permitted unless the character in the film was punished for his crime. As the film historian Carlos Clarens summarizes the result, "No real-life criminals were portrayed in American films from *Dillinger* in 1945 until *Baby Face Nelson* in 1957 (roughly the heyday of the *film noir*)."[37]

A completely "ethnic" treatment of Italian American Wise Guys would therefore be extremely difficult until the Production Code was abolished in 1967, as Hollywood studios reeled from the threat of television competition and sought to loosen up the rules and to allow more mature, adult themes in their pictures to sell tickets. It is not by accident that the gangster film with

the greatest ethnic content in the history of the Hollywood cinema was released only in 1972 (*The Godfather*) after the Production Code was no longer
the arbiter of how such themes could be treated. Nonetheless, pressure
groups and anti-defamation leagues were still active enough to force director
Francis Ford Coppola to avoid any single mention of the words *Mafia* or *La
Cosa Nostra* in the greatest of all Mafia films. One of these pressure groups,
the Italian-American Civil Rights League, was organized by Joe Colombo,
head of a powerful New York Mafia family, and Colombo was even shot in
the course of one of the group's protests in 1971.[38] Unfortunately, Colombo's
exploitation of the legitimate fears of honest Italian Americans that the cinema had stereotyped them by virtue of their national origin cast doubt on legitimate discussions of the problem for some time afterward. With *The
Godfather's* phenomenal success and the demise of the Production Code,
however, virtually no restrictions were left to hinder the use of Italian American Wise Guys in the cinematic depiction of organized crime.

The Road to The Godfather

Hollywood movies about gangsters from the mid- and late-1930s down to
The Godfather were often reluctant to emphasize the ethnic origins of their
protagonists, following the Production Code. Indeed, a new protagonist appeared—one that might be called the Midwest Desperado, modeled upon
the many famous gangsters such as Bonnie and Clyde, John Dillinger, Pretty
Boy Floyd, Baby Face Nelson, or Ma Barker. These criminals were anything
but foreign, spoke only English with an accent that was 100 percent American, and were anything but organized in ways that resembled the Mafia or
any other Italian American criminal association. Because in most respects
they resembled the traditional villain in the American Western, such as Jesse
James or the Younger Brothers, they made the perfect foil to the lawman, the
figure that now begins to dominate the gangster film.

   In spite of this change in the direction of the genre, a number of important
films during this period depict characters who reflect Hollywood Italian Wise
Guys, although the role such ethnic criminals play is often muted and almost
concealed by providing far fewer ethnic signifiers than we encounter in *Little
Caesar* or *Scarface*. One means of handling the problem of possible stereotyping was to combine an Italian American criminal figure with a member of the
WASP majority who attempts to understand how society might have produced such a criminal, turning the figure into the product of social or economic conditions—in short, a victim. Hollywood Italian Wise Guys also may
have their ethnic edges softened by joining them to positive Hollywood Italian figures—for example, a crusading district attorney or a lawman with the

same ethnic background as the criminal he is fighting. By playing the "bad-wop-and-good-wop-cop" card, film studios hoped to anticipate any criticism of ethnic stereotyping. After all, they did not want Italian Americans boy-cotting their products. Balancing negative figures with positive ones from the same ethnic group has always been a simple means of deflecting such criti-cism. In some cases, the Hollywood Italian gangsters themselves play down their ethnic identities, signaling a desire to pass from the violent, uncouth, and unrespectable kind of gangster Rico Bandello or Tony Camonte repre-sented toward a more socially acceptable and highly regarded figure occupy-ing an important place in respectable society. After all, even though this period was actually the high-water mark of Italian American organized crime in the United States in terms of its influence upon politicians, labor unions, and society in general, Italian American criminal figures received very little publicity after the disappearance of Al Capone. The most intelligent and pow-erful Wise Guys learned the obvious lesson Capone's real life or his fictional-ized life in the movies taught: publicity for a gangster almost certainly leads to his downfall. Any real discussion of organized crime in America would have to wait until 1950 when Senator Estes Kefauver, a Democrat from Tennessee with presidential ambitions, whipped up popular interest in what came to be known as the Kefauver Committee Hearings on crime. His hearings took place in fourteen different cities and lasted for fifteen months, and they cre-ated in the public mind the conviction that there was a national organization of predominantly Italian American Mafiosi who corrupted politicians, con-trolled gambling and most illegal activities, as well as many law officials and public servants. Millions of Americans watched the proceedings on the new medium of television. New York crime boss Frank Costello took the stand to-ward the end of the hearings on March 13, 1951. The results of his testimony were almost as momentous as those following the television debate between Richard Nixon and John F. Kennedy. Body language and a thick, five o'clock shadow destroyed Nixon for those who witnessed the debate on television, while those who heard it on radio gave the nod to Nixon. In like manner, tel-evision struck the first major blow against the Wise Guys. Costello's lawyer persuaded the Kefauver Committee not to show his face (he had sense enough to know that Costello's swarthy beard in the late afternoon would make him look like a crook). But the picture of his twisting fingers as he squirmed under questioning, his raspy voice, and his use of the Fifth Amend-ment guaranteeing him against self-incrimination left millions of viewers be-lieving that he was a mobster mastermind. Later, on November 14, 1957, the discovery that some sixty Italian American hoodlums had gathered at Apalachin in New York, a story spread immediately by television news, would only confirm the view of organized crime as an octopus stretching all over the nation. The facts were far more complex than this simplistic conspiracy-theory interpretation of the Mafia. It would take Hollywood some time before its cinematic reality caught up with the stereotypical televised image that Italian American Wise Guys were part of a vast, national conspiracy.

Marked Woman (1937; Lloyd Bacon, director) is perhaps the classic case of ethnic erasure in the treatment of Hollywood Italian Wise Guys. Yet, it opens with intertitles claiming quite falsely that the narrative is completely fictitious, an obvious tribute to the Production Code's negative view on any truly biographical treatment of a criminal figure. In fact, anyone reading the newspapers carefully would realize that the film's account of how five "hostesses" agree to testify against a New York crime czar was obviously an account of how Charles "Lucky" Luciano (1897–1962) was convicted on prostitution charges in 1936 by rising politico and crusading Special Prosecutor Thomas E. Dewey based on the testimony of several women "in the life." Luciano received a record sentence (thirty to fifty years) and languished in prison until 1946, when he was paroled with Dewey's approval, allegedly because of his efforts to keep the docks in New York clear of foreign saboteurs.

Before they died, both Luciano and his Jewish mobster friend Meyer Lansky (1902–83) alleged that at least one act of apparent sabotage (the arson attack on the liner *S.S. Normandie* in 1942) was actually arranged by the Mafia to give Luciano the excuse to keep the docks clear of sabotage, thereby gaining favor with the authorities.[39] The facts of the case against Luciano were strange at best. Luciano always maintained that Dewey had forced witnesses to perjure themselves to get him, and in fact after the trial and sentencing, key witness Florence Brown (known as "Cokey Flo" for her cocaine habit), and others signed sworn affidavits in Paris that they had lied on the stand in order to gain immunity from prosecution and financial reward.[40] Certainly the sentence of three-to-five decades of prison time was unheard of for such a noncapital offense. Dewey's racket-busting reputation won him election to the governorship of New York, but after his unsuccessful presidential campaign against Harry S. Truman, Dewey became involved in a number of business affairs that raised serious ethical questions in his later career. He invested heavily in the Mary Carter Paint Company controlled by none other than Meyer Lansky from the Bahama Islands through Swiss bank accounts, so cutting corners on the Luciano trial would not have been impossible to imagine. One wag commented that Dewey had progressed "from racketbuster to racketbacker."[41]

Marked Woman is a fascinating and unusual film. Naturally, following Production Code requirements, the prostitutes in the headlines became "hostesses" in a "clip joint," rather than whores in a brothel. "Lucky" Luciano, "Cokey Flo" and Dewey are transformed into Johnny Vanning (Eduardo

Ciannelli), Mary Dwight (Bette Davis), and David Graham (Humphrey Bogart). Although Vanning is certainly not an Italian name, Eduardo Ciannelli's performance as the Luciano figure does not conceal his Italian American origins. Ciannelli's accent is clearly that of an educated Italian who speaks English well—not the usual bad English spoken by working-class Hollywood Italian types. This is discernible from his pronunciation of certain letters in English. He combines a very slick appearance, dressing immaculately with very conservative taste as if he were a banker, with a steely gaze and an imperious manner. He even arrives on the scene with a Pekinese on a leash (obviously something he thinks connotes good breeding), and one of his mobsters is assigned to walk it. Vanning enters the Club Intime, where the girls work, and announces that he has taken over the clip-joint rackets in the city and that he will cheat the chumps in a "high class" manner. "Anybody that sticks with me gets taken care of," he tells the skeptical women, but of course the phrase "gets taken care of" can also point to the impending violence of which Vanning is capable if he is crossed by the girls. But underneath the elegant tailoring and the slick surface, Vanning is still just a hoodlum, a fact revealed by his misunderstanding of the meaning of the club's French name ("Club Intime"), which he changes to Club Intimate, a translation his upper-crust customers certainly do not require.

Director Lloyd Bacon's point of view in this film is original, since the entire narrative unfolds from the perspective of Mary Dwight, played brilliantly by Bette Davis, and the other prostitutes. Mary is brave, intelligent, tough, and street-smart and knows how to take care of herself in a callous racket. As she says as the film begins, she thinks she can handle Vanning and his new group of thugs:

> I know all the angles, and I think I'm smart enough to keep one step ahead of them, 'til I get enough to pack it all in and live on Easy Street the rest of my life. I know how to beat this racket.

Mary does not, however, reckon with her younger sister, Betty (Jane Bryan), who is being sent to college with money Mary makes from prostitution. At first, Betty knows nothing about how Mary makes her living. One evening Betty goes to a party with Emmy Lou (Isabel Jewell), and after an encounter with Vanning, she is knocked down a flight of stairs and killed accidentally, forcing Vanning to dispose of her body. Emmy Lou is a witness to this crime, but she is afraid to tell Mary, who threatens Vanning if she finds any connection between her sister's disappearance and him. She vows to get Vanning "even if I have to crawl back from my grave to do it." Mary goes to Dwight Graham, where she learns that Betty's body has been discovered, but since earlier she had helped Vanning trick Graham in a court case involving Vanning, Graham refuses to believe her this time.

When it becomes clear to Vanning that Mary and the other girls have been speaking to Graham, he wants to make sure they do not talk. Vanning goes to the boardinghouse where the girls live together, and after threatening them all, his hoods beat and disfigure Mary, leaving her almost dead in the hospital. This violence on Vanning's part inspires the girls to a courageous decision to testify against Vanning. Vanning's lawyer advises the criminal to cut a deal with Graham, since the testimony of the five women is damning. But in his arrogant reply, Vanning reveals what makes him tick, and it is exactly the same kind of drive for power that explains Rico Bandello or Tony Camonte:

> Me, I don't make no deals wit nobody. They make deals wit me. All the time I been dat way, since I was dat big. You think I care for money? All I care about is to make people do what I tell 'em . . . I ain't goin' to let no five crummy dames put the skids on me now!

It is important to note that Vanning's lower-class, Italian accent becomes much more pronounced during this diatribe about his will to power than it appears at the beginning of the film, when Vanning managed to maintain a higher-class tone. No matter how far he may wish to rise in the polite society whose vices he serves, he is still an uncouth hoodlum. Rather than wearing a scar himself, like his cinematic ancestor Scarface, Vanning scars the women he terrorizes. The trial results in a brilliant victory for Graham (the press predicts his victory might even make him the next governor, like Dewey), and Vanning receives exactly the same sentence as Luciano received at the real trial: thirty to fifty years.

Marked Woman is unusual in that it makes a woman the heroine in a courageous stand against a Hollywood Italian mobster modeled on Little Caesar or Scarface, even if the ethnic traits typical of these two earlier characters are more muted. It is Mary Dwight, and not David Graham, who emerges at the conclusion of the film as the heroine. In fact, Graham's concluding speech to the jury, which convicts Vanning, emphasizes the fact that "leading citizens" and "men of righteousness" did absolutely nothing to stop Vanning's evil rampage of crime: they were too busy or too afraid. "Frankly," Graham continues as he admits that his star witnesses are no angels, "they are everything the defense has said they are. Their characters are questionable, their profession unsavory and distasteful." But they are the only people in the entire city brave enough to stand up to Vanning. Most Hollywood Italian Wise Guy films quite naturally focus upon male protagonists. Women in the gangster film are either "molls," mistresses, wives, or mothers, but they never really take part in the world the gangsters inhabit. In *Marked Woman*, led by Bette Davis's remarkably strong and convincing performance, women take center stage.

It is amusing that while Hollywood was busily erasing ethnic traits from gangster films on a regular basis, its business relationships with Italian American gangsters sharply increased during the 1930s and the 1940s. Hollywood had more than an artistic relationship with the Mob, finding material for its films from the pages of the daily newspapers. In fact, there is a long history of a relationship, both legal and illegal, between organized crime in America and the movie industry.[42] These dealings included both personal relationships, since celebrities have always enjoyed socializing with gangsters, racketeering in movie industry unions, and even some gangsters dabbling in film production. The friendships between Frank Sinatra, Dean Martin, and various gangland figures (especially Sam Giancana), and in turn the connection between the Rat Pack, the Chicago Mob, and the Kennedy family have already been mentioned. Such a close relationship began with the arrival of Benjamin "Bugsy" Siegel (1905–47) on the West Coast, sent there by his partners in crime Meyer Lansky and Lucky Luciano to run the profitable wire services that were a key to bookmaking on the West Coast. Well before Siegel was dispatched by the syndicate to develop the casinos in Las Vegas, his base of operations for the Mob was Los Angeles, where his charm and reputation as a gangster attracted the friendship of such movie stars as Jean Harlow, Cary Grant, George Raft, Gary Cooper, and Clark Gable.

Attempts to extort money from the film industry began as early as the reign of Al Capone in Chicago, and the Chicago Mafia always played a key role in the West Coast operations, both in Hollywood and later in Las Vegas. By 1939, columnist Westbrook Pegler revealed a scandal that uncovered a great many of the illicit dealings between the Mob and Hollywood studios. Willie Bioff, the West Coast representative of the powerful Hollywood Local 2 of the International Alliance of Theatrical Stage Employees (IATSE), turned out to have a prostitution arrest dating from 1922 in Chicago. Bioff's colleague George Browne, supported by votes from mobbed-up union locals in the East Coast, became president of the IATSE. Together, Bioff and Browne aided the Mob in all sorts of illegal extortion schemes: taking payoffs to avoid projectionist strikes, protection money from all of the major studios, as well as a tax on membership dues of 2 percent. The ensuing uproar over the tax on membership led to the Pegler columns and eventually to racketeering charges leveled at both Browne and Bioff, who were sentenced to jail in 1941. The investigation also revealed that Joseph M. Schenck, president of the MPAA, acted as the middleman in the transactions, resulting in a charge of perjury and income-tax evasion, for which Schenck served a year in prison. Bioff and Browne began to talk to federal investigators by 1944 in an effort to reduce their sentences, and their testimony implicated a number of important Chicago mobsters, including Frank Nitti, Paul "the Waiter" Ricca, and John Roselli. Nitti, made famous by Eliot Ness and his "Untouchables" as Capone's underboss, actually committed suicide rather than go to prison for labor racketeering in the film studios. Bioff was later blown up in a car bomb in 1955 while living under an assumed name in Phoenix, apparently after he stupidly went to work for the manager of the Riviera Hotel in Las Vegas. Since the Riviera was a front for Chicago Mob interests, that was the end of Bioff.

Hollywood Italian Wise Guys in the Postwar Gangster Film: T-Men, Kiss of Death, Cry of the City, Knock on Any Door, Key Largo, *and* The Big Heat

Production Code regulations made it difficult to indict an entire ethnic group for being criminals, but they did not prevent a number of films from identifying their most malevolent figures with Italian American heritages. In many cases, as was previously mentioned, Italian American Wise Guys were coupled with positive members of the Italian American community, even lawmen, in order to achieve some balance. One of the most interesting of these gangster films may also be classified as one of the truly first-rate *films noir* of the period: *T-Men* (1947; Anthony Mann, director).[43] Besides the stupendous photography of *noir*-cinematographer John Alton, *T-Men* features what will become a common narrative strategy, juxtaposing the "bad wop" character with the "good wop cop" figure. Alton's photography becomes a model for low-key lighting as a major ingredient in creating the atmosphere typical of *film noir,* while Mann's visual style employs frequent low-angle shots, single-camera setups, and faces reflected in glass or mirrors to create the particularly expressionist tone so typical of the genre. But Mann also succeeds in combining this expressionist style with a semidocumentary quality by employing a voice-of-God narrator to open the film with a newsreel-like celebration of the Treasury Department's law-enforcement units and their undercover agents. This narrator continues to fill in information during the course of the film while the narrative—purporting to be a composite case file of actual T-Men activities—unfolds. The identification of Italian Americans with mobsters begins in the Treasury Building in Washington, where one high official (unlike J. Edgar Hoover, who claimed for years that crime was not organized on a national level) describes "some tie" among the various mobsters around the country, argues that to break up a counterfeiting ring in Los Angeles, the agents must work through the Vantucci gang in Detroit, and calls for two undercover agents capable of passing for mobsters with some knowledge of Italian. Obviously, without saying so directly, the Treasury executive identifies organized crime with Italian Wise Guys. One of the two men chosen is Dennis O'Brian (Dennis O'Keefe), who has apparently already worked against Italian American mobsters, since he is described as the man who previously broke up the Maserati gang. O'Brian is Irish but grew up on Mulberry Street—the famous Little Italy of New York City. His partner is an Italian American named Tony Genaro (Alfred Ryder), who speaks fluent Italian, has graduated from the University of California, and comes from the Indianapolis office.

Assigned to penetrate the Italian American Vantucci mob in Detroit headed by Luigi and Carlo Vantucci, O'Brian, and Genaro—calling themselves Manny Harrigan and Tony Galvani—present themselves after extensive rehearsals of their roles at a local hotel where the owner, a figure well known to local policemen, named Pasquale (Tito Vuolo), sizes them up as fugitive gangsters that might be of interest to his patron, Vantucci (Anton Kosta). This allows Mann to have Galvani and Pasquale engage in a conversation in excellent Italian. When O'Brian goes to Los Angeles, he encounters an important Mob boss, another Italian American Wise Guy named Triano (John Wengraf) who lives in a mansion in Beverly Hills and who has received a favorable report about him from Vantucci in Detroit. Triano resembles Johnny Vanelli with perfect English grammar and a slight but educated Italian accent. In one of the film's climactic scenes, Triano discovers that Galvani is a treasury agent and has him killed beneath the eyes of the other undercover agent, who, unable to stop the murder, must remain silent in order to protect the investigation. *T-Men* thus makes a number of statements about gangsters: they are mostly Italian American, they are organized on a national scale (in spite of Hoover's protests to the contrary), and they are vicious, requiring other Italian Americans with a knowledge of Italian American culture and language to put their lives on the line in order to infiltrate their ranks. The irony of the film is that when O'Brian eventually breaks the case, the top man turns out to be named Oscar Gaffney, clearly not an Italian American, and a well-known philanthropist and antiques dealer who cooperates with the Vantuccis and other Wise Guys.

Other ironies are connected with the production of *T-Men*. Los Angeles hoodlum John Roselli served a three-year sentence for entertainment-industry racketeering, a conviction made possible by the testimony of Bioff and Browne. After his release, he returned to Hollywood and produced a number of minor gangster films without, however, receiving wide public credit for them. In fact, one of those three films he produced was *T-Men*. Roselli also produced *He Walked by Night* (1948; Alfred Werker and Anthony Mann [uncredited], directors), a police procedural drama about a psychopathic cop-killer; and *Canon City* (1948; Crane Wilbur, director), a film about a prison break. Obviously a mobster with a sense of humor, Roselli returned to working for the Chicago Mob in Hollywood after he was released from jail.[44] Years later, both Sam Giancana and Roselli were implicated in the infamous Operation Mongoose, the alleged plot organized by the CIA and the Mafia to assassinate Castro. Most accounts of Operation Mongoose conclude that the Mafia simply defrauded the CIA out of money, realizing that any such assassination scheme in Cuba (a place they knew much better than the CIA after years of running casinos there) was doomed to failure. Nevertheless, it was dangerous even to speak of such affairs. Giancana was assassinated before he could testify before Senator Frank Church's Senate committee investigating the alleged plot. Roselli did, in fact, testify five days after Giancana's murder and although he revealed very little, he, too, was in turn murdered, his body eventually turning up in an oil drum floating in the ocean off the coast of Florida.

Kiss of Death (1947; Henry Hathaway, director) ranks as one of the most important *film noir* narratives Hollywood produced. Its urban realism may well reflect the filmmaker's admiration for the Italian neorealist classics that were becoming popular at the time. Hathaway's *noir* version of New York City in *Kiss of Death* opens with an intertitle statement affirming that all the interior and exterior scenes in the film are real, and indeed one of the work's most interesting features is this photographic realism, capturing such landmarks as the skyline, the Chrysler Building, and the city's mean streets. These real locations are particularly effective in the opening sequences that narrate a jewel robbery in the Chrysler Building and make particularly impressive use of the cramped elevators filled with passengers but traveling at extremely slow speeds while the anxious robbers must act calm and cool as they descend to the ground floor. Like *T-Men* and so many other *films noir*, *Kiss of Death* has a narrative voice-over providing explanatory commentary on the film. In this case, the narrator is a woman, Nettie Cavallo (Coleen Gray), an Italian American girl who we later discover has become the second wife of Wise Guy Nick Bianco (Victor Mature).

For the first time in a film considered in this book, the point of view of the film—identical with that of the narrative voice—explains and partially condones the crimes committed by a Hollywood Italian Wise Guy. Basically, the film contends that Nick Bianco's mistakes are caused by poverty and a disadvantaged childhood. As the film begins, the camera focuses upon busy New Yorkers (most of them prosperous) doing their Christmas shopping. But Nettie's voice informs us that Nick Bianco is unable to find a job because of his background and so a jewel robbery is how he buys presents for his two daughters. Nick is apparently a decent person but he is plagued by bad luck that runs in the family. As he tries to get out of the building after the robbery, he is shot in the leg by a policeman. Nettie's voice immediately provides us with extenuating circumstances, as she explains that the same thing happened to Nick's father when he was killed by a policeman in a robbery as Nick looked on. His father's murder was one of Nick's earliest memories. Little Caesar and Scarface were psychopaths, and their depiction left the audience with the feeling that the gangsters had deserved their death in a hail of police bullets. But excuses are found for Nick, excuses that derive from sociological or economic explanations of criminal behavior, especially among disadvantaged ethnic groups in urban ghettos.

Nettie's narrative voice gives the film its tone and moral dimension. Because of it, we know that Nick, who is decent at the core, can be redeemed. Two other Italian American figures are included in the film, as if the director wished to provide two examples of a continuum—one positive Hollywood Italian, one negative Hollywood Italian, and Nick Bianco in the middle with the potential for going toward one of these two opposite moral positions. The good Hollywood Italian is the Assistant District Attorney Louie DeAngelo (Brian Donlevy), who demonstrates that there is nothing genetic about Italian crime. Such casting goes beyond the more simplistic "bad-wop-and-good-wop-cop" technique, since DeAngelo has gone beyond the working-class occupation of policeman to attend college and then law school, proof that Italian American social mobility is possible in American society of the period. Like Nick, he has a family, and he attempts to persuade Nick to give up the other members of the gang (two out of three were Italian Americans) who robbed the jewelry store by an appeal to Nick's two daughters. Nick's refusal signals that he clings to the Mafioso's code of *omertà* and trusts in the syndicate's usual promises to take care of a felon's family during the time he spends in prison without talking.

In direct contrast to DeAngelo's successful career as an Italian American lawyer defending justice is Italian American psychopath Tommy Udo (Richard Widmark), who informs DeAngelo that "I wouldn't give you the skin off a grape." He admires Nick's refusal to become a squealer, pronouncing him a "stand up guy." The Udo part was Widmark's first screen role, and for his outstanding performance, he received an Oscar nomination for Best Supporting Actor. Udo's opinion of squealers is low in the extreme (as reflected in his famous statement cited at the beginning of the chapter), and he viciously murders an old woman, the mother of Nick's partner in the jewel robbery, Pete Rizzo, in an effort to find out where Rizzo has hidden when the syndicate falsely believes that Rizzo has begun to talk about the organization. Nick goes to prison without revealing anything, a place where, as Nettie's voice-over announces, there are "plenty of jobs and no prejudice" of the kind that kept Nick from finding a job before. Thus, while the Rizzos and the Udos represent Italian American contributions to the Mob, the Cavallos and the DeAngelos stress another possible ethnic outcome: Nick Bianco remains in the middle and ultimately goes straight because of the love of his wife more than the aid of the assistant district attorney.

Three years pass after Nick goes to prison. Meanwhile, he discovers that his first wife has committed suicide, in despair, because of her poverty and the false promises of the syndicate to reward Nick for his silence. Moreover, Nettie (once the babysitter of the family) has told Nick that his first wife was also having an affair with Pete Rizzo, his partner in crime. Driven to desperation by news of his wife's death and the fact that his children are in an orphanage, Nick decides to "squeal" and to become the underworld's most hated figure—the informer. He works with DeAngelo to jail Udo, who has now become one of the underworld's most vicious enforcers. The district attorney suggests to Nick that they put out the word that it is Pete Rizzo who is informing on Udo. "Your side of the fence is almost as dirty as mine," remarks Nick, and DeAngelo retorts: "With only one big difference, we hurt bad people, not good ones."

Kiss of Death *(1947; Henry Hathaway, director). Italian Americans on different sides of the law: Assistant District Attorney Louis DeAngelo (Brian Donlevy), psychopathic murderer Tommy Udo (Richard Widmark), and Nick Bianco (Victor Mature).*

No *film noir* could possibly accept such a cut-and-dried separation of good and evil in its moral universe, and *Kiss of Death* immediately uncovers the weakness of the forces of good and the power of those of evil. The cruel outcome of the false report that Rizzo has begun to talk is the brutal murder of Rizzo's Italian mother in a scene that is among the most famous murder scenes in *film noir,* as the giggling and smiling Udo pushes the paralyzed woman down a staircase in her wheelchair. Nick hands DeAngelo all the information he should need to convict Udo, but in contrast to the original deal he made with Nick, DeAngelo forces Nick to provide testimony personally, thereby marking him as a stool pigeon in the eyes of the syndicate, including especially the vengeful Udo. Then DeAngelo fails to deliver on any of his promises: newspapers provide publicity about Nick's testimony and DeAngelo even loses the case to the shyster Mob lawyer Earl Howser (Taylor Holmes), who runs circles around DeAngelo.

After his acquittal, Udo warns Nick with a demented grin: "We are going to have some fun together just like we used to" and that his wife and two daughters are "going to have some fun too." Nick rejects DeAngelo's ineffectual attempts to offer help and compares him unfavorably with Udo: "He's nuts and he's smarter than you are . . . there's only one way to get Udo and that's my way." Nick decides to use Udo's fixation with shooting squealers in the belly to keep him away from his wife and two daughters, but in so doing he has to risk sacrificing his own life. Provoking a confrontation with Udo outside a restaurant, Nick taunts him to do his own dirty work so that he, and not one of his gang, will be the one to shoot him in the belly. Nick has promised DeAngelo that he will deliver Udo on a "silver platter," and the crazed gangster forgets that he is a three-time loser and that even being arrested carrying a gun will send him to prison for life. He shoots Nick in the stomach five times just as the police arrive and shoot Udo. Nettie's voice-over accompanies Nick in the ambulance to the hospital, emphasizing the fact that he may well survive: "Sometimes out of the worst comes the best . . . I got Nick" she informs us.

Nick Bianco represents quite a different kind of Hollywood Italian Wise Guy. Although born in poverty and with a father who is a criminal, Nick can still be redeemed by an act of will but not by society's legal institutions. He must run the risk of dying in order to defeat the psychotic killer Tommy Udo, whose constant repetition of his determination to become a "big man" recalls the drive to power typical of not only Little Caesar and Scarface but also Johnny Vanning. Redemption for Nick is found in a personal act of courage in defense of his family and not in adherence to a more lofty set of values. It is *la famiglia,* that bedrock Italian American institution, which makes his redemption possible and provides what link exists in the film between the good Italian American (DeAngelo) and the Italian American capable of redemption (Nick). Only Tommy Udo has no family, and he is, therefore, beyond saving.[45]

Cry of the City (1948; Robert Siodmak, director) repeats some of the elements of *Kiss of Death*, which made that film such a hit with the public. Victor Mature is recast as a Hollywood Italian policeman, Lieutenant Candella. Like Nick Bianco, he has come from the slums but has made something of himself. The film contrasts Candella to another Hollywood Italian gangster, Martin Rome (Richard Conte), who at the opening of the film lies wounded in a hospital bed. Candella and Rome are childhood friends, and the policeman has spent many happy moments around the Rome family table, eating with the boy who has become a hardened criminal. The Italian American ethnic background shared by the protagonists of *Kiss of Death*, muted in many respects, is now emphasized in *Cry of the City*, and Martin Rome's parents have a heavily pronounced Italian American accent. Siodmak's expressionist background relies more heavily upon studio-created settings than did Henry Hathaway's film, which emphasizes real urban locations in both interiors and exteriors. Both films exploit the dark skyline of New York City as a visual motif, an almost obligatory image for a *film noir* set in this city.

The plot of *Cry of the City* seems more contrived and confused than the relatively simple narrative of *Kiss of Death*. A shyster Mob lawyer named W. A. Niles (Berry Kroeger) appears at the hospital bed of Martin Rome, who he thinks is dying, and tries to persuade Rome to confess to a crime that he did not commit—the De Grazia jewel robbery and murder—in order to save another of his clients. Rome refuses and throws the lawyer out of his room. The old childhood friendship of Candella and Rome is emphasized by a scene that features Candella visiting the Rome household, where the policeman even calls Mrs. Rome "Mamma," showing how close their ties really are. There are Italian and American flags in the living room on either side of a portrait of the Virgin Mary, calling attention to the Rome family's patriotism and their Catholicism. The family speaks Italian as well: they are first-generation Italians whereas their criminal son, like Candella, was born in America. Martin's younger brother Tony (Tommy Cook) shows how easily immigrant children could head for the wrong side of the tracks, however, because of the contempt he shows for Candella's profession as a law-enforcement officer, rudely calling him "a copper." He seems ready to follow his brother into a life of crime. Candella takes some of Mamma Rome's soup to the hospital for his criminal friend Martin, where the exchange cited at the beginning of the chapter takes place, juxtaposing an honest Candella, who works for a living, to the dishonest Rome, who thinks "only suckers work" and wants anything but to "be a square." Although everything about Martin Rome's actions is reprehensible, Richard Conte's performance makes him a thoroughly likable criminal, a man worthy of Candella's friendship.

Martin escapes from the hospital and goes to the shyster lawyer's office to hide. When Niles shows up, Rome offers to sign a false confession to the De Grazia strangulation and robbery if the lawyer will give him $10,000, but the conversation degenerates and Rome eventually kills the lawyer and empties the office safe containing the De Grazia jewels. He then goes to his mother's house where his honest father orders him out of the family home. His long-suffering Italian mother (another traditional theme in the depiction of the gangster family) first bandages his wounds but then, realizing that her son will never become an honest man, orders him to leave. At that moment Candella arrives, suspecting that Rome has come home, but Rome pulls a gun on him in the family kitchen and escapes in a car driven by his moll Brenda (Shelley Winters).

The film's plot becomes even more intricate than the simple juxtaposition suggested by the theme of the "bad-wop-and-good-wop-cop." Rome discovers that a demented masseuse named Rose Given (Hope Emerson), with

Cry of the City *(1948; Robert Siodmak, director). Italian Americans on different sides of the law: gangster Martin Rome (Richard Conte) with his brother Tony (Tommy Cook) by his side holds a gun on childhood friend Lieutenant Candella (Victor Mature) in the kitchen where both men used to share Mrs. Rome's (Mimi Aguglia) meals.*

incredibly strong hands, has strangled Mrs. De Grazia and is one of the criminals behind the De Grazia jewel robbery. He goes to her massage parlor to strike a bargain: her assistance in his escape in return for some of the jewels she has stolen that had been hidden in the lawyer's safe by her accomplice, the lawyer's client, where Rome found them. Hope Emerson's performance as the psychotic Rose is almost as sinister as that of Richard Widmark as Tony Udo in *Kiss of Death*, and like Widmark, Emerson almost steals the show.

Ultimately, good must triumph over evil, and at the conclusion of the film a confrontation of the two former childhood friends results in the shooting of Martin Rome by Candella. Just before Candella shoots, he shouts "In the name of the law, Rome, stop!" That final exclamation separates the two friends into very different moral worlds. Martin's brother Tony arrives on the scene, and in a rather sudden and unexpected transformation of his attitude about Candella, he informs Candella that Martin is dead, and the two men walk away from the dead gangster, Tony crying on Candella's shoulder. Apparently, Tony and the Rome family have lost a son and brother but have gained a surrogate son and brother in Candella, a change foreshadowed by Candella's earlier address to Mrs. Rome as "Mamma."

The classic gangster film of the 1930s suggests no mitigating factors in the delineation of the character of its protagonist. Little Caesar and Scarface are psychopaths, pure and simple. Between the advent of these early films and the end of World War II, other, more understanding and compassionate explanations of crime had begun to undermine this simplistic explanation for the existence of the Bandellos and Camontes produced by Italian American ghettos. One such important study was William Foote Whyte's *Street Corner Society: The Social Structure of an Italian Slum*, first published by the influential University of Chicago Press in 1943.[46] Whyte's analysis of the members of Italian American street gangs has become a sociological classic, republished dozens of times since and required reading for social workers in the inner cities of America. *Street Corner Society* offers a basically compassionate explanation for Italian American crime and argues for more efforts on society's part to engage immigrants so that their desire to become assimilated Americans is not thwarted by prejudice and poverty. *Kiss of Death* offers a similar sociological argument in favor of disconnecting the popular prejudices linking Italian heritage and crime, particularly by the narrative voice-over provided by Nick Bianco's second wife, Nettie, who argues that ethnic prejudice against Nick's background made it impossible for him to find honest work. Extenuating circumstances are also implied in *Cry of the City* and *T-Men*: each film argues that Italian Americans may well succeed not only in honest work but as law-enforcement officers if their character and drive are strong enough to prevent their environment from corrupting their positive values, as it had in the case of their criminal Wise Guy adversaries. *Knock on Any Door* (1949; Nicholas Ray, director), on the other hand, seems determined to include every possible cliché about innocents in a disadvantaged environment who are forced to turn to a life of crime.

Knock on Any Door opens with a scene shot on a studio location: the brutal murder of a policeman by a man fleeing the scene of a robbery. In a subsequent police roundup of suspects in the area, Nick Romano (John Derek in his debut), known as "Pretty Boy" Romano for his handsome looks and fulsome head of jet-black hair, is arrested. He calls Andrew Morton (Humphrey Bogart), a prominent lawyer who, we later learn, also grew up in the same city slums but made something of himself. Romano plays on Morton's liberal guilt, since he had earlier defended Romano's father but through inattention had allowed his father to be sentenced to prison for murder, where he died shortly thereafter, when he clearly should have been released because the so-called crime was done in self-defense to protect his business. Morton decides to take Nick's case not only because of his own guilt over Nick's father but also because he comes from the same milieu, but his uptown law employers tell him bluntly that taking such a case will destroy any chance he might have of becoming a partner in the firm.

True to his liberal leanings, Morton takes the case. His adversary, District Attorney Kerman (George Macready), is something of a fanatic. He seems to have a personal grudge against Romano because of his good looks. Interestingly, Kerman has an *X*-shaped scar on his face that reminds us of the protagonist of *Scarface*. Most of the film is narrated in a series of flashbacks that uncovers Nick's background, while Morton is somehow allowed to ramble on to the jury about Nick Romano's past and Nick's relationship to Morton. Through these flashbacks, the spectators come to understand that Morton's argument that environment causes crime constitutes his best defense of his client. We discover that Nick's father was sentenced in part because he could not speak English well and the prosecution "made a monkey out of him" during the trial. Ray offers one more variation on his scene of the long-suffering Italian immigrant mother who speaks a very good form of Italian (certainly not any Southern dialect), as does John Derek. A social worker arrives, Miss Patterson (Candy Toxton), who apparently understands Italian, and she eventually becomes Morton's wife. After his father dies in prison, Nick grows up in a Chicago slum where other Italian American kids attack him and eventually bring him into a street gang like the ones studied by Whyte. Nick fights with his mother, who says he is a bad boy who has stopped going to Mass and contrasts his present delinquency to his past service in the church choir. But his negative environment and bad company land Nick in reform school, which offers no reform but nurtures his propensity toward criminality. At this point in Nick's story, Morton tells the jury "life is based on one law—fear" and that Nick and others in this hellish reform school live "without hope—except some day, get out, get even."

By the time Nick Romano leaves reform school, he has become—at least in Morton's bleeding-heart-liberal opinion—a hardened case. His transformation from choir boy to potential criminal is best embodied in his famous motto: "Live fast, die young, have a good-looking corpse." He delivers this personal philosophy while in the local Italian American barber shop, where he obviously spends a great deal of time attending to his distinctive hairdo. As if to signal to others than he desires to be a real gangster, Nick wears the same kinds of sharp clothes (fedoras, double-breasted suits) that gangsters both in the movies and in the newsreels sported at the time that the film was made. From Morton's perspective, shaped as it is by sociological apologies for criminal behavior, Nick attempts to fight the inevitable fate awaiting him, falling in love with a good girl named Emma (Alene Roberts).

From time to time in the film, Morton returns from narrating a flashback to the present and directly addresses the jury, telling them that Nick tried to hold jobs but was constantly the victim of peer pressure at the pool hall from his ghetto buddies or from overbearing bosses, whose criticisms caused him to break out in fits of rage. When he is fired for smoking on the job by a particularly unpleasant boss, Nick explodes and decides to turn to crime rather than honest work, and even his wife's protestation that she is expecting a child does not deter him: "No baby! Give it away to somebody . . . what I used to say still goes: live fast, die young, and have a good-looking corpse." In short order, Nick goes off the deep end, takes part in a robbery, and is immediately arrested. During this robbery, his desperate wife commits suicide with the gas oven in their small apartment. Ray's camera cuts from Romano's discovery of his dead wife's body to a high-overhead shot from the rooftop down on the entrance to a church, where his wife's coffin is being placed in a hearse. Nick is now on the run and soon afterward is arrested for his second robbery in which a policeman is killed.

Largely persuaded by his own impoverished background and his liberal guilt, Morton believes Romano's claim that he is innocent. The entire film delivers what must be considered the textbook version of the argument that nurture, not nature, causes crime. Ray's flashbacks and Morton's explanations advance the thesis that Romano was made a criminal by society and virtually exonerates him of any personal responsibility. Morton's skill as a courtroom lawyer essentially demolishes all the witnesses against Nick, but the aggressive district attorney's constant use of the nickname "Pretty Boy" begins to undermine Nick's confidence. Incredibly, in a fit of rage at the district attorney's mention of his wife's death by suicide and his own sense of guilt, Nick breaks down under questioning and admits his guilt when a verdict of innocent was virtually assured.

Morton's argument before Nick's sentencing seems not to have been undermined at all by Nick's confession. In his plea for mercy, Morton says that Nick is guilty of many things—of knowing his father died, of being reared in poverty, of having bad friends, of hanging around in pool halls and bars as a boy, of receiving brutal treatment in reform school. Basically, in a declaration that explains the film's title but should strike even modern audiences, constantly bombarded by claims of victimhood from one minority group or another, as ridiculous, Morton declares that society must be blamed for the crimes attributed to Nick, who implicitly becomes the real victim:

> Nick Romano is guilty, but so are we . . . and so is that precious thing called society . . . society is you and you and you [pointing to the jury] and all of us. We, society, are hard and selfish and stupid. We are scandalized by environment and we call it crime. We denounce crime and yet we disclaim any responsibility for it. And we lack the will to do anything about it. Until we do away with the type of neighborhood that produced this boy, ten will spring up to take his place . . . a hundred . . . a thousand. Until we wipe out the slums and rebuild them, knock on any door and you may find Nick Romano! [here, the camera cuts to another obviously Italian American "Guido" in a tight T-shirt who is combing his long black hair with a comb like "Pretty Boy" Romano] . . . If he dies in the electric chair, we killed him!

Ray's camera then cuts to a very high angle shot (that of the sentencing judge) down on both Morton and Romano, showing that the judge will condemn Romano to death. In the last sequence of the film, we see Nick from behind in a long shot down a corridor leading to the execution chamber: his head has been tonsured so as to allow the electricity to pass more easily through his body. True to his nickname, "Pretty Boy" Romano, as he stares back to look at Morton, he turns around and combs his hair one last time before dying. While Morton stands in the left of the frame and THE END partially covers Romano in the distant long shot at the end of the corridor, the condemned man enters a room bathed in a diffused light that symbolizes his martyrdom.

The questionable premise of *Knock on Any Door*—that an Italian American slum automatically produces crime and turns innocent boys into hardened criminals—provides an unintentional parody of postwar sociological studies like Whyte's *Street Corner Society*, few of which ever

Knock on Any Door *(1949; Nicholas Ray, director). Lawyer Andrew Morton (Humphrey Bogart) attempts to defend "Pretty Boy" Romano (John Derek), a punk gangster who relies on his looks and innocent face to convince a jury he is not guilty.*

argued such a simple-minded and direct link between environment and criminality. Ray seems completely unaware that Morton's own slum background provides a persuasive counterargument, and the fact that absolutely no sympathy is aimed during the film at the true victims in the story—the dead policeman, his family, or Nick's dead wife—makes *Knock on Any Door* difficult to take seriously when compared to the far more complex narratives of *T-Men, Kiss of Death,* or *Cry of the City.* These films hold criminals responsible for their actions. At the same time, Ray's film offers the strongest case Hollywood cinema produced for explaining Italian American Wise Guys by the poverty-stricken slums in which they were reared rather than simply blaming their bad behavior on their ethnic background. Morton's argument at least has the merit of being applicable to any minority ethnic group in any urban ghetto. It also belies the popular prejudice held by most Americans who were not of Italian descent during the era in which the film was produced that Italian American culture and criminality were virtually synonymous.

American society had changed markedly during and immediately following World War II, and with the end of Prohibition organized crime changed as well. In spite of the admittedly attractive cinematic qualities of gangsters like Rico Bandello and Tony Camonte, in the real world such psychopathic, publicity-seeking mobsters were a real threat to the true business of criminals—making money. Two famous films made within a decade after the cessation of hostilities—*Key Largo* (1948; John Huston, director) and *The Big Heat* (1953; Fritz Lang, director)—reflect Hollywood's search for a different environment within which to place its Italian American Wise Guys. The first work by Huston is based upon a 1939 Broadway play by Maxwell Anderson, whose earlier play *Winterset* (1935), originally a loosely based retelling of the Sacco and Vanzetti case, had become in 1936 a gangster film directed by Alfred Santell. The film version of Anderson's play starred Edoardo Cianelli in the role of Italian American gangster Trock Estrella. Since Santell's film argued that Sacco and Vanzetti were innocent of a crime actually committed by Trock Estrella, it naturally appealed to Italians abroad who had been incensed over the execution of the two famous anarchists. Santell's *Winterset* won the Best Cinematography award at the Venice Film Festival of 1937 and was even unsuccessfully nominated for the Mussolini Cup, the festival's most prestigious award. Paul Muni, the star of *Scarface*, played the leading role in Anderson's play on Broadway, a Spanish American war deserter who fights off bandits. Huston changed the plot of Anderson's play dramatically, focusing upon mobsters who take over a Key Largo resort hotel on the off-season as a jumping-off place for their trip to Cuba, and the war deserter becomes war hero Major Frank McCloud (Humphrey Bogart), who visits the key in order to pay a visit to the family of one of his soldiers who died in the battle of San Pietro in the Italian campaign. Interestingly enough, John Huston was also the director of what has been called the greatest documentary film about World War II, *The Battle of San Pietro* (1945), a masterpiece virtually cut into pieces by wartime censorship. Huston's film detailed the great human costs (some 1,100 American lives) that were incurred in a fierce battle between American troops and German forces near Rome. No doubt, Huston meant to honor the bravery of the men he observed in that bitter Italian campaign.

Although McCloud is presented as a cynical, hardened man whose war experiences have turned him into someone who rejects the kinds of heroics that resulted in the death of his comrade in Italy, Bogart plays the same kind of cynic that he made so famous in the role of Rick Blaine in *Casablanca* (1942; Michael Curtiz, director). No matter how much he protests in *Key Largo* that he has put aside heroism, the audience knows that in the final confrontation between McCloud and Johnny Rocco (Edgar G. Robinson, the coarse gangster trying to make his escape to Cuba), the cynical McCloud will prevail. Johnny Rocco represents one of Robinson's finest performances as an Italian American Wise Guy, and in many respects *Key Largo* recalls *Little*

Caesar much in the same way that Raoul Walsh's *White Heat* (1949) starring James Cagney playing the role of Cody Jarrett provides an intentional commentary upon the famous James Cagney performance as Tom Powers in *The Public Enemy* (1931; William Wellman, director). Since the gangster genre was virtually created by *Little Caesar, Scarface,* and *The Public Enemy,*—all released within a brief, two-year period (1931–32), Huston's re-creation and modification of the Rico Bandello role in the character of Johnny Rocco makes an important contribution to the creation of a very different kind of Hollywood Italian Wise Guy.

Johnny Rocco represents the last of a dying breed. His nostalgic description of the "old days" when he was the top mobster in the United States and visited Florida for his vacations to sample the pompano and champagne reminds us both of Al Capone's habitual vacation spot, and Scarface's Florida vacation, which provides his sister Cesca the opportunity to marry his main enforcer. McCloud calls Rocco "the one and only Rocco," and marvels that he has not been deported, prompting Rocco's famous retort about his mistreatment by the American authorities as if he were a communist. Huston was certainly attuned to the contemporary fears about communist infiltration of American life that eventually grew into the McCarthy-era persecutions of dissenters, but he was not above a humorous description of mobsters as super-patriots. McCloud's description of Rocco as not just the biggest of the big mobsters—not just a king but an emperor—is meant to be taken ironically. But Rocco, a megalomaniac after the models of *Little Caesar* and *Scarface,* interprets McCloud's words literally and proves in an outburst how out of step he is with the postwar period, a time requiring a more sophisticated Wise Guy: "When Rocco talked, everybody shut up and listened. What Rocco said went. Nobody was as big as Rocco. I'll be like that again, only more so. I'll be back up there one of these days, and then you're gonna really see something." Before long, Rocco claims, he will be back bribing politicians and policemen and controlling people. Rocco's motto is that he simply wants "more," just like the character Nick Bandello upon whom his persona is modeled. Moreover, when McCloud tells him he is no hero and that all he desired from the war was a world without the likes of Johnny Rocco, the gangster tries to humiliate McCloud by daring him to shoot him with a pistol (one he has, of course, unloaded).

McCloud, however, only rises to the occasion when he has a chance to succeed. Even dressed in gangster chic—two-tone shoes, Panama hat, double-breasted suit with a white handkerchief in the lapel pocket, and a Havana in his mouth—Johnny Rocco, the epitome of the Hollywood Italian Wise Guy, proves no match for the hardened Army veteran of the Italian campaign. McCloud's decency and belief in another and better world, which must follow after the high price he and his soldier comrades paid during the war, triumph over Rocco's egotism and his evil values. True to his character, Rocco makes outlandish claims about his invincibility: "You're not big enough to do this to Rocco. I'll kill you! You'll never bring me in, never!" But McCloud has met tougher enemies in Europe than this two-bit punk, and Rocco meets his inevitable end, his well-tailored body lying on the deck of the boat that he has tried to force McCloud to pilot to Cuba. During the entire length of *Key Largo*, Rocco and his henchmen continue to look nostalgically back at the Prohibition era and the good old days. But their day (that is, the kind of era that permitted the egotistical and publicity-grabbing mobster like the real Capone, or the cinematic Bandello and Camonte) has passed, thanks to the actions of brave soldiers such as McCloud who, having proved their valor abroad, must now do so again on the home front.

Key Largo is justly famous for its great performances, but its visual texture is far inferior to such works as *T-Men*, *Cry of the City*, or *Kiss of Death*. Designed as a kind of epitaph for Edward G. Robinson, it is essentially a star vehicle rather than a cheaply made film that exploits the kinds of expressionistic visuals so familiar in the greatest *films noir* of the period. In fact, except for a few shots of Florida employed in the opening scenes, virtually all of the film was shot on a Warner Brothers studio lot in California with special effects to simulate (not always very skillfully) the buildup of a Gulf hurricane. Virtually the entire film takes place within a small home, closed up to the impending storm. After Rocco's death, Nora Temple (Lauren Bacall), the sister of McCloud's dead comrade in arms, flings up the shutters and light enters the house again, announcing visually that perhaps a new day has dawned as a result of McCloud's heroism, and suggesting that the postwar era may well see fewer Johnny Roccos.

Johnny Rocco and his ilk are doomed by a certain kind of progress, but the mobster kingpin, the Hollywood Italian boss of bosses, begins to take on entirely different characteristics. American cinematic depictions of Wise Guys eventually lead to an entirely different kind of Mob boss as developed by Coppola's *Godfather* trilogy. One step in that direction may be found in the classic *film noir* by Fritz Lang, *The Big Heat* (1953), a distant forerunner of five urban vigilante films in a series beginning with *Death Wish* (1974; Michael Winner, director), and starring Charles Bronson as a liberal pacifist inspired by the murder of his wife to become the avenging angel of urban criminality against criminals.[47] In Lang's film, Dave Bannion (Glenn Ford), an honest cop but one who does not bend to the political whims of local law enforcement officials who are totally corrupted by organized crime, goes to investigate the apparent suicide of another policeman, Sergeant Thomas Duncan. Duncan's widow Bertha (Jeanette Nolan) conceals the confessional note her husband has left, detailing his dishonest dealings with the Mob boss of the city of Kenport, a fictitious city with an amazing resemblance to Los Angeles. Bertha lies to Bannion, telling him that her husband was despondent and ill, and she telephones Mike Lagana (Alexander Scourby), the city's crime lord, blackmailing him with the information she discovers in her husband's letter, a document she keeps hidden from the police. Shortly thereafter, Bannion meets Lucy Chapman (Dorothy Green), Duncan's girlfriend, who tells him that Duncan was most certainly neither ill nor despondent and casts doubt on the widow's sorrow: "The only difference between me and Bertha Duncan is that I work at being a B-girl, and she has a wedding ring and a marriage certificate."

Bannion confronts the widow with Lucy's testimony but Bertha refuses to give him any details that could assist his investigation. Shortly thereafter, the police Teletype recounts the murder of an unidentified woman (it is Lucy), who has also been tortured by cigarette burns all over her body. Bannion is then summoned by his superior, who orders him to lay off the investigation and is forced to close the case because of pressure "from upstairs." Clearly, Bannion surmises, there must be some connection between Lucy Chapman's death after speaking to him, Bertha Duncan, to whom he gave the gist of what Lucy said to him, and the police department's attempts to distance itself from the case. Subsequently, his wife receives a threatening and obscene telephone call and Bannion is warned to mind his own business since "some *big* people" are becoming annoyed. Without any evidence but realizing who controls the town of Kenport, Bannion immediately suspects the boss of bosses in the city, Mike Lagana, and rushes to confront him.

In Mike Lagana, Fritz Lang shows us an Italian mobster who has developed far beyond the likes of Nick Bandello, Tony Camonte, or even Johnny Vanelli. We share Bannion's glance into Lagana's world, and it is that of the exclusive country club, not the pool halls, the bars, and clip joints typical of most of the earlier Hollywood Italian mobsters. His residence is that of a captain of industry, a palatial mansion. His property is patrolled by a round-the-clock detail of the city's policemen, so tight is his control over the men running the police force. When Bannion goes inside the mansion, there is an exclusive party in progress for Lagana's daughter, and the butler escorts him inside. Lagana receives Bannion in his library/study, the kind of room one would not expect to find in the home of such an individual. Lagana represents an assimilated Hollywood Italian mobster, his power manipulated behind the scenes, his corrupt tentacles intertwined with all of the most important economic and political officials of the city. He is a goombah "passing for white" in the parlance of the period. Unlike Rico Bandello or Tony Camonte, Lagana realizes that publicity can destroy his power. What most upsets him is any reference to the good old days, Lucy Chapman's "old fashioned" killing or anything associated with Prohibition-style gangsterism. As he tells Bannion, "This is my home, and I don't like dirt tracked into it."

Lagana's desire to manipulate behind the scenes by political rather than violent means is effectively juxtaposed to his brutal second-in-command, Vince Stone (Lee Marvin), whose girlfriend Debby Marsh (Gloria Grahame) eventually is horribly disfigured when Stone throws hot coffee on her face for coming on to Bannion. Stone also organizes an attempted car bombing aimed at Bannion, but Bannion's wife unfortunately starts the car and is killed. Lagana goes to Stone's luxurious penthouse apartment, and on the balcony looking out on the lights and the skyscrapers of this city of the imagination, he worries about upsetting the voters in the coming elections with too much violence, a practice that might alert them to his machinations:

> Vince, you worry me. We've stirred up enough headlines. The election's too close. Things are changing in this country, Vince. A man who can't see that hasn't got eyes. Never get the people steamed up. They start doing things. Grand juries. Election investigations. Deportation proceedings. I don't want to land in the same ditch with the Lucky Lucianos.

While attempting to achieve complete economic and social assimilation into polite society, Lagana—like Johnny Rocco—fears deportation more than anything else.

But Lagana's carefully laid plans begin to come unglued because of Stone's callous and cruel disfigurement of his girlfriend (now she has a reason to talk to Bannion about his schemes), Bertha Duncan's grasping demands for blackmail payoffs, and the fallout from the growing pressure from Bannion's investigation, pursued as an angry private citizen after he quits the police force. Basically, Bannion becomes a vigilante. Bannion nearly chokes the gangster named Larry Gordon to death. Gordon was the killer Stone sent to kill Lucy Chapman, who most probably also put the bomb in Bannion's car. Bannion subsequently spreads a rumor that Gordon has confessed to him. Then Bannion confronts Bertha Duncan with the information that he has on her blackmail scheme, and he is tempted to choke her as he almost choked Gordon. Unlike Stone and Lagana, Bannion cannot bring himself to commit murder, but he is not above making sure that malefactors like Gordon or Bertha receive their just desserts. He is indirectly responsible for Gordon's death, because Lagana's gang kills him after the false rumor Bannion has spread. And when he tells Debby that Bertha has a document—her insurance policy—detailing her husband's corruption and all of Lagana's evildoings that will be released in the event of her death, Debby shoots her and releases the information to the public. Again, Bannion is indirectly responsible for her actions, since he not only told Debby about the document but also gave her the gun used in shooting Bertha. Moreover, Debby subsequently returns to her boyfriend Vince and scalds him with burning coffee before he shoots her, an act of violence impossible without Bannion's information.

The end result of this complicated denouement leads to the exposure of the crime syndicate's corruption, and the arrest of Lagana and Police Commissioner Higgins (a habitual card player with Vince Stone and mobsters from Lagana's gang). Bannion seems to be completely oblivious to the violence created in his wake, and in the final sequence of the film, one that has depicted two frightening scaldings by hot coffee, he goes out to investigate another case (he has returned to the police force) and orders one of the men in the office to "keep the coffee hot"!

The Godfather: *the Return of History and Ethnicity*

Before the international success of Mario Puzo's novel and the film trilogy Francis Ford Coppola produced from it made "Mafia" a household word all over the world, a few films appeared to mark a gradual return to an interest in the historic roots of Italian American contributions to organized crime that will constitute one of *The Godfather* trilogy's most original features. In addition, like Coppola's trilogy, a number of these films posited the existence of a crime syndicate in the United States that was run predominantly by Italian Americans, something even the Federal Bureau of Investigation, under J. Edgar Hoover, continued to deny until the mid-1950s. These films include *Black Hand* (1950; Richard Thorpe, director); *The Brothers Rico* (1957; Phil Karlson, director); *Pay or Die* (1960; Richard Wilson, director); and *The Brotherhood* (1968; Martin Ritt, director).[48]

Black Hand and *Pay or Die* both refer to the death of the famous Italian American detective from New York City, Joseph Petrosino (1860–1909), who was personally responsible for cracking down upon Black Hand extortion plots among Italian Americans (including a plot directed at the famous opera star, Enrico Caruso). Petrosino was murdered by the Mafia in Palermo after what was supposed to be a secret anti-Mafia mission there revealed by the press. These two films also hark back to the era before Prohibition when, as discussed earlier, disconnected bands of extortionists calling themselves the Black Hand preyed upon the Italians newly arrived in America, and who lived in the major urban ghettos of the country. In the first film, a young man named Johnny Colombo (Gene Kelly) seeks revenge for the murder of his Italian father by a Black Hand gang years ago. A character based upon Petrosino, called Louis Lorelli in the film (J. Carrol Naish), provides information about the murder just before his own death in Naples while carrying on an investigation abroad. Whereas *Black Hand* uses a character inspired by the historical Petrosino, *Pay or Die*—in which Ernest Borgnine plays Petrosino—is a movie biography of the Italian American policeman. In both films, there is an interest in the historical origins of Italian American criminality as well as in the reconstruction of the Little Italies of the beginning of the twentieth century that produced such criminals.

The Brothers Rico and *The Brotherhood*, on the other hand, both assume the existence of organized crime (a Mafia) and a very important role in it for Italian Americans. Coppola's *Godfather* trilogy naturally assumes that such an organization exists and, furthermore, has historic roots that can be traced in a dramatic story line. In the first film, Richard Conte plays Eddie Rico, a syndicate accountant whose naiveté about the true nature of the Mob leads to the death of his brother Johnny, an event that moves Eddie to kill his uncle, the head of the Syndicate, named Sid Cubik (Larry Gates) who lives in the heart of Little Italy in New York. Eddie leaves Mulberry Street and the Syndicate for a prosperous middle-class life in Florida in a laundry business, but it will take more than the passage of a few years living without the Mob to wash his past and his conscience clean.

The Brotherhood appeared only a few years before *The Godfather*, and its commercial failure led many Hollywood producers to fear even doing an adaptation of Mario Puzo's best-selling novel. Like *The Brothers Rico, The Brotherhood* assumes the existence of an organized Syndicate—in this case run by a committee in New York City composed of both Italian Americans and other ethnic groups (Jewish, Irish). But its plot attempts to go back to the beginnings of organized crime in America—Lucky Luciano's removal of Salvatore Maranzano (1868–1931), the "Boss of Bosses"—and the creation of a crime Syndicate that included not only Italian Americans but also others. The film contrasts the "old" ways of the entirely Sicilian Mafia of Maranzano with that very different group of criminals associated after 1931 with Lucky Luciano.

Two brothers—Frank (Kirk Douglas) and Vince Genetta (Alex Cord)—are the sons of one of the Sicilians murdered by Luciano when Maranzano's rule over the Mafia had been destroyed some three decades previously.

Frank, a member of the crime syndicate running New York operations, discovers that one of the other Italian American mobsters on the syndicate—Dominick Bertolo (Luther Adler)—was the non-Sicilian who betrayed his father and forty other Sicilians of the Old School years before. This knowledge is complicated by the fact that Frank's brother is married to Bertolo's daughter and that Frank has opposed the ambitious plans of the syndicate to move into the electronic industry and defense or space projects. One of the few survivors of the old Sicilian "Mustache Petes"—the old Mafiosi who followed the old codes of honor and who never allowed non-Sicilians into their midst—reveals Bertolo's treachery to Frank and demands satisfaction for "la Santa Mamma" or the Mafia. The role of this older Sicilian mobster figure, named Don Peppino, is played admirably by Eduardo Ciannelli—the unforgettable mobster Johnny Vanning (the Lucky Luciano figure) in *Marked Woman*—in one of Ciannelli's last screen performances. Challenged by Don Peppino's directions to behave honorably and to revenge his father's death, Frank kills Bertolo and flees to Sicily. Frank eventually allows himself to be killed by his own brother Vince, since the Syndicate will kill Vince if he does not carry out this assignment.

The Brotherhood may well be said to foreshadow some of the major elements of Coppola's *Godfather* trilogy. In the first place, it employs on-location shooting in Sicily to portray the atmosphere and the environment that originally produced the Mafia in Italy. Coppola will later use the Sicilian sequences in his trilogy to even greater effect. Secondly, the major conflict in the film is between a purely "Sicilian" definition of Mafia and a broader "American" definition of the Mafia that includes ventures into sophisticated electronic industries. Frank's objections to this attempt to subvert a key defense industry are based upon the federal reaction he foresees, one that he believes will destroy the Syndicate. In a similar argument, Don Corleone in *The Godfather* sets off a gang war by refusing to go along with the drug traffic, since he believes that the stiff sentences handed out to dope dealers will crack the *omertà* protecting mobsters and will cause the mob's political support to evaporate. Unlike *The Godfather*, however, where organized crime in New York City is primarily an Italian American operation, run by five different families, in *The Brotherhood*, organized crime is more accurately shown as being directed by a variety of ethnic groups in which Italian Americans may play a dominant but not an exclusive role—something that has been historically true since the Luciano era. Even with such potentially interesting material, it is easy to understand why *The Brotherhood* was a commercial failure. Its very weak script and rather bad acting pale in comparison with the stellar performances of the protagonists of *The Godfather* or that film's brilliant script.

An Ethnic Antidote to the Hollywood Italian Wise Guys:
Hollywood Italian Cops in Serpico, Prince of the City,
Donnie Brasco, Above the Law, *and* Out for Justice

Hollywood Italian cops appeared as early as the silent film *The Detectives of the Italian Bureau* in 1909. That first example of the "bad-wop-and-good-wop-cop" theme would not be the only time films juxtaposed positive and negative ethnic figures in a single film. It was Inspector Ben Guarino who confronted Tony Camonte in *Scarface*. The courageous Tony Genaro working for the Treasury Department loses his life while working undercover against Italian American gangsters in *T-Men*. In *Kiss of Death*, it is Assistant District Attorney Louie DeAngelo who relies upon Nick Bianco's testimony to prosecute Tommy Udo. Of course, the best example of this theme may be found in *Cry of the City*, where Lieutenant Candella brings in Martin Rome even though they are childhood friends. Just as the long-suffering Italian mother becomes a staple minor theme in Hollywood Italian films about Wise Guys, so, too, the "good-wop-cop" figure juxtaposed to the "bad-wop" Wise Guy becomes popular. Such a doubling of ethnic characters not only makes for good drama but also serves to deflect criticism that hints at discriminatory treatment of a particular ethnic group.

Although the Hollywood Italian policeman or law-enforcement officer may often be found in gangster films whenever Hollywood Italian Wise Guys turn up, it is important to point out that despite the international success of a film such as *The Godfather*, the 1960s and the 1970s (and indeed several decades later) were actually not so much characterized by numerous gangster films as by numerous films in which cops were the major focus. Hollywood films also became more and more violent at the same time, but in most cases individuals on the "right" side of the law were to blame for this rise in film violence. In an attempt to win back audiences being lost to television, the industry basically dropped the Production Code in the mid-1960s and moved toward more violence, more shocking language, and less reticence to offend various minority or ethnic groups. A rating system was established in 1968 in place of the Production Code. Many of the era's most popular and most controversial films were cop films, and the violence portrayed in them seemed to increase exponentially with each new film. They included: *Bullitt* (1968; Peter Yates, director); *Madigan* (1968; Don Siegel, director); *The French Connection* (1971; William Friedkin, director); *Dirty Harry* (1971; Don Siegel, director); *Walking Tall* (1973; Phil Karlson, director); *Magnum Force* (1974; Ted Post, director); and *The Enforcer* (1976; James Fargo, director). Given the role that Italian Americans played in organized crime (an influence either actual or imagined), it is not surprising that a number of important films portraying Hollywood Italian cops emerged during this period.

Hollywood Italian cops seem to have been identified with undercover work based upon the obvious assumption that people who have grown up in an ethnic neighborhood and have ties to a community where gangsters are produced will have a greater chance of understanding how they operate and how they may be brought to justice. This emphasis on the ethnic quality of such policemen also raises the interesting question of their loyalties, which may be potentially divided due to their neighborhood origins. *Serpico* (1973) and *Prince of the City* (1981), both directed by Sidney Lumet, are excellent examples of this kind of narrative. Serpico is basically a hippie cop who likes classical music and opera, does not believe that hamburgers and doughnuts are health food (unlike his fellow cops), and is such a nonconformist that he is immediately assigned to undercover work. Based on a true story about a New York Italian American cop named Frank Serpico who blew the whistle on endemic corruption in the police department, the film provides a showcase for Al Pacino's acting talents, displayed in his numerous disguises, which directly followed on his rise to stardom in *The Godfather* the previous year. We see Serpico's Italian mother for a brief scene, during which the two speak Italian (without subtitles), but paradoxically this quintessentially Italian American New Yorker relies so much on costumes in his undercover work that his ethnic identity is almost concealed. Many of the criminals he encounters are not Wise Guys but are black drug dealers. Yet, Serpico's real enemies are the corrupt policemen who seem to infest every precinct in the city and who fail to give him backup after they learn he is speaking to an investigative commission. Only one man (presumably also an Italian American) seems to be a truly honest cop—Inspector Barto (Ed Crowley). Serpico and Barto together hit a numbers house and discover that Barto's own precinct is just as corrupt as the other precincts!

Perhaps the most dramatic moment in the film concerns Frank's attempt to work on his own to avoid the corruption of his fellow cops: he concentrates on a loan-sharking and numbers operation run by an Italian American Wise Guy who wears expensive suits and a Panama hat (continuing the constant identification of Wise Guys with high-fashion statements). Arresting the man, Serpico drags him into the station house and while he is doing paper work for the arrest, the gangster sits around the office chatting and laughing with Serpico's colleagues in a friendly manner. It is obvious that he has been paying them off for some time. Doing his job, Serpico discovers that the man actually has a rap sheet as a cop killer and loses his temper, beating the mobster up and berating the cops around him. Presumably, his anger derives from the fact that the gangster is an Italian American like Ser-

Serpico *(1973; Sidney Lumet, director). A publicity still distributed by the studios that includes some of the many disguises Frank Serpico (Al Pacino) employed while working as an undercover cop in New York City.*

pico. Seriously wounded in the line of duty (without receiving much assistance from his fellow policemen), Serpico testifies for some five years in the corruption investigation and becomes a pariah in the department. As the film concludes, he packs his bags to leave for France and a concluding intertitle informs us that he has resigned from the force and is living in Switzerland. Apparently the New York Police Department is so corrupt that it is beyond repair.

Prince of the City presents an equally depressing account of New York policemen. Its plot is far more interesting than that of *Serpico*, even though Lumet's direction drags the story out for far longer than necessary. *Prince of the City* focuses on Danny Ciello (Treat Williams), the head of an elite Special Investigative Unit (SIU) that fights drug dealers and engages in corrupt activities at the same time. Lumet's film presents a universe literally filled with Hollywood Italians on both sides of the law. Many of the detectives in the SIU have Italian names: Dom Brando (Kenny Marino), Joe Marinaro (Richard Foronjy), and Gino Moscone (Carmine Caridi). For ethnic balance, the squad also boasts one Jew—Gus Levy (Jerry Orbach)—who predictably works undercover in the garment industry, and one Anglo, Bill Mayo (Don Billet). A number of the important district attorneys or federal officials are Italian Americans: Rick Cappalino (Norman Parker); District Attorney Polito (James Tolkan); Mario Vincente (Steve Inwood). With the exception of the odd drug addict (predictably black), the serious criminals are either Latin American drug dealers or local Italian American Wise Guys.

What makes *Prince of the City* more interesting, in some respects, than *Serpico* is that the protagonist of the film has close and important ties to his old ethnic neighborhood and the mobsters who inhabit it. Ciello's contacts there include his cousin Nick Napoli (Ronald Maccone), a crooked bail bondsman named Dave DeBennedeto (Ron Karabatsos), a local gangster named Rocky Gazzo (Tony Munafo), and a big-time drug importer named Marcel Sardino (Cosmo Allegretti). His cousin hangs out at a Mulberry Street social club (presumably the center of the criminal world for the Hollywood cinema), and Ciello frequently goes there for information, espresso, and conversation. Over espresso, Nick once asks him: "I mean, you get your rocks off putting Italians in jail? Ain't enough niggers out there for youse?" Nick makes no secret among his Mafia associates that his cousin is a cop, always making sure that is the way he introduces him to his colleagues. But he does wonder at the profession Ciello has chosen, especially since he knows that on occasion Ciello can be corrupted.

Lumet obviously wants to portray Danny Ciello as a tortured soul trying to get back to the honest ways he professed when he first became a policeman to help people, not to steal from drug dealers and to become like the Mafiosi he knows from his old neighborhood. Indeed, the cynical manner in which the federal prosecutors use Ciello's testimony—resulting in the suicide of at least two of his friends and the disgrace of many policemen—and the corruption rampant among lawyers and judges that the film also documents suggest that Ciello's Mafia relatives are no worse than the federal officials who dominate Ciello's life for over six years of testimony and living in hiding. Nobody emerges unscathed in Lumet's sordid portrait of big-city corruption: Ciello's life is almost destroyed for telling the truth about police corruption while important criminals and drug dealers pay their bail and are out of the country in a day. His cousin Nick is decapitated for the damaging effects of Ciello's testimony on Mob contacts within the police department. The film holds out no moral message, but it is clear that Lumet believes the New York Police Department's detectives resemble the Wise Guys too much to trust them.

Donnie Brasco (1997; Mike Newell, director) represents by far the most intricate and most original expression of this "bad-wop-good-wop-cop" theme. *Serpico* questions the very nature of ethnic identity with its many disguises. *Prince of the City* explores the difficulty of turning against men you have for years trusted with your life. It also highlights the strong ethnic ties that come with growing up in a particular neighborhood, ties that may call into question more universal values such as justice and obeying the law. *Donnie Brasco* goes to the heart of what makes a criminal by showing us a policeman who works undercover so long and so successfully that he begins to think, talk, and act like a Wise Guy. Donnie "Don the Jeweler" Brasco (Johnny Depp) is actually an Italian American FBI undercover cop named Joe Pistone. He befriends a lower-level Mafia "made man," a soldier with twenty-six murders under his belt for the Mob, named Benjamin "Lefty" Ruggerio (Al Pacino). Lefty comes from Mulberry Street in New York City, and after Donnie has earned Lefty's trust and friendship, he introduces Donnie to the other "made men" of the Mafia crew to which he belongs. These unsavory characters include Dominick "Sonny Black" Napolitano (Michael Madsen), Nicky Santora (Bruno Kirby), Paulie (James Russo), Alphonse "Sonny Red" Indelicato (Robert Miano), Bruno "Whack-Whack" Indelicato (Brian Tarantina), and Richie Gazzo (Rocco Sisto). They hang out at the usual neighborhood social club and many have, as the above list of names suggests, the characteristic gangster nicknames that seem to be so important in Hollywood.

What is extraordinary about *Donnie Brasco* is that without building up the kind of epic atmosphere that is so characteristic of *The Godfather* trilogy and constitutes so much of its charm, British director Newell manages to make the audience feel real empathy for Lefty, and admiration for his obvious friendship—even love—for his younger friend Donnie Brasco. Moreover, he achieves this insight into the complex emotional ties between Wise Guys and into the scary world these mobsters inhabit by replacing the kinds of epic figures of Coppola's films with protagonists that come from the far more gritty, dirty, and objectionable world depicted in Scorsese's portraits of the mob in such films as *Mean Streets, Goodfellas,* and *Casino* (1995).

Newell's gangsters, on the Scorsese model, are despicable people: they beat up Japanese waiters when they ask them to take off their shoes in a Japanese restaurant; they spend most of their time playing cards, drinking, and complaining about how much work being a gangster entails (and their complaints are real ones); and they are capable of brutally killing men they have known for years and then cutting up their bodies with butcher knives and saws to dispose of them (again, a nod to Scorsese, as we shall see later). *Donnie Brasco* also enters their world, an ethnic enclave where some very strict rules exist. Lefty explains to Donnie that Wise Guys carry money clips, not wallets. "Connected" guys (those involved in the life) are introduced as "friends of mine," while "made" guys (those who have killed for the Mob and have been inducted into it as official members when the "books" are opened to allow new membership) are introduced as "friends of ours." One of the best scenes of the film involves Joe Pistone explaining to his very square FBI colleagues what the ubiquitous phrase "fuhgeddaboutit" means in Mob-talk. Basically, the phrase means just about anything depending on the context.

Being a Mafioso is an often terrifying, difficult, and stressful enterprise in Donnie Brasco's world, just as it is in every episode of *The Sopranos*. As Lefty explains to Donnie, the fact that Lefty is vouching for Donnie means that if Donnie turns out to be a rat, Lefty's life is forfeit: "In our thing [Lefty is obviously referring to the Italian term *Cosa nostra* here], you get sent for. You go in alive, you come out dead, and it's your best friend that does it." As Sonny Black explains after he is kicked up in the organization, he and his crew owe the bosses $50,000 per week from loan sharking, numbers, prostitution, hijacking trucks, or general misbehavior—if he and his crew are not "good earners," as the new boss puts it, "somebody gets clipped." "Getting sent for" is the nightmare of every Mafioso.

The dramatic conflict of *Donnie Brasco* comes from the deepening malaise felt by Joe Pistone as he infiltrates the Mob so successfully that he begins to surpass his mentor Lefty in the estimation of Sonny Black, their over-boss. He tells his real-life wife Maggie (Anne Heche) during one of the few times he is able to have any contact with her: "I'm not becoming like them, Maggie, I am them!" Joe realizes that doing his job as a policeman will eventually cause the bosses to "send for" Lefty, and he is also aware of the fact that Lefty loves him more than a son. Joe Pistone's impersonation of a Wise Guy has been so effective that when the FBI confronts Sonny Black and all his crew with pictures of Donnie Brasco in the FBI Academy, they deny, at first, that he could possibly be an undercover agent. Naturally, it takes an Italian American raised in an ethnic neighborhood in a Northern city—at least this is the film's basic premise—to know, understand, and finally arrest an individual of the same ethnic group from the same kind of neighborhood who has somehow failed to follow the honorable path in life.

Two outstanding performances by Johnny Depp and Al Pacino make *Donnie Brasco* a first-rate movie. The portrayal of the emotional and psychological problems associated with a life of crime in the mob and with the betrayal of a close friend has rarely been depicted better on the screen. At the conclusion of the film, neither Lefty nor Joe Pistone finds much satisfaction in their lives. As Lefty watches animal documentaries (his favorite kind of film) on television, he receives the dreaded telephone call—he is "sent for" to pay for his mistake in trusting and vouching for Donnie Brasco. This iron law of the Mafia led to the same conclusion in *Prince of the City:* Danny Ciello's cousin Nick Napolitano is murdered because Nick vouched for the fact that Danny was a crooked cop, not an informer. Lefty no longer wants to struggle against his fate, and as he tells his girlfriend Annette (Ronnie Farer), "If Donnie calls, tell him . . . if it's got to be anyone, I'm glad it was him." Then, he empties his pockets of anything valuable, removes his ring and his watch and even his crucifix, and places in a drawer these meager tokens of a life spent entirely in the Mob so that Annette will have at least something to remember him by after what will obviously be his assassination. A shot in the FBI gun range immediately follows this poignant scene, emphasizing the fact that Joe Pistone has killed Lefty by testifying against the Mob as surely as if he had pulled the trigger himself. But Joe's reward for years of undercover work, psychological pressure, guilt, and sometimes sheer terror that threatened to destroy his marriage and his life, is almost insulting: a cheap medal, a $500 check, and some meaningless words from a high-ranking FBI official who cannot stay at the ceremony long enough to exchange a few pleasant words. This is the reward for betraying a friend. And in spite of the intertitle that announces Pistone's testimony created more than 200 indictments and 100 convictions (not to mention a $500,000 contract on him that still remains open, or, at least, did remain open at the time of the production of *Donnie Brasco* in 1997), we are left with the very real feeling that Lefty's friendship was, in most respects, something far more valuable.

Quite a different picture of the Hollywood Italian policeman emerges from two action films starring Steven Seagal: *Above the Law* (1988; Andrew Davis, director) and *Out for Justice* (1991; John Flynn, director). In some circles, Seagal's martial-arts action films have replaced the Dirty Harry series of films starring Clint Eastwood or the Death Wish franchise starring Charles Bronson as the reactionary, right-wing cinema they love to hate. In the first film, Seagal plays Nico Toscani, an ex-CIA agent and special-ops soldier with extraordinary martial-arts ability who saw duty in Vietnam and returns to his hometown Italian American neighborhood in Chicago to work for the police. There Nico encounters a villain named Zagon (Henry Silva) he knew previously in Vietnam, a man who is the kingpin behind a CIA-related scheme to smuggle dope into America. Thus, Seagal combines what might be called a leftist Hollywood plot (the ubiquitous CIA as the agency of evil and dope dealing) with a rightist martial-arts approach to the problem—giving something to everyone on each extreme of the political spectrum. In *Above the Law*, the only people who can be trusted are people from the ethnic "neighborhood"—in this case, other Italian American policemen who guard Nico's family (including Sharon Stone as Nico's wife Sara in one of her earlier roles), or the Italian priest murdered by Zagon and his CIA-affiliated goons.

The film ends with the colorful deaths of Nico's enemies after he thwarts their attempts to assassinate a U.S. Senator investigating ties between drug dealers and the CIA. The politically loaded narrative is best captured by an exchange between Nico and Nelson Fox (Chelcie Ross), his former partner in Vietnam, now totally corrupted by the CIA's schemes to smuggle drugs into America:

NICO: Do we kill our own senators now?
Fox: Why not? The Romans did!
NICO: Are we the fucking Romans?
Fox: We're an empire too![49]

Out for Justice opens with an intertitle citing a statement by Brooklyn playwright Arthur Miller: "While to the stranger's eye one street was no different from another, we all knew where our 'neighborhood' somehow ended. Beyond that, a person was . . . a stranger." This action film resembles *Prince of the City*; its major theme is the neighborhood and the ethnic and cultural links that exist between the honest Italian American policeman Gino Felino and the Italian American Wise Guys with whom he grew up in New York City. Unlike Danny Ciello, whose contacts with his cousin Nick and other mobsters eventually led to his corruption, Gino is incorruptible. And given the violence associated with contemporary action films, Gino Felino is a Hollywood Italian cop who is quite different from most of those we have examined.

The plot of *Out for Justice* is not challenging. Gino Felino, Bobby Lupo (Joe Spataro), and Richie Madano (William Forsythe) are three Italian American kids "from the neighborhood" in Brooklyn: Gino and Bobby become cops, whereas Richie seeks to become a Wise Guy. When Richie discovers that he and Bobby have been sharing a girl, Richie goes berserk, kills Bobby in front of his wife and children in the middle of a Brooklyn street, and high on coke, he goes on a killing spree that includes bystanders in traffic jams. Only Gino, it seems, has the will and the killing power to stop him. Even the local Wise Guys are after Richie because he is giving them a bad name in the neighborhood. Few films in the history of Hollywood Italian gangsters have emphasized man-to-man violence of the martial-arts variety, although most have contained a good deal of graphic violence. Consequently, when we see the opening credits of *Out for Justice* rolling over the red snakeskin books of a pimp sticking out of a car windshield through which Gino has thrown him for beating up on one of his prostitutes, we realize even before the film begins that the Hollywood Italian world of Steven Seagal is an entirely different kind of place. When Gino goes to Richie's bar, rousts everyone, and beats them into bloody pulps (calling them "finokes," a corruption of *finocchio*, the Italian expression meaning "queers" that is also a general expression of contempt), Seagal demonstrates his prowess as an Aikido master and combines the Wise Guy film with the martial-arts movie.

Nevertheless, the violent-action sequences should not prevent the viewer from linking *Out for Justice* to the tradition of Wise Guy films, especially those featuring honest Hollywood Italian cops. In fact, one important scene of this action film recalls quite explicitly Siodmak's *Cry of the City*. Gino goes to Richie's home, where in Italian and without the assistance of English sub-titles, Richie's long-suffering Italian American mother begs Gino not to kill her boy. Like Lieutenant Candella in *Cry of the City*, who spent much of his youth in Mamma Rome's kitchen but finds himself forced to kill her son Martin, Gino has been practically brought up in the Madano household. Richie's father (Dominic Chianese) tells Gino that he cannot understand what went wrong with his son: he has worked for fifty years at the same job since arriving in America, fixing subway cars and trying to do the right thing by his sons. Later, we learn that Mr. Madano acted as a second father to Gino when his own father died, slipping Gino a bit of spending money now and then when he was young. Unlike Lieutenant Candella, whose compassion for the Rome family and the memory of his long friendship with Martin color his response to what is a difficult personal situation, Gino merely responds that Richie was always bad and always crazy. At the inevitable showdown concluding the film when Gino kills Richie, it is also done in a brutal, partic-ularly violent manner that completely reverses the rather noble confronta-tion that concludes *Cry of the City*. Gino basically beats Richie almost to death, shoving a corkscrew into his brain, and when his Mafioso friend Frankie (Sal Richards) arrives on the scene, Gino grasps his pistol and fires it several times into Richie's body, ordering Frankie to tell his boss Don Vitto-rio (Ronald Maccone) that Frankie has fulfilled his orders. This action is not that of a policeman firing in the line of duty—it is savage vigilante justice. In effect, the line between the Mafia and the police is blurred almost beyond recognition.

Gino Felino may well be even more violent than his childhood friends who have graduated into the Cosa Nostra. Many of them are stereotypes, almost all with the now-obligatory nicknames associated with Wise Guys: Bobby "Arms" (Jay Acovone); Joey "Dogs" (Nicky Corello); and Buchi—Butchie spelled with an Italian American flair (Robert Lasardo). Physically, they are believable because they are obviously recruited from Brooklyn and seem to come out of Mafia Central Casting. Don Vittorio and Frankie are far more interesting figures, for they represent "the neighborhood" (that recurrent phrase in the film) in a manner not unlike Gino Felino. In fact, Felino and the Mob are both trying to stop Richie and even consult on how to do so, giving Seagal the opportunity to speak Italian (he is, after all, partly Italian American) at a sit-down with a Mafia Don. Subtitles are provided as if we are watching a foreign film. Gino addresses Don Vittorio with the customary Southern Italian expressions of respect (translated as "Don Vittorio, my honor and respect to you. God bless you."). While Don Vittorio wants to take care of Richie with "our ways," Gino says he knows the neighborhood better than anyone and, of course, Bobby Lupo was his best friend.

In short, Gino seeks a *vendetta* in the best Sicilian fashion, not a simple arrest or even a simple killing. There is even what might be called a "Hood montage" in the film, where scenes of Gino searching through the neighborhood, beating up various people to get information on Richie, are juxtaposed to Frankie's men doing the same thing for the Mafia. Gino becomes so engaged at Ritchie that in another sit-down with Don Vittorio, after the mobster says to Gino that "we're family," Gino insults him by declaring "I'm not one of you, and I'm not with you." Of course, exactly the opposite is true. Outside the restaurant after insulting Don Vittorio, Frankie asks Gino why he did, and their exchange is interesting:

> NICO: I always wanted to be a Wise Guy . . . who would have ever thought I would of become a cop.
> FRANKIE: You're lucky, you know. Maybe God's a puppeteer, and we're just on the end of the string.

Similarly, Bobby Lupo, the victim of the original murder that opens the film and motivates the narrative until Richie's death, is a policeman like Gino. He is also described as a man who always wanted to be a mobster. It appears that in the martial-arts Brooklyn of Steven Seagal, such a career choice represents the highest aspiration for Italian American youngsters. In a sense, Gino is a Wise Guy: he simply has a badge that allows him to do things for which real Wise Guys would go to prison.

Out for Justice is no great work of art. But judged from the standards of action films, neither is it completely without interest. Perhaps more than anything else, such a film shows us the extent of the impact of *The Godfather* trilogy and the Scorsese mobster films that preceded it. It may not be too far-fetched to see Frankie's reference to God as a humorous puppeteer, making some of the Brooklyn Italian American cops and others gangsters, as a meta-literary and metacinematic allusion to the much more famous puppet strings that serve as the now-classic logo for Puzo's novel and Coppola's adaptation of *The Godfather*. The distance *Out for Justice* has traveled since the appearance of the novel in 1969 and the film in 1972 may be judged after our analysis of the most important Wise Guy films ever made: Coppola's *Godfather* trilogy and Scorsese's *Goodfellas*.

The Godfather *Trilogy and* la famiglia: *The Apotheosis of Hollywood Italian Wise Guys*

The Historical and Economic Context of The Godfather *Trilogy*

Francis Ford Coppola's trilogy—consisting of *The Godfather* (1972), *The Godfather Part II* (1974), and *The Godfather Part III* (1990)—is the single most significant work in the history of Hollywood Italians.[50] The first film received ten Oscar nominations and won in three categories: Best Picture, Best Actor, and Best Screenplay Adaptation from Other Material. *Part II* received another ten nominations and won in six categories: Best Picture, Best Director, Best Screenplay Adaptation from Other Material, Best Supporting Actor, Best Music, and Best Art Direction. *Part III* received an additional six nominations but did not win a single award. Twenty-six nominations and ten Oscars represent an amazing achievement, given the fact that the three films were made in such completely different circumstances and over almost two decades. Many bad films receive Oscars, but in the case of Coppola's trilogy, the wonder is that it did not receive even more than ten awards. The greatest injustice was done to the third film in general (it was far more deserving of merit than the Academy's judges and voters determined) and to cinematographer Gordon Willis in particular, whose lighting and direction of photography created one of the landmarks of cinematic art in the twentieth century.

Almost everything about the first film that launched the *Godfather* franchise seems serendipitous. Paramount Pictures bought the rights to Mario Puzo's novel, *The Godfather* (1969) for a relatively small amount of money before the book really took off as a best seller and a long seller. By some miracle, Paramount paid only $80,000 for the rights to the novel three months before it was published. After its publication, it sold over 400,000 hardcover copies in less than six months and remained on the best-seller list for almost seventy weeks. Coppola (who was about to win an Oscar in 1971 for his work on the screenplay of *Patton*) had only directed three films before *The Godfather* and, by his own admission, would never have been hired to shoot the adaptation of the novel had it been such a blockbuster when he signed the contract. Almost everything about the film that is recognized as the touch of genius was opposed by Coppola's studio. Nino Rota's evocative music displeased the studio bosses. Coppola was told that Marlon Brando would never play in any film unless he did so for free. Virtually everyone who was cast in *The Godfather* was not a star at the time the film was made, but almost every one of them became famous as a result of their work on *The Godfather*. Yet, their selection was opposed vehemently by Paramount. The studio in particular came very close in the first week of shooting to a decision to fire Al Pacino, and for some time Coppola himself was almost dismissed for a variety of reasons—spending too much money in a work that had originally been budgeted with little money; not putting enough action and violence in the film; selecting actors that the studio preferred not to employ; making a period film instead of putting Puzo's historical best seller in a contemporary setting. In retrospect, it seems incredible that Paramount wanted to turn the vast American historical panorama suggested by Puzo's novel and elaborated upon by Coppola's brilliant script, written in collaboration with Puzo, to a picture set in the 1970s—in Kansas City! Had Paramount's executives succeeded in making the kind of film that they wanted, it would have become something much like the mediocre *The Brotherhood*, which Paramount had released unsuccessfully early in 1968, or like the unimpressive gangster films made for television from other Puzo novels that have followed in the wake of *The Godfather*, such as *The Last Don* (novel 1996; television film, 1997) or *The Last Don II* (television film, 1998), both directed by Graeme Clifford.

Fortunately for Paramount, Coppola's *The Godfather* virtually saved the studio, which was practically bankrupt at the time and had just been gobbled up by Gulf and Western in what looked like a very bad economic decision. Its success also invigorated the American film industry, which at the time was experiencing many financial difficulties. When the completed film hit the theaters, it opened in an age long before the present era of openings, which sees more than a thousand screens and enormous advertising budgets aimed at creating an automatic hit to protect huge investments. Different figures are quoted for the cost of the movie—Coppola's commentary on the film cites the figure of less than three million dollars, whereas other sources put the total at some six million dollars. In almost no time at all (six months), the film surpassed the ticket sales of Victor Fleming's masterpiece, *Gone with the Wind* (1939), a box-office record of sales figures that had taken more than three decades and numerous releases and re-releases to accumulate. By 1975, worldwide ticket sales had reached the phenomenal sum of $330,000,000! In short, the film made history. Many of the lines from the scripts of the three films have become part of the American language and have subsequently been reused and parodied in subsequent gangster films or in *The Sopranos*. *The Godfather* remains one of the most popular films ever made. George Lucas (who worked with Coppola on certain uncredited portions of the film) and

Stephen Spielberg would follow Coppola's pioneering example in changing the face of Hollywood in the 1970s and the 1980s with other block-
buster films in a series that revived the industry's fortunes, such as the *Star
Wars* films, the *Jaws* films, or the *Indiana Jones* films.

Mario Puzo's The Godfather: *From Bestseller to Blockbuster*

Puzo's novel is certainly the work of Italian American fiction that has
had the greatest impact upon popular culture. In celebrating Coppola's
achievement in the film version of the book, most critics generally underestimate the importance of Puzo. In fact, the novelist made substantial
contributions to all three scripts in *The Godfather* trilogy, and virtually all
of the memorable lines in the screenplay of the first and second parts of the
trilogy are taken practically verbatim from the novel. Eloquent testimony
to the dominant role the novel played in directing Coppola's adaptation
may be found in one of the supplementary sections in the special DVD
Collection of the trilogy entitled "Francis Ford Coppola's Notebook," a
page of which is illustrated and the importance of which is outlined also in
one critical work on the films.[51] Coppola calls this notebook a "prompt
book," and he produced it himself, carefully cutting out the pages from the
hardback edition of the novel and then inserting them into pages that contained a cutout space for the novel's pages. He then made copious notes on
the novel, indicating how he would use the passage, what he might delete,
and filling the huge notebook with numerous observations about details to
include in the film adaptation. The prompt book contained information
on several topics: notes on the historical context of the film, the imagery
and tone he wished to create, as well as the pitfalls he wanted to avoid.
What is most important about this prompt book is that it was not only
produced before the screenplay was written but that Coppola maintains he
could have easily shot the film using the prompt book without ever having
a script. Needless to say, this argues for an enormous contribution from the
novel itself.

Coppola's major changes from novel to film involve deletions. Puzo's
novel is divided into nine books. Book 1 opens, like the film, with a meeting between an undertaker named Amerigo Bonasera and Don Vito Corleone, the Godfather of the title. The book introduces all of the members
of Don Vito's family (Sonny, Fredo, Michael—Don Vito's three natural
sons—his daughter Connie, who is about to marry Carlo Rizzi on the day
Bonasera appears at his home; and Tom Hagen, his adopted son). It also
presents members of Don Vito's other "family," his Mafia family. These
characters include his two underbosses, Clemenza and Tessio, as well as

some of the lesser Mafiosi that work for them, such as the traitor Paulie Gatto. The mysterious assassin Luca Brasi who fears only Don Vito Corleone joins the others. Non-gangster figures include Don Corleone's famous godson Johnny Fontane, the most important crooner of the period probably modeled after Frank Sinatra, as well as his son Michael's girlfriend, Kay Adams.

Book 1 of Puzo's novel contains the majority of the famous episodes in the film: Johnny Fontane's ruined voice and his need to land a role in a new picture made by Hollywood mogul Jack Woltz; the Godfather's plan to make Woltz an offer he cannot refuse, resulting in a bloody horse head in Woltz's bed and a role in the film for Johnny Fontane; Don Corleone's refusal to deal in drugs after Victor "The Turk" Sollozzo requests his participation and assistance; subsequent assassination attempts on the Godfather by Sollozzo's men with the tacit permission of the other Mafia families in the city who want to expand their illicit business into narcotics; and finally Michael's assassination of Sollozzo and his police-captain bodyguard, the corrupt cop Captain McCluskey. All of this material and many famous lines come directly out of Puzo's Book 1. Coppola wisely decided to focus upon these tightly connected episodes and only took from the rest of the book what he needed to bring his film to a conclusion.

Book 2 mainly relates the story of Johnny Fontane and events in Hollywood and Las Vegas, most of which are deleted from the film. Book 3 presents the historical information about Don Corleone's origins and development into a gangster leader that becomes central to *The Godfather Part II*. Book 4 contains important elements Coppola used to continue the plot of Book 1: the Don's recovery after his attempted assassination and the death of his son Santino, known as Sonny; and the Don's agreement to meet with the other families to make the peace. Book 5 focuses at length on Don Vito's meeting with the other families. It also contains a subplot cut entirely from the screenplay: a love affair between an abortionist doctor named Jules and Lucy Mancini, a woman with whom Sonny had an affair before his death. Jules operates on Johnny Fontane's voice, curing his problems and allowing him to continue his singing career, and he also operates upon Lucy, who has a difficult problem with her sexual organs that his expert surgery removes. In Book 6 Puzo describes Michael Corleone's time hiding from the law in Sicily, his marriage, and the death of his young bride when an assassination attempt on him mistakenly kills his wife, Apollonia. This material becomes part of Coppola's screenplay. In Book 7, Michael returns to New York and marries for a second time, now to his old girlfriend Kay Adams. Coppola cut out entirely a subplot in this book about Johnny Fontane's friend Nino Valenti. The Corleone family's move from New York to Las Vegas is treated, along with Moe Greene, the "Bugsy" Siegel surrogate, whom Michael wants to buy out to set up his own casino. In a rather brief Book 8, Don Vito Corleone dies, he has a huge gangland funeral, and then Michael (now in charge of the Mafia family) assassinates all of the heads of the families who oppose him plus the traitor Tessio, who had gone over to the other side, thinking that the Corleone family was too weak to protect him. After serving as the godfather for Carlo's son, Michael kills his brother-in-law Carlo Rizzi, since he was the man who betrayed Sonny to the other side in the gangland struggle for supremacy. When Michael's wife Kay asks her husband if Connie's accusation that he had Carlo murdered is true, Michael denies this, but Kay realizes that he is lying. In the concluding Book 9, Tom Hagen explains to Kay the reasoning behind Michael's murders. The novel concludes as Kay Adams, now a convert to Catholicism, goes every day to church to light a candle and to pray for the immortal soul of Michael Corleone.

Coppola's prompt book and the subsequent screenplay are thus integrally related, and Coppola's reliance on his prompt book more than on the subsequent screenplay demonstrates the important role of the novel in shaping the final film. By his many deletions and abbreviations of the original literary text, Coppola produced a far more concise plot, one with most of the same characters but none of the interesting and extraneous events and figures that populated Puzo's sprawling work. The Nino Valenti/Dean Martin character disappears entirely. Johnny Fontane, Valenti's Frank Sinatra-like sidekick, remains in the film but is infinitely less important. Indeed, it could be argued that Johnny Fontane serves in the film only to provide the excuse to present the episode of the horse's head in the arrogant and prejudiced film producer's bedroom, the ultimate emblem of Don Corleone's far-reaching power. The relationship between Jules the surgeon and Lucy Mancini also disappears, and Las Vegas (far more important in the novel) becomes the ultimate destination of the Corleone family only after they pay all their "debts" in New York City.

Coppola's Mafia as Metaphor for America and as Classical Family Tragedy

Two often cited quotations from Coppola have rightly dominated discussions of his masterpiece. Interviewed in 1972, the director maintained that he employed the Mafia as a symbol for something much larger:

I always wanted to use the Mafia as a metaphor for America. If you look at the film, you see that it's focused that way. The first line is "I believe in America." I feel that the Mafia is an incredible metaphor for this country. Both are totally capitalistic phenomena and basically have a profit motive.[52]

Interpreting the film in following Coppola's suggestion that the Mafia is a metaphor for America places the work into the context of the 1970s, an age of demonstrations, lack of faith in democratic institutions, and the protests surrounding the Vietnam War. The justly famous opening sequences of the Corleone wedding and Don Corleone's reception of supplicants for favors in 1945 as World War II has just drawn to a close indeed clearly prompt the viewer to consider the film as making an important statement about America. The film opens with titles in white letters on a black background, along with the logo of the puppeteer's hands pulling the puppet's strings that was rendered so famous by the cover of Puzo's novel. Nino Rota's haunting trumpet version of the film's major musical theme is heard on the sound track as the titles slowly fade to black and Bonasera, the undertaker (Salvatore Corsitto) pronounces the famous words "I believe in America" in a thick, Italian accent. We see Bonasera in close-up, but one of the most famous shots in the history of cinema using a computerized zoom attached to a Mitchell camera that pulls back in an extremely slow reverse zoom reveals the true subject of this sequence: Don Corleone in a low-keyed lighting in a dark study that combines the rich textures of oaken desks and leather chairs. The somber hues of the room are increased by the fact that cinematographer Gordon Willis uses the familiar shade and shadows cast by Venetian blinds frequently employed in the *film noir* for graphic effects. The negative of this sequence was apparently underexposed as well. Carlos Clarens, always the most sensitive critic of the gangster genre, declares quite rightly that this and other similar interiors of the film may well reflect Coppola's encounter with Luchino Visconti's masterpiece, *Il gattopardo* (1963, *The Leopard*) as Coppola establishes the dominant image in the film—as Clarens puts it, "one lingering, controlling image, that of hushed ceremonials among men in darkened rooms"—that will return with even greater force at the conclusion of the film as Don Corleone (Marlon Brando) is replaced by his son Michael (Al Pacino) in a slightly altered room, now decorated in the style of the 1950s but equally sinister.[53] The darkened colors recall the painters of the Old Masters, particularly those from the European Baroque (Caravaggio, Georges de La Tour, and Rembrandt all come to mind), painters who combined such interiors with strangely illuminated details to emphasize their themes. All these darkened but richly textured interiors in the trilogy are associated with conspiracies and confessionals. Bonasera's supplication for justice for his daughter who

The Godfather *(1972; Francis Ford Coppola, director). Undertaker Bonasera (Salvatore Corsitto) asks Don Vito Corleone (Marlon Brando) for a special favor on his daughter's wedding day.*

has been beaten by two non-Italian boys at first meets with the Godfather's refusal, since Bonasera has never treated the Don with "respect" even though the don's wife was godmother to his only child: Bonasera had relied on American justice and had erroneously believed that American-style justice would prevail. But he has learned that courts function to support those with power, not to assist patriotic immigrants. Only when Bonasera calls Vito Corleone "godfather" and kisses his ring can he receive the kind of justice he expects from America's courts—the two boys will very shortly be beaten within an inch of their lives by some of the gangster's underlings, and Bonasera will someday perform a "service" for Don Corleone. Eventually he prepares the bullet-ridden body of Sonny Corleone (James Caan) after his assassination by killers from the other Mob families in the gang war touched off by the failed attempt on the don's life.

An abrupt cut takes us to the festive Italian music outside the dark den of iniquity where the Godfather conducts his dirty business into the world of sunlight—the wedding of Connie (Talia Shire) and Carlo Rizzi (Gianni

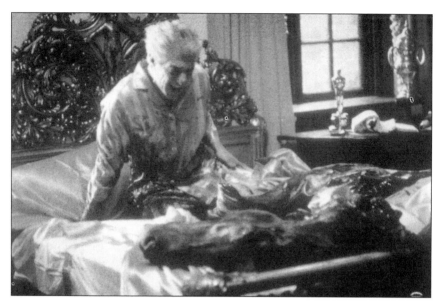

The Godfather *(1972; Francis Ford Coppola, director). Hollywood mogul Jack Woltz (John Marley) receives an offer he cannot refuse from Don Corleone—the severed head of his prized stud-racehorse Khartoum—convincing Woltz that Johnny Fontane is the perfect star for his new film.*

Russo). We now see the whole family: Tom Hagen (Robert Duvall), the don's adopted son and lawyer; Michael, Sonny, and Fredo (John Cazale), along with the other principal players. Other members of the Mafia are present on this important day in the life of the don's family: Clemenza (Richard Castellano), Tessio (Abe Vigoda), Luca Brasi (Lenny Montana), another powerful Mafia boss, Barzini (Richard Conte), who will be revealed as the brains behind the plot to overthrow the Corleone empire, Kay Adams (Diane Keaton), Michael's girlfriend and future wife, Johnny Fontane (Al Martino), and the don's wife (Morgana King). Here, the other family in the don's life—not the Mafia family but that of his private life—gathers for a group photograph, an event that takes place again in the subsequent two films of the trilogy after their opening sequences.

And here, in the golden sunshine of the exterior scene, the second important quotation from Coppola about his intentions in *The Godfather* becomes relevant:

But as I've said, this movie was never about a Mafia family. I think it was about a classic noble family. It could be about kings in ancient Greece or in the Middle Ages. It could just as well be about the Kennedys or the

Rothschilds, about a dynasty that transcends even one's obligations to one's country. It is about power and the success of power.[54]

Coppola's two important declarations about his goals in making his movie are not in conflict but central to his creation. Coppola's first statement about the metaphoric nature of the film might have more precisely stated that the Corleone Mafia family has adopted American-capitalist business principles—principles that they extend to a monopolistic logic by being willing not only to compete with other gangsters but by being willing, when necessity commands, to kill their competition! Their cutthroat ultra-Americanism, however, always serves to advance the interests of a private nuclear family, not an economic class, a corporate body, or a national group as would be expected in a more traditional business arrangement. Puzo's novel constantly repeats this same theme, and Coppola's film embraces it completely. Don Corleone has become famous because of his use of reason, backed up by force. His criminal methods are celebrated in the underworld precisely because he organizes crime as a corporation, as an economic entity that elevates profit over personality. But the mailed fist inside the velvet glove that the don professes to wear is always the final solution to any "commercial" problem. This "business logic" is perfectly expressed in the line that Michael uses to explain to Kay Adams in the wedding scene how Don Corleone managed to relieve Johnny Fontane, his godson, from a contract with a recalcitrant bandleader. As Michael says, "My father made him an offer he couldn't refuse. Luca Brasi held a gun to his head, and my father assured him that either his brains or his signature would be on the contract . . . That's a true story . . . That's my family, Kay. It's not me."

The element of *The Godfather* that makes it resemble a Greek tragedy derives from the fact that Michael's belief he can remain outside the business logic of his father's iron fist ultimately proves to be false. In order to protect first his wounded father, and then the entire Corleone criminal empire, Michael will be forced to become like his father. He will be obliged to murder Sollazzo "The Turk" (Al Lettieri), Sollazzo's corrupt police accomplice and bodyguard Captain McCluskey (Sterling Hayden), and eventually all the major associates of the opposing Five Families in New York—Barzini, Cuneo (Rudy Bond), Phillip Tattaglia (Victor Rendina), and Moe Greene (Alex Rocco) in Las Vegas, when he takes revenge for his father's attempted assassination attempt and Sonny's murder. For good measure, Michael also kills his brother-in-law Carlo Rizzi for betraying Sonny to the Corleones' enemies, and in a scene cut from the final version of the film, he also murders Fabrizio (Angelo Infanti) who betrays him personally in Sicily in a failed assassination attempt that results in the death of his first wife, Apollonia (Simonetta Stefanelli).

The metaphor of business pervades the film and is intertwined with the theme of the family. In refusing to give Sollazzo protection from the legislators and judges he controls in expanding the drug trade, Don Corleone at first declares that "It doesn't make any difference to me what a man does for a living" but he adds that drugs are a "dirty business." After he tries to kill the don, Sollazzo repeats Don Corleone's logic by telling Tom Hagen that the drug expansion is "good business": "I don't like violence, Tom. I'm a businessman. Blood is a big expense." Later, when Tom, Sonny, Michael, Fredo, and the Corleone underbosses meet to discuss strategy, Tom declares that "this is business, not personal, Sonny!" and Sonny's anger prompts him to forget his father's teachings: "They shot my father. That's business? Your ass!"

At this dramatic meeting Michael, the "nice college boy" as Sonny calls him, persuades them all that there is no other choice but for him—and not the other family members who have always been involved in the family's criminal enterprises—to kill both Sollozzo and McCluskey in order to protect his wounded father. In the film, this is the moment when Michael begins to become his father and to ascend as the undisputed underworld boss of New York City. Like his father, he declares: "It's not personal, Sonny. It's strictly business." Michael's tragedy is that every one of his subsequent actions negates this statement. Puzo's novel makes his transformation into the future Don Michael Corleone much clearer. Without the visual resources of the cinema, Puzo spells it all out:

> Michael stood up. "You'd better stop laughing," he said. The change in him was so extraordinary that the smiles vanished from the faces of Clemenza and Tessio. Michael was not tall or heavily built but his presence seemed to radiate danger. In that moment he was a reincarnation of Don Corleone.[55]

And Puzo then spells out what the Corleones always mean when they claim that criminal affairs must be regulated by business logic, not personal feelings, when Tom Hagen accuses Michael of taking the don's assassination attempt personally:

> For the second time he saw Michael Corleone's face freeze into a mask that resembled uncannily the Don's. "Tom, don't let anybody kid you. It's all personal, every bit of business. Every piece of shit every man has to eat every day of his life is personal. They call it business. OK. But it's personal as hell. You know where I learned that from? The Don. My old man. The

Godfather. If a bolt of lightening hit a friend of his the old man would take it personal. He took my going into the Marines personal. That's what makes him great. The Great Don. He takes everything personal. Like God. . . . Tell the old man I learned it all from him and that I'm glad I had this chance to pay him back for all he did for me. He was a good father.[56]

Unlike *The Godfather Part II*, a film that contains numerous jumps between the past and the present, the narrative structure of *The Godfather* follows a classical linear narrative with only one major shift in location— the sequences dealing with Michael's exile in Sicily, his marriage to Apollonia under the protection of Don Tommasino (Corrado Gaipa), Don Vito's Sicilian friend and fellow Mafia boss. Here, Coppola suggests but does not elaborate upon the possible historical explanation for the birth and expansion of the phenomenon of the Mafia in Italy. Given the meager resources placed at his disposal, Coppola follows the novel rather closely in this section of the film, but the material he cuts out of the novel in the first film will be exploited quite extensively in the second. The Sicilian sequences are something of an interlude designed to show the growth of a Sicilian consciousness in Michael, once the "nice college boy" destined by his gangster father to become a member of America's ruling elite, as Don Vito later explains while father and son plan their revenge against the Five Families:

I never wanted this for you. I work my whole life, I don't apologize, to take care of my family. And I refused to be a fool, dancing on the strings held by all those big shots. I don't apologize, that's my life, but I thought that . . . that when it was your time . . . that you would be the one to hold the strings. Senator Corleone . . . Governor Corleone. . . .

The Godfather Part II will elaborate upon this theme, showing how Vito Corleone was forced into exile from Sicily by the Mafia and then, against his will, into criminal activity to defend his family in America, resulting in the criminal empire he eventually constructed for himself and his children. It is Vito's tragedy that his crimes ensnare his son, trapping Michael in a web that is even tighter than the one that made him a criminal. What is most impressive about Coppola's treatment of this larger-than-life character is that he is a completely sympathetic figure in spite of his criminal actions. Through the entire trilogy, Coppola presents gangsters with noble possibilities: another turn of fate would have made Vito Corleone a leading figure in politics or business, just as he thought his youngest son would become in America. Their destinies resemble those of a Greek tragedy, inexorably moving toward horrible results even though they begin with the best of intentions. These tragic overtones remain one of the reasons why some critics quite wrongly complain that Coppola romanticizes his criminal figures, a charge that cannot be sustained when the denouement of *The Godfather Part III* finally plays out.

Michael's experience, and the loss of his first wife, drive him to return to New York once his safety seems assured and he is cleared of the charges against him for the assassinations of Sollazzo and McCluskey. Immediately he assumes the leadership of the Corleone crime family with his still-weakened and convalescent father as his consigliere. The deadly "business" of Mafia life has faded into the background, forgotten for a brief moment of nuptial bliss in Sicily until the traitor's car bomb quickly brings Michael back into the game.

In order to bring Michael safely back to America, Don Corleone agrees to a dangerous tactical decision. He calls a meeting that includes not only the Five Families of New York but also an assembly of gangsters associated with the dominant New York families from all over the country. He offers his protection to the expanding drug market in return for his son's safe passage home. Coppola shoots this dramatic meeting in one of the most impressive offices he could find in New York, the actual corporate head-

The Godfather *(1972; Francis Ford Coppola, director). Don Corleone (Marlon Brando) embraces Philip Tattaglia (Victor Rendina) and makes the peace between the five Mafia families of New York while Mafia chieftain Barzini (Richard Conte) claps in approval nearby.*

quarters of a major American corporation identified with the expansion of American capitalism in the late nineteenth and early twentieth century: the New York Central Railroad's board of directors meeting room located in New York City.[57] Similar meetings in corporate settings will later take place in the second and third films of the trilogy evoking the business theme: in *The Godfather*, the "board meeting" is national and strictly limited to American Mafia "business"; in *The Godfather Part II*, a similar meeting takes place in Battista's Havana before the Castro revolution and is attended by numerous heads of American corporations with huge investments in Cuba; in *The Godfather Part III*, Michael's Mafia family attempts to cleanse its dirty Mob money by investing in a Vatican-dominated multinational and the meeting takes place in the Vatican itself! In all three instances, the link between criminal activity and business cannot be hidden, and the higher Michael rises, the more obvious it becomes that the entire world of business resembles a criminal organization like the Mafia.

During Don Vito's meeting with his colleagues, he first repeats his objections to drugs, believing it will prove to be the ruin of the Mafia (a word, by the way, that is never uttered during the entire film). But Don Barzini, who emerges during the meeting as the eminence grise behind the plots against the Corleone empire, counters his arguments with those of changing times:

> Times have changed. It's not like the old days when we can do anything we want. A refusal is not the act of a friend. If Don Corleone had all the judges and the politicians in New York, then he must share them, or let us others use them. He must let us draw the water from the well. Certainly he can present a bill for such services. After all, we are not communists!

Barzini's line draws laughter from the assembly, and another Mafioso insists that drugs must be controlled as a business to "keep it respectable": this translates into not selling drugs near schools or to children (an *infamia*, as he calls this practice in Italian); he observes that in his own city (Buffalo), he would limit drug traffic to "the dark people, the colored . . . they're animals anyway, so let them lose their souls." Don Corleone's famous powers of reason prevail, and the drug traffic will be controlled and permitted with Corleone's assistance and protection from his political connections in the East. As Barzini concludes, "And there will be the peace." When he receives assurances that Michael can safely return, Don Corleone and Philip Tattaglia embrace while Don Barzini (now obviously the dominant figure in the underworld) stands by giving his blessing to the cessation of hostilities. In a subsequent scene cut from the final film but included in the longer television version of the film, Don Corleone admits that the peace is a sign of his family's weakness and reminds his son Michael that he has pledged his word not to take revenge, but Michael reminds the old don that he never promised forgiveness, and makes plans for a final solution to their family problems, a settling of accounts that will take place only after the Godfather's death.

Michael's ascension to assume his father's position becomes clear in the Las Vegas sequence where Michael meets Moe Greene and informs the gangster–casino manager that the Corleone family wants to buy his share of the Corleone-financed casino and move all its business interests to Las Vegas. Michael's posture is strictly businesslike, and he coldly and brusquely rejects the Las Vegas style entertainment—broads, booze, and free gambling chips—that Fredo, Michael's elder brother, offers in Moe Greene's name from the casino. Fredo has served as the family's representative in the casino the Corleone family now wants to purchase from Moe Greene to establish the place as a beachhead in their drive to control the city's gaming industry after they leave New York City. When Fredo objects that the man he works for there will never sell, Michael's curt answer ("I'll make him an offer he can't refuse") confirms his destiny. Moe Greene refuses and insults Michael in front of his older brother, Johnny Fontane (the key to Michael's plans to expand Hollywood entertainment in the Las Vegas casinos), and Tom Hagen. Losing his temper, Greene yells at Michael: "Sonofabitch—do you know who I am? I'm Moe Greene! I made my bones when you were going out with cheerleaders!" Greene's refusal to deal marks his doom. Michael's steely, passionless, cold, calculating behavior reflects the hard business logic that marks his family's enterprises as well as the state of the soul of a man who embraces the diabolical.

Michael's revenge, carried out with military precision, comes during the extraordinary and justly famous baptism sequence when he stands as godfather to the son of Carlo Rizzi and Connie. This scene represents one of the most skillful and original innovations that Coppola added to the novel. In Puzo's version of this material, Moe Greene has already been murdered as almost an afterthought following the meeting in Las Vegas. The dramatic rhythm of the film is not even hinted at by Puzo's version. In fact, the settlement of accounts is even interrupted in the novel by a long digression about Al Neri (Richard Bright), a zealous policeman who has been sentenced to prison for excessive force and manslaughter in the arrest and killing of a black pimp who beat up his prostitutes. Coppola retains Neri in his adaptation of the novel, primarily because Neri serves as a parallel to the fearless Luca Brasi, the faithful retainer of Don Vito Corleone. The baptism sequence moves in a series of thirty-seven abrupt cuts between the church where Michael stands as the actual godfather to his sister's son (played by his daughter Sofia who will play an important and much disputed role in *The Godfather Part III* as Michael's daughter Mary) and other locations.

As the priest conducts the ceremony in the Latin of the traditional pre-Vatican II Catholic ritual, making the scene seem even more unfamiliar than it might otherwise be, the scene shifts alternately and abruptly from the church to many different locations: a hotel room where Rocco Lampone (Tom Rosqui), now the leader of a group Michael has secretly assembled for the task, prepares a machine gun; Clemenza walks to his car carrying a shotgun and then goes up the stairs of a building; Al Neri ironically dons the costume of a policeman and loads his pistol; Barzini walks through the corridor of a building toward the steps outside; Willi Cicci (Joe Spinnell) gets a shave in a barbershop of a hotel and then waits outside a revolving door; Moe Greene receives a massage. Cuts back to the baptism carry the priest's voice as he addresses the ritual questions of baptism in the name of the infant being baptized but which Michael Corleone, the child's godfather, answers. The entire sequence is filled with irony as the priest intones: "Michael Francis Rizzi, do you renounce Satan and all his works? . . . and all his pomps?" The new godfather (a literal godfather, who now presides over the baptism of his godson, and a figurative godfather, who has planned the assassination of all those men who oppose his power) replies twice in the affirmative: "I do renounce them." After his first renunciation, the gruesome and dramatic killings begin: Moe Greene is shot in the eye through his glasses; Rocco Lampone kills Philip Tattaglia in bed with one of his prostitutes; Cicci shoots Don Cuneo inside the revolving door after blocking its gyrations; and Al Neri shoots not only Barzini's bodyguard and chauffeur but also Barzini himself.

Coppola cuts back to the church where Michael Corleone affirms that his godson will be baptized, and as the priest pours holy water on the baby's head and blesses him in Latin, the camera cuts back to a succession of dead bodies—Tattaglia, Don Cuneo, Barzini, and his men. When the priest sends the newly baptized infant out with the blessing "Go in peace, and may the Lord be with you," the camera dissolves from the shadowy interior of the church to the church steps in the light of day. The overlapping of the sound track, with its ominous organ music that gradually builds up toward resolution, and the Latin service makes the religious ceremony, which symbolically represents rebirth and salvation, seem strange and even diabolic, since precisely at the time Michael is renouncing Satan in public, he is embracing Satan in private. Here, and elsewhere in the trilogy, Catholic ritual becomes an integral part of Coppola's brilliant and very faithful re-creation of Italian American Catholic culture. But here as elsewhere, the director also turns this religious imagery into something quite frightening, in this case a new kind of judgment day for the Corleones' enemies.

After literally disposing of all opposition to his power from the other families, Michael takes care of business at home by having both of the traitors in his own "family" executed: Tessio, who has gone over in secret to Barzini; and Carlo, his brother-in-law, whose son he has just honored by becoming his godfather. The film ends in a brilliant fashion, back in the darkened office in which it opened. Dean Tavoularis, the highly talented production designer for the trilogy, changes the décor slightly to indicate that time has passed since we first met Don Vito Corleone in 1945: now, the room has been slightly altered to fit the style of the present (1951). But nothing really has changed except the identity of the leader of the Mafia family. After denying to his wife Kay that he had anything to do with Carlo's murder (a cold, blatant lie), the penultimate medium long shot through the frame of the study door reveals Michael in his father's place, now with his own Mafia "family": Michael's henchmen congratulate him and kiss his hand (the sign of respect in the trilogy). The final shot includes Kay looking at her husband in disbelief as Al Neri closes the door on her, effectively shutting her, and Michael's genetic family, away from his Mafia family. Fate has traveled full circle, and the film has delivered a devastating account of how a good man has been corrupted by power, the thirst for revenge, and the vagaries of circumstance and birth. The second and third parts of *The Godfather* trilogy investigate how Michael Corleone sinks deeper and deeper into the moral abyss of violent crime while, all the while, attempting to move his "business" toward legitimacy and to turn his power into a force for good. It will be his tragedy that such a purification of his evil actions will prove to be impossible and will have dire consequences for those he loves.

The Godfather Part II: *A New Kind of Narrative and Italian American History*

The unexpected and unprecedented commercial and artistic success of *The Godfather* obscures the fact that the original project was intended to be a relatively low-budget film shot by a virtually unknown director based upon a script derived from a book the rights for which were purchased long before it became a best seller. Moreover, the studio's objections to virtually everything about the film that made it a great work of art stood as almost insurmountable obstacles to the completion of the project, and Coppola, Brando, and Pacino were very nearly either not hired initially or very nearly fired during the process of the production. But the brilliance of the script, the camera work, lighting, and its sets should not also obscure the fact that

The Godfather is a relatively conservative, traditional film made on what to-day would be considered a shoestring budget. Except for the touch of genius added by Coppola to the plot of the novel at the conclusion of the film, with the tour de force of the cross-cutting parallel sequences between baptism and assassination and the one jump in place (but not in time) from New York to Sicily and back, Coppola created a classic dramatic narrative that re-sembles the traditional five-stage structure of a classical play, as one percep-tive critic has demonstrated.[58]

With a much larger budget, complete control over script and production, and lavish plans to film strategic portions of the movie in Italy and in his-torically accurate sets on various New York City streets, Coppola's second venture into Godfather country also experimented with a much different and much more complex kind of narrative structure. Working with novel-ist Mario Puzo and combining his own plot inventions with historical ma-terial he had discarded from the novel to tighten the classic narrative structure of the first film, Coppola now approached his subject matter with far more ambitious intentions. Not one but two story lines are presented and narrated through cross-cutting between them. From the novel (with additions of his own invention), Coppola traces the early life and career of the young Vito Corleone (Robert De Niro) from his childhood in Sicily through his arrival at Ellis Island as a fugitive from Mafia *vendettas* in Italy to the streets of New York's Little Italy (lovingly re-created by Dean Tavoularis). Roughly one-quarter of the film is devoted to this story, taking place between 1901 and 1918, on Don Corleone's origins, and a full quarter of an hour of the dialogue is delivered in Sicilian with subtitles, so that in many respects *The Godfather Part II* resembles a foreign film. The second narrative strand traces the development of Vito's son Michael (Al Pacino) and takes place in the fictional present of the late 1950s as Vito's successor has moved operations to Nevada (his family compound is now in Lake Tahoe, not suburban Long Island) where he launches an expansionist plan with a Jewish mobster-financier (modeled on the real gangster mastermind Meyer Lansky), a character named Hyman Roth (Lee Strasberg) in the film. Roth as a young boy appeared in sequences from the first *Godfather* film that were cut from the final film: Vito Corleone helped Roth when he was starving, much like Tom Hagen, a boy Vito Corleone adopted and groomed into one of his closest collaborators and who became his foster son. But Roth betrays Michael, draws his brother Fredo into his web, and forces Michael one more time to launch a murderous campaign of self-defense that results not only in the deaths of Hyman Roth and his underling Johnny Ola (Dominic Chianese, later to become famous in *The Sopranos* television series as Uncle Junior), but also his brother Fredo. Eventually, Michael must also force the gangster who inherited the Corleone family in New York after the move to Las Vegas to commit suicide for his decision to testify against Michael before a Senate hearing on organized crime. This colorful, old-fashioned Sicilian criminal is named Frankie Pentangeli or Frankie "Five Angels" (Michael Gazzo). Coppola was obliged to invent Frankie Pentangeli after Richard Castellano, who played the key role of Clemenza in the first film, proved impossible to sign to a contract for the sequel. Coppola places one important sequence of the film in Washington, D.C. of the 1950s. Michael is summoned to testify at a Senate investigation on organized crime that bears a resemblance to the actual Kefauver or McClellan hearings on the Mob in America. Another important section of the film takes place in Havana on the eve of Castro's revolution, an event that destroyed Mob power and its gambling empire on that small island.

By intertwining two different but related narratives in *The Godfather Part II*, Coppola adds a deeper historical dimension to the material he first presented in *The Godfather*. The theme of the sequel thus becomes quite literally the relationship of past and present, which are inextricably linked, as well as the power of the past over the present and even the future. Six major shifts in time occur between the historical past and the present. Coppola's purpose is to illustrate not only how the original godfather became a mobster but also how that heritage came to dominate his son Michael's life: continuing the suggestions of Greek or Shakespearian tragedy that Coppola employed to structure the first film, he now demonstrates how the sins of the fathers are visited upon their sons.

The Godfather Part II opens in the early years of the twentieth century in Sicily. A young Vito Andolini's father and brother have been killed by the local Mafia boss Don Francesco, aka Don Ciccio (Giuseppe Sillato). Vito's mother goes to Don Ciccio to plea for the young boy's life, claiming he is a bit of a simpleton, but the Mafioso replies that "when he's older, he'll come for revenge" and murders her as well while Vito escapes. Relatives and friends arrange for Vito to be saved and smuggled to America. Coppola then films a beautiful immigrant scene of the arrival of the *Mosholu* at Ellis Island (a set reconstructed carefully in the fish market of the Italian city of Trieste). When young Vito is asked his name, instead of Andolini from Corleone, the Irish immigration official misunderstands and registers him incorrectly, using his birthplace as his last name. This frequent mistake upon arrival in America becomes a portent of the confusion of Italian and American values that will haunt *The Godfather Part II*. Titles inform the viewer that the date is 1907 and that the boy's name is now Vito Corleone.

While the young Vito sits in a darkened room lit in a manner reminiscent of the carefully crafted interiors of the first film, awaiting the moment his quarantine for smallpox can be lifted and he can enter the United States, Coppola abruptly cuts to the future with an intertitle: HIS GRANDSON ANTHONY VITO CORLEONE. LAKE TAHOE NEVADA 1958. The scene recalls the wedding sequence that followed Bonasera's supplication to Don Corleone in the first film. One of the most powerful means at Coppola's disposal now becomes the subtle repetition of motifs, themes, and sequences from the first film, all set in an entirely different context to provide a commentary on each work. The location is now Nevada, not New York, but the same priest from the baptism scene in the first film now presides over the Eucharist. Things have obviously changed, since the policemen outside the family mansion are now served drinks rather than being vituperated. The Corleone family celebrates its power and search for legitimacy, surrounded by powerful figures, including the corrupt Senator Geary (G. D. Spradlin). The bright light of the celebration is once again contrasted to the dark, menacing lighting of Michael's study (even his windowpanes contain a spiderweb design, a metaphor for the evil deeds planned there).

Outside in the light, Geary praises Michael for contributing a huge check to the University of Nevada. Inside he attempts to shake Michael down for casino licenses while insulting his Italian heritage, a mistake for which he will eventually pay a very high price. During the rest of the celebration, Michael receives Johnny Ola, Hyman Roth's "Sicilian messenger boy," and attempts to smooth the feelings of Frankie Pentangeli, who is brooding over the friction with Roth's Italian allies in New York, the Rosato brothers. The distance Michael has moved from his Sicilian roots and his father's culture may be measured by Pentangeli's humorous attempts to convince the band to play a Sicilian tarantella: in spite of everything, only "Pop Goes the Weasel" comes out of their instruments. With Pentangeli's old-fashioned style of being a gangster, the impossibility of playing Sicilian music, which his father enjoyed at Connie's wedding in the first film, his international alliance with a Jewish mobster, and his meetings with a United States Senator, Michael has not only changed but the Mob itself has become more Americanized, less Sicilian, more global, and more multinational, just like other "businesses." The Corleone family has begun to disintegrate just like other contemporary American families: Connie now drags around men who do not love her, while Fredo's American wife is a drunk who shouts "never marry a wop" to the assembled guests. That evening an assassination attempt on Michael's life nearly succeeds, casting suspicion upon Pentangeli (in reality, Roth ordered the hit with intelligence gathered by Johnny Ola from Michael's own brother Fredo). This dramatic and somewhat confused event leads Coppola to his second important historical flashback, again introduced by an intertitle:

The Godfather Part II *(1974; Francis Ford Coppola, director). Don Fanucci (Gastone Moschin), the gangster boss of Vito Corleone's New York Italian neighborhood, strolls through the crowds at the San Gennaro Festival, a historical flashback to a now vanished Little Italy re-created by Coppola's set designers.*

VITO CORLEONE NEW YORK CITY 1917. Coppola reconstructs Little Italy from several streets in New York City and even includes a weepy melodrama, *Senza Mamma*, about the immigrant experience written by Coppola's maternal grandfather, which emphasizes family ties. This play finds echoes in the rest of the film, during which Michael continues to break down, even to destroy, the sacred bonds of family, all in the name of "business." In the theater during the performance of the melodrama, Vito first encounters a member of the Black Hand, Fanucci (Gastone Moschin), who preys on the Italians of the neighborhood by demanding protection money and a cut of any of the criminal activities in the quarter. Eventually, Vito meets his future criminal associates—a much younger Clemenza (Bruno Kirby) and Tessio (John Aprea). Although initially an honest man who only thinks of working hard to support his family, Vito loses his position at the Abbandando grocery story after Fanucci forces the owner to hire one of his relatives. Subsequently, young Clemenza demonstrates to Vito how easily money can be made through crime, earning Vito a rug lifted from the home of a rich family under the nose of a cop on the beat.

As Michael plays with his son Santino (later Sonny) on the stolen rug, we are once again abruptly jerked back into the present. This time, Coppola's treatment of the present becomes more complicated and consists of a number of different sequences in different locations, all of which concern the complex plot against his power. Michael visits Hyman Roth in Florida and then Frankie Pentangeli in New York, who now lives in the old family home of Don Vito Corleone that had first passed to Clemenza before his death. Uttering one of the most famous Sicilian sayings employed in the three scripts—"keep your friends close but your enemies closer"—Michael informs Pentangeli that Hyman Roth was behind the bungled assassination attempt at Lake Tahoe and urges him to make the peace with the Rosato brothers in order to lure Roth into the error of thinking that Michael has failed to realize Roth is behind his problems. In another brief sequence in this section, we see Fredo talking to Johnny Ola on the telephone, informing Roth's underling that Pentangeli has agreed to meet with the Rosato brothers and that he will not be bringing a bodyguard. When Pentangeli arrives and attempts to negotiate with the Rosato brothers following Michael's instructions, Tony Rosato (Danny Aiello) sneaks behind him with a garrote, declaring: "Michael Corleone says hello!" Since Pentangeli survives the strangulation, he will naturally later believe Michael had betrayed him and will agree to testify against Michael before a Senate hearing. But in reality, Roth and the Rosato brothers were behind the attempt on Pentangeli all along. The narrative then moves quickly (and somewhat confusingly to many first viewers of this section of the film) to a Nevada brothel run by Fredo where the arrogant Senator Geary falls into the Corleone family hands because a prostitute with whom he played sado-masochistic sexual games is found dead. Either the Senator killed the girl in a drunken frenzy (a possible hypothesis) or, what is more likely, the Corleones have arranged her murder to ensnare the Senator. Whatever the real explanation may be (and Coppola purposely keeps it unclear), there is no mistaking the meaning of Tom Hagen's words to the frantic Senator: "This girl has no family, nobody knows that she worked here. It'll be as if she never existed. All that's left is our friendship."

Another long, complicated series of sequences takes place in Battista's Cuba, where Michael has gone to meet Roth to seal a deal for investing millions of dollars in the Cuban casinos. Once again, Coppola returns to the important theme of *The Godfather*—comparing Mafia activities to business. The boardroom meeting of the Mafia dons in that first film, unfolding in the New York Central Railroad corporate office, now takes place in Battista's presidential palace, where representatives of gigantic American corporations—General Fruit, United Telephone and Telegraph, Pan-American Mining, South American Sugar—all sit around the table. Both Roth and Michael join them as equal capitalist partners: as Battista puts it, they represent "our

associates in tourism and leisure activities"! Battista is given a solid-gold telephone by one company, an almost too obvious symbol of rampant and exploitive capitalism. In yet another important sequence in Cuba, to celebrate
his birthday, Roth divides up a cake with the image of Cuba on it for his
criminal associates, waxes eloquent about the fact that "there are wonderful
times" and that in Cuba, the Mob finally has a governmental partner that
"knows how to help business." Later, in private, Roth makes the justly famous
statement about the Mob: "Michael, we're bigger than U.S. Steel" and says
that now with a beachhead ninety miles from American shores with a
friendly government, all they need is a man who wants to be president badly
enough to take their money.

More and more subplots are developed in this Cuban section. Fredo arrives with briefcases of money for Roth, and Michael reveals to Fredo that
he intends to kill Roth before Roth manages to murder him. Senator Geary
(now in the Corleones' pocket) shows up to be entertained by Fredo, while
Roth reveals, in spite of himself, why he hates Michael so much. He was a
close friend of Moe Greene, killed at the conclusion of the first film. Like
Michael, Roth maintains that he forgot that murder because he supposedly
thinks only about business: "So when he turned up dead, I let it go. And I
said to myself, this is the business we've chosen. I didn't ask who gave the
order. Because it had nothing to do with business!" Of course, like Michael,
who always preached that business was not personal in the first film, Roth
in fact considers everything to be personal. By accident, Fredo reveals that
he is the family traitor, breaking Michael's heart, and almost at the same
time, Michael's bodyguard (Amerigo Tot) is killed by the Cuban police
guarding Roth in the hospital; Fredo escapes after Michael tells him he
knows that he has betrayed the family ("I know it was you Fredo, you broke
my heart . . . you broke my heart!"), and the entire enterprise in Cuba collapses as Castro's guerrilla forces occupy the capital city of Havana. Relent-
lessly pursuing his nemesis, Michael hounds Roth all over the globe before
finally having him assassinated at the airport when he returns home to the
United States to face arrest by the authorities.

Back in Lake Tahoe, Michael hears that Kay has lost a child and angrily demands to know if it was a boy. Many of the flashbacks to the past are linked
to the Corleone children, emphasizing the ties between generations in the
family history. In this case, the child Kay and Michael have lost triggers a
flashback to the young Vito Corleone, desperately watching attempts to cure
the young, just-born Fredo of pneumonia. The two children link the narrative sequences from present and past, so different in place and time.

It is in this flashback to Vito Corleone's youth that the godfather is born.
Fanucci insists on having a share of the proceeds (he wants "to wet his

beak," as he puts it in the Sicilian manner) from the criminal activities of Clemenza, Tessio, and their friend Vito. But Vito has looked around the city and has realized that Fanucci really has little power and no organization. He tells his two friends that he will take care of Fanucci by "reasoning" with him (these powers of reason that later become proverbial) and will "make an offer he don't refuse . . . don't worry." At first he toys with Fanucci to lull him into a false sense of security, meeting him as he takes his ritual espresso coffee in an Italian bar. But during the local celebrations and processions devoted to San Rocco, Vito kills Fanucci at the door to his apartment. The scene is ingeniously choreographed as Vito Corleone runs over the tops of the tenement houses while spotting his prey. Down below, on the street level, Fanucci prances down the street in his signature white suit and receives adulation and signs of respect from his "clients." Like the baptism sequence and its dramatic cross-cutting in the first *Godfather* film, this sequence is a tour de force of editing that employs a meaningful moment in Italian American Catholic culture (a religious procession) to narrate a dramatic crime. After the murder of Fanucci, and just before the narrative abruptly returns us back to the present, Vito sits on the front porch steps of his tenement with his family, picks up the baby Michael (the future Don Michael Corleone), and tells him in Italian: "Michael, your father loves you very much, very much."

In this section of the film devoted to the fictive present, a number of important events occur. Michael confronts a Senate subcommittee hearing on organized crime whose star witness—Frankie Pentangeli—was no doubt modeled upon the real super-witness Joseph Valachi who turned on the Mob and was guarded in an FBI compound like the film character.[59] Haunted by the fact that his brother is a traitor, Michael asks his mother if Don Vito, by being strong to protect his own family, ever thought he might lose it. When his mother insists that you can never lose your family, Michael replies in Italian "i tempi cambiano" ("times are changing"). As if to emphasize that the old days were perhaps not only different but better, another important flashback occurs here in the narrative, returning us to Vito Corleone, who has become an important person in the neighborhood now that the fate of Fanucci has become known. Besides receiving free fruit as a sign of respect, Vito's wife asks him to intercede with a greedy Italian landlord, Signor Roberto (Leopoldo Trieste), to help a poor widow keep her apartment and her dog. Vito does not respond to Roberto's insults, he merely tells him to ask around the neighborhood about him, and later when Signor Roberto returns with the information he has received, he is so afraid of Vito that he can barely find his voice to agree to Vito's demands.

The Godfather Part II *(1974; Francis Ford Coppola, director). Signor Roberto (Leopoldo Trieste), the local Italian American landlord, argues with the young Vito Corleone about an old woman's rent in a historical flashback to a now-vanished Little Italy in New York City.*

In a comic skit that is perhaps almost unique in the three *Godfather* films, the Italian actor Leopoldo Trieste does a superb job of struggling to open the door to escape from the dreaded presence of Don Vito. Coppola nailed the door shut without telling Trieste before he performed this scene, so his discomfort at being unable to escape through the office door is genuine. It is exactly the kind of scene that Coppola must have seen in the two Fellini films starring Trieste that formed part of his cinematic heritage—*Lo sceicco bianco* (1952, *The White Sheik*) and *I vitelloni* (1953). It is not by accident that in the historical flashbacks, Coppola employs two Italian actors, Trieste here and Gastone Moschin as Fanucci. If Trieste is an homage to Fellini, Moschin pays tribute to another and younger model Coppola admires—the Bernardo Bertolucci of *Il conformista* (1970, *The Conformist*), a brilliant film in which Moschin played a murderous Fascist secret agent to great effect. In the one case, Coppola uses Fanucci to show how Vito's strength of mind and his courage made him fit to be a criminal mastermind. In the other, Trieste underscores how Don Vito always uses his public persona as a dispenser of justice and fair treatment to build his reputation among the Italian American community, since he realized that it was an essential ingredient in creating his power base.

Coppola returns us from this humorous vignette filled with Italian American cultural symbols to the Senate hearing. The Valachi testimony before the McClellan Senate subcommittee on organized crime had blown the lid off the history and practices of the Mafia in a way that no other investigation had ever done. Understandably, this information also made Italian Americans nervous, and the prejudicial idea that all members of this ethnic group were criminals had led to some very hyperbolic editorials in the Italian American newspaper *Il progresso*. Partly in fun and partly because Coppola resented the charges that they were playing to ethnic prejudice, the screenplay of the second film incorporates the strident defense of Italian American "genius" into the unctuous declaration that Senator Geary utters at the hearing: "These hearings on the Mafia are in no way whatsoever a slur upon the great Italian people. Because I can state from my own knowledge and experience that Italian-Americans are among the most loyal, most law-abiding, patriotic, hard-working American citizens in this land." Such a statement presents quite a contrast to the insulting, ethnic slurs Geary pronounced in Michael's Lake Tahoe office. In this statement and in Michael's subsequent written statement he reads to the subcommittee, we find the first occurrences of the word "Mafia" and the phrase "Cosa Nostra" in the *Godfather* trilogy.

Subsequently, Michael quizzes Fredo about the Roth conspiracy, then tells him that he must leave the family and orders Al Neri to kill Fredo after the death of their mother. Even though Italians consider family relationships sacrosanct, there is no lack of betrayals within their nuclear families, just as there is no absence of traitors in their Mafia families. At the hearing, Michael arranges for Frankie's Sicilian brother Vincenzo, who speaks no English, to appear at the hearing. Vincenzo simply nods toward Frankie, and this apparently results in Frankie's refusal to testify against Michael, saving him from a charge of perjury and allowing him to turn the tables on the investigating subcommittee. It is important to understand exactly what has occurred in this scene. Michael is not threatening Frankie by bringing his brother to the hearing, implying that Vincenzo will be killed if Frankie talks. Quite the reverse is happening according to the ancient logic of the Mafia code of *omertà* that forbade talking to the police in the old Cosa Nostra. Frankie's brother is threatening Frankie's family, for according to the old ethos, if Frankie breaks the iron rule of *omertà*, Vincenzo will be forced to destroy Frankie's family to restore his own honor. A remark in Italian left untranslated by Coppola's subtitles at this point shows that this is so: Tom Hagen leans over to Vincenzo Pentangeli and says at the end of the hearing: "l'onore della famiglia sta apposto" ("the honor of the family is intact").

Michael's success as a gangster is not matched by a similar success with his family. Besides his brother Fredo's betrayal (that must eventually be punished by death), Michael's wife Kay has begun to realize that Michael will never manage to legitimize the Corleone family business and in an effort to leave the marriage and to take her children with her, she has had an abortion on her last pregnancy, throwing the fact into Michael's face in order to force him to break with her. Once again, the mention of children provides the transition to another flashback, this time to follow the young Vito Corleone who travels from New York to Sicily for two kinds of business: revenge on Don Ciccio for murdering his family years earlier; and collaboration with his friend Don Tommasino (Mario Cotone) in their new Genco olive-oil business which eventually serves Vito as a legitimate front for his criminal enterprises. Kay's rather exaggerated definition of the Sicilian thirst for *vendetta* in the previous sequence—"This Sicilian thing that's been going on for two thousand years"—dominates this historical return to Sicily, resulting in Don Ciccio's assassination and Don Tommasino's paralysis from a crippling shotgun blast. As Vito boards the train to return to America, his business finished, he now holds Michael in his arms and tells his son (and future heir to the same thirst for revenge): "Michael, say good-bye."

In the final series of sequences in the present which concludes the film, a number of things occur. Michael's paranoia has become monstrous. When Tom asks him is it worth it to wipe everyone out after he has won, Michael replies: "I don't feel I have to wipe everyone out—just my enemies, that's all." But by now, his enemies include members of his own family as well as his gangster opponents. As in the first film, Michael settles the family's accounts, although not in as brilliant and as economic a manner as in the baptism sequence. Hyman Roth is shot at the airport after he has been expelled from all the countries in which he has attempted to hide from Michael's wrath (a parallel to the death of Barzini and the other heads of the Five Families). Frankie Pentangeli commits suicide after being promised by Tom Hagen that his family will be taken care of (a parallel to the death of the once faithful Tessio). Before this occurs, he and Tom reminisce about the better times, when the Mafia families were organized along the lines of the Roman legions: "We was like the Roman Empire," Pentangeli remarks before he kills himself in a bathtub by slitting his wrists like a Roman patrician. Finally, even Michael's brother Fredo is killed by Al Neri for his part in the Roth plot (a parallel to the murder of Carlo Rizzi, Michael's brother-in-law). As the shot rings out on the lake when Fredo is shot, Michael bows his head down and ponders the depths to which he has just sunk. Coppola then dissolves to December 7, 1941, on the day Pearl Harbor was bombed and when Michael's sister Connie was first introduced to her future husband Carlo Rizzi by Sonny. The occasion is a surprise birthday party for the don, coincidentally born on Pearl Harbor Day though many years before, and while they wait for Don Vito to return home, Sonny, Michael, and Fredo discuss the impending war. Sonny declares that the thirty thousand men who enlisted that day were "saps" because they were risking their lives for strangers, not their family, and when Michael says, "That's Pop talking," Sonny tells him: "Your country ain't your blood, you remember that!" In spite of all his plans and his desire to escape the kind of life his father has led, Michael Corleone ultimately chooses, in a situation of necessity, to follow the same path. As the whole family runs off to greet the don at the door, Michael remains alone at the dinner table: Coppola then dissolves to Vito holding Michael's hand and waving good-bye from the train in Sicily, dissolves to the future where the now victorious don sits alone in his Lake Tahoe compound, and finally fades to black. Michael Corleone has emerged from the many attempts on his life and power completely victorious. But he now stands alone, the murderer of his brother and without a wife and family at home. In the end, one "family" has destroyed the other.

The dramatic cross-cutting between the two worlds of the young Vito Corleone, the future godfather, and his modern son Michael, the man who will eventually wear the godfather's mantle, forces the viewer to consider the evolution and collision of two entirely different kinds of moralities. There is the ancient, traditional Mediterranean morality that some students of southern Italian culture have labeled as "amoral familism." Best stated in Edward Banfield's *The Moral Basis of a Backward Society*, first published in 1958, this world is dominated by the basic rule: "Maximize the material, short-run advantage of the nuclear family; and assume that others will do likewise."[60] Such characters as Don Ciccio, Don Tommasino, Fanucci, and the Pentangeli brothers certainly do follow the old ways of "amoral familism" that are as old as Homeric poetry. Such values, if they are practiced in America, are imported from Mediterranean culture.

Vito Andolini (aka Corleone) was born into an impoverished and lawless world of blood feuds and endless *vendettas* that spawned the breeding ground for first the disorganized Black Hand and later the Cosa Nostra, or the Mafia in America. Although he attempted to live an honest and law-abiding life in America, he found that injustice (in the form of Fanucci) and economic prejudice (in the form of a lack of opportunities for Italian American immigrants) were almost as daunting as the conditions he left behind him. He thus returned to the "amoral familism" described by Banfield and dedicated his life to maximizing the power of family or clan. This is the world of both *The Godfather* and *The Godfather Part II*, but perhaps it is best described in a portion of the original script for the first film that was eventually discarded in the final cut as Don Corleone gives an important piece of advice to his son Michael:

> Believe in a family. Can you believe in your country? Those *pezzonovante* of the state who decide what we shall do with our lives? Who declare wars they wish us to fight in to protect what they own. Do you put your fate in the hands of men whose only talent is that they tricked a bloc of people to vote for them? . . . Believe in a family, believe in a code of honor, older and higher, believe in roots that go back thousands of years into your race. Make a family, Michael, and protect it. These are our affairs, *sono cosa nostra*, governments only protect men who have their own individual power. Be one of those men . . . you have the choice.[61]

Living in the twenty-first century according to such rules would presuppose a frightening return to a premodern era, but it is impossible to understand the appeal of the *Godfather* trilogy without understanding the primordially satisfying appeal of such a system. A part of every contemporary audience expresses satisfaction in the defeat of the "system," cheering when Don Vito or Don Michael settles the family's "debts" at the end of each of the three films in a hail of gunfire.

A second set of values, appealing to many Americans, may be said to reside in the "business logic" that Italians like Don Vito seem to have acquired after they reached America. Over and over again in the first and second films of the trilogy, both Don Vito and then Michael Corleone are identified with the power of reason and with a business logic, a situational morality that calls for the compromise of absolute moral principles like those held by an amoral familist who believes in the ancient codes of honor of southern Europe when business demands compromise. It is this strict business logic that drives Vito to make the peace, and encourages Michael to strike a deal with Hyman Roth, and when Frankie Pentangeli, a representative of the old ways, what the Italians call *la via vecchia*, indignantly exclaims that Michael has "loyalty to a Jew before your own blood," he expresses the older morality. In principle, then, the two worlds should be different and in fact seem to be: family, clan, blood feud, *vendetta*, on the one hand; and business, profit, the iron law of the market (albeit an illegal market), on the other.

Yet the ultimate irony in the *Godfather* trilogy is that the business enterprise in question—organized crime—is called a "family," not a corporation. At its core, in spite of the Americanization of certain elemental values from the world of "amoral familism," the attempt to apply strictly business principles to criminal life ultimately proves to be a failure because of the survival of a rugged residue of the old ethos. Ultimately, in spite of what everyone says, everything is personal, not just business. Thus, the demands for revenge—and not merely profit—are the motives that truly drive the protagonists of each of the three films, no matter how much Michael may try to deny this or to reform his activities into Anglo-American directions. Michael's efforts to create a new and completely Americanized—that is to say, legitimate commercial lifestyle for his "family"—are doomed to failure. Perhaps the most distressing aspect of this situation is that the treachery and betrayal always seems to come from within a man's true family as well as from his Mafia family (Carlo Rizzi, in the first film; and Fredo in the second). Michael's every effort to protect his family eventually results in his family's destruction.

The Godfather Part III *and the Search for Michael's Redemption*

Coppola finally agreed to create a second sequel to *The Godfather* in large measure because he did not feel that Michael Corleone had been punished sufficiently in the first two films. As he has remarked in the DVD

The Godfather Part III *(1990; Francis Ford Coppola, director). Joined by shyster lawyer B. J. Harrison (George Hamilton) and Archbishop Gilday (Donal Donnelly), an aging Michael Corleone (Al Pacino) celebrates an honor from the Catholic Church for his donation of $100,000,000 to Catholic and Sicilian charities.*

commentary on the film, there is no worse way to pay for your sins than to have your children pay for them. Also according to the DVD commentary, *The Godfather Part III* was originally intended to open with a meeting between Michael and Archbishop Gilday (Donal Donnelly), the manager of the Vatican bank. That important business deal would have been followed by the scene that opens the film as it was finally edited—a title reading NEW YORK CITY 1979 with a sequence showing Michael about to receive membership in the Order of Saint Sebastian (a thinly disguised fictional version of the real Order of Malta), while his voice-over reads a letter he sends to his children, asking them to attend the ceremony. In a sense, the archbishop would have replaced Bonasera of the original film as a supplicant to a Mafia don, but now the fact that the supplicant would be a prince of the Catholic Church bargaining with a gangster for many hundreds of millions of dollars would provide an accurate measure of the power and influence Michael has accumulated to the present time of 1979.

The prelate would have opened his request for funds with an ironic citation from Dante's *Inferno* XIX, 115–17, a denunciation of the corruption of the Church because of the wealth it obtained from the famous (but historically nonexistent) Donation of Emperor Constantine: "Ah, Constantine! Of how much ill was mother, / Not thy conversion, but that marriage-dower / Which the first wealthy Father took from thee!"[62] Since the archbishop will prove to be thoroughly corrupt himself during the course of the film, his cynical citation of Dante's denunciation of ecclesiastical wealth would have been a humorous, but perhaps too overly intellectual, opening to the film. According to Coppola, Michael's response was to have been: "You quote Dante beautifully, but we are talking about business!"

That response would have thus returned the spectator to the main theme of the first and second films in the trilogy. Then Michael would have agreed to give the Church six hundred million dollars to cover shortfalls in their accounts, and in return, he and his family would be virtually guaranteed legitimacy and the laundering of their remaining wealth plus a controlling interest in a global holding company owned in large measure by the Vatican. The metaphorical parallel between washing or laundering dirty money and washing away sins was completely intentional, since *The Godfather Part III* represents Michael's desperate attempt to find redemption for his horrible crimes. In this movie, he also attempts to put his family back together—not only repairing his relationship to his estranged wife Kay but also reconciling his life and career with his children—his son Anthony (Franc D'Ambrosio), who wants to be an opera singer and hopes for his father's blessing, and with his daughter Mary (Sofia Coppola), who he has named as the director of the wealthy charitable foundation he has created to distribute funds to the needy in Sicily, the land of his father's birth. In contrast to the first two films, where Michael always emerges victorious after having outsmarted his enemies, now the weary mobster boss desires only to achieve redemption, forgiveness, and to wash away his sins and those of his gangster family by charitable works and good deeds. He is no longer very interested in the illegal activities of his past. Audiences who had loved the first two parts of the trilogy were naturally disappointed at not experiencing the return of the clever young Mafia don who never missed a trick. In the third film, Coppola focuses his camera on Michael's soul.

Thus, the third installment repeats many of the motifs of the first and second films with variations, but now these seemingly familiar events— family gatherings, Catholic rituals, betrayals, ritual killings—are viewed from an entirely different viewpoint—that of Christian redemption. The festive occasion that opens the third film with Michael's induction into the super-elite Order of Saint Sebastian may superficially recall the wedding and the confirmation ceremonies of the first two works (including the family portraits taken at such group events), but here the Church is involved and the protagonist's motives concern his immortal soul. Moreover, Michael takes under his wing Vincent Mancini (Andy Garcia), the illegitimate offspring of the liaison between Sonny Corleone and the barely seen Lucy Mancini of *The Godfather*. Destined to become the successor to Don Vito and Don Michael, Vincent stands in contrast to Joey Zaza (Joe Mantagna), the flashy kind of mobster probably modeled on John Gotti. Zaza has taken over the Corleone-family crime business in New York, which had earlier passed first to Clemenza and then to Frankie Pentangeli. Preoccupied with his search for legitimacy and the charitable works designed to save his soul, Michael has paid little attention to the original source of his family's wealth and power, and Vincent objects to the manner in which Zaza has recruited blacks to deal in drugs in Italian American neighborhoods and has generally corrupted the old ways of doing "business," methods that would have appealed to the old Don Vito Corleone. Ultimately, Vincent will succeed Michael as the godfather of the family, and both Puzo and Coppola pondered the possibility of making a fourth film in the series that would have dealt with two separate time periods and narratives, much like the style of *The Godfather Part II*. The modern story would have focused upon Vincent, while flashbacks would have examined the rise to power of Don Vito Corleone and Sonny Corleone in the years leading up to World War II. Such a film might still be made some day in the future, but Coppola would have to work without the contributions of Mario Puzo, who died in 1999.[63]

One observant critic of the *Godfather* trilogy has quite rightly underscored their indebtedness to grand opera in many ways other than the fact that the ending of the third film coincides with events in the conclusion of Mascagni's *Cavalleria rusticana* on the Palermo opera stage.[64] The ending of the film—Mary is shot on the steps of the opera house when the assassin misses her father Michael—recalls Giuseppe Verdi's great tragic opera *Rigoletto* (1851), where the tragic death of Gilda, Rigoletto's beautiful daughter, occurs by accident and as a way of punishing the hunchback protagonist. Like Michael, who seems to have been cursed by a cruel fate to repeat the path of his own father, Rigoletto is hoisted by his own petard with the fatal curse "La maledizione."

There is also an operatic or at least a musical quality in Coppola's technique of repeated motifs, repetitions with variations, in each of the three films. Many film historians have pointed to the obvious Italian cinematic precedents for Coppola's trilogy—Visconti's *Il gattopardo, La caduta degli dei* (1969, *The Damned*), or Bertolucci's *1900* (1976, *Novecento*). All three films provide a detailed study of a family saga and a historical panorama Coppola could not have failed to appreciate. Visconti and Bertolucci are the two Italian directors most indebted to melodrama and Verdian or Wagnerian opera in their films, and the manner in which grand opera introduces musical themes, varies them, sets them in different keys and unusual contexts, corresponds exactly to the manner in which Coppola introduces sequences that have parallels in the rest of the trilogy.

We have already mentioned how each of the three films opens with a family ceremony, and who could forget the bloodbaths that conclude each of them? Religious ceremonies and rituals are also employed in similar ways: the baptism sequence framing the murders in the first film; the procession in Little Italy that highlights Fanucci's assassination by Vito Corleone in the second film; the similar procession in Little Italy in the third film during which Vincenzo assassinates Joey Zaza, as well as the religious procession on the opera stage that serves as commentary on the action in the audience concluding the third film. In each film, characters show up at such ceremonies who are unwelcome and uninvited (Luca Brasi at Connie's wedding; Frankie Pentangeli at Anthony's confirmation; Joey Zaza and Vincent at the ceremony inducting Michael into the Order of San Sebastian). If Vito has his Luca Brasi, Michael has his Al Neri. Traitors abound in successive films: Paulie Gatto, Carlo Rizzi, and Tessio; Frankie, Fredo, and Hyman Roth; Don Altobello, Joey Zaza, and a series of corrupt priests and financiers (Lucchesi, the Archbishop, Keinszig). The meeting in the New York Central Railroad boardroom where Vito makes the peace with the Five Families returns in Havana in Battista's presidential palace, and once again in the third film, where the Commission gathers in Atlantic City before they are all murdered by Joey Zaza. Specifically Italian foods also attain symbolic significance in each film. Clemenza carts off the can-noli but leaves the pistol in the first film and instructs Michael on how to make Italian American spaghetti sauce. The cannolis return in the third film when Connie poisons Don Altobello at the opera, and in the same work, Vincent teaches Mary how to make gnocchi. In the second film, a melodrama (*Senza mamma*) with an immigrant audience makes an ironic comment on the importance of family, while in the third, a puppet show "La Baronessa di Carlini"—about a father who kills his daughter for being in love with her cousin—symbolizes Michael's fear that Vincent will marry his cousin, who is Michael's daughter, Mary.

In each film, the rule governing an attempted overthrow of the Cor-leone dynasty follows the same pattern: enemies always come at you through those you love. Crime is always described in terms of business deals, not personal *vendettas*, but inevitably business becomes personal and results in a search for revenge. When Michael finally meets the sinis-ter Lucchesi at the first meeting to discuss the control of Immobiliare (the name of the Vatican holding company), Lucchesi remarks: "Yes, you will take control. We'll gladly put you at the helm of our little fleet. But our ships must all sail in the same direction. Otherwise, who can say how long your stay with us will last? It's not personal, it's only business. You should know, Godfather." Michael replies that if Lucchesi is ready to do business with him, he is prepared to do business with them, but as he leaves the sumptuous Vatican palace, he remarks "We're back to the Borgias!"—for-getting that he has committed enough heinous crimes himself to rival that famous Renaissance family.

Even simple visual images weave a thread throughout the three films, perhaps the most famous being the appearance of oranges at important moments in the film.[65] In the first film, Vito shops for that fruit just before he is shot, and Coppola photographs the fruit rolling around the dark street in an unusual overhead shot near where Don Vito's body falls. Tes-sio (a future traitor) is introduced with an orange in his hand. Oranges are placed on the table at Woltz's mansion. At the meeting of the Five Fami-lies, oranges are placed in front of Vito's enemies on the table. In the sec-ond film, this motif continues: Johnny Ola brings an orange from Florida from Hyman Roth. Both the young Vito and Fanucci pick up an orange from a grocer's cart. When Michael declares that if history has taught us anything, it instructs us that anybody can be killed, he is eating a whole orange. In the third film, when Michael has a diabetic attack before con-fession to Cardinal Lamberto, he asks for orange juice and later, when he dies, an orange drops from his dying hand. Their appearance in the three films becomes an operatic leitmotif, and oranges are particularly relevant in a film about Sicilian American gangsters. Sicily is famous for a particular kind of orange, the so-called blood orange whose juice is so dark it might be taken for tomato juice or blood. *"Sangue chiama sangue"* ("blood demands blood") exclaims the faithful Sicilian retainer Carlo who once served Michael as his bodyguard in Sicily in the first film and will eventually revenge the murder of his patron Don Tommasino in the third film. The Sicilian blood orange punctuates the killings of the three films and the treacherous dealings of their protagonists.

The result of these many interrelated sequences in the three films and a consistent use of imagery and situations throughout the trilogy produce a richness of cinematic texture that is without parallel in American films of the postwar period. It is not overstating the case to say that the interrelated and interwoven themes of the *Godfather* trilogy recall two great works of Italian literature, *The Divine Comedy* and *The Decameron*, in which much the same technique is exploited to great effect between the various cantos of the poem or the *novelle* of the prose collection. If film directors must act like God when they create, as Federico Fellini often claimed many times in the course of his long career, then Francis Ford Coppola surely endowed even the smallest of details in each of these three masterpieces with divine inspiration.

Coppola intended *The Godfather Part III* to portray his belief that the higher up the ladder of society you climb, the more corrupt things are. Saddam Hussein, he has remarked, was a devoted fan of *The Godfather!*[66] Much of the plot of this third film came directly from newspaper headlines of the period. In the screenplay, Michael makes huge investments in a Vatican-owned company run by corrupt prelates and financiers backed by equally corrupt Italian politicians. Such a theme of corruption in the highest places, especially corruption in the Church, was probably suggested to him by the fact that the Italian Società Generale Immobiliare (a huge firm in which the Vatican owned some 15% of its shares) actually invested in Paramount, his production company.[67] Archbishop Gilday seems to have been modeled after Bishop Paul Marcinkus, an American priest from Chicago whose management of the Vatican bank was seriously criticized for Mob connections in both Italy and the United States. The fact that Marcinkus came from Cicero, Illinois (long the capital of Mafia activities in the Chicago area since the time of Al Capone), and the remark he reputedly made that the Church could not be managed with Hail Marys alone certainly raises interesting questions about his stewardship of the Church's finances. Marcinkus was very friendly with Michele Sindona (1920–86), a financier deeply involved in Vatican banking and with large investments in Immobiliare. Sindona was selected by Pope Paul VI as a financial adviser to the Vatican, but his empire crashed and he ended his life in prison, where he was poisoned. It is probable that his own bank in the United States, the Franklin Bank, was deeply involved in Mafia money laundering before it collapsed in 1974. Sindona had a powerful friend in Italy, Licio Gelli, the leader of the P2 Masonic Lodge that included most of the powerful and influential people in Italy. The figure of Lucchesi (Enzo Robutti), the powerful eminence grise behind all the skullduggery at the Vatican aimed at Michael's power and money, probably derives from various characteristics of Gelli, Sindona, and a famous Italian politician named Giulio Andreotti, many times prime minister of various Italian governments and a Christian Democrat frequently linked to the Mafia in Sicily. When Carlo kills the master criminal Lucchesi by plunging his broken eyeglasses into his neck, he has just whispered into his ear a famous cynical remark famously uttered by Giulio Andreotti: "*Il potere logora chi non ce l'ha!*" ("Power wears out those who don't have it"), a humorous modification of the better-known Anglo-Saxon adage attributed to Lord Acton that "power corrupts and absolute power corrupts absolutely." No doubt Coppola based the figure of Keinszig (Helmut Berger), another corrupt banker in the film, on Roberto Calvi, the administrator of the Vatican-owned Banco Ambrosiano and a close collaborator of Sindona who died a mysterious death in 1982 in London by hanging from the Blackfriars Bridge. He was probably murdered there (just as Keinszig is certainly murdered by Michael's emissaries in the film), since his death at a bridge named for the Blackfriars (the English term for Dominican Order) provides a pointed reference to the Vatican and the financial scandals associated with Calvi, Sindona, and Marcinkus.

To understand completely the political, economic, and cultural background of the Vatican corruption that Coppola employs as a backdrop to Michael's search for redemption would require extensive reading and knowledge of contemporary Italian history.[68] As if these nefarious Italian and Vatican figures did not provide a complex enough plot, Coppola adds details obviously related to the sudden and mysterious death of Pope John Paul I in 1978 after only about a month as supreme pontiff. This pope had demanded an investigation of the Vatican finances managed by Calvi, Marcinkus, and others, and his unexpected death was clearly helpful to those involved in the financial morass at the Vatican. Coppola creates a similar religious figure, the honest Cardinal Lamberto (Raf Vallone), a good man determined to clean up Vatican finances who dies in similarly mysterious circumstances while Michael tries desperately to save him. Upon this very complex series of references to contemporary Italian history, much of which was unfortunately lost on American audiences, Coppola overlays the narrative of Pietro Mascagni's melodrama *Cavalleria rusticana*, an opera about revenge and adultery at Easter time, in which Anthony Corleone is to debut his operatic career at a performance in Palermo with the entire family in the audience. Naturally, this musical premier becomes the dramatic moment when Michael's enemies will try to have him killed, and in like measure, Michael goes to the opera after dispatching his own agents to dispose of the men plotting against the pope and himself to conceal their financial misdeeds.

The structure of *The Godfather Part III* thus resembles nothing else more than a complex baroque opera, with several main plots and various interconnected subplots. In fact, the conclusion of the film plays itself out as Mascagni's opera draws to a close on the Palermo stage. It is not surprising that the theme of Mascagni's opera is that of revenge—*vendetta*—the core motif of the entire *Godfather* trilogy. But the revenge theme, so central to the entire *Godfather* story, often must struggle for emergence in such a collection of complicated subplots, and it stands in opposition to the other important theme in this third part of the trilogy, Michael's search for redemption.

Although Michael searches desperately to atone for his crimes, Coppola denies him even that satisfaction. When the guilt-ridden Mafia boss meets Cardinal Lamberto, the kind priest to whom he has gone to uncover Vatican corruption, he says he is "beyond redemption," and initially, when Michael asks what the point of confession is if he does not repent, Lamberto replies that he is a practical man and has nothing to lose by confessing his sins. When he hears the horrible news that Michael has murdered his brother, Lamberto utters a heretical denial of the possibility of Michael's redemption. Absolving him almost automatically, he declares that Michael's life *could* be redeemed, but that he knows Michael does not believe it. Michael's terrible punishment is to lose his faith—even in Dante's world of the damned, only "una lagrimetta" ("one little tear") will save a soul if the sinner has faith in the cleansing power of redemption, but Michael lacks that simple faith. Medieval Christians would know the term for his condition—it is despair, the most grievous sin imaginable, since it denies the possibility of salvation. The figure representing Despair is the most heartrending figure in Giotto's Arena Chapel fresco cycle, and it would provide the perfect commentary upon Michael Corleone in his mature old age. When he utters his now-famous line that is parodied so humorously in *The Sopranos* on more than one occasion—"Just when I thought I was out, they pull me back in!"—he is being false to himself. It is not "they" who pull him back in but it is he who refuses to leave. Perhaps the most ironic aspect of *The Godfather Part III* is that Michael launches

another bloody settlement of accounts at the conclusion of the film motivated both by his other personal thirst for revenge and for the salvation of
a pope. But while the bodies pile up at the end of the film, he is left alone,
an old and embittered man, with only a stray dog to witness his death. Even
Vito Corleone died at home with his grandson as company. As noted, Coppola once intended the title of the final work to be "The Death of Michael
Corleone," and in truth, this theme represents the destination to which the
whole trilogy inexorably moves. But what a stupendous cinematic journey
that trek of a condemned soul provides for his audiences!

Martin Scorsese's Goodfellas *(1990) and* Casino *(1995):*
Mafia famiglia *versus Mafia "Crew" and the Eclipse of*
the Wise Guys

It would be impossible to understand Scorsese's two important forays into
the gangster genre, or to appreciate fully the developments that take place
in David Chase's masterful series of television films, *The Sopranos*, without
viewing them against the backdrop of Coppola's *Godfather* trilogy. To ig-
nore the intertexual links between all these works would be something
similar to evaluating the place of the Civil War in American popular culture without taking into account the impact of *Gone with the Wind*. Coppola's trilogy aimed at an epic sweep of American (and Mafia) history that
could serve both as a metaphor for America and a tragic family saga worthy of comparison to Greek drama or Shakespeare, and an inevitable result
of his talent and the films' impact upon the popular imagination naturally
romanticized, to a certain extent, the theme of the Italian American Wise
Guy. Scorsese's take on the Mob was quite different. Whereas Coppola followed such European epic films as those made by Italian directors Visconti
or Bertolucci, Scorsese—who elsewhere admits to following Italian models
for such works as *Mean Streets* (Fellini's *I vitelloni*) or his contribution to
New York Stories in 1989 entitled "Life Stories" (Italian episode films such
as *Boccaccio '70*)[69]—developed a personal style beyond that of *Mean Streets*
by incorporating many of what he himself calls "all the basic tricks of the
New Wave from around 1961." These include freeze frames, repetitions of
various shots or sequences from different points of view, and jump cuts.[70]
More than is typical of Coppola's cinematic style, there is the hint of the
cinéphile or film buff in Scorsese's technique, as well as the inevitable
metacinematic touches that mark the European auteur. But Scorsese is also
highly indebted to the native American tradition of the gangster film and
the documentary, as well as that hybrid European-American tradition of
film noir. These influences are particularly evident in his frequent use of

voice-overs in both films to tie the sometimes disparate sequences together (typical of both *film noir* and documentary) as well as the extensive use of establishing captions to mark the different narrative divisions of the film into segments (a technique used frequently in realistic documentaries). The extremely explicit use of coarse language marks a step beyond Coppola's much more measured use of such vulgar expressions. The "F" word dominates the conversation of his Wise Guys just as it does the language of the television series indebted so much to Scorsese's example, *The Sopranos*. And Scorsese's use of music in both films stands apart from Coppola's Italian and Italian American compositions (interspersed with a few popular songs) written specially for his trilogy by Nino Rota and his father Carmine Coppola. The screenplay for *Goodfellas* lists, for example, forty-three different popular songs on the sound track, all following Scorsese's guiding principle that he would only use music that could have actually been heard in concert or on the radio at the time the events on the screen unfold. Rather than establishing time and place with popular music, Scorsese emphasizes that such an approach is "lazy" and that he wanted to "take advantage of the emotional impact of the music."[71] Thus, the sound track contains everything from Tony Bennett and Dean Martin oldies to Italian doo-wop, rhythm and blues, soul music, and hard rock that replace the more traditional orchestrated musical score by film composers hired specifically to write original scores for films.

More important than either his cinematic style or the musical accompaniment he employs, Scorsese's intentions are clearly different from those of Coppola. In both *Goodfellas* and *Casino*, he sets about to attack a number of myths about mobsters in general and Italian American Wise Guys (also called "goodfellas" in the film) in particular. Carlo Clarens summarizes these myths nicely in discussing *The Godfather*, noting that they were "carried to a claustrophobic extreme in Coppola's trilogy: namely, that there is a code of honor among thieves, and that this perfectly self-contained (and self-sustaining) world rarely touches the man in the street."[72] Scorsese shows that these defining myths developed in Coppola's view of the Mob are, at best, cinematographic conventions useful to concoct a great story. While Scorsese also employs a briefer history of the Mob in these two works than that larger and more epic expansion of historical time in Coppola's trilogy, he, too, presents his treatment of gangland as a kind of metaphor about American culture between the 1950s and the 1980s, taking aim at two key locations: the Italian American neighborhoods of New York; and the gambling casinos of Las Vegas, once dominated by the Mob because of the city's usefulness in employing the "skim" in the Mob-dominated gambling establishments to earn hundreds of millions of illegal dollars. Las Vegas casinos functioned as the Mob's laundry for dirty money from all of its many illegal activities.

Goodfellas presents a significantly different picture of organized crime. If Coppola's trilogy showed Italian American gangsters as the primary motivating force behind organized crime (with some important exceptions, such as the Jewish Hyman Roth), Scorsese represents the ethnic origins of criminals in a far more realistic manner. Coppola's works stress *la famiglia*—the blood ties between primarily Sicilian mobsters who set up crime "families" that are generally ruled by members of their own personal families. In Scorsese, the double-edged meaning of "family" has lost most of its emotive power. Like the world of Tony Soprano, it is the mobster's "crew" that matters—the men gathered around him regardless of ethnic origin who can become "good earners." It is true that Italian Americans seem to play a vital role, but at least in the world of the two Scorsese movies, major participants in criminal activity are not only Italian American, but are also Irish, Jewish, African American, and even Mormon.

Goodfellas provides the best example of this criminal "diversity." Henry Hill (Ray Liotta), the protagonist of the film who travels from being a gofer for the local crooks to robber and drug dealer to a "rat" who testifies against his colleagues and ends up in a witness protection program, is half-Irish and half-Sicilian. Although the fact that he is not completely Sicilian prevents him from ever becoming a "made guy," it does not hinder him in the slightest from working for a "crew" run by the local Sicilian mobster, Paulie Cicero (Paul Sorvino). Cicero seems connected to the powerful Gambino crime family, but his status is closer to that of the underbosses of Coppola's trilogy—Clemenza, Tessio, Frankie Pentangeli, or Joey Zaza—than any larger-than-life godfather. Moreover, organized crime lacks in Scorsese's world that mythic quality celebrated by Coppola. Henry explains exactly what the Mob means in an important voice-over:

> Hundreds of guys depended on Paulie and he got a piece of everything they made. It was tribute, just like in the old country, except they were doing it here in America. And all they got from Paulie was protection from other guys looking to rip them off. And that's what it's all about. That's what the FBI could never understand. That's what Paulie and the organization does—offer protection for people who can't go to the cops. That's it. That's all it is. They're like the police department for Wise Guys.

After giving Henry a one-hundred-dollar bill when he is first arrested, Jimmy informs Henry that he learned "the two greatest things in life . . . Never rat on your friends . . . and always keep your mouth shut." When he betrays his crew members and goes into the Witness Protection Program at the end of the film, Henry breaks the two cardinal rules of being a gangster.

Henry forms a tight group of three friends who work for Paulie, the other two being the psychotic killer Tommy DeVito (Joe Pesci) and the equally murderous but less mentally disturbed Jimmy Conway (Robert De Niro). Of the three, only Tommy is completely Sicilian. Henry Hill not only represents a different kind of crime organization than Coppola, but his marriage to a woman who is not Italian American (like Michael Corleone's marriage to Kay Adams, the purest kind of WASP) represents a step away from the old ways of marrying strictly Italian American girls. Karen Hill (Lorraine Bracco, later to become famous as Tony Soprano's psychiatrist) comes from a Jewish background, and her reaction to the Italian Americans who seem all to be named either Peter or Paul or Maria, and who all sport huge gold crucifixes that she must hide from her Jewish mother, shows how very different the cultures of these two groups really are.

Coppola's narrative in *The Godfather* and *The Godfather Part III* is basically a traditional story line with beginning, middle, and end. In *The Godfather Part II,* two interconnected story lines were juxtaposed, one explaining something about the other. Scorsese presents a far more discontinuous narrative, beginning with the opening scene that an establishing caption sets in New York in 1970. Henry, Jimmy, and Tommy are carrying the body of "made guy" Billy Batts (Frank Vincent) out of town to be buried after Tommy's psychotic anger has resulted in his murder, but we do not see the actual event until much later in the film. Although this opening segment of the film is the only one presented out of chronological order, the length and intensity of the other six segments of the story line vary tremendously and challenge the viewer perhaps even more than the two story lines Coppola developed in *The Godfather Part II.*

The first segment, EAST NEW YORK, BROOKLYN, 1955, shows a young Henry caught in the same trap that we have previously examined in *A Bronx Tale:* faced with a choice between imitating his father and the gangster across the street, Henry travels a different road than the young Italian American boy in that film and joins Paulie's crew, even receiving a "graduation gift" of money when he "loses his cherry" and is first arrested. A freeze frame underscores the smiling faces of the other "goodfellas" who have become Henry's new, true family.

An establishing caption labeled IDLEWILD AIRPORT, 1963 moves the film forward quickly almost a decade when Henry has become a "good earner" for Paulie. Henry's greatest achievement is to have taken part in the Air France robbery at the nearby airport, a caper organized by Jimmy. Here the main focus of the segment examines Henry's marriage to Karen, and like everything else in the world of the gangsters, love and sex are connected to money, to Wise Guy deals. Instead of being shocked at Henry's violent attack on a neighbor who has tried to force himself on her and who receives a pistol whipping for his impertinence, Karen confesses on a voice-over that Henry's lifestyle excited her: "I know there are women like my best friends who would have gotten out of there the minute their boyfriend gave them a gun to hide. But I didn't. I got to admit the truth. It turned me on." The connection of money, power, and sex becomes even more obvious at the conclusion of the segment when Karen asks Henry for a wad of cash to go shopping. When asked how much she needs, she replies "this much" and holds her thumb and forefinger a few inches apart, and when she receives a wad of cash that large, she then says "this much," places her hand on his crotch, then goes down on her knees and unzips his fly to perform oral sex on him. During the brief time Scorsese examines the evolution of their marriage in this segment, Karen has gone from being swept off her feet to negotiating money for sex. Their marriage has become a "deal" like everything else about Henry's life.

Another establishing caption sets us in QUEENS, NEW YORK, 11 JUNE 1970. We have now returned to the time opening the film, and now we see the details behind the murder of Billy Batts. In order to emphasize just how desensitized Henry has become to the kind of vicious, senseless, and psychotic violence of which Tommy and Jimmy are capable, Scorsese portrays the trio driving Tommy's car with the body of Batts in the back, as they go to retrieve a shovel from his mother's home (played by Scorsese's own mother, Catherine). The three men eat, being treated by Tommy's mother as if they were just a group of young boys over for a meal, and afterward she shows them her dog paintings. On their way to bury the body, they hear a thumping noise and discover that Batts is still alive. Jimmy and Tommy finish him off; Henry's voice-over informs us that in reality, the so-called rules governing Wise Guys had already begun to come unglued, because their execution of a "made guy" was an infraction for which Tommy is executed later in the film:

> Murder was the only way that everybody stayed in line. You got out of line, you got whacked. Everybody knew the rules. But sometimes, even if people didn't get out of line, they got whacked. I mean, hits just became a habit for some of the guys. . . . Shooting people was a normal thing. It was no big deal.

As a freeze frame shows us Henry's face, the screen turns fiery red and a sizzling noise can be heard on the sound track. Always the Catholic moralist as well as the sophisticated auteur, Scorsese seems to be suggesting with this intervention in the narrative that Henry's soul is already destined for Hell. In like manner, during the violent explosion that destroys the car belonging to casino manager and underworld accomplice Ace Rosenthal (Robert De Niro) in *Casino*, Ace's body somersaults down toward flames lapping at the bottom of Scorsese's frame as the credits for *Casino* run, reminding the audience how Ace's infernal occupation as money launderer and skim-manager for the Mob will eventually be rewarded.

Even more troubling than the murder of Billy Batts is the shooting and murder of a young apprentice hood named Spider (played by Christopher Imperioli, who later becomes a star in *The Sopranos*). Tommy DeVito's psychotic behavior once again emerges when Spider takes too long to bring him a drink, and Tommy accidentally shoots Spider in the foot while pretending that he is imitating the actions of Humphrey Bogart in *The Oklahoma Kid*. Later when Spider returns with a bandaged foot and Tommy mocks him, Spider tells him, "Why don't you go fuck yourself, Tommy?" and Tommy responds by shooting him six times with his automatic pistol. Rules exist, but Wise Guys seem to have a habit of breaking them, and their

Goodfellas *(1990; Martin Scorsese, director). Without any provocation, psychopath Tommy DeVito (Joe Pesci) shoots a waiter in the Mafia social club frequented by the Wise Guys, while Henry Hill (Ray Liotta) looks astonished in the right foreground.*

personalities, Scorsese reminds us, are those of psychopaths. Reflecting the gradual disintegration of Mob discipline, Henry's marriage begins to dissolve as well with his many infidelities, to the point that Karen even threatens to kill him with his own pistol.

In another segment announced by the caption TAMPA, FLORIDA, TWO DAYS LATER, Henry and Jimmy manage to be arrested in Florida running a bill-collecting errand for Paulie and land in jail. Henry finds Paulie there serving a year for contempt, and in this prison he begins the drug dealing that will eventually destroy him. In jail, perhaps in imitation of Coppola's many references to Italian American cuisine, the Wise Guys feast on lobster, steak, prosciutto, wine, Italian bread, and Scotch. Scorsese derives particular pleasure from showing how Paulie prepares garlic in a very special way, slicing it with a razor to produce extremely thin slices that become translucent while they are sautéed. As Henry describes this incredible situation: "Everyone else in the joint was doing real time, all mixed together, living like pigs. But we lived alone. And we owned the joint."

Now Scorsese moves his narrative quickly forward to emphasize the process of corruption undermining the Wise Guy lifestyle. In a subsequent segment labeled FOUR YEARS LATER, Henry continues to deal drugs in spite of Paulie's explicit warning not to do so (a theme that continues the Mafia's reluctance to get involved in drugs that is one of Coppola's most important themes), and Henry acquires a new girlfriend who snorts about as much of his product as he sells. Jimmy masterminds the famous Lufthansa airport robbery, netting almost six million dollars, but then decides that killing his accomplices is more profitable and safer than sharing. A massacre follows in this segment with gruesome murders of everyone associated with the theft except for Tommy, Henry, and Jimmy. But Tommy must now pay for the murder of Billy Batts (obviously Paulie has given him up to the Gambino family who rules over him). Hearing he is being taken into the Mafia as a "made guy," he is abruptly shot in the head. Scorsese captures his death with an overhead shot that shows blood seeping out of his head and over the carpet.

After this pivotal event that demonstrates the ultimate corruption of the gangster world to which Henry and his friends belong, Scorsese presents a masterful segment labeled SUNDAY, MAY 11TH, 1980, 6:55 A.M. that is subdivided into nine different times, ranging from early morning to late evening. During this hectic day, when Hill's world finally collapses, a desperate Henry tries to sell gun silencers; takes his crippled brother home from the hospital avoiding a collision on the road; prepares supper with an amazing amount of Italian food (all of which is detailed, from braising the beef, pork butt, and veal shanks for the tomato sauce to the ziti with meat gravy, roasted peppers, string beans with olive oil and garlic, veal cutlets for appetizers, and so forth); delivers dope; cooks supper; and does any number of things difficult for any normal person—while also high on drugs. As he pulls out of the driveway, he is arrested as his wife flushes the heroin down the toilet.

With the concluding segment entitled THE AFTERMATH, Henry fears his former friends, since they are afraid he will rat them out (as he does). He and Karen accept the FBI's offer to testify and enter the Witness Protection Program. As the film ends and Henry goes to the witness stand to testify against his friends, he has no remorse but only regrets the loss of his wealth and power. Speaking directly to the camera (and to us), he says:

> See, the hardest thing for me was leaving the life. I still love the life. And we were treated like movie stars with muscle. We had it all, just for the asking.... When I was broke, I would go out and rob some more. We ran everything. We paid off cops. We paid off lawyers. We paid off judges. Everybody had their hands out. Everything was for the taking. And now it's all over.

Scorsese's camera then cuts to a tracking shot down a street of new tract homes in what appears to be a place as far from Brooklyn as could be imagined. Henry Hill opens his door in a bathrobe and picks up his morning paper, continuing his voice-over commentary to the audience:

> That's the hardest part. Today everything is different. There's no action. I have to wait around like everyone else. Can't even get decent food. Right after I got here I ordered some spaghetti with marinara sauce and I got egg noodles and ketchup. I'm an average nobody. I get to live the rest of my life like a schnook.

Tommy suddenly reappears in a concluding image, firing six shots at the camera and toward the audience, a typical New Wave homage to a silent film, Edwin S. Porter's *The Great Train Robbery* (1903). Concluding titles inform us of the fates of the principal players: Henry Hill remains in the Witness Protection Program although he has divorced his wife; Paulie dies in Federal Prison at the age of seventy-three; and Jimmy serves a prison term and will be eligible for parole only in 2004. The last music played on the sound track is a bad version of Frank Sinatra's famous song "My Way," a version sung by rocker Sid Vicious, a musical degradation that parallels Henry's descent into Hell and the end of the Mob's heyday.

Scorsese offers nothing at all noble or uplifting in his portrait of Wise Guys in *Goodfellas*. Mobsters are simply working-class guys unafraid to break any codes of conduct in order to make money, pure and simple. If Coppola's *Godfather* trilogy provides a history for organized crime that leaves room for tragic protagonists and epic sweeps of chronology, Scorsese actually chronicles the breakup of the power of the Mafia and its associated "good earners" in the last two decades of the twentieth century as law-enforcement officials exploit new investigative techniques, new technologies, and new legislation to break up the Mob's power. *Casino* confirms this fall from grace and continues the story of the Mob's decline by showing how organized crime eventually lost control of the casinos in Las Vegas.[73] Shooting took place for many weeks in the Riviera Casino in Las Vegas, and Italian production designer Dante Ferretti created a fine display of the proper casino opulence that matched the over fifty wardrobe changes—virtually all pastels in color and consisting of matching colors in ties, shirts, trousers, and even shoe leather!—sported by the casino manager working for the Mob, Abe Rothstein. De Niro's performance in *Casino* is even better than in *Goodfellas* (where he is not the main character), and he is paired with another Joe Pesci role as the psychotic killer Nicky Santoro sent out to protect Kansas City Mob interests in how Ace manages the casino skim for the Mafia. Much of the film focuses upon Ace's pill-popping and alcohol-guzzling wife Ginger (Sharon Stone), whose work in the film was admirable but actually detracted from the tightness of the plot, which runs nearly three hours.

As in *Goodfellas,* Scorsese's style is semidocumentary with establishing captions and extensive use of voice-overs by Ace and Nicky. With another pairing of De Niro and Pesci, there is some sense of repetition and of old territory already traveled when *Casino* is compared to *Goodfellas.* For the Mob, at least in Scorsese's version of Las Vegas, the casinos represent paradise on earth and the last chance for working-class gangsters to make enormous profits and, in effect, to have the chance to wash away their sins by skimming money from the counting room or laundering money earned in other illegal operations elsewhere. One of the most impressive shots in the film is a long Steadicam sequence that follows the money through the bowels of the huge casino hotel. In addition, Scorsese's narrative documents the operation set up by the Kansas City Mob (a gang under the control of the Chicago Mafia, the branch of organized crime that controlled virtually everything west of the Mississippi River) that was eventually penetrated by the FBI.

By controlling the Teamsters' Union and their lucrative pension funds, the Mob obtained cash to finance their casinos in Las Vegas. Front men managed the casinos only in the imagination of the law-enforcement officials, whereas trusted Mafia representatives, such as Ace Rothstein, who were very often not Italian Americans but more often Jewish in ethnic origin, would make sure that the Mafia received their skim without any problems. What is most amusing about the image of the Mob in *Casino* is that the Italian Mafiosi who control the Tangiers Casino in the film are basically old-timers back in Kansas City who hang out in places like the San Marino Italian Grocery. Remo Gaggi (Pasquale Caiano) and Artie Pescano (Vinny Vella) seem more like superannuated Italian grandfathers than dangerous Mafiosi. No Don Vito Corleone or Don Michael Corleone would ever been have arrested in the humiliating circumstances the FBI creates to destroy what was a perfect setup for making hundreds of millions of dollars. In the San Marino Italian Grocery, owned by Pescano's mother (as in *Goodfellas*, another role played by Scorsese's own mother), with a wiretap placed there for an entirely different matter, the FBI discovers all the pertinent details about the skim in Las Vegas and the people involved in it. Moreover, when the old Mafiosi geezers are finally arrested, Pescano's detailed account of his travel expenses incurred while working for the Mob shuffling back and forth from Kansas City and Las Vegas sinks all those involved with the skim. Basically, the Mob's power in Las Vegas falls apart in much the same manner as the crew of *Goodfellas* self-destructs.[74]

Scorsese's intention is to make a metaphor of America through his image of the gaudy, excessive Las Vegas casinos. With the disappearance of men such as Santoro and Rothstein and the destruction of many of the traditional casinos in Las Vegas, the old world of Sinatra's Rat Pack and the gambling houses financed by the Teamsters' Union Pension Fund—including the Sands, the Argent, the Fremont, the Flamingo, the Stardust, the Tropicana, the Aladdin, the Dunes, the Desert Inn, the Thunderbird, the Sahara, and the Riviera—changed abruptly. With the government crackdown on Mob operations described in *Casino*, however, junk bonds replace Teamster cash, and large corporations replace the Mob, turning Vegas into a kind of Disneyland for families who could gamble away their life savings while their children play in theme parks. In the last sequence of the film, Scorsese shows us—with more than a touch of nostalgia—the destruction of some of these more traditional gambling houses and the appearance of the kind of theme-park gambling house represented by such establishments as Treasure Island, MGM, or Excalibur, themselves overtaken since the appearance of Scorsese's film by even more enormous billion-dollar gambling hotels that now cater to the high roller with sophistication, such as Bellagio and the Venetian. Replacing the cheap buffet dinners serving Surf 'n Turf are expensive

French, Italian, and Asian gourmet restaurants surrounded by art works painted by Picasso and other modern masters.

Wise Guys and American Cinema in Retrospect

Despite any actions against ethnic stereotyping that may be undertaken by the National Italian American Foundation (NIAF), the close identification of gangsters of Italian heritage and Hollywood Wise Guys will doubtless survive into the future. Because of the long tradition ranging back to silent cinema of depicting Hollywood Wise Guys as Hollywood Italians, and particularly because of the high artistic merits of many of these films—culminating in the *Godfather* trilogy by Coppola or the gangster films created by Scorsese—a century of artistic tradition now seems to have become almost a cliché that may be joined to other cinematic or literary clichés. Thus the popular culture may define Jews as naturally clever and wealthy; blacks may be considered natural athletes and sexually potent; East Asians (thanks mainly to World War II and Vietnam) may still be considered inscrutable; Arabs, of more recent date, may be linked to terrorism and treachery. And finally, Italian Americans may continue to provide models for both criminal masterminds as well as deranged, psychotic killers in the gangland trenches, courtesy of the impact of films by Coppola and Scorsese. Of course, very few people really think that all Italian Americans are gangsters, just as very few believe that all Jews are rich and clever like Meyer Lansky or Bernard Baruch, or that all blacks are basketball All-Americans, pimps, or powerful sex machines.[75] But ethnic stereotypes take on a life of their own in the arts, and Hollywood Italian Wise Guys have at least the satisfaction of not only being represented in many works of genius but also of being considered the best in their illegal profession. At least in the popular or cinematic imagination, Hollywood Italian Wise Guys have eliminated or exterminated most of their other ethnic competitors. As Scorsese suggests with *Goodfellas* and *Casino*, the real Wise Guys probably experienced far greater difficulty when they were confronted by the recent determined efforts of the Federal government to destroy their influence in casinos, trade unions, and both legitimate and illegitimate businesses. Nonetheless, the postmodern version of the Hollywood Italian Wise Guy produced by the television series *The Sopranos* has made the identification of organized crime with Italian Americans even more inevitable in the popular imagination.

5

❦

Comic Wise Guys: Hollywood Italian Gangsters Yuk It Up

CHARLIE PARTANNA (Jack Nicholson): "Do I ice her, do I marry her? Which one o' dese?"

MAEROSE PRIZZI (Anjelica Huston): "Marry her, Charlie. Just because she's a thief and a hitter doesn't mean she's not a good woman in all the other departments. If she was some kind of fashion model, it wouldn't last more than thirty days. But you and she is in the same line of business, you are lucky you found each other, you know that, Charlie? . . . She is an American. She had a chance to make a buck so she grabbed it."

> Hit man Partanna discusses his new love with
> Don Corrado Prizzi's daughter in *Prizzi's Honor* (1985)

"I want a normal life. I'm sick and tired of the gambling, the guns, bailing you out of jail, never knowing when you're gonna come home, *if* you're gonna come home . . . look at this place! Everything we wear, everything we eat, everything we own fell off a truck!"

> Angela DeMarco (Michelle Pfeiffer) to her gangster husband, Frank
> "The Cucumber" DeMarco (Alec Baldwin), in *Married to the Mob* (1988)

"By the way, my name is Shaldeen."

"Hi ya, Shaldeen. My name is Tod. . . . it's Italian for extra special."

> Exchange between Tod Wilkerson, Witness Protection Program
> name for gangster informant Vinnie Antonelli (Steve Martin) to a girl
> (Carol Kane) he meets in the supermarket in *My Blue Heaven* (1990)

CLARK KELLOGG (Matthew Broderick): "Robbery is still a crime in New York, is it not? It's not legal."

VICTOR RAY (Bruno Kirby): "That depends on the circumstances."

> The young student who comes to New York University
> to study film discusses morality with one of the local hoods
> who has just robbed him in *The Freshman* (1990)

"I'm not my father, Diane, just as you're not your father. If we were our fathers, what we did last night would only be legal in Arkansas."

> In a parody of Michael Corleone's remarks to Kay Adams at the opening
> wedding sequence of *The Godfather*, Anthony Cortino (Jay Mohr)
> explains things to Diane (Christina Applegate) in *Mafia!* (1998)

PAUL VITTI (Robert De Niro): "You're good. Nah, nah, you're good, Doc! You're good! I'm gonna be gettin' in touch with you. . . . Just one more thing. If I talk to you and you turn me into a fag, I'm gonna kill you, you understand?"

BEN SOBEL (Billy Crystal): "Could we define 'fag'? Because some feelings may come out. . . ."

PAUL: "I go fag, you die . . . got it? . . . You're good, you're good!"

> A Jewish psychoanalyst encounters resistance in therapy with his
> Italian American mobster patient in *Analyze This* (1999)

With the striking impact of Hollywood Italian Wise Guys upon the popular imagination following the appearance of *The Godfather* trilogy and the subsequent success of *Goodfellas*, it was only natural that the cinematic fiction created by such talented directors as Coppola or Scorsese would spawn a series of films to parody the cinematic conventions their works had created, or at least popularized, by their treatment of the traditional gangster genre film. John Huston's *Prizzi's Honor* (1985) may be credited as the film that popularized the Mobster comedy. It was nominated for eight Oscars,[1] won four Golden Globe awards,[2] earned fulsome praise from many film reviewers, and in its wake a number of other Mob comedies soon followed. They include: Jonathan Demme's *Married to the Mob* (1988); Herbert Ross's *My Blue Heaven* (1990); Andrew Bergman's *The Freshman* (1990); Jim Abrahams's *Mafia!* (1998; also entitled *Jane Austen's Mafia!*); Harold Ramis's *Analyze This* (1999); Kelly Makin's *Mickey Blue Eyes* (1999); Rob Pritts's *Corky Romano* (2001); and *Analyze That* (2002; Harold Ramis, director).

A number of the special conventions associated with Hollywood Italian Wise Guys become crucial elements in Mafia comedy. First, the place of the "family"—both that of the Italian American family at home and the metaphoric Mafia family—becomes as vital to comic action as it is to the Mob films. The image of the Hollywood Italian of Little Italy recurs, since many of the Hollywood Italian Wise Guy comic protagonists tend to be Guidos or Guidettes and exhibit the physical characteristics of many of their more serious ancestors: Brooklyn or New York accents; working-class backgrounds; an only seemingly paradoxical contrast between good taste in clothes or food, in some films, with a total lack of taste in dress, in others; frequent discussions about or appearances of Italian food; a preference for the fish-out-of-water comic plot; and an obvious fascination with Mob violence. Mobsters still reflect a lawless lifestyle, but the comic mobsters may well reflect even more of an ethnic stereotype than their more realistic counterparts, in large measure because any form of comedy, film or literary, relies heavily upon stereotypical characters and stock situations.

Prizzi's Honor (1985; John Huston, director). Mob hit man Charlie Partanna (Jack Nicholson) and hit woman Irene Walker (Kathleen Turner), who have been hired to kill each other, share a pleasant lunch together.

Prizzi's Honor relies less on comedy than on black humor. Based on a novel by Richard Condon, the film has an all-star cast, including Jack Nicholson as Prizzi-family hit man Charlie Partanna; Anjelica Huston as Don Corrado Prizzi's daughter Maerose; Kathleen Turner as hit woman Irene Walker; and William Hickey as the Prizzi boss. Charlie and Irene are professional killers, and they meet quite by accident when Irene is called in from outside the Prizzi family to clean up some messy business. Charlie somewhat unbelievably falls in love with Irene the minute he sees her during a church wedding. Since the Italian literary tradition from Dante, Boccaccio, and Petrarch celebrates sudden emotional changes based solely on the sense of sight, it is not surprising to find such improbable passions in a film comedy dealing with people of Italian ancestry. The film sets in conflict the romantic love between Charlie and Irene, on the one hand, and the Prizzi-family honor, on the other.

Charlie's love for Irene causes him to betray the family honor and to cover up the theft of Vegas casino money owed to the Prizzi, a theft that has been engineered by Irene and her husband (a man Charlie murders for the

Prizzi family). Although Charlie manages to retrieve the money, he is given a mission: he must kill Irene in order to defend the family honor. When given this task, Charlie can only answer: "Family is the only place I can be. I know that." To which his father replies, in an ironic echo of *The Godfather*: "It's business, Charlie, only business." Charlie then flies to Los Angeles to kill his beloved, but as a murderer herself, Irene does not trust him. After they make love, she takes a silenced pistol from her dressing table and in the traditional military stance with two hands on the weapon she tries to kill Charlie before he kills her. But Charlie is too quick and kills her with a fast knife through the throat.

Prizzi's Honor emphasizes irony and sardonic black comedy, but most of the rest of the Wise Guy comedies are far closer to slapstick than to tragicomedy. Although the gangster film has traditionally been a man's world, the fact that this film sports a female assassin departs somewhat from that formulaic plot. Even though Irene dies at Charlie's hands, Maerose Prizzi seems to be the most complex character in the film, because she manipulates all of the other protagonists to gain her goals, including marriage to Charlie, and she may well be the true successor to her cunning Mafia father. *Married to the Mob* continues this novel interest in viewing the Italian Mafia from a woman's viewpoint. Women in the first two Coppola *Godfather* films were largely superfluous appendages to male characters that were at the core of the action. In *The Godfather Part III*, Michael's sister Connie, however, becomes one of the cleverest and most powerful of the Corleone family, eventually supplanting Michael and sponsoring the rise of Sonny Corleone's illegitimate son to head the family. She shows her ruthlessness by murdering Don Altobello (Eli Wallach) at the opera with poisoned cannoli. Scorsese's *Goodfellas* asked his audience to consider the plight of Henry Hill's wife, who shares the voice-overs with her husband and whose unhappy status as a Mafia wife provides a great deal of the pathos in the film.

Married to the Mob examines the world of working-class mobsters almost completely from a female point of view. Angela DeMarco (Michelle Pfeiffer) may have big hair, and she may decorate and dress in a style that can be best be described as dago kitsch, but during the course of the film, she exhibits a capacity to change and to grow out of her subservient role as a Mob bimbo. After her husband Frank "The Cucumber" DeMarco (Alec Baldwin) meets his death because his love affair with the mistress of his Mafia chieftain, Tony "The Tiger" Russo (Dean Stockwell), leads to his assassination, Tony casts his lustful eyes upon the DeMarco widow—even though Angela makes every effort to abandon the life of a Mafia wife. FBI agent Mike Downey (Matthew Modine) enters the picture, falls in love with Angela, and at the ending of the

Married to the Mob *(1988; Jonathan Demme, director). Mob boss Tony "The Tiger" Russo (Dean Stockwell) tries to romance Angela DeMarco (Michelle Pfeiffer) after her mobster husband has been killed.*

film, love conquers all; Angela emerges from her murky past as a Mafia princess, and she enters the legitimate world presumably by the traditional ending of comedy—love and marriage.

Blessed by a fine script written by Nora Ephron and the comic talents of Steve Martin playing Vinnie Antonelli, a gangster who has agreed to enter the Federal Witness Protection Program in return for resettlement in a new and legitimate life as Tod Wilkerson, *My Blue Heaven* is arguably the best of all of the mobster comedies. Employing the fish-out-of-water plot to great comic effect, Vinnie lands in Fryburg, California, and in a tract home in what may be a reference to the fate of Scorsese's Henry Hill from *Goodfellas.* Like Henry Hill, Vinnie cannot find any good Italian food there in the suburbs, and like so many other Mafia figures, his slick silk suits and stylish Italian clothes mark him unmistakably as a comic form of John Gotti, the so-called Dapper Don. Also like *Goodfellas, My Blue Heaven* relies on explanatory caption titles from Vinnie's point of view. For example, the title I ATTEMPT TO ADJUST TO MY NEW ENVIRONMENT shows Vinnie shopping in a Fryburg grocery store where so many people tell him "Have a nice day" and address him with a friendly "Good morning!" that Vinnie, in stereotypical

New York response, tells them: "Fuck you!" Vinnie stands out like a fish out of water in a virtually crime-free small town, and within almost no time he meets other former Mafia members and participants in the Witness Protection Program who have been exiled to Fryburg. Predictably they are all named Rocco, Vinnie, Nicky, Dino, Richie, and they all hate the suburbs: as Vinnie says, "The way I look at it, this is where you go when you die."

My Blue Heaven sports a number of metacinematic references, drawing attention to its status as a film rather than a docudrama or biography offering realistic portrait of gangsters in a Witness Protection Program. Perhaps the most unexpected twist of the plot is that of a sympathetic informer. In almost all gangster films, traitors, informers, and squealers are depicted in an extremely unsympathetic way, as "rats." Vinnie Antonelli, however, is impossible to dislike. He is not only cleverer than all the law-enforcement officers in whose custody he is, but he has style, wit, class, pizzazz, and moxie. He is also apparently a film buff. When Vinnie meets one of his ex-friends, now most improbably running a pet store, they engage in a comic contest imitating James Cagney's famous tough-guy lines—"You dirty rat!"—from *Taxi!* (1931; Roy Del Ruth, director). Later when Vinnie tries to persuade Barney he is really on his side, Vinnie parodies the lines Michael Corleone speaks to his wounded father in the hospital ("I'm with you now, Pop") but does so with a contorted Brooklyn accent, saying over and over again "I'm wit' chu," a comic routine that anticipates the more famous multifaceted explanation of the Mob phrase "fuhgeddaboutit" by Donnie Brasco in the film of the same name. Finally, leaving the pet shop, Vinnie does an obvious imitation of Sylvester Stallone in *Rocky*, shadow-boxing his way across the street. *My Blue Heaven* thus toys with the entire tradition of gangster films and previous depictions of Hollywood Italians.

Like *Married to the Mob*, pairing the Mafia character with the law-enforcement officer succeeds in making the comic plot more complex. Eventually, Vinnie marries Crystal (Melanie Mayron), one of the local policewomen, and settles down. But he does so only after creating chaos in Fryburg with his Mafia cohorts in a scheme to defraud the local citizens with a campaign to raise money for the local Little League stadium. Even further complicating the plot is a secondary love affair between local District Attorney Hanna Stubbs (Joan Cusack) and FBI agent Barney Coopersmith (Rick Moranis), who is in charge of Vinnie until he completes his testimony against the Mob in New York.

The trip to New York fuels much of the comic power of the film. Vinnie easily gives Barney the slip at the airport when his noisy Italian American mother and a host of his relatives crowd around him. Vinnie cannot be bothered with secrecy, since he has an appointment with his Italian tailor.

My Blue Heaven *(1990; Herbert Ross, director). Merengue! Uptight FBI agent Barney Coopersmith (Rick Moranis) receives a lesson in "dago cool" from gangster Vinnie Antonelli (Steve Martin), who is in Barney's care in a witness protection program somewhere in the very un-Italian American Southwest.*

Since Barney is a complete nerd, Vinnie drags him along and outfits him in a slick Italian silk suit. Of course, the pair eventually ends up in a night club, which provides the setting for the zippiest dancing scene to appear in the cinema for some time. The sequence involves Vinnie teaching Barney to do the merengue dance step. In a beautifully edited series of shots, Vinnie inspires Barney to shed his nerdy personality and to enjoy life's simple pleasures. The comic dance then culminates in a shootout between Barney and Mafia goons sent to kill Vinnie before his testimony the next morning at the federal courthouse.

In a complete and hilarious reversal of character, Vinnie actually builds the Little League stadium in Fryburg and outfits his team in imitation Wise Guy uniforms: a cool white suit with broad, extra-padded shoulders and a red shirt with yellow tie. The uniforms are a comic version of what a hip Mafia gangster might wear if he played baseball. His mother bribes the umpire to make sure the home team wins, while his ex-Mafia friends hawk the traditional baseball stadium peanuts and hot dogs along with stolen CDs and car stereos. Everyone on both sides of the law is reconciled as Vinnie's last explanatory title announces: YOU KNOW, SOMETIMES I EVEN AMAZE MY-SELF. Crystal and Vinnie begin a family, while Hanna and Barney are to-gether. Crime may not pay, but in Nora Ephron's comic universe, opposites attract, language matters, and the result is laughter through a clever ma-nipulation of a number of comic stereotypes about Italian Americans in general and Mafia members in particular.

The Freshman takes even more liberties with the tradition of film come-dies. Its protagonist, a first-year film student at New York University from Vermont named Clark Kellogg (Matthew Broderick), encounters the perils of the big city when he is robbed of his luggage and money by Victor Ray (Bruno Kirby). Being indignant rather than scared, Clark manages to find Victor again, threatens to go to the police if his belongings are not returned, and receives a job offer from Victor's Uncle, Carmine Sabatini (Marlon Brando), a shady Italian American importer who quite naturally bears a perfect resemblance to the protagonist of Coppola's *The Godfather*—one of the running gags of the movie. Sabatini hires Clark to transport rare and ex-otic animals from the airport to New Jersey, where they will apparently be served up as a feast for the idle, disgusting rich for fabulous amounts of money—in the case of Clark's first animal, a Komodo dragon, $350,000 a plate!—depending on how rare they are.

My Blue Heaven alludes in clever ways to film history and to other depic-tions of gangsters or Hollywood Italians. *The Freshman* goes a step beyond, showing Clark meeting his faculty adviser in his office and attending film classes taught by his adviser, who is the egomaniac film professor Arthur Fleeber (Paul Benedict). Fleeber assigns everything he has ever written to his class (with the obvious motive of selling his books). But he is supremely uninterested in Clark's problems: when informed of Clark's inability to buy all of his books because of the theft of his property, Fleeber tells him curtly: "I'm your faculty adviser, not your caseworker." To Fleeber, Clark represents just one more book and one more royalty payment, and Fleeber has no in-terest in anything that is not connected with his academic specialty.

The most obvious reference to the gangster tradition in the cinema is the presence of Marlon Brando playing Carmine Sabatini, not to mention Bruno Kirby as Victor, who was the young Clemenza in *The Godfather Part II*. Sabatini frequents the kind of Italian social club in Little Italy that was the preferred hangout of the young Vito Corleone in *The Godfather Part II*. There he offers his guests Italian espresso (although he does not like it him-self), and when Clark asks Sabatini if the portrait on the wall is really that of Italian dictator Benito Mussolini, Sabatini sarcastically replies that "it ain't Tony Bennett!" Hastening to say that the portrait has no political value, he describes it as no more than a vestige of the nostalgic past of some of his

The Freshman *(1990; Andrew Bergman, director). Bearing a startling resemblance to a certain godfather of cinematic fame, Carmine Sabatini (Marlon Brando) hires college student Clark Kellogg (Matthew Broderick) to do a job for him, making him an offer Clark cannot refuse.*

older club members, something akin to hanging a portrait of the Beatles in Clark's dorm room!

Back in class, Clark listens to Fleeber discussing the Fleeber treatise *Guns and Provolone,* a book on the gangster film that compares Marx's *Das Kapital,* Kant's *Critique of Pure Reason,* and the Lake Tahoe scene from *The Godfather Part II.* Only those who have read little recent film theory would imagine that this kind of film writing was only a figment of the scriptwriter's imagination! The clip Fleeber screens in class shows the exchange between Michael Corleone and the corrupt Nevada lawmaker Senator Geary, and it is not without significance to the unfolding of the plot, since we shall eventually discover that federal agents working for the Fish and Wildlife Service, who attempt to arrest Sabatini for his exotic-animal feasts, are actually corrupt officers of the law, not unlike Senator Geary, who are trying to assassinate him with Clark's unwitting assistance.

Several other allusions to the first *Godfather* pique our curiosity about Clark's adventure. When Carmine extends the "hand of friendship" handshake to Clark, Victor explains that this means you have become part of the group. When Carmine gives Clark the "kiss of kisses" ("*bacci di tutti bacci,*" as Victor explains it in his unidiomatic Italian), that is even more important and signifies that Clark has become part of the family and worthy of marrying Carmine's daughter Tina (Penelope Ann Miller), who suddenly—and to Clark's surprise—begins to act as if she is to marry Clark in the near future. Perhaps the most interesting metacinematic element in *The Freshman* occurs as Clark watches Carmine saunter down the street near his social club, purchasing fruit, particularly *The Godfather*'s symbolic oranges, from the nearby Oriental greengrocer and having his money refused by the proprietor. Sabatini insists on paying the grocer's little boy.

The Freshman must end happily to follow the rules of comedy, and at the conclusion of the film, we discover (somewhat unbelievably) that Carmine had planned everything that occurs in the film, including the defeat of the two corrupt police agents, since he has decided to abandon his exotic gourmet-club business. Furthermore, his crazy chef Larry (Maximilian Schell) informs us that the rich guests are eating perfectly normal haute cuisine, because the exotic animals are only there to further the scam of their filthy-rich clients. When all is said and done, Carmine Sabatini is a kinder and gentler version of Don Corleone and does not have the heart to kill the animals he supposedly serves up for dinner. The last comic shot of the film shows Carmine and Clark walking through a cornfield with the Komodo dragon.

The lighthearted spoofing of certain well-known features of the Coppola *Godfather* trilogy in *The Freshman* is taken to absurd lengths in *Mafia!*, a film with stylistic affinities to the *Airplane!*, *Police Academy*, or *Hotshots!* series. The humor is always heavy handed, of the *Mad* magazine variety, and almost every line delivered by the actors seeks to make a pun or parodies some well-known sequence in a famous gangster film. When Don Cortino (Lloyd Bridges), the head of the powerful Mafia family satirized in the film, is shot full of holes with a machine gun, he jerks around as if he were dancing the Macarena. Like Don Corleone, he lies in a deserted hospital, and when the don's son Anthony Cortino (Jay Mohr) hears from his girlfriend Diane (Christina Applegate) that Don Cortino is all alone in his bed, Anthony supplies what he believes to be the obvious explanation: there are no assassins coming to kill him; but as Anthony complains, "He belongs to an H.M.O." Other Coppola scenes parodied include the murder of Sollazzo and McCluskey, as well as the death of Vito Corleone in the garden (now with a huge watermelon slice in his mouth rather than an orange slice) from *The Godfather;* and the flashbacks to Sicily in *The Godfather Part II*. The conclusion of the film also includes a parody of the baptism scene from *The Godfather. Mafia!* goes beyond the satire of the Coppola films, opening with a very successful parody of the beginning of Scorsese's *Casino*. With a voice-over also reminiscent of Scorsese's style, we see Anthony

Cortino being blown up in a car with religious music on the sound track, but all sorts of silly things occur during the scene in which he floats through the air: for example, he dunks a basketball and catches a Frisbee with his mouth. *Mafia!* is merely a succession of one-liners and comic gags, some of which are amusing and others of which fall flat. Still, constructing an entire film based upon Italian gangster gags serves to illustrate the tremendous impact that works by Coppola and Scorsese have had upon American popular culture.

Quite a different approach to gangster comedy emerges from a good film, *Analyze This.* Opening to the tune of Italian American Louis Prima's jazz singing (one of the musical motifs that made *Big Night* interesting), *Analyze This* shares with *The Sopranos* an interest in the psychoanalysis of a gangster. Dr. Ben Sobel (Billy Crystal) becomes the analyst of mobster Paul Vitti (Robert De Niro), who is cracking under the stress of his job and the threat of rival mobster Primo Sidone (Chazz Palminteri). Like Tony Soprano, Vitti has panic attacks, and as the film unfolds, we discover that the root cause of his problems lies in the fact that he witnessed the assassination of his father in a restaurant to which he takes Sobel for lunch. Vitti's problems take many forms. Not only does he have panic attacks, but he cannot sleep easily, he is nervous, he has chest pains, and he cries uncontrollably, even while watching television commercials. Of course, there are the predictable sexual side effects:

> PAUL: I couldn't get it up last night.
>
> BEN: Do you mean sexually?
>
> PAUL: No, I mean for the big game against Michigan State. Of course sexually—what the fuck's the matter wit' you? ... If I can't get it up, that makes me less of a man, and I can't have that. In my world, I deal with animals, Doctor, they may seem dumb to an educated guy like you, but make no mistake about it, Doctor, animals are very cunning and they sense weakness.

Perhaps even more amusing is the reversal of roles that takes place in the film. Vitti is understandably reluctant to accept Freudian explanations of his predicament:

> PAUL: Fuckin' Greeks! ... What are you saying? That I wanted to fuck my mother?
>
> BEN: No, it's a primal fantasy.
>
> PAUL: Have you ever *seen* my mother? Are you out of your fucking mind?

Analyze This (1999; Harold Ramis, director). New York mobster boss Paul Vitti (Robert De Niro) congratulates psychiatrist Ben Sobel (Billy Crystal) for his talents as an analyst.

BEN: It's Freud.
PAUL: Then Freud's a sick fuck and you are, too, for bringing it up! . . .
   Yuk!

But in spite of his reluctance to accept the classic Freudian line about the oedipal complex, Paul recognizes that Ben, too, has problems dealing with his super-successful analyst father who is also the author of best sellers and ignores Ben's accomplishments, even refusing to take time to attend Ben's second wedding because of a book signing.

The fact that both Paul and Ben share a common weakness in their tenuous and tense relationship to their fathers is seen most clearly in a satire of a famous sequence from *The Godfather* (one also parodied in *The Freshman*): Ben imagines himself being shot in the street in precisely the same manner that occurred to Don Vito Corleone, and it is Paul who portrays the Fredo role, since he is too afraid and nervous to react to the shooting. Even the overhead shot of the oranges rolling on the street during the attempted assassination is repeated in Ben's dream. When Ben relates the dream to Paul, the mobster remarks: "I was Fredo? I don't think so."

Like *My Blue Heaven* and *The Freshman*, and unlike *Mafia!*, *Analyze This* has a literate, entertaining script. And like the other two films, the metacinematic references in *Analyze This* advance the narrative and provide important commentaries on the plot and characters; they are not merely excuses for gags or one-liners as in *Mafia!* Yet, *Analyze This* shares one major characteristic with *Mafia!*—its style combines elements from both Coppola and Scorsese. Paul Vitti is essentially a comic version of a medley of Scorsese characters played by De Niro and other actors in Scorsese's gangster films. His mannerisms, like those of Marlon Brando in *The Freshman*, have become part of our collective cinematic memory. Audiences immediately think of Don Vito Corleone when they see Brando dressed in a shabby suit offering espresso coffee to his guests in Little Italy, just as they think of Jimmy Conway or Ace Rothstein as they hear the New York accent and see the familiar facial expressions of De Niro. All of this gangster humor works in *Analyze This*. The sequel, entitled *Analyze That* (2002; Harold Ramis), is far less successful. Even De Niro singing lyrics from *West Side Story* in Sing Sing Prison cannot save this sequel from being a pale shadow of its comic predecessor.

Light comedy requires a literate script, and the quality of the screenplay in *Mickey Blue Eyes* sets it far above a film like *Corky Romano*, a vehicle for *Saturday Night Live* star Chris Kattan. This movie is sometimes so badly scripted that even its actors seem embarrassed to recite their lines. *Mickey Blue Eyes* is another fish-out-of-water comedy, with Hugh Grant playing Michael Felgate, an art auctioneer at Cromwell's, an art dealership similar to Sotheby's in New York City. Michael falls in love with Gina Vitale (Jeanne Tripplehorn), daughter to Mob boss Frank Vitale (James Caan). Afraid to involve Michael in her family affairs and knowing too well that he will be tainted by the criminal environment she inhabits, Gina declines to marry him. The plot consists of a complicated process of making the marriage possible by the end of the narrative: once again, marriage brings a traditional comedy to a close. Caan's presence in the film recalls his important performance in *The Godfather*. Many familiar Italian American faces appear in the film. Besides the inimitable Joe Viterelli of *Analyze This*, there are a number of character actors who have become identified with *The Sopranos*—Burt Young, Vincent Pastore, and John Ventimiglia.

In *My Blue Heaven*, gangster Vinnie Antonelli was totally out of his element in suburban California. In *Mickey Blue Eyes*, Englishman Michael Felgate must pretend to be a gangster from Saint Louis named "Mickey Blue Eyes" and he fails miserably to pronounce certain by now legendary phrases, including the obligatory "fuhgeddaboutit." Equally predictable but always entertaining is a sound track featuring Dean Martin and Louis Prima. Although the great gangster films depicting Hollywood Italians may depart from the usual ethnic stereotypes that too easily identify men of Italian descent with criminal activity, these films usually go beyond the facile identification of an entire group of people with a specific illegal behavior and achieve the status of true works of art. Since they are so skillfully defined, so aesthetically created, and so uniquely cinematic in their presentation, few Italian Americans should feel embarrassed by the figures portrayed in the films of Coppola or Scorsese. These characters are larger than life and at times, they border on the sublime and the tragic. Although one may approach a figure like Don Vito Corleone with negative feelings, it is extremely difficult not to have conflicting opinions about the nature of his character. In spite of ourselves, we grant Don Corleone a modicum of our respect and not a small amount of our envy for being able to avoid dancing to the puppeteer strings of the powerful, as so many "average" people are obliged to do.

Gangster comedies, on the other hand, depend almost entirely upon the acceptance of stereotypes, as do most traditional comedies. We laugh at them because we recognize their features immediately for their stereotypical nature: gangster girlfriends chew gum, have big hair, and buy hideous home furniture; gangsters dress better than the average American and pay great attention to the food that they consume; mobsters kill each other but, on occasions, they may do so in such a manner that their activities cause us to laugh. Unlike the sinister protagonists that make up the rogues' gallery of Hollywood Italian Wise Guys, their comic counterparts in Wise Guy comedies merely amuse us. The idea that senators, politicians, and presidents act exactly like mobsters—an idea advanced in Coppola's *Godfather* trilogy but one that becomes a common thread in the contemporary gangster film—represents a troubling thought. Reducing such a frightening and powerful figure as Michael Corleone to comic proportions would inevitably mean making him smaller and less important, less frightening, and less troubling to our consciences. When Wise Guys yuk it up, we sense that sooner or later, bullets will stop flying and a wedding celebration will bring the story to a happy ending.

6

Sopranos: The Postmodern Hollywood Italian *Famiglia*

"Uncle Junior and I, we had our problems with the business. But I never should have razzed him about eating pussy. This whole war could have been averted. Cunnilingus and psychiatry brought us to this!"

> Tony Soprano (James Gandolfini) comments on the disastrously destructive effects of letting it be known that Mafia leaders practice oral sex and see therapists in "Boca" (I, 9)

MEADOW SOPRANO (Jamie-Lynn Siegler): "It's the '90s. Parents are supposed to discuss sex with their children."
TONY SOPRANO: "Yeah, but that's where you're wrong! You, see, out there it's the '90s, but in this house it's 1954!"

> Tony Soprano counsels his daughter about the facts of life in "Nobody Knows Anything" (I, 11)

TONY SOPRANO: "When America opened the floodgates and let us Italians in, what do you think they were doin' it for, because they were trying to save us from poverty? No, they did it because they needed us, they needed to build their cities and dig their subways and make 'em richer. The Carnegies and the Rockefellers, they needed worker bees, and there we were. But some of us didn't want to swarm around their hive and lose who we were, we wanted to stay Italian and preserve the things that meant something to us—honor, and family, and loyalty. And some of us wanted a piece of the action. Now we weren't educated like the Americans, but we had the balls to take what we wanted, and those other fucks, those . . . uh, uh, the J. P. Morgans, they were crooks and killers too, but that was the business, right?, the American way . . ."
JENNIFER MELFI (Lorraine Bracco): "That might all be true, but what do poor Italian immigrants have to do with you and what happens every morning when you step out of bed?"

> Tony Soprano explains his theory of Italian immigration to his therapist in "From Where to Eternity" (II, 9)

"In this house, Christopher Columbus is a hero. End of story."

> Tony Soprano's comment to his son after Anthony Junior (Robert Iler) reads a passage from a revisionist history of the United States branding the discoverer of America as responsible for what is described as the "genocide" of native American populations in "Christopher" (IV, 3)

Television Series or Art Film?

The Sopranos debuted in 1999 on HBO, the pay-cable television network that hired producer David Chase to create the series. Four years and fifty-two episodes later, at present count, the series has raised HBO's subscription numbers by leaps and bounds, made David Chase the toast of the film world, and turned the cast of the show, most of whom were relatively unknown but very talented New York character actors, into household names. Audiences are guaranteed at least six years, or twenty-six more episodes, of the program. But regardless of the impact of the last two years of the series, *The Sopranos* has changed the face of American television and has done more to popularize Hollywood's vision of Italian Americans than any single film or group of films since *The Godfather* trilogy. Perhaps less noticeable to the general public is the fact that *The Sopranos* also represents the historical culmination of a long process of assimilation of Hollywood Italian images into the mainstream of American popular culture. Because of its unique place in the history of representations of Italian Americans in American show business, *The Sopranos* deserves to be considered one of the most original artistic creations of our time.

Including *The Sopranos*, a series created for television (albeit a pay-for-view channel) in a discussion of the Hollywood Italians in the movies requires some explanation. Perhaps the obvious and best reason is that producer Chase shoots his television series with film, not video. Everything about the production values of each individual episode of *The Sopranos* resembles a "stand-alone feature film," as Chase himself states, rather than a hastily made and hastily shot television program. Even a cursory glance at the visual texture of any individual episode on the proper television equipment (high definition compatible receivers with stereo sound) reveals that Chase has succeeded in creating a television series that is, in fact, a series of real movies, not just a long run of episodic narratives. Most importantly in this regard, no commercial interrupts any of the episodes (something no television network would permit), and Chase produces only thirteen episodes each year (fewer than a normal television series would require to fill in a year's programming). Chase combines the best aspects of traditional Hollywood studio production (teams of scriptwriters who work together on numerous rewrites of the screenplays) with the guiding vision of the single director as auteur (Chase edits all the films even if he is not the director of a particular individual episode).[1] Great artistic risks are taken in the series, and to date, they have invariably paid off with stellar performances and fascinating twists and turns of plot that have captivated a huge national audience.

The Sopranos quickly earned the attention and respect of film and tele-vision critics and historians.[2] The cast of the program is enormous, and the plots extremely complicated. The narratives unfold from one episode to the next in as complicated and as sophisticated a manner as a reader might expect from the great cycles of novels associated with late nineteenth- and early twentieth-century literary realism.

The Complex Cast of Characters

The Sopranos focuses upon several Italian American families who live in New Jersey. Both Corrado "Junior" Soprano (Dominic Chianese)—Tony's uncle—and "Johnny Boy" Soprano (Joseph Siravo)—Tony's deceased fa-ther—established careers in the Mob, a vocational path Tony chose even after he spent at least some time in college. Tony Soprano lives in North Caldwell, one of the wealthiest towns in the area and the United States (also the area where producer David Chase grew up). He is married to Carmela (Edie Falco) and has two children—Meadow and Anthony, Jr. Tony is clearly a man on the way up, while Uncle Junior has less talent as a gangster, and although both men have their own crews, during the course of the unfolding of the narrative, both men come into conflict to the extent that Junior actually puts out a contract on his nephew that is never actually enforced. Tony's life is made miserable by the machinations of his mon-strous mother Livia (Nancy Marchand) and by the often screwball actions of his sister Janice (Aida Turturro). Tony's "crew" consists of a psychotic gangster named Paulie "Walnuts" Gualtieri (Tony Sirico); Silvio Dante (Steven Van Zandt), the crew's consigliere and the manager of the Bada Bing strip joint where the gangsters hang out; "Big Pussy" Bonpensiero (Vincent Pastore), who eventually betrays the group with the FBI, for which Tony and Silvio execute him; and Tony's nephew Christopher Molti-santi (Michael Imperioli). Furio Giunta (Federico Castelluccio) is brought into the gang from Naples when Tony runs short of trusted underlings. Hesh Rabkin (Jerry Adler), not officially a member of the crew, represents the Jewish financial wizard traditionally associated with Italian gangs. Re-lated to the Soprano family by ties of affection and business is the Aprile family: Jackie Aprile (Michael Rispoli), the boss of the crews led by Tony and Junior, dies from cancer, pitting Tony against Junior over who will suc-ceed him. Richie Aprile (David Proval) returns from prison expecting to succeed Jackie but finds Tony in his path, thereby creating another source of conflict. It seems as if the Apriles and the Sopranos will be brought to-gether by the marriage of Richie and Janice, but in a fit of anger Janice shoots Richie, obliging Tony to dispose of his body. Ralph Cifaretto (Joe

Pantoliano) becomes the lover of Jackie's widow Rosalie Aprile (Sharon Angela), and he is eventually called on to murder Rosalie's son Jackie Jr. (Jason Carbone), who has attempted to rob a card game run by the Mob. Other principal players include: Artie Bucco (John Ventimiglia) and Charmaine Bucco (Katherine Narducci), owners of an Italian restaurant frequented by the protagonists; Johnny "Sack" Sacrimoni (Vincent Curatola), a New York gangster who moves to New Jersey with his enormous wife; Carmine Lupertazzi (Tony Lip), a New York boss with authority over New Jersey operations—another source of friction and potential mayhem; Dr. Jennifer Melfi, Tony's psychiatrist; her husband Richard La Penna (Richard Romanus) and son Jason (Will McCormack); Jennifer's psychiatrist Dr. Elliott Kupferberg (Peter Bogdanovich); Tony's suburban neighbors, Dr. Bruce Cusamano (Robert Lupone) and his wife Jean (Saundra Santiago). Tony has a number of extramarital affairs, with two Russian women—Irina (Oksana Babiy) and Svetlana Kirilenko (Alla Kliouka)—a Mercedes saleswoman named Gloria Trillo (Annabella Sciorra); and various mistresses ("goomahs"), prostitutes, or party girls.

Italian Americans in Sopranoland: The Minority Becomes the Majority

Italian Americans make up the fifth-largest ethnic group in the last census (almost sixteen million people) in the United States. Some Italian Americans, supported to some degree by the National Italian American Foundation (NIAF), have objected strenuously to David Chase's creation on the grounds that his program demeans members of a single ethnic group, focusing upon Italian American criminals rather than more edifying professions that are followed by the Sons of Italy. Yet, even while Chase views Italian American life and culture through the lens of the Hollywood Italian Wise Guy, it would be unfair to the program to describe it in so superficial and cursory a fashion.

In fact, what Chase actually creates in *The Sopranos* is a fictional universe in which Italian Americans become the norm by which everything is measured. Other ethnic groups appear (African Americans, Jews, Russians, Hispanics) as well the traditional WASP, but these groups are always marginal to the Italian American majority. Based upon an examination of the cast of the first fifty-two programs, *The Sopranos* contains ninety-eight "continuing" or principal players and six hundred and fifty-two "featured" players, characters that are in every episode. Of the continuing characters, seventy-four are Italian Americans and only twenty-four are non-Italian, and of these continuing characters, fifty-seven are played by actors of Italian American origin. Of the featured characters, at least two hundred and fifteen are Italian American characters, many of whom are actors of Italian American origin.

To understand the significance of this critical mass of "dagos" and "Wise Guys," it is sufficient to turn to some of the classic movies treating Hollywood Italians. *Little Caesar* had twenty-six major characters, of which only nine were Italian characters, and not a single actor of Italian origin was in the picture. *Scarface* had a total of thirty-four characters, of which thirteen were of Italian origin. But only two actors of Italian origin were in the picture besides George Raft, whose mother was Italian American. In *Christ in Concrete*, eleven of the fifteen main characters were Italian Americans, but only two of the actors were of Italian origin. Only with the *Godfather* trilogy do we experience an on-screen saturation by Italians, either fictional characters or actors, that may be compared to the percentages found in *The Sopranos*. In Coppola's three gangster films, there are one hundred thirty-eight major figures, one hundred of which represent Italians or Italian Americans. A total of eighty-three actors playing these roles are of Italian origin.[3]

The examples of Coppola and Scorsese no doubt encouraged Chase to cast so many "New York" or East Coast actors of Italian origin for the authenticity of their facial features, their accents, and their familiarity with Italian American culture. But in neither Coppola's nor Scorsese's fictional universe, populated primarily by gangsters, are there Wise Guys surrounded by so many other Italian Americans in such a wide variety of professions, economic classes, and interests. We have priests—Father Phil Intintola (Paul Schultz); psychiatrists—Jennifer Melfi; Richard La Penna; and Dr. D'Alessio (Robert Cicchini); agents from the Federal Bureau of Investigation—Skip Lipari (Louis Lombardi), Grasso (Frank Pando), Deborah Ciccerone (Lola Gladini), Robyn Sanseverino (Karen Young), Tancredi (Jay Christianson), and Malatesta (Colleen Werthmann), as well as local bureau chief Frank Cubitoso (Frank Pellegrino); policemen—Detective Giardinia (Vince Viverito); physicians—Dr. Bruce Cusamano, Dr. Rotelli (Victor Truro), and Dr. Donna Dechristafolo (Ava Maria Carnevale); restaurant owners—the Buccos; financial advisers—Brian Cammarata (Matthew Del Negro); car salespersons—Gloria Trillo; dental students—Finn Detrolio (Will Janowitz); hardware store owners—Dave Scatino (Robert Patrick); Columbia University fundraisers—Mr. Ross, whose family name was changed from Rossetti (Mark Kamine); nightclub owners—not only Silvio Dante but also Rocco De Trolleo (Richard Petrocelli); university feminists—Professor Longo-Murphy (Roma Maffia); art dealers—Virginia La Paz; hospital administrators—Barbara Giglione (Nicole Burdette) and Miss Antoinette Giacolo (Candy Trabucco); contractors—Jack Massarone (Robert Desiderio); painters and interior decorators—Vic Musto (Joe Penny); owners of sanitation companies and their employees—Dick Barone (Joe Lisi) and Connie De Sapio (Jennifer Albano); funeral-home directors—Mr. Cozzerelli (Ralph Lucarelli); dentists and periodontists—a screaming football dad named Romano (Peter Napoliello); fast-food workers—Jesus Rossi (Mario Polit), part-Italian and also a rapist; butchers—Francis Satriale (Lou Bonacki); educators—Principal Cincotta (Daniel Oreskes), Principal Charles Cirillo (Anthony Patellis); labor-union leaders and their employees—Dave Fusco (Mark Lotto), Bobbi Sanfilippo (Robyn Peterson); Italian Anti-Defamation League activists—Philip DiNotti (Joseph R. Sicari); plumbers—Mr. Ruggiero; tennis coaches—Ed Rusticcia (Robert Bogue); and real-estate agents—Virginia Lupo (Cynthia Darlow). Even an American Indian activist named Maggie Donner (Alex Rice) admits that she is one-eighth Italian, since she is related to one of the cavalrymen who fought her ancestors on the Great Plains, a trooper of Italian origin! In the United States, Italian Americans may well be only one group out of many, but in David Chase's Sopranoland, they have replaced the WASP as the norm.

David Chase and the Italian American Experience

Such a strange concentration of Hollywood Italians in a single locale is clearly motivated by something other than demographic precision. From everything David Chase has said to the press and in an extensive interview with Peter Bogdanovich that is included in the DVD collection of the first year's episodes, it is quite clear that Chase utterly rejects any concern with defaming the image of Italian Americans by producing a show about Hollywood Italian Wise Guys. Chase's mother was an Italian American (family name DeCesare) and his daughter Michele DeCesare appears in the series as Hunter Scangarelo, one of Meadow Soprano's closest friends. Rejecting the politics of victimization and entitlement that too frequently color discussions about ethnic groups in America, Chase provides what he calls a "long answer" to Bogdanovich's question about ethnic prejudice:

> The Italian American experience is an advertisement for America, for the democratic experiment. It's hard for me to think of a group who's come from so little who's done so well. . . . If you have so little self-esteem at this point that these movies bother you, I have to wonder why. Also because this Italian Mob thing has become, for whatever reasons, a national myth. . . . In the end, if your self-esteem is that shallow and you have a problem with the fact that this tiny minority called gangsters make it tough for the rest of you, I think you should take your case to them . . . I don't think it will happen, but I think that's what you should do.

Chase believes that one of the most significant facts about Italian Americans is that they have never played the ethnic card as a group. They have never postured as victims, nor have they ever claimed compensation for ills—imaginary or real—that they have suffered during their migration to America. Instead, with the exception of a very few gangsters, they have worked hard and diligently to pull themselves up from poverty to become valuable members of American society. Even as gangsters, Tony Soprano and his crew are completely integrated into American society. How more assimilated could a family be when an Italian American princess is named Meadow Soprano, while her best friends include a Hunter Scangarelo and a MacKenzie Trillo? Italians traditionally name themselves after saints, but there is no record of saints named Meadow, Hunter, or MacKenzie. In the Hall of Fame of preppies and WASPs, however, such names are quite common. In short, the names of the Italian Americans are carefully chosen by Chase to underscore his belief that Italian Americans are completely assimilated and, indeed, constitute the majority of the population in his fictional universe.

Chase takes on those who have attacked *The Sopranos* as creating prejudicial media images of Italian Americans in several episodes at various times. In "46 Long" (I, 2), Paulie "Walnuts" searches the city's upscale coffeehouses for the thief who stole a car belonging to Anthony, Jr.'s science teacher. Seeing the crowds of people ordering coffee, Paulie sees the vogue of espresso in America as an instance of the exploitation of Italian culture by others who profit from it unfairly: "We invented this shit and all these cocksuckers are getting rich on it," declaring that non-Italians "ate *pootsie* until we gave them the gift of our cuisine." When his partner Big Pussy Bonpensiero loses his patience and exclaims, "Oh, again with the rape of the culture?", we can be sure that he echoes David Chase's own opinion. True to his criminal nature, Paulie steals an espresso coffeepot from the national chain, the name of which is humorously misidentified by one of Big Pussy's auto-stripper mechanics as "Buttfucks" rather than "Starbucks." Later in an episode shot in Italy and set in Naples ("Commendatóri," II, 4), the same Paulie arrives in the Old Country, eager to recover his ethnic roots, try real Italian cuisine, and to make personal connections with the Neapolitans. Paulie's visit to Naples turns out to be a complete disaster: he thinks the natives are unfriendly; he hates the food, rejecting a delicacy (black pasta with squid ink), asking, instead, for "macaroni and gravy," a request that the locals translate as spaghetti and tomato sauce; and he must hire a bored prostitute with whom he can discuss the tiny town from which his ancestors immigrated to America. One of the Neapolitan mobsters eating with Paulie and observing his gauche response to Paulie's ancestral home remarks in Italian: "And you thought the Germans were classless pieces of shit!" If Chase can be criticized for anything, it is the implication in *The Sopranos* that Italian Americans— unlike their more "authentic" counterparts in Italy proper—often exhibit bad taste in dress, food, and style due to the lower-class origins of some of his characters. The Cusamanos, Tony's upscale Italian American neighbors, basically think Tony is gauche, someone to be excluded from a refined and educated inner circle of friends (one of whom is Tony's analyst, Jennifer Melfi) or their country club. On the other hand, Tony considers the Cusamanos "Wonderbread wops," "Mayonnaises," or "Meddigan" (the Italian American pronunciation for "Americans")—so assimilated that they have lost the bedrock Italian values of honor, family, and loyalty, the qualities Tony lists for Dr. Melfi in his explanation of Italian immigration. He even employs the term "white" to refer to assimilated Italian Americans. Yet, measured against the real Italians of Naples, Tony and Paulie seem completely American and not at all integrally linked with the foreign culture from which their ethnic roots sprang.

Another important episode dealing with the issue of Italian American images much later in the series ("Christopher," IV, 3) analyzes the general sense of victimhood in American culture today. When the New Jersey Council of Indian Affairs threatens to disrupt the annual Columbus Day Parade, Silvio Dante wants to organize the Wise Guys to form a counter-demonstration. During the same episode, Father Phil Intintola sponsors a lecture by Montclair State College professor Longo-Murphy, an Italian feminist, on "Italian American Women and Pride." In her lecture to Carmela and her Italian American lady friends, Longo-Murphy makes the argument that Americans associate Italian Americans with Wise Guys because "that is the way the media depict us," but Chase also has her reject the findings of another study's conclusions that Americans realize such images are pure fictions and do not really think all Italian Americans are gangsters any more than they think all Italians are artists or opera singers. This kind of information, counter to the prevalent mood of victimhood in America, would undermine the search for past wrongs to be righted by today's entitlements. Interestingly, Tony Soprano argues with Silvio that his own self-esteem does not depend upon identifying himself as Italian (even though he informs his son that Columbus is a hero in the Soprano home) and that Silvio has succeeded in his chosen profession (admittedly an illegal one) because of merit and hard work, not because of his ethnic heritage. When Silvio and Tony's crew fail to cancel the Native American protest, they turn to a Native American leader who operates a casino on Indian land for help, but their free day in the casino's high-roller room costs Tony the promise to book Frankie Valli for the casino. The Indian casino manager admits that he was totally uninterested in his Native American ancestry until he found a way to turn his ethnic identify into cold, hard cash.

The episode contains a number of moments that all center on the corruption of the politics of victimization. As a Jew, Hesh naturally sympathizes with the plight of the Native Americans but becomes incensed when a Cuban friend of many years compares Columbus with Hitler. Hesh angrily declares that equating the Holocaust with anything else is tantamount to anti-Semitism and orders his long-time friend out of his home. Anthony, Jr.'s history teacher apparently spouts the ludicrous opinion that Columbus would today stand trial for slavery and genocide alongside Yugoslavian dictator Slobodan Milosovic (that silly opinion prompts Tony's remark about Columbus being a hero in his home). On a television program, an African American initially supports the Italian American "right" to an ethnic holiday but becomes as angry as Hesh when his Italian American interlocutor employs the expression "middle passage," a term usually used to refer to the passage of blacks as slaves to America, to refer to Italian immigrants. To demonstrate just how ridiculous such a focus upon victimization really is, the only true Italian gangster in Tony's crew, Furio Giunta, declares that as a Neapolitan, he cannot stand Columbus, who came from Genoa and was therefore a Northern Italian, part of the class that always had the power and money in the peninsula and that treated all southerners as if they were peasants. Basically, in Chase's fictional world, not to mention the real world of American politics, being a victim is very much about influence, privilege, and occupying a prime spot on the pecking order of groups who feel that they are entitled to be paid for past offenses, real or imagined. That much of this kind of talk represents posturing is then demonstrated by the fact that the irate Silvio Dante, having a wonderful time at the Native American casino, completely forgets about the Columbus Day Parade as he cavorts with prostitutes, eats the expensive food, and gambles away all his free comps. By the time he remembers what brought him there in the first place, Columbus Day has come and gone.

Linguistic Comedy

There are numerous reasons why *The Sopranos* is such an impressive show, but primary among them is the quality of the writing. Humor lurks everywhere in the midst of murder, mayhem, corruption, and dirty dealing. For example, Tony and his associates actually exhibit a good level of intelligence, but their lack of university polish opens them up to a number of linguistic mistakes and malapropisms that the scriptwriters obviously delight in inventing. Christopher Imperioli must be corrected by Big Pussy when he calls the character in *The Godfather* who sleeps with the fishes Louis Brassi instead of Luca Brasi (I, 1); later in discussing the impact of the FBI upon the Mafia, Christopher describes "dysentery among the ranks" rather than dissension. Anthony, Jr. mixes anarchists up with "antichrists" and later, in speaking of his new-found belief that God does not exist, attributes this idea to Nitch, not Nietzsche (I, 8). Meadow describes an Italian American singer as "that Mario Lasagna guy," not Mario Lanza (II, 2). Tony mistakes Cap d'Antibes—the resort—for Captain Tibes, a man he thinks owns a string of luxury hotels (I, 2). Tony also confuses Prince Machabelli—the brand of perfume—for Niccolò Machiavelli, author of *The Prince* (as noted, one of the frequently cited books by Wise Guys); calls the Spanish painter Goyim rather than Goya (III, 12); speaks of "indigenous" rather than "indigent" people (IV, 4); and characterizes Ralph Cifaretto's sexual performance as "penissary contact with a Volvo" rather than a vulva! Perhaps the most amusing of all these linguistic jokes is a discussion initiated by Bobby "Baccala" Baccalieri (Stephen Schirripa), who believes that the predictions of Quasimodo foretold the events of 9/11. When Tony corrects him—"Nostradamus and Notre Dame—it's two different things altogether"—Bobby nevertheless is not persuaded, noting that Quasimodo was a hunchback and Notre Dame has a quarterback and halfbacks: "You ever pondered that? The back thing with Notre Dame?" This kind of banter continues throughout the many episodes and constitutes a comic backdrop to many of the more violent actions.

Critical Views on The Sopranos

To explain the extraordinary appeal of *The Sopranos*, literary critic Sandra Gilbert has neatly summarized the major themes of the critics into three viewpoints: the Sopranos R Us; the Sopranos R Art; and the Sopranos R Postmodern Art.[4] The first theory sees Tony's New Jersey family and his Mob associates as representative of contemporary America. The second view is linked to the first, for it praises *The Sopranos* for its links to the serious realistic literature of the last century (Dickens, Zola, Balzac). I find the arguments associated with viewing the series as a realistic portrait of contemporary America or a spin-off of nineteenth-century realism unconvincing. Much more on the mark, however, is the third point of view, one that sees the series as incorporating a postmodern approach to Hollywood Italians.

Postmodern Hollywood Italians

There is no better or no more amusing definition of the postmodern impulse in contemporary culture than that provided by best-selling novelist and semiotician Umberto Eco in his *Postscript to "The Name of the Rose"*:

> The postmodern reply to the modern consists of recognizing that the past, since it cannot really be destroyed, because its destruction leads to silence, must be revisited: but with irony, not innocently. I think of the postmodern attitude as that of a man who loves a very cultivated woman and knows he cannot say to her, "I love you madly," because he knows that she knows (and that she knows that he knows) that these words have already been written by Barbara Cartland. Still there is a solution. He can say, "As Barbara Cartland would put it, I love you madly." At this point, having avoided false innocence, having said clearly that it is no longer possible to speak innocently, he will nevertheless have said what he wanted to say to the woman. . . . Irony, metalinguistic play, enunciation squared.[5]

Elsewhere in his discussion of the postmodern impulse, Eco notes that in literature, books "always speak of books, and every story tells a story that has already been told."[6] In parallel fashion, a postmodern movie or a series of postmodern movies like the many episodes of *The Sopranos* will feature an ironic and intertextual revisitation of other movies. Eco's definition of postmodernism certainly applies to *The Sopranos*. As Chase himself has stated, every episode of his four-year-long narrative cycle has been designed like a real movie, not an episode in a soap opera or a television serial. Consequently, metacinematic references to other movies, and in particular to other gangster films, abound. As might be expected, allusions to Francis Ford Coppola's *Godfather* trilogy—what has rightly been called "the Rosetta Stone of Mafia folklore"[7]—are extremely common. Running throughout the fifty-two programs, they provide an important theme that links Chase's creation to a cinematic tradition. Recognizing such references becomes one of the most satisfying experiences of watching the shows. Such references may be stylistic or thematic. For example, in several crucial episodes, Chase employs the same kind of dramatic cross-cutting in his film editing that made the conclusion of *The Godfather* so powerful. In the third episode of the first year ("Denial, Anger, Acceptance"), Chase cross-cuts between a choir concert in which Meadow sings a religious solo song with her family in the audience, on the one hand, and a hit on Christopher's sidekick Brendan Filone (Anthony DeSando), on the other. The reference to the concluding baptism scene of

The Godfather is unmistakable. Later, editing between a religious moment—Carmela's confession to Father Phil—and an act of Mob violence—Tony's murder of a Mob informer hiding in a town where he has taken Meadow for a college interview—makes the fifth episode of the first year ("College") one of the best in the entire series.

Other references rely more on knowing the dialogue from the *Godfather* trilogy. The fact that Tony and company all know the trilogy practically by heart reflects the very real fact that federal wiretaps have revealed how true-life Wise Guys actually imitate the expressions and mannerisms they see in these movies. In "Meadowlands" (I, 4), Big Pussy describes the manner in which Brendan has been killed as a "Moe Greene special," since he was shot in the eye in imitation of the execution of the Las Vegas casino manager in *The Godfather*. Paulie Walnuts then argues with Big Pussy about the hit sending a message, arguing that Coppola just framed the shot in that manner to shock his audience. Immediately thereafter in the same episode, Uncle Junior tells a Godfather joke. In "Boca" (I, 9), the girl's soccer coach must accept an offer he cannot refuse, a clear reference to Don Vito Corleone's habitual remark. Gangsta rapper and music impresario Massive Genius (Bookeen Woodbine) argues that *The Godfather Part III* has been misunderstood and is actually the best of the three movies in "A Hit Is a Hit" (I, 10). In the same episode, Bruce Cusamano and his friends ask Tony how real *The Godfather* actually is while on the golf course at the exclusive country club to which Tony is later denied membership. In revenge, Tony gives Cusamano a box of sand, allowing his neighbor to think the box contains weapons or drugs—at any rate, something illegal. In doing so, he is copying Peter Clemenza's actions in *The Godfather Part II* when he forces Vito Corleone to hide a sack full of illegal pistols in the family tenement. In "Nobody Knows Anything" (I, 11), Paulie's car horn even sounds Nino Rota's musical theme from *The Godfather*.

The second year continues the ongoing *Godfather* references. In "Guy Walks into a Psychiatrist's Office" (II, 1), Philly Parisi (Dan Grimaldi) takes over Uncle Junior's crew when Junior is sent to jail, and just before leaving the house he is told "Don't forget the pastries," in imitation of Clemenza's order to take the cannoli but leave the pistol after the assassination of Paulie Gatto. Parisi is subsequently murdered by Gigi Cestone (John Fiore). In "Commendatóri" (II, 4), Tony's crew becomes angry as they attempt to watch alternate outtakes from *The Godfather* from advance DVD copies of Coppola's trilogy that they have stolen. Paulie's favorite line is "It was you, Fredo," the words spoken by Michael Corleone in *The Godfather Part II* that peg his brother as a traitor. Since Big Pussy is betraying the Soprano family while sitting in their presence, Paulie's remark comments on

Big Pussy's treachery. In the same episode, Tony's statement that his favorite scene in Coppola's trilogy is Don Vito's trip to Sicily foreshadows his own trip to Italy to arrange the importation there of stolen luxury cars. In "Funhouse" (II, 13), Silvio does one of his many imitations of lines from the Coppola trilogy ("Our true enemy has yet to reveal himself"—Michael Corleone's remark after he has had a diabetic attack in *The Godfather Part III*), and his words are as true with reference to *The Sopranos* as they are in Coppola's film. But the true enemy—Big Pussy—reveals himself in Tony's dream that contains an obvious reference to Luca Brasi "sleeping with the fishes" in *The Godfather*. Big Pussy appears in the dream as a talking fish that will subsequently sleep with the other fishes after Tony, Paulie, and Silvio kill him and throw his body into the ocean.

In the third year in "Proshai, Livushka" (III, 4), an undertaker repeats Don Vito's line about using all his powers and skills to make Tony's mother Livia look good after her death (the reference is to the first movie in the trilogy when Don Vito brings the dead body of Sonny Corleone to be prepared for burial). Later ("To Save Us All from Satan's Power", III, 10), Tony recalls Silvio Dante's imitation of Michael Corleone's line from *The Godfather Part II* ("It was you, Fredo"), and he suddenly realizes that Big Pussy was wearing a wire for the FBI at that precise moment. In the same episode, Meadow gives Tony a talking fish for Christmas, not realizing that this reminds him of Big Pussy, the dear friend he has been forced to kill for his betrayal of their business to the FBI. Ironically, Meadow's gift reminds Tony both of Luca Brasi sleeping with the fishes in *The Godfather* and of the best friend he has been forced to murder. In "Everybody Hurts" (IV, 6), Anthony, Jr.'s friends compare Satriale's Pork Shop to the Genco Oil Company run by Don Vito Corleone in *The Godfather*, while Anthony's girlfriend Devin assumes incorrectly that Tony's home will look like the mansions from the same film.

Chase employs references to the Coppola masterpieces in a clever manner, using them both to delight us when we recognize them and to add layers of meaning to his own stories. In effect, he realizes that Coppola has already established a grammar for dealing with the Mafia, and he exploits Coppola's treasure trove of ideas, images, and situations, revisiting the trilogy in such a way that the hippest viewers will derive pleasure from recognizing the citations.

As we might expect from the style of his own series, Chase's also cites the works of Martin Scorsese. In fact, Chase wants *The Sopranos* to represent the Mob in a more sinister light—following Scorsese's example in *Goodfellas* and *Casino*—rather than the epic tragedy that Coppola creates. The use of aggressively coarse and obscene language in the series follows, and even surpasses, Scorsese's practice. And like Scorsese (and unlike Coppola), Chase prefers source music to new compositions. His sound tracks comprise a list of appropriate pop tunes from the contemporary period, except for a few throwback songs included for nostalgic or ironic purposes, like Bob Dylan's bad rendition of a Dean Martin classic. Indeed, a Martin Scorsese look-alike even appears in the second episode of the first year, entering a nightclub while Christopher and Adriana (Drea de Matteo) stand in line waiting to be admitted. It is not surprising, therefore, that in the first episode of the first year—the pilot episode entitled "The Pilot"—Father Phil asks Carmela what Tony thinks of Scorsese's *Goodfellas* as if being in the Mafia made him a movie critic. In "College," Meadow tells Tony that she and her friends prefer *Casino* to *The Godfather*. Scorsese's Las Vegas movie depicts the Mob in decline, and one of Tony's preoccupations is the feeling that his father Johnny Boy enjoyed the heyday of the Mob, whereas Tony came into the family "business" when things began to fall apart. The most interesting reference to Scorsese of all in the series takes place in "The Legend of Tennessee Moltisanti" (I, 8). Christopher angrily shoots a kid in the foot while he waits impatiently to be served pastries in a bakery, just as Tommy DeVito (Joe Pesci) shot a young boy to death during a card game in *Goodfellas*. The in-joke here is that the actor playing Christopher—Michael Imperioli—also played the young boy who was murdered in *Goodfellas*. Moreover, actor Imperioli does actually script other episodes of the series, and in this one, he plays a Wise Guy attempting to write scripts. The references to other films are emphasized by the fact that in this particular episode, Christopher toys with the idea of becoming a scriptwriter of Mob movies but is doomed only to play out the role of gangster in real life. After Uncle Junior's hit on Tony fails, the FBI offers Tony a chance to enter the Witness Protection Program. Carmela is interested but Tony refuses in an obvious reference to the fate that awaited Henry Hill at the conclusion of *Goodfellas:* "You want to move to Utah, be Mr. and Mrs. Mike Smith? We can sell some Indian relics by the road. Maybe start a rattlesnake ranch. . . . . Have some Mounties over to dinner. Eat some tomatoes that have no taste" ("Isabella," I, 12). When Christopher finally becomes "made" and is about to be initiated into the Mafia by Tony and his crew ("Fortunate Son," III, 3), his mistress Adriana worries that Christopher will be killed instead. She believes this is possible because she (like David Chase) has watched a similar event in *Goodfellas* where Tommy DeVito (Joe Pesci again) is easily lured into a convenient place to kill him since he believes he is about to be "made." Christopher tells Adriana what Tony tells him: that she and he have seen "too many movies." Of course, it is David Chase who has seen too many movies, much to the audience's delight.

Chase does not limit his references to the obvious Coppola and Scorsese classics. There are also citations, some much more subtle, to the classics of the gangster genre. One of the running jokes at the Bada Bing Strip Club involves an inept Wise Guy delegated to answer the telephone who cannot ever quite figure out how call waiting or the hold button works ("46 Long," I, 2). His failure to take important calls drives Tony, with whom he almost sympathizes, to beat him with the telephone. An inept but comic assistant of Tony Camonte has similar problems with telephones in *Scarface*. In "A Hit Is a Hit" (I, 10), Paulie cites Rico Bandello's dying words—"Mother of Mercy, is this the end of Rico?"—when Christopher leaves a crew orgy to have dinner with his girl. In "Boca" (I, 9), Uncle Junior hits his mistress with a cream pie rather than a grapefruit, as occurs in the famous grape-fruit-in-the-face scene from William Wellman's *The Public Enemy* (1931). Chase admits that this James Cagney classic movie was his favorite as a child. Thus, it is not surprising that Tony watches the movie during the episode in which his mother Livia's death is reported ("Proshai, Livushka," III, 2), and he cries over the fact that movie gangster Tom Powers had a mother who loved him, unlike his unnatural mother—a sinister and pow-erful figure suggested not only by Chase's own mother but also by the con-niving Empress Livia from the television series *I, Claudius*.

Besides these winks at the three classic gangster movies that established the genre in the 1930s, Chase's characters mention a number of other, some-times surprising films. Since Chase's entire series rests upon the fact that Tony Soprano consults a psychiatrist, Dr. Jennifer Melfi, there is one amusing reference to *Analyze This*, the Wise Guy comedy based upon the same prem-ise. During a moment when Tony believes he should break off his sessions with Dr. Melfi and consults another doctor (also an Italian American), he tries to hide his true identify by giving the doctor a false name, but to no avail ("Guy Walks Into a Psychiatrist's Office," II, 1):

> DR. D'ALESSIO: Mr. Spears. I watch the news like everyone else. I know who you are, and I saw *Analyze This*. I don't need the rami-fications that could arise from treating someone like yourself.
> TONY SOPRANO: *Analyze This*? Come on, it's a fucking comedy!

In "Big Girls Don't Cry" (II, 5), Tony meets Paulie in front of the monu-ment in Paterson, New Jersey, which is dedicated to movie comedian Lou Costello (Louis Francis Cristillo), a pointed commentary on Paulie's posi-tion in the crew as he is being demoted by the arrival of the Neapolitan Fu-rio Giunta. The psychotic Ralphie is fixated upon Ridley Scott's *Gladiator* (2000), especially the line "What we do in life echoes through eternity."

Ironically, as a murderer, Ralphie remains quite unconcerned about his fate in eternity: that task belongs primarily to Carmela Soprano. When Ralphie uses the address the Roman warriors exchange before battle in *Gladiator*— "Strength and honor"—Tony sarcastically replies, "Scotch and soda" ("Employee of the Month," III, 4). When Tony and his crew are not involved in complex family problems or engaged in criminal activities, it seems that they are always watching movies. Ralphie's cell phone even plays the theme music from the film *Rocky* ("Christopher," IV, 3). Tony takes in Frank Capra's *It's a Wonderful Life* (1946), even the Mob's favorite Christmas movie, before picking one of his crew to play Santa Claus at the Bada Bing's annual Christmas party for neighborhood kids ("To Save Us All from Satan's Power," III, 10). And in "For All Debts Public and Private" (IV, 1), the fact that Tony watches Howard Hawks's 1959 Western, *Rio Bravo*— the sequence where Dean Martin sings "My Rifle, Pony and Me"—helps to set the stage for Tony's false sense of security while, unbeknownst to him, the FBI is closing in on his criminal activities. Like the heroes of Westerns, Tony always praises the strong, silent hero (roles he identifies with Gary Cooper) and believes they are a model for Italian American manliness.

Tony and Christopher, along with Tony's cronies, are all movie addicts. But others habitually pattern their behavior after film characters. When Artie Bucco tries to collect a debt from a dishonest Frenchman, he first practices his threatening gestures in front of his mirror just as Travis Bickle (Robert De Niro) does in Martin Scorsese's *Taxi Driver*. Even Adriana, Christopher's mistress and future wife, watches *The Last Don* (1997), a television movie adapted from one of Mario Puzo's less successful novels following *The Godfather*. Presumably, she thinks she can learn something about how she should behave from watching the mobsters' women in that film.

Chase's references to classic gangster films are expected in a postmodern revisitation of the gangster genre. Other citations in the series are perhaps even more interesting. In the Neapolitan sequence ("Commendatóri," II, 4), Chase shoots himself at a city bar in an obvious reference to the famous cameo appearances Alfred Hitchcock always inserted in each of his pictures. We have already discussed Martin Scorsese's debts to Italian cinema, especially that of *Mean Streets* to Federico Fellini's *I vitelloni*. True to his own Italian origins, Chase also pays homage to both Fellini and Roberto Rossellini in several fascinating sequences. Psychoanalysis provides Chase's series with a fundamental framework. Much of the narrative development spins out of Tony's sessions with Dr. Melfi. In "Funhouse" (II, 13), the concluding episode of the second year, Tony experiences six different nightmares brought on by food poisoning, most of which occur on the Asbury

Park boardwalk near the ocean front as their setting. In one of these nightmares, Tony's men—Hesh, Silvio, Christopher, Paulie, Big Pussy—stand with him on the boardwalk in a pose that must certainly be indebted to similar scenes on the Adriatic beaches of Rimini in Fellini's *I vitelloni*. In that film, Fellini's young slackers all post themselves near the water during the winter when the tourist season is over. The winter season sets the sad tone of both dream sequences. In another of Tony's nightmares in this installment, Chase borrows from what may be the most famous movie of all time indebted to psychoanalysis, Fellini's *8½* (1963). As Tony imagines himself kissing Dr. Melfi, Dr. Melfi morphs into Annalisa (Sofia Milos), the beautiful, alluring woman he meets in Naples who is the boss of the Camorra family with which he has business ties. A similar dream sequence earlier in the series—"Meadowlands" (I, 4)—depicts a nightmare during which Dr. Melfi—the classic object of the patient's sexual desire during Tony's analysis—becomes his mother Livia during a kiss. Here Chase reverses the sequence in Fellini's *8½* in which the protagonist Guido kisses his mother at his father's graveside and she becomes his wife. For Chase, the movement from Melfi to Livia is far more frightening.

The Neapolitan episode of the second year ("Commendatóri," II, 4) contains a number of references to *The Godfather*. But beyond these obvious citations usually discussed by critics, another interesting movie reference occurs in the same episode: Tony and Annalisa repeat one of the events in Roberto Rossellini's *Viaggio in Italia* (*Voyage in Italy*, 1953). *Viaggio in Italia* was one of the films most highly praised by the French New Wave, whose directors delighted in a kind of referential citation that has since been associated with postmodern style. In Rossellini's original, a stodgy English couple, played by George Sanders and Ingrid Bergman, visit the famous sights of Naples—Vesuvius, the site of a Sybil of Cumae, Pompeii, the National Museum and its Farnese sculpture collection, the lava fields. At each spot, Mediterranean sensuality and a zest for life assault their dead sensibilities. Annalisa also takes Tony to visit the site of the Cumean Sybil. But from the first moment that Tony and Annalisa meet, the air sizzles with an obvious sensuality that contrasts markedly to Rossellini's sexually repressed Brits. In fact, Tony dreams of having sex with Annalisa from behind, dressed in a Roman toga (a dream that we see), and Annalisa bluntly asks Tony if he wants to "fuck" her during their visit to the Cumean Sybil's cave. Quite a distance has been traveled from Ingrid Bergman's iceberg performance as a frigid foreigner to Annalisa's direct solicitations! For once in his life, Tony refuses the opportunity, fearing to mix pleasure with business ("I don't shit where I eat," he remarks). Annalisa is the only beautiful and willing woman with whom Tony does not sleep during the four years of the program.

By means of his many citations from the long tradition of gangster movies and other cinema classics, David Chase forces the attentive viewer into a very active position when watching *The Sopranos*. Everyone learns to understand Hollywood Italian Wise Guys by watching the movies. Chase's Hollywood Italians function best before a sophisticated audience that knows how to decode the postmodern citations in the many episodes. For the vast majority of his audience, however, such concerns are less important than those linked to Chase's focus on the family, rather than criminal activities. To structure such a series on Hollywood Italian Wise Guys around a real family and real family problems—and not simply around a crime family—Chase turns to psychoanalysis.

Therapy and the Contemporary Hollywood Italian Famiglia

In his interview with Peter Bogdanovich, David Chase points out that the classic gangster figures, such as Little Caesar, Tony Camonte, and Vito or Michael Corleone, were probably all depressed characters who needed psychoanalysis. His own gangster Tony Soprano requires medical assistance because he has panic attacks that incapacitate him. Moreover, at the beginning of the series, Tony suffers from nightmares about ducks flying away with his penis; as the series progresses, he continues to have bad dreams that point to a traitor in his gang. It is inaccurate to say that *The Sopranos* is a successful venture because they portray gangsters as if they were ordinary people. Chase's gangsters are individuals who live under extraordinary pressures, dealing with stressful situations that most people could not survive. In addition, they are forced to deal with all the normal problems that the average citizen faces: kids taking drugs and getting in trouble, marriage and divorce, infidelity, broken friendships, depression, illness, and so forth. Tony exercises a profession that forces him to kill his best friends, to commit mayhem even when he prefers another more peaceful solution to his problems, to live in constant fear of arrest and punishment, and what is worse, to fear for his very life and the future of his wife and children. Nothing about this situation is normal. What is normal about Tony is that in addition to these very unusual conflicts in his life, he also has a wife who feels neglected; a daughter graduating from high school and looking for a college to attend, who also questions her father's occupation and has the usual adolescent crises; a son who has typical teenage problems with drinking and bad behavior; and bills to pay to maintain the upper-middle-class lifestyle to which his family has become accustomed.

Other films about life in the Mob—like Coppola's *Godfather* trilogy—have invented the situation Chase exploits: the conflict between one family (the nuclear family of husband, wife, children, and relatives) and the other "family" (the Mafia). But no other director has made the conflicts that arise from the first family more important than those that emerge from the second. In *The Godfather*, for example, there is a great deal of talk about the "family"; but most of the action concerns the criminal activity of the second family, not the very real problems of the first family or their daily lives. As Chase has stated, after the traditions of the gangster film created by such figures as Coppola or Scorsese, "the only place to go was the private life." What is truly remarkable about *The Sopranos* is that the interaction between the members of the first and traditional family produces results that are almost as deadly as the interaction between members of the second, criminal family. Tony not only has panic attacks, an off-the-wall sister, policemen and federal agents breathing down his neck, but he also has an uncle who tries to kill him, a mother who encourages his uncle to do so, other Mafiosi who would like nothing better than to replace him, and a gang of murderers who are his best friends but who, nevertheless, have such easily damaged egos over their place in the mobster pecking order that they may turn against Tony at any moment to ally themselves with his enemies or testify against him to avoid prosecution. All this is more than enough to produce *agita*, the word Chase's Hollywood Italians use for stress.

Tony works in a profession the members of which do not approve of telling anyone—neither priest nor psychoanalyst—about their business. This secrecy is partly because Hollywood Italian gangsters embrace a macho refusal to admit weaknesses. Still, the fundamental reason is that such information can send them to jail or get them killed. When Tony's associates finally learn that he is seeing a psychiatrist, their reaction is surprising and basically positive: although Christopher (not yet a made man) harbors doubts, the veteran mobsters are more understanding, since they have lived for years with the same stress. Paulie admits he has gone himself to consult a shrink, and Silvio Dante says he has no problem with it: "Look, uh, this thing of ours, the way it's going, be better if we could admit to each other these are painful, stressful times. But it'll never fuckin' happen" ("I Dream of Jeannie Cusamano," I, 13).

As the series unfolds over four years, Tony discovers his mother has a borderline personality disorder. Even though his father, Johnny Boy Soprano, was one of the toughest mobsters in the area, Livia reduced him, as Tony puts it to Dr. Melfi, to "a squeaking gerbil." Livia refused to allow Johnny Boy to go to Las Vegas, where he would have made a fortune during the heyday of the Mob's control of the city's casinos, and she never really showed any love for her three children—Tony, Janice, and Barbara. She threatened to put Tony's eyes out with a meat fork when he was a young child ("Down Neck," I, 7). As a grandmother, she is equally destructive. To young Anthony, Jr., upset because he has read Nietzsche and considers the possibility that God is dead, Livia delivers a devastating tirade about the lack of meaning in life:

> LIVIA: Why does everything have to have a purpose? The world is a jungle, and if you want my advice, Anthony, don't expect happiness. You won't get it, people let you down, and I'm not naming any names, but in the end, you die in your own arms.
>
> ANTHONY, JR: You mean, alone?
>
> LIVIA: It's all a big nothing. What makes you think you're so special?

Livia conspires with Uncle Junior to have Tony killed, and when the plot fails, she pretends to Junior that he misunderstood her. When Junior's incompetent assassins cannot do the job, Livia provokes Artie Bucco to try to complete the task by revealing to him that Tony has had his restaurant torched. This is true, but Tony committed this arson to help Artie, since Uncle Junior was about to have a rival gangster murdered in his restaurant, a crime that would have ruined Artie's business. Livia ignores the fact that Tony ensures that Artie has his restaurant rebuilt even better than before with insurance money. Although he continues to deny that his mother could be trying to have him killed, Tony cannot avoid this conclusion when FBI agents force him to listen to tapes containing proof of his mother's complicity. In one of the most compelling scenes in any of the episodes to date ("I Dream of Jeannie Cusamano"), after he hears that his mother has conveniently suffered a stroke upon learning that Tony is on to her schemes against him, Tony rushes to the hospital to suffocate her with a pillow but arrives too late: as Livia is carried off on a stretcher covered with an oxygen mask, she wears a smile. The program and the first year conclude with a poignant note about the importance of family. During a severe storm, Tony, Carmela, Meadow, and Anthony, Jr. take shelter in Artie's new restaurant. There they are taken in by Tony's old friend and discover Paulie, Silvio, Christopher, and Adriana. Tony tells his wife and children that they must savor the "little moments" in family life that are good, and try to repeat them when they have their own families later in life.

Family life and Mob family life both have their dangerous sides in Tony's crazy world. Tony holds to the belief that the profession he has chosen requires certain sacrifices that force him to do things he wishes he did not have to do, but to Dr. Melfi, he strongly rejects the idea that he and his gangster friends are monsters on the level of child molesters or dictators like Hitler or Pol Pot: "We're soldiers. Soldiers don't go to Hell. It's war. Soldiers kill other soldiers. Everybody involved knows the stakes, and if you're gonna accept those stakes, you gotta do certain things. It's business . . . soldiers, we follow codes, orders . . ." ("From Where to Eternity," II, 9). Nonetheless, Tony cannot accept the fact that his mother wants him dead, and he finds it equally diffi-cult to believe that his best friend, Big Pussy, has betrayed him and has turned into a "rat" who wears a wire to gather information against him. Such behavior seems to run in Tony's families. His sister Janice pressures her boyfriend, Richie Aprile, to cause Tony problems, insinuating that he de-serves more power than Tony has given him, thus initiating a series of devel-opments that almost leads Richie to betray Tony. Before that occurs, however, Janice manages to kill her lover in a fit of pique, and her target—Tony—must, as usual, clean up the mess.

By the third episode of the third year, ironically entitled "Fortunate Son," some psychoanalytic explanations for Tony's panic attacks and fainting spells emerge. In a flashback, Tony remembers that as a boy of eleven, he saw Johnny Boy chop off one of the butcher Satriale's fingers for not paying his gambling debts. Ultimately, Johnny Boy and the Soprano crime family ac-quire Satriale's Pork House for unpaid debts, and Tony's first fainting spell comes after he sees this traumatic attack on the kindly family butcher. After Livia cooks Johnny Boy a roast-beef dinner, Tony overhears Johnny Boy mix-ing sex and meat. "You like it with the bone standing in it," he says, and he re-marks that "the lady loves her meat." As Dr. Melfi notes, Tony's relationship to meat is not unlike that described by Marcel Proust with his famous madeleines—it opens the passages to his memory. In fact, one of Tony's fainting spells occurs just after he has eaten a snack of cold cuts (capicola) from the family refrigerator. Unlike most children, however, Tony remem-bers being fascinated rather than disgusted by the violence he witnessed. Yet, the future gangster confronts his mother's sexuality at an early age and asso-ciates it with meat, which sometimes brings on his spells and panic attacks.

Sopranoland and Contemporary Hollywood Italians

It would be impossible to discuss all the fascinating details of David Chase's original and provocative series in a brief space. But *The Sopranos* may well be defined as the high-water mark for Hollywood Italians in the movies. His imaginary America becomes a land chiefly populated by Ital-ian Americans. Set in an ethnic New Jersey that actually boasts a popula-tion where Italian Americans are made to seem as if they form the majority, Chase's Sopranoland treats Italian Americans as completely as-similated into the American mainstream. It is true that Hollywood Italian Wise Guys—and not Hollywood Italian brain surgeons or Hollywood Italian Secretaries of State—are Chase's focus. But virtually every kind of profession is exercised by Italian Americans in Chase's world, and it would be difficult to see *The Sopranos* as proof that Italian Americans are only lower-class manual laborers completely without power or influence in society. If the history of the American cinema represents Hollywood Italians primarily as Dagos, Palookas, Romeos, and Wise Guys, David Chase adds an enormous number of other professions to this list, providing a fuller and more compelling portrait of contemporary Hollywood Italians than any other movie or group of movies to date.

David Chase believes (as I do) that few people in the audiences who admire *The Sopranos* really believe all Italian Americans have ties to the Mafia. But Chase does believe (as I do) that a playful, postmodern approach to Hollywood Italian Wise Guys can make for great entertainment. A very wise professor of literature once announced in a Dante seminar many years ago that, sad though it may be to relate, great literature really constitutes no history of virtue. Quite the contrary is true. The same is true of great movies. Would millions of Americans set everything aside on Sunday evenings to glue themselves in front of their television sets to watch *The Sopranos* if it narrated the lives of soccer moms or of opera singers, as its title amusingly implies, rather than Wise Guys? The answer is obvious.

Italian Americans need not fear such representations in the movies since Italian Americans have achieved too important a place in American society and have made too many significant contributions to American culture to allow such a superficial summation of their contributions to stand uncontested. Mobsters are unfortunately a part of the Italian American heritage, but only a small part. Even if the Hollywood cinema has focused upon such Hollywood Italian images as Dagos, Palookas, Romeos, Wise Guys, and Sopranos, the reality of Italian Americans has been a steady and progressive march toward full membership in American society. But it has taken an Italian American, David Chase, to represent this most vividly. Yet, the history of Hollywood Italians in the American movies can still tell us all about how difficult such a road was and how long it took to travel it.

Notes

Introduction

1. Cited by Giorgio Bertellini in "New York City and the Representation of Italian Americans in the Cinema," in Philip V. Cannistraro, ed., *The Italians of New York: Five Centuries of Struggle and Achievement* (New York: The New York Historical Society and the John D. Calandra Italian American Institute, 1999), p. 115.

2. I am indebted to Tim Long, my colleague in Indiana University's Department of Classical Studies, for this precise information. The line may be found in H. Rushton Fairclough, ed., rev. ed. G. P. Goold, *Virgil, Aeneid VII-XII—Appendix Vergiliana* (Cambridge: Harvard University Press, 2000), pp. 524–27.

3. Native New Yorkers usually refer to a specific neighborhood around the historic Mulberry Street in Manhattan when they call an area "Little Italy." I use the term more loosely to refer to any Italian ethnic enclave in an urban area, whether in the various boroughs of New York City—such as Manhattan, Brooklyn, Queens, or Staten Island—Philadelphia, New Orleans, Chicago, or parts of Connecticut and New Jersey.

4. An excellent discussion of Anglo-Italian cultural relationships during the Renaissance may be found in Mario Praz, *The Flaming Heart* (New York: Norton, 1973; org. ed. 1958).

5. For a discussion of European émigrés and their impact upon Hollywood, see: John Russell Taylor, *Strangers in Paradise: The Hollywood Émigrés, 1933–1950* (New York: Holt, Rinehart and Wilson, 1983); and Neal Gabler, *An Empire of their Own: How the Jews Invented Hollywood* (New York: Doubleday, 1989). For a bibliography of works on ethnicity and the American cinema, see Lester D. Friedman, ed., *Unspeakable Images: Ethnicity and the American Cinema* (Urbana: The University of Illinois Press, 1991).

6. For Hollywood as a reflection of American history, see Kenneth M. Cameron, *America on Film: Hollywood and American History* (New York: Continuum, 1997).

7. For discussions of the role of *la famiglia* in Italian American life, see: Richard Gambino, *Blood of My Blood: The Dilemma of the Italian-Americans* (Toronto: Guernica, 1998); Jerre Mangione and Ben Morreale, *La Storia: Five Centuries of the Italian American Experience* (New York: Harper Collins, 1992); and a number of essays in *Beyond "The Godfather": Italian American Writers on the Real Italian American Experience*, eds. A. Kenneth Ciongoli and Jay Parini

(Hanover: University Press of New England, 1998). To be avoided at all costs is any naïve reliance on the so-called "Banfield thesis" of "amoral familism" that was popularized by Edward Banfield in *The Moral Basis of a Backward Society* (New York: The Free Press, 1958). This book that has done more to foster the acceptance of stereotypes about the role of the family in Italian or Italian American culture than any other single academic work ever printed. There is little doubt that *some* Italians or their Italian American relatives reflect Banfield's "amoral familism," but to claim that this is a universal trait makes about as much sense as saying Italians are natural opera singers.

1. Dagos: Hollywood Italian Histories of Immigration

1. Unless otherwise noted by a reference to a specific script in print, all references to film dialogue in this book are transcribed by the author from available prints, DVDs, or videocassettes.

2. Cited by Richard Gambino, *Blood of My Blood*, p. 77.

3. Israel Zangwill, *The Collected Works of Israel Zangwill* (New York: AMS Press, 1969), p. 95.

4. Marie Hall Ets, ed., *Rosa: The Life of an Italian Immigrant* (Madison: University of Wisconsin Press, 1970), p. 254.

5. For a fine history of Italian Americans, see Mangione and Morreale, *La Storia*, pp. 97, 110, 159, from which I have taken these statistics.

6. See Mangione and Morreale, *La Storia*, pp. 181–86, for a discussion of emigration to Louisiana and New Orleans.

7. For the detailed account with numerous documents appended to the text, see Richard Gambino, *Vendetta: The True Story of the Largest Lynching in U.S. History* (Toronto: Guernica Editions, 2000).

8. Gambino, *Vendetta*, pp. 103–04.

9. Gambino, *Vendetta*, reprints the entire text of the speech, which was widely reprinted all across the nation in newspapers with apparent approval.

10. For a discussion of representations of Italians in the early silent cinema, see: Lee Lourdeaux, *Italian and Irish Filmmakers in America: Ford, Capra, Coppola, and Scorsese* (Philadelphia: Temple University Press, 1990), pp. 65–85; Kevin Brownlow, *Behind the Mask of Innocence* (Berkeley: University of California Press, 1990), pp. 309–20; Ilaria Serra, *Immagini di un immaginario: L'Emigraziana Italiana negli Stati Uniti fra i due secoli (1890–1924)* (Treviso: Cierre Edizioni, 1998), pp. 110–59; and Paola Casella, *Hollywood Italian: gli italiani nell'America di celluloide* (Milan: Baldini & Castoldi, 1998), pp. 19–48. The fundamental research tools for the early American cinema from the Biograph era to 1930, with numerous indices arranged by subject matter (Italy, immigration, gangsters, etc.) that are particularly helpful when examining the images of Hollywood Italians in the period are the following volumes: *Biograph Bulletins 1896–1908*, ed. Kemp R. Niver (Los Angeles: Artisan Press, 1971); *Biograph Bulletins 1908–1912*, ed. Eileen Bowser (New York: Octagon Books, 1973); *The American Film Institute Catalogue*

of Motion Pictures Produced in the United States, Feature Films, 1911–1920, 2 vols., ed. Patricia King Hanson (Los Angeles: University of California Press, 1988); and *The American Film Institute Catalogue of Motion Pictures Produced in the United States, Feature Films, 1921–1930*, 2 vols., ed. Kenneth W. Munden (New York: R. R. Bowker, 1971).

11. The theme of a Jewish girl or boy falling in love with an Irish Catholic boy or girl was also very popular, culminating in the very successful Cohen & Kelly series, or in various versions of *Abie's Irish Rose*: first a comedy written by Anne Nichols; then a film by Victor Fleming by the same title in 1929; and then refilmed with the same title in 1946 by A. Edward Sutherland.

12. Brownlow, *Beyond the Mask of Innocence*, pp. 315–20, discusses this film and *The Italian* in some detail; see also Lourdeaux, *Italian and Irish Filmmakers in America*, pp. 67–69; and Serra, *Immagini di un immaginario*, pp. 137–55.

13. Charles Musser, "Ethnicity, Role-playing, and American Film Comedy: From *Chinese Laundry Scene* to *Whoopee* (1894–1930)," in Friedman, ed., p. 66. I am indebted to Musser's interpretation of ethnicity in *Animal Crackers* for this discussion.

14. Fred L. Gardaphé, "Introduction" to Pietro Di Donato, *Christ in Concrete* (New York: Signet, 1993), p. xi. For additional commentary on the novel, see: Fred L. Gardaphé, *Italian Signs, American Streets: The Evolution of Italian American Narrative* (Durham: Duke University Press, 1996), pp. 66–75, as well as his treatment of Di Donato in "Italian American Novelists" in Pellegrino D'Acierno, ed., *The Italian American Heritage: A Companion to Literature and Arts* (New York: Garland, 1999), pp. 167–70; Arthur D. Casciato, "The Bricklayer as Bricoleur: Pietro Di Donato and the cultural politics of the popular front," *Voices in Italian Americana* (Fall 1991), pp. 67–76; and Harry Geduld, "*Christ in Concrete*: dal romanzo al film," *Cinema & Cinema* 11 (1984), 17–25, the most important discussion of the adaptation of the novel into the film under discussion. Much of the material here is taken from my earlier article "*Christ in Concrete* di Edward Dmytryk e il neorealismo italiano," *Cinema & Cinema* 11 (1984), 9–16. Dmytryk's film was also released under another title in the United Kingdom as *Give Us This Day*; in America it was released under an alternate title, *Salt to the Devil*; the Italian title *Cristo fra i muratori* was perhaps the most appropriate title for the film adaptation.

15. As this book was being completed, a DVD edition of a beautiful print was released by a small company specializing in rescuing important but undistributed films—All Day Entertainment. The DVD includes important interviews and commentaries.

16. Edward Dmytryk, *It's a Hell of a Life but Not a Bad Living: A Hollywood Memoir* (New York: Times Books, 1978), p. 118.

17. For information about the Italian reception and distribution of the work, see *Schedario cinematografico* (Rome: Centro dello spettacolo e della communicazione sociale, 1972).

18. For a discussion of *la via vecchia*, see Gambino, *Blood of My Blood*.

19. For an excellent discussion of this key novel of the 1950s, see David Halberstam's *The Fifties* (New York: Ballantine Books, 1993), pp. 523–27.

20. For details on *Good Morning Babylon,* see Peter Bondanella, *Italian Cinema: From Neorealism to the Present,* 3ʳᵈ rev. ed. (New York: Continuum, 2002), pp. 395–97, which cites Griffith's speech from the script.

21. For discussions of such sequences in the neorealist cinema or in Scola, see my *Italian Cinema,* chapters 2 and 10.

22. I am treating *A Bronx Tale* as a film primarily on the Little Italy of the 1960s and not as a gangster film because the work's focus is upon Calogero's coming of age and the environment in the Italian ghetto, not upon the Mob. In any realistic portrayal of a Little Italy, it would, however, be difficult to avoid some mention of organized crime.

23. See Ellen Draper, "'Controversy Has Probably Destroyed Forever the Context': *The Miracle* and Movie Censorship in America in the Fifties," *The Velvet Light Trap* 25 (1990), 69–79. For a discussion of Rossellini, Fellini, and their Christian themes—an important influence on Martin Scorsese according to his recent documentary on Italian cinema—see Peter Bondanella, *The Films of Roberto Rossellini* (New York: Cambridge University Press, 1993) and *The Cinema of Federico Fellini* (Princeton: Princeton University Press, 1992).

24. For discussions of Scorsese's works, see the following useful books: Lawrence S. Friedman, *The Cinema of Martin Scorsese* (New York: Continuum, 1998); David Thompson and Ian Christie, eds., *Scorsese on Scorsese* (London: Faber & Faber, 1996); and Lourdeaux, *Italian and Irish Filmmakers in America.* See also various essays in *Scene italoamericane: Rappresentazioni cinematografiche degli italiani d'America,* eds. Anna Camaiti Hostert and Anthony J. Tamburri (Rome: Luca Sosella Editore, 2002).

25. Pellegrino D'Acierno, "Cinema Paradiso: The Italian American Presence in American Cinema," in D'Acierno, *The Italian American Heritage,* p. 628. See also Donald Tricarico, "Guido: Fashioning an Italian-American Youth Style," *Journal of Ethnic Studies* 10 (1991), 41–66; and especially "Bensonhurst" in Maria Laurino's outstanding book, *"Were You Always an Italian?": Ancestors and Other Icons of Italian America* (New York: Norton, 2000), pp. 121–55.

26. Marion Weiss, *Martin Scorsese: A Guide to Reference and Resources* (Boston: G. K. Hall, 1987), p. 10; or David Thompson and Ian Christie, eds., *Scorsese on Scorsese* (London: Faber and Faber, 1996), p. 41.

27. Raymond Chandler, "The Simple Art of Murder," in Howard Haycraft, ed., *The Art of the Mystery Story* (New York: Carroll & Graf, 1992; org. ed. 1946), p. 237. Chandler's definition refers, of course, to the character of the detective in the hard-boiled detective novel that made his fortune.

28. In the original Italian versions of his films, Fellini sometimes employed voice-overs spoken by the director himself, as for example in both *Roma* (1972, *Fellini's Roma*) and *Amarcord* (1974, *Amarcord). I Vitelloni's* voice-over is delivered by an unspecified narrator who seems to be identified with the one character that leaves his provincial home and goes to Rome to seek his fortune there (Moraldo), something Fellini did himself.

29. In *Scorsese on Scorsese,* the director notes that when Robert Altman saw the film at the New York Film Festival, he told Scorsese he very much enjoyed the

film but would have employed more tracking shots rather than shots using a hand-held camera. Scorsese replied that if he had done all those particular shots with a tracking camera, he would still be there shooting, and he added that the "economics dictated the style, and the style just happened to work" (p. 47).

30. *Scorsese on Scorsese*, p. 45.

31. For a consideration of the impact of Catholicism upon the cinema, see Les and Barbara Keyser, *Hollywood and the Catholic Church: The Image of Roman Catholicism in American Movies* (Chicago: Loyola University Press, 1984). For recent discussions of Catholicism's role in the "Little Italies" of New York City, see two books by Robert A. Orsi: *The Madonna of 115th Street: Faith and Community in Italian Harlem 1880–1950* (New Haven: Yale University Press, 1985); and *Thank You, St. Jude: Women's Devotion to the Patron Saint of Lost Causes* (New Haven: Yale University Press, 1996).

32. For Lee's cinema, see: Donald Bogle, *Toms, Coons, Mulattoes, Mammies & Bucks: An Interpretative History of Blacks in American Films*, 4th ed. (New York: Continuum, 2001), pp. 318–23, 352; Mark A. Reid, ed., *Spike Lee's "Do the Right Thing"* (New York: Cambridge University Press, 1997); and Spike Lee with Lisa Jones, *"Do the Right Thing": A Spike Lee Joint* (New York: Simon & Schuster, 1989).

33. For information in this regard, see Catherine Pouzoulet's essay "The Cinema of Spike Lee: Images of a Mosaic City," in Reid, ed., *Spike Lee's "Do the Right Thing*," pp. 31–49, to which this discussion of the demographically accurate account of the neighborhood at the time the film was made is indebted.

34. Ibid., p. 37.

35. Spike Lee with Lisa Jones, *Spike Lee's "Do the Right Thing*," pp. 186–87.

36. For an enlightening discussion of Italian American language, see Laurino's essay "Words," in *"Were You Always an Italian?,"* pp. 100–20; see also Pellegrino D'Acierno's "Cultural Lexicon: Italian American Key Terms," in D'Acierno, ed., *The Italian American Heritage*, pp. 703–66.

37. Spike Lee with Lisa Jones, *Spike Lee's "Do the Right Thing*," pp. 243–44.

38. Ibid., p. 38. That Lee's remarks about the portrayal of African Americans in the Rocky series are incorrect will be clear from our discussion of the topic in the chapter devoted to Hollywood Italian Palookas.

39. Ibid., p. 45.

40. Douglas Kellner, "Aesthetics, Ethnics, and Politics in the Films of Spike Lee," in Reid, ed., *Spike Lee's "Do the Right Thing*," p. 93.

41. W. J. T. Jackson, "The Violence of Public Art: *Do the Right Thing*," in Reid, ed., *Spike Lee's "Do the Right Thing*," p. 111.

42. Bogle, *Toms, Coons, Mulattoes, Mammies & Bucks*, p. 243.

2. *Palookas: Hollywood Italian Prize Fighters*

1. *The American Heritage Dictionary of the English Language* (Boston: Houghton Mifflin, 1969), p. 946.

2. Michael Quinion, *World Wide Words* (*www.quinion.com/words*), 29 January 2000.

3. Gerald Early, *The Culture of Bruising: Essays on Prizefighting, Literature, and Modern American Culture* (Hopewell, NJ: The Ecco Press, 1994), p. 11.

4. Early, *The Culture of Bruising*, p. 6.

5. Norman Mailer, "King of the Hill," in Joyce Carol Oates and Daniel Halpern, eds., *Reading the Fights* (New York: Henry Holt, 1988), p. 126.

6. Joyce Carol Oates, *On Boxing* (Garden City, NY: Doubleday, 1987), p. 25.

7. S. Kirson Weinberg and Henry Arond, "The Occupational Culture of the Boxer," *American Journal of Sociology* 57, #5 (1952), 460.

8. Weinberg and Arond, 462.

9. The theme of the "great white hope" inspired a 1970 play by Howard Sackler, *The Great White Hope*. The play was filmed with the same title by Martin Ritt in 1970. Johnson's career was the first major boxing career to be extensively filmed by documentary filmmakers.

10. For the discussions of boxing's symbolic, racial, and political history in twentieth-century American culture, I have relied on three excellent books: Jeffrey T. Sammons, *Beyond the Ring: The Role of Boxing in American Society* (Urbana: University of Illinois Press, 1988); John Sugden, *Boxing and Society: An International Analysis* (Manchester: Manchester University Press, 1996); and the previously cited book by Gerald Early, *The Culture of Bruising*.

11. Curtiz's *Kid Galahad* has also been titled *The Battling Bellhop* for screening on television. Another remake appeared in 1941, some years before the Presley movie: Ray Enright's *The Wagons Roll at Midnight*. In this picture, a young man (Eddie Albert) saves someone from a lion in a circus run by Humphrey Bogart and becomes chief lion tamer.

12. John Sugden, *Boxing and Society*, pp. 23, 24.

13. Rocky Graziano with Roland Barber, *Somebody up There Likes Me* (New York: Pocket Books, 1955), p. 35.

14. Graziano, *Somebody up There Likes Me*, p. 191.

15. Graziano (ibid., p. 271) also notes that he fought a man named Milo Theodorescu, winning a first-round technical knockout, who was called "Golden Boy" because he played the violin like the William Holden character in *Golden Boy*. Life copies art even in the boxing ring.

16. Ronald Levas, "Reading the Fights: Making Sense of Professional Boxing," in Oates and Halpern, eds., *Reading the Fights*, p. 11.

17. Oates, *On Boxing*, p. 60.

18. Early, *The Culture of Bruising*, pp. 102, 100–101.

19. Early, *The Culture of Bruising*, p. 102.

20. Here and elsewhere, I take figures on film costs and gross receipts, as well as information about nominations for awards and awards received, from the invaluable International Movie Data Base (*www.imdb.com*).

21. For a collection of these reviews, as well as six articles written especially for the book, see Steven G. Kellman, ed., *Perspectives on "Raging Bull"* (New York:

G. K. Hall, 1994). Marion Weiss, *Martin Scorsese: A Guide to References and Resources* is an excellent guide to much of the critical literature on the film. For additional commentary on this film, see the previously mentioned Friedman, *The Cinema of Martin Scorsese*, pp. 113–133; Paola Casella, *Hollywood Italian: gli italiani nell'America di celluloid*, pp. 343–348; and David Thompson and Ian Christie, eds., *Scorsese on Scorsese*, pp. 78–87. See also: David Alan Mellor, "The Ring of Impossibility, or, the Failure to Recover Authenticity in the Recent Cinema of Boxing," pp. 81–91; and Nick James, "Raging Bulls: Sexuality and the Boxing Movie," pp. 112–119, in David Chandler, ed., *Boxer: An Anthology of Writings on Boxing and Visual Culture* (Cambridge: MIT Press, 1996).

22. Morris Dickstein, "Stations of the Cross: *Raging Bull* Revisited," in Kellman, ed., *Perspectives on Raging Bull*, p. 78.

23. Ibid., pp. 80, 79.

24. The critics who stress the homoerotic elements in *Raging Bull* include Friedman, *The Cinema of Martin Scorsese*; the Nick James essay in Chandler, ed., *Boxer*; and the Michael Kimmel essay, "Ethnicity and the Erotics of Violence," in Kellman, ed., *Perspectives on "Raging Bull,"* pp. 84–95, which compares the film to a pornographic film.

25. Jake La Motta with Joseph Carter and Peter Savage, *Raging Bull: My Story* (New York: Da Capo, 1997, orig. ed. 1970), p. 178.

26. David Denby, "Brute Force," in Kellman, ed., *Perspectives on "Raging Bull,"* p. 44.

27. Cited by Friedman, *The Cinema of Martin Scorsese*, p. 126.

28. Scorsese, *Scorsese on Scorsese*, p. 84.

29. Cited in Kellman, ed., *Perspectives on "Raging Bull,"* p. 27.

30. Scorsese, *Scorsese on Scorsese*, p. 77.

31. Ibid.

32. Cited in Kellman, ed., *Perspectives on "Raging Bull,"* p. 27.

33. This point is made by Friedman, *The Cinema of Martin Scorsese*, p. 114.

34. Paul Schrader, *Schrader on Schrader*, ed. Kevin Jackson (London: Faber & Faber, 1990), p. 133.

35. As Scorsese himself notes, when the picture was completed it was screened for Schrader, who did not like it very much but as he wrote to Scorsese when shooting began on the film: "Jake did it his way, I did it my way, you do it your way" (*Scorsese on Scorsese*, p. 77).

36. For additional information about Wepner, see his website at: *www.users .nac.net/subliminal/chuck.html.* The site also contains photographs of the Wepner-Ali match and bills Wepner as the "real Rocky."

37. Maria Laurino's *"Were You Always an Italian?,"* pp. 136–37. The complete essay, entitled "Bensonhurst" (pp. 121–57), is the most interesting discussion of the Italian American culture of this famous neighborhood currently available.

3. Romeos: Hollywood Italian Lovers

1. Cited by Irving Shulman in *Valentino* (New York: Pocket Books, 1968), p. 94. The most recent biography of Valentino is Emily Leider's *Dark Lover: The Life and Death of Rudolph Valentino* (New York: Farrar Straus & Giroux, 2003).

2. Quoted in Kitty Kelley, *His Way: The Unauthorized Biography of Frank Sinatra* (New York: Bantam, 1987), p. 289.

3. Cited by Shawn Levy in *Rat Pack Confidential* (New York: Anchor, 1998), p. 227.

4. Ibid., p. 36.

5. Nick Tosches, *Dino: Living High in the Dirty Business of Dreams* (New York: Delta, 1992), p. 166.

6. Lawrence J. Quirk and William Schoell, *The Rat Pack; Neon Nights with the Kings of Cool* (New York: Avon, 1998), p. 182.

7. Tosches, *Dino*, p. 330.

8. For a survey of such characters, see Victoria Thomas, *Hollywood's Latin Lovers: Latino, Italian and French Men Who Make the Screen Smolder* (Santa Monica: Angel City Press, 1998).

9. These connections to Valentino are noted by Thomas in *Hollywood's Latin Lovers*, pp. 49–50.

10. There is an interesting bio-sketch of Valentino by John Dos Passos in *The Big Money* (1936)—the third novel of the *U.S.A.* trilogy—entitled "Adagio Dancer."

11. This film is included in the materials on the DVD that contains both *The Sheik* and *Son of the Sheik*, most likely shot to publicize Valentino after the appearance of the first of these films.

12. According to Jeanie Basinger's *Silent Stars* (New York: Knopf, 1999), p. 274, Valentino had only one rival in film history when smoking a cigarette with style and sexuality—Marlene Dietrich—and remarks: "What a shame they were never paired—two androgynous figures in tuxedos with their cigarettes aglow . . . what a loss to film history." I would add Humphrey Bogart and Lauren Bacall to her cigarette and sex list after the birth of the talkies. For a feminist view of Valentino, see Miriam Hansen, "Pleasure, Ambivalence, Identification: Valentino and Female Spectatorship," in Jeremy G. Butler, ed., *Star Texts: Image and Performance in Film and Television* (Detroit: Wayne State University Press, 1991), pp. 266–97.

13. Ibid., p. 266.

14. For an excellent survey of Italian American musical culture to which my discussion is indebted, see Robert Connolly and Pellegrino D'Acierno's "Italian American Musical Culture and Its Contribution to American Music," in D'Acierno, *The Italian American Heritage*, pp. 387–490. One excellent analysis of Sinatra's singing style may be found in Gene Lees, *Singers and the Song II* (New York: Oxford University Press, 1998), pp. 91–103.

15. For a complete biography of Sinatra, to which my discussion of his career is indebted, see Kitty Kelley's controversial but always interesting *His Way.*

16. *Silent Stars*, p. 307.
17. Cited by Kelley, *His Way*, p. 91.
18. Cited in ibid., p. 124.
19. These figures are reported in Kelley, ibid., p. 125.
20. Ibid., p. 134.
21. Ibid., p. 212. But according to Kelley (p. 212), Cohn apparently had close ties to Johnny Roselli, the Mafia man in Los Angeles in charge of labor racketeering at the time in the film industry. Lest I be accused of besmirching Frank Sinatra's character while admiring only his talent by mentioning friendships with known mobsters, many of whom were regrettably Italian Americans in their ethnic background, let me repeat an assessment of his character by Anthony Quinn with which I am in essential agreement: "I don't love everything that Frank does or the way he treats people at times, but anyone who sings like he does cannot be a really bad man" (cited by Levy, *Rat Pack Confidential*, p. 314).
22. See Tom Kuntz and Phil Juntz, eds., *The Sinatra Files: The Secret FBI Dossier* (New York: Three Rivers Press, 2000).
23. For my discussion of Dean Martin's life and career, in addition to the books listed in the bibliography on the Rat Pack, I am deeply indebted to Nick Tosches's remarkable and previously cited biography *Dino*.
24. Tosches, *Dino*, p. 145.
25. Ibid., p. 46.
26. Ibid., pp. 204–205.
27. Ibid., p. 246.
28. Ibid., p. 272, cites these figures.
29. Levy, *Rat Pack Confidential*, p. 91.
30. Tosches, *Dino*, p. 323.
31. Levy, *Rat Pack Confidential*, p. 84.
32. Ibid., pp. 86–87.
33. Ibid., p. 109.
34. Tosches, *Dino*, p. 325.
35. Ibid., p. 52.
36. Ibid., p. 323.
37. Quirk and Schoell, *The Rat Pack*, p. 182.
38. Ibid., p. 184.
39. James Ellroy is best known as the author of the novel *L.A. Confidential* (1990), the source of one of the most important films made in Hollywood during the last decade of the twentieth century. But two other Ellroy novels—*American Tabloid* (1995) and *The Cool Six Thousand* (2001)—explore the many links, real or imagined, between the Kennedy brothers, the Kennedy patriarch, the Mob in Las Vegas, plots against Fidel Castro, and the assassinations of both JFK and RFK.
40. Tosches, *Dino*, p. 330.
41. The author must confess to a touch of nostalgia for the setting of the Nevada casinos in the mid-1960s, the Rat Pack era. As a graduate student, I

worked as a craps dealer in Harrah's Club in Reno during the summers of 1966 and 1967. Gamblers and visitors to casinos in general simply dressed better in those days, even in what was then a very small casino far removed from the glamour of the Las Vegas Strip. There was none of the theme-park atmosphere that now dominates Las Vegas gambling. But then again, the restaurants were not so sophisticated as they are today.

42. This song was written specifically for *Ocean's Eleven* and for Martin by James Van Heusen and Sammy Cahn. It is interesting that Frank Sinatra does not sing in the film. A self-professed "whore for his music," Sinatra apparently thought that his singing was too sophisticated for the low-brow film he was making, even though he sang in other Rat Pack films.

43. For a discussion of the sexual activities on the sets of these two westerns, see Quirk and Schoell, *The Rat Pack*, pp. 214–18. Kelley, *His Way*, p. 242, also reports on Sinatra's use of prostitutes as extras on the set of *4 for Texas*.

44. For a description of his reaction, as well as for his relationship to Kennedy and Sam Giancana after the election until the president's assassination, see Kelley, *His Way*, pp. 308–58.

45. Tosches, *Dino*, p. 331.

46. Levy, *Rat Pack Confidential*, p. 323.

47. Levy goes on to explain our nostalgia for this moment in American pop culture: "If anyone grew nostalgic for it, if it ever seemed like a more innocent time, that was because it was the last moment of cultural unanimity. For the first sixty years of the century, save a couple dozen months after Elvis made the scene, everybody in every house in America found pleasure in the same type of comedy, music, movies. The Rat Pack bunched it altogether in an unprecedented height and pitch—and for the last time. And nobody seemed to agree about anything ever again after they were toppled from their golden aerie" (ibid.).

48. For a discussion of the "Guido" or the "cugine" image of blue-collar Italians, see the previously cited Tricarico, "Guido: Fashioning an Italian-American Youth Style"; D'Acierno, "*Cinema Paradiso*" in *The Italian American Heritage;* and Laurino, "*Were You Always an Italian?*"

49. Nik Cohn, "Tribal Rites of the New Saturday Night," *New York* 9, #23 (7 June 1976), 31–43.

50. Ibid., pp. 33–34.

51. Nik Cohn, "Saturday Night's Big Bang," *New York* (8 December 1997), 34.

52. See her essay "Bensonhurst" in *"Were You Always an Italian?"*, pp. 134–41.

53. Ibid., p. 141.

4. *Wise Guys: Hollywood Italian Gangsters*

1. The line in the screenplay is slightly different: "Better quit the racket, Arnie. You got so you can dish it out, but you can't take it no more." Cited in Gerald Perry, ed., *Little Caesar* (Madison: University of Wisconsin Press, 1981), p. 132.

2. Cited from Martin Scorsese and Nicholas Pileggi, *Goodfellas* (London: Faber and Faber, 1990), p. 4.

3. Cited by Mangione and Morreale in *La Storia*, p. 247.

4. Ibid., 245. See Herbert Asbury, *The Gangs of New York* (or. ed. 1927: New York: Thunder's Mouth Press, 2001) for details about gang life before the rise of truly organized crime during and after Prohibition.

5. Mangione and Morreale, *La Storia*, p. 251.

6. Ibid., p. 248.

7. Cited by ibid., p. 166.

8. For a discussion of the Black Hand, see ibid., pp. 167–69; or Humbert Nelli, *The Business of Crime* (New York: Oxford University Press, 1976).

9. It is an interesting bit of trivia that Thomas Ince's brother Ralph would play the part of a gangster in *Little Caesar*.

10. Mangione and Morreale, *La Storia*, p. 167, cite a letter to the *New York Times* from an Italian landlord named Salvatore Spinelli who defied Black Hand extortion notes and who suffered five bomb attacks on his rental properties, ruining his business.

11. Three books are to be recommended here: Browlow's *Behind the Mask of Innocence*; Gevinson's *American Film Institute Catalog—Within Our Gates: Ethnicity in American Feature Films, 1911–1960*; and Carlo Clarens, *Crime Movies: An Illustrated History of the Gangster Genre from D. W. Griffith to "Pulp Fiction,"* updated by Foster Hirsch (New York: Da Capo, 1997; original edition, 1980). My discussion of Hollywood Italian Wise Guys is deeply indebted to these sources. In addition, I have found extremely useful information in Jack Shadoian, *Dreams and Dead Ends: The American Gangster/Crime Film* (Cambridge: MIT Press, 1977); the collected essays of Robert Washow, *The Immediate Experience: Movies, Comics, Theatre and Other Aspects of Popular Culture* (Cambridge: Harvard University Press, 2001, enlarged edition); and Thomas Schatz, *Hollywood Genres: Formulas, Filmmaking, and the Studio System* (New York: Random House, 1981), a study that contains an entire chapter devoted to the genre (pp. 81–110).

12. Cited by Brownlow, *Behind the Mask of Innocence*, p. 312.

13. Browlow's classic study presents numerous films on drug traffic, white slavery, crime, political corruption, and prohibition. Taken together, only a small percentage of these works identify the criminals as Italian Americans.

14. Gerald Perry, "Introduction: Little Caesar Takes over the Screen," in *Little Caesar*, p. 9.

15. Cited by Clarens, *Crime Movies*, p. 33.

16. The film was later remade in 1951 by John Cromwell staring Robert Mitchum and Robert Ryan, and the co-writer credited by the script was W. R. Burnett, author of the original novel on which *Little Caesar* was based.

17. For Kevin Brownlow's discussion of *The Racket* on the stage and the screen, to which I owe most of the details outlined here, see his *Behind the Mask of Innocence*, pp. 276–81.

18. I am indebted to Clarens's discussion of *Doorway to Hell* in *Crime Movies*, pp. 53–54, for most of the details about this film.

19. Figures reported by ibid., p. 60.

20. Schatz, *Hollywood Genres*, p. 82.

21. Warshow, "The Gangster as Tragic Hero," in *The Immediate Experience*, p. 100.

22. Warshow, "Movie Chronicle: The Westerner," in ibid., p. 106.

23. Warshow, "The Gangster as Tragic Hero," in ibid., p. 102.

24. Clarens, so frequently convincing in his discussions of crime films, calls Rico's friendship a "nonerotic homosexual attachment" (*Crime Films*, p. 59). Shadoian's perplexed attitude about this question in *Dreams and Dead Ends* (p. 29) is far more to the mark: "The homosexual nature of the Rico-Joe relationship has often been remarked, and I suppose it is true, although it is not explicit. . . . Joe's crime, in Rico's eyes, is a betrayal of male solidarity and friendship."

25. Clarens, *Crime Movies*, pp. 89–91, has an excellent discussion of the problems Hawks faced from censorship and distribution.

26. For a mass of information about the Mafia, its leaders, and its history, I have found two books very useful: Carl Sifakis, *The Mafia Encyclopedia: From Accardo to Zwillman* (New York: Facts on File, 1987); and Jerry Capeci, *The Complete Idiot's Guide to the Mafia* (Indianapolis: Alpha, 2002).

27. Clarens, *Crime Movies*, p. 84, reports this fascinating information.

28. Ibid., p. 93, makes this important point.

29. The lines falsely attributed to Machiavelli by the scriptwriters, later replaced in the film by the biblical quotation about how those who live by the sword die by it, read: "The first law of every being is to preserve itself and life. You sow hemlock, and expect to see ears of corn. –Machiavelli." Cited in Perry, *Little Caesar*, p. 45. Machiavelli was an important source for *A Bronx Tale*, as we have noted in the first chapter. The moral principles governing the behavior of the Corleone Mafia family may be compared to many of the ideas of Machiavelli's *Prince* with profit, and I do believe that Mario Puzo was directly inspired by Machiavelli (or at least the evil legend of Machiavellianism) for this relationship.

30. Francesco Guicciardini, *The History of Italy*, trans. Sidney Alexander (New York: Macmillan, 1969), p. 123. For a complete discussion of the Borgia legend, see my *Francesco Guicciardini* (Boston: Twayne, 1976), pp. 111–13. Modern scholars are all in agreement that this rumor has absolutely no truth in fact. Another important source of an Italianate legend of family incest would be provided by Shelley's "Elizabethan" tragedy, *The Cenci*, which was banned in England for over a century and a half, a drama that deals with the incestuous relationship between Beatrice Cenci and her father.

31. Mario Puzo, *The Family*, completed by Carol Gino (New York: Harper Collins, 2001).

32. Clarens, *Crime Movies*, p. 93.

33. Michael Munn, *The Hollywood Connection: The True Story of Organized Crime in Holly*wood (London: Robson Books, 1993), pp. 87–93, provides this report of the real personal link between *Scarface* and Capone.

34. In my outline of the history of the Production Code and its impact upon the gangster film, I follow Schatz, *Hollywood Genres*, pp. 96–110; and Clarens,

Crime Movies, pp. 71–73, 81–101, 114–15, 192, 251, 271–72, 293–94; and Giuliana Muscio, "L'era di Will Hays. La censura nel cinema Americano," in Gian Piero Brunetta, ed., *Storia del cinema mondiale: Gli Stati Uniti*, vol. II, part I (Turin: Einaudi, 1999), pp. 525–55.

35. See Ellen Draper, "'Controversy Has Probably Destroyed Forever the Context': *The Miracle* and Movie Censorship in America in the Fifties," *The Velvet Light Trap* 25 (1990), 69ff.

36. Cited by Clarens, *Crime Movies*, p. 272.

37. Ibid., 192.

38. For a detailed account of Colombo and his civil rights group, see Capeci, *The Complete Idiot's Guide to the Mafia*, pp. 213–21.

39. Sifakis, *The Mafia Encyclopedia*, pp. 104–6 and 242–43, presents an excellent account of Dewey's career and the *S. S Normandie* incident.

40. Clarens, *Crime Movies*, pp. 156–57, contains an excellent discussion of the actual facts behind the film, to which I am indebted.

41. Sifakis, *The Mafia Encyclopedia*, p. 106, cites this comment and provides information about the connection between Dewey and Lansky's paint company.

42. For a detailed discussion of these links over the years as both Hollywood and organized crime developed, to which my summary outline of these links is indebted, see: Munn, *The Hollywood Connection;* Otto Friedrich, *The City of Nets: A Portrait of Hollywood in the 1940's* (Berkeley: University of California Press, 1997); Clarens, *Crime Movies*, 166–68 and passim; and Sikafis, *The Mafia Encyclopedia*, entries on "Movie Racketeering," pp. 229–30;" and "John Roselli," pp. 284–85.

43. For a discussion of Mann's film noir production, including *T-Men*, see Andrew Dickos, *A Street with No Name: A History of the Classic American Film Noir* (Lexington: The University Press of Kentucky, 2002), pp. 206–13. For a detailed discussion of *film noir* style, see Foster Hirsch, *Film Noir: The Dark Side of the Screen* (New York: Da Capo, 1983), which contains stupendous photographs; for the history of the concept of *film noir,* closely related to the gangster film in this period, see James Naremore, *More than Night: Film Noir in Its Contexts* (Berkeley: University of California Press, 1998).

44. Allegedly his boss Sam Giancana said of him: "He's perfect for Hollywood. Out there you gotta have class. And Roselli's smooth as fuckin' silk" (cited in Munn, *The Hollywood Connection*, p. 219).

45. One of the most detailed analyses of *Kiss of Death* is to be found in Shadoian's *Dreams and Dead Ends*, pp. 121–33. Shadoian emphasizes the contribution of Ben Hecht (the scriptwriter for *Scarface* and the uncredited writer for *Cry of the City* as well), although I believe his sees much more Christian symbolism in the film than its structure will allow.

46. William Foote Whyte, *Street Corner Society: The Social Structure of an Italian Slum* (Chicago: University of Chicago Press, 1993; 4ᵗʰ rev. ed.). The original first edition of the book only identified the city as "Cornerville," but in the fourth edition (p. 342), Whyte identifies the actual location as the famous North End of Boston, Massachusetts, the scene of the Boston Tea Party.

47. *Death Wish* created a franchise much like *Rocky*, and like the *Rocky* franchise, the five films in the series are of very different quality, generally declining as the story idea degenerates over time. The other four films in the series were: *Death Wish II* (1982; Michael Winner, director); *Death Wish 3* (1985; Michael Winner, director); *Death Wish 4: The Crackdown* (1987; J. Lee Thompson, director); and *Death Wish 5: The Face of Death* (1994; Allan A. Goldstein, director).

48. For critical or historical commentary on these films, see: Clarens, *Crime Movies*, pp. 270–77; or a very detailed discussion of *The Brothers Rico* in Shadoian, *Dreams and Dead Ends*, pp. 250–64.

49. Comparisons between the Mafia and the Roman Empire are not uncommon. In *The Godfather II*, during a conversation between Tom Hagen and Frankie Pentangeli while Frankie is in Federal custody, the claim is made that the Mafia's organization derives from the Roman legions. This is probably the source of the citation in *Above the Law*. In the third episode ("Denial, Anger, Acceptance") of the first year of *The Sopranos*, the claim is advanced by Tony Soprano that the contemporary Mafiosi are the direct descendants of Roman legionnaires.

50. As might be expected, the literature on *The Godfather* trilogy is substantial. Of special interest are Coppola's own comments on the three films plus supplementary materials included in the essential *The Godfather: DVD Collection* (released in 2001); and Michael Schumacher's *Francis Ford Coppola: A Filmmaker's Life* (New York: Crown, 1999). I have relied upon three excellent books for details on the productions of the films, awards, budgets, and the like: Harlan Lebo, *The Godfather Legacy* (New York: Fireside, 1997); Peter Cowie, *The Godfather Book* (London: Faber and Faber, 1997); and Peter Biskind, *"The Godfather" Companion: Everything You Ever Wanted to Know about All Three "Godfather" Movies* (New York: HarperCollins, 1990). For a detailed study of Puzo's novel, see Chris Messenger, *"The Godfather" and American Culture: How the Corleones Became "Our Gang"* (Albany: State University of New York Press, 2002). Nick Browne, ed., *Francis Ford Coppola's "The Godfather" Trilogy* (New York: Cambridge University Press, 2000) contains a number of interesting essays on the productions, the Mafia, music, and the artistic style of the three works. William Malyszko's *"The Godfather": Director, Francis Ford Coppola* (London: York Press, 2001) presents an excellent analysis of the first film in the trilogy, of particular use for students.

51. See Peter Cowie, *"The Godfather" Book*, pp. 28–35. Cowie calls it "Coppola's bible." The single copy of this priceless document is housed in the American Zoetrope Research Library in Rutherford, California. As Cowie notes, "If ever proof were needed that auteurist theory—and practice—was alive and well in North America in 1971, this hefty volume provides it" (p. 35).

52. Cited from an interview in 1972 given to Manny Farber in Browne, ed., *Francis Ford Coppola's "The Godfather" Trilogy*, p. 118.

53. Clarens, *Crime Movies*, p. 277.

54. Cited in Lebo, *The Godfather Legacy*, p. 216.

55. Mario Puzo, *The Godfather* (New York: Signet, 1978), p. 132–33.

56. Ibid., p. 145.

57. For important and significant details about the film's production, see Coppola's own commentary in the DVD collection containing the three films.

58. See Malyszko, *The Godfather*, pp. 25–29, who shows how the film follows quite closely the traditional Hollywood three-act structure or even the more ancient five-part Aristotelian dramatic structure (of which the three-act structure may be considered a variant).

59. See Peter Maas, *The Valachi Papers* (New York: Putnam's, 1968). As Peter Cowie notes in *The Godfather Book* (p. 214), Puzo had complete access to his friend Peter Maas's Valachi documents and no doubt used these documents to good effect in the extraordinary character he created in Frankie Pentangeli.

60. Banfield, *The Moral Basis of a Backward Society*, p. 83. My previously stated reservations about using this book as a scientific description of all Italian culture remain correct, I believe; but Banfield's definition of "amoral familism" certainly describes perfectly the values held by the Mafia of the early decades of the last century.

61. Cited in Lebo, *The Godfather Legacy*, pp. 159–60. A *pezzonovante* is an old Italian slang word for "big shot" and apparently refers originally to a ninety-caliber cannon, a large artillery piece at the time the expression was coined.

62. Dante, *The Inferno*, trans. Henry Wadsworth Longfellow, ed. Peter Bondanella (New York: Barnes & Noble, 2003), p. 100. This statement is found in the canto devoted to the punishment of simony, the sale of church offices for money—an appropriate citation to mark Michael's meeting with a priest about money.

63. In 2003, Random House announced that author Mark Weingardner had been signed to do a sequel to *The Godfather* novel. This could spell the possibility of yet another film in the future, directed by Coppola or by someone else.

64. See Naomi Greene's essay "Family Ceremonies; or, Opera in *The Godfather* Trilogy," in Browne, ed. *Francis Ford Coppola's "The Godfather" Trilogy*, pp. 133–55, to which my own discussion of this film is much indebted.

65. Biskind, *The Godfather Companion*, pp. 46–47, 112, and 177 provides a detailed list of the appearances of oranges in the three films but other than remarking that they were the symbol of evil in the film, he does not note their peculiar relevance to a film about death and violence in Sicily or among Sicilian mobsters. Malyszko, *The Godfather*, p. 42, notes oranges as visual motifs in *The Godfather*.

66. DVD commentary to the film by Coppola.

67. See Peter Cowie, *The Godfather Book*, pp. 114–18, for a discussion of the actual political or economic events alluded to in the film, to which my outline is indebted.

68. For more details, consult some of the following books on the subject: Robert Cornwell, *God's Banker: An Account of the Life and Death of Roberto Calvi* (New York: Dodd, Mead, 1983); Nick Tosches, *Power on Earth* (New York: Arbor House, 1986); and Luigi DiFonzo, *St. Peter's Banker* (New York: Watts, 1983); and Leonardo Cohen and L. Sisti, *Il caso Marcinkus* (Milan: Mondadori, 1991). The details of these interrelated scandals will seem so incredible that they pass even

the boundaries of fiction or cinema. Like the literature on the Kennedy assassinations, the information on these scandals ranges from the fanciful to the factual, interspersed with various conspiracy theories. Running a simple Internet search on any of the principals in these conspiracies will uncover all sorts of strange theories ranging from papal elections influenced by either the Russians or the CIA to ideas that Coppola or Puzo could never have imagined possible.

69. Thompson and Christie, eds., *Scorsese on Scorsese*, p. 147, notes Scorsese's interest in this episode film made up of segments by Federico Fellini, Vittorio De Sica, and Luchino Visconti.

70. Thompson and Christie, eds., *Scorsese on Scorsese*, p. 151. For important discussions of *Goodfellas* and *Casino*, see the following works. The films' sources are two non-fictional accounts written by Nicholas Pileggi: *Wise Guy: Life in a Mafia Family* (New York: Pocket Books, 1987) and *Casino* (New York: Pocket Books, 1995). The screenplays for the two films may be found in Martin Scorsese and Nicholas Pileggi, *Goodfellas;* and Martin Scorsese and Nicholas Pileggi, *Casino* (London: Faber & Faber, 1996). The *Scorsese on Scorsese* volume above contains important statements by the director on his intentions in making the two films. For other criticism, see: the previously cited works on Scorsese in chapter one and especially Friedman, *The Cinema of Martin Scorsese;* Ian Colley, *Goodfellas: Director Martin Scorsese* (London: York Press, 2001); Stella Bruzzi, *Undressing Cinema* (London: Routledge, 1997); Robert Kolker, *A Cinema of Loneliness*, 3rd ed. (New York: Oxford University Press, 2000); and Marilyn Yaquinto, *Pump 'em Full of Lead: A Look at Gangsters on Film* (New York: Twayne, 1998).

71. *Scorsese on Scorsese*, pp. 160–61.

72. Clarens, *Crime Movies*, p. 277.

73. *Casino* is a film based on actual people and historical events, although there have been some liberties taken with the truth by scriptwriters Pileggi and Scorsese. Actually, the two wrote the script before Pileggi's book *Casino* appeared in print, employing Pileggi's research on the Mob in Las Vegas. This is why a title at the opening of the film announces: "Adapted from a true story." For another look at the Mob in Las Vegas, see William F. Roemer's *The Enforcer—Spilotro: The Chicago Mob's Man Over Las Vegas* (New York: Ivy Books, 1994). Roemer is an ex-FBI agent who spent his career chasing Wise Guys, and *The Enforcer* focuses upon the man called Nicky Santoro in the film and played by Joe Pesci—in real life, Anthony "The Ant" Spilotro—and his friend, bookmaker and casino operator for the Mob Frank "Lefty" or "Mr. Inside" Rosenthal who is called Sam "Ace" Rothstein in the film.

74. Perhaps the best outline of how the Mob built Las Vegas is found in an entire chapter devoted to this subject in Capeci's *The Complete Idiot's Guide to the Mafia*. For a more scholarly study of the phenomenon, see Ronald A. Farrell and Carole Case, *The Black Book and the Mob: The Untold Story of the Control of Nevada's Casinos* (Madison: University of Wisconsin Press, 1995), a work that also discusses the role of Tony Spilotro and Frank Rosenthal in the Mob's operations in Las Vegas. One of the most interesting pieces of information provided by

Farrell and Case is a table outlining the ethnic origins of the men inscribed in the Black Book (the list of gangster-associated individuals, such as Spilotro, who were denied access to casinos by Nevada regulators) and the ethnic origins of the regulators themselves. In the first case, 62.9 percent of the people in the Black Book were Italian in origin, followed by 22.6 percent of men who were Jewish in origin. 74.1 percent of the regulators were Anglo-Saxon in origin.

75. Rich Cohen's *Tough Jews: Fathers, Sons, and Gangster Dreams* (New York: Simon & Schuster, 1998), as well as Sergio Leone's brilliant film, *Once Upon a Time in America* (1983), should set the record straight that all historical gangsters in the United States were not Italian American. For stereotypes of blacks, see David Bogle's *Toms, Coons, Mulattoes, Mammies, and Bucks.* A more general discussion of ethnic or racial stereotypes in the movies may be found in Friedman's anthology, *Unspeakable Images: Ethnicity and the American Cinema*, which contains an excellent bibliography on this subject.

5. *Comic Wise Guys: Hollywood Italian Gangsters Yuk It Up*

1. The film received only a single Oscar, given to Supporting Actress Anjelica Huston for her performance as Maerose Prizzi, the daughter of the Mafia don in the film. It was nominated for Best Picture, Best Director, Best Actor, Best Supporting Actor and Actress, Best Adapted Screenplay; Best Costume Design; and Best Editing.

2. Nominated for Best Picture, Best Director, Best Actress, Best Actor, and Best Supporting Actress, the only category in which *Prizzi's Honor* did not win was Best Supporting Actress, the category for which the film received its single Oscar.

6. *Sopranos: The Postmodern Italian* Famiglia

1. For David Chase's discussion of the series, see his introduction to a collection of five scripts from the first three seasons of the program, *The Sopranos: Selected Scripts from Three Seasons—Series Created by David Chase* (New York: Warner Books, 2002), pp. vii–x; or his lengthy discussion with Peter Bogdanovich (who plays the role of Jennifer Melfi's psychoanalyst in the program) included in the DVD collection of the entire first year of the program.

2. An excellent guide to the individual episodes in the first four years of the program may be found in Maurice Yacowar's *The* Sopranos *on the Couch: Analyzing Television's Greatest Series*, 2nd rev. ed. (New York: Continuum, 2003). David Bishop's *Bright Lights, Baked Ziti: The Unofficial, Unauthorized Guide to* The Sopranos (New York: Virgin Books, 2001) covers the first three years of the show. A now somewhat outdated guide to the first two seasons may be found in Stephen Holden, ed., *The New York Times on* The Sopranos (New York: Pocket Books, 2000). David Lavery, ed., *This Thing of Ours: Investigating the Sopranos* (New York: Columbia University Press, 2002) contains a series of academic essays assessing the series from a variety of critical perspectives. Regina Barreca, ed., *A Sit-*

down with the Sopranos: Watching Italian American Culture on T.V.'s Most Talked-About Series (New York: Palgrave MacMillan, 2002) contains essays by various hands, all written from an Italian American perspective that views *The Sopranos* positively and not as a negative image of Italian Americans. Glen O. Gabbard's *The Psychology of the* Sopranos*: Love, Death, Desire, and Betrayal in America's Favorite Gangster Family* (New York: Basic Books, 2002) examines the series from the perspective of psychotherapy. Chris Seay's *The Gospel According to Tony Soprano: An Unauthorized Look into the Soul of TV's Top Mob Boss and His Family* (New York: Tarcher/Putnam, 2002) examines the show from the somewhat surprising vantage point of religion. And finally, David Simon's *Tony Soprano's America: The Criminal Side of the American Dream* (Boulder: Westview Press, 2002) sees *The Sopranos* as proof that something is rotten in America.

3. I have compiled these figures from the cast listings in the following sources: Yacowar's *The Sopranos on the Couch;* the International Movie Data Base on the Internet *(www.imdb.com);* and Lebo's *The Godfather Legacy.* Even admitting some slight errors in my calculations, the drastic changes in percentages from the early gangster films through the 1940s and Coppola to David Chase are perfectly apparent.

4. See Sandra M. Gilbert, "Life with (God)Father," in Barreca, ed., *A Sitdown with the Sopranos*, pp. 11–25, for the complete argument.

5. Umberto Eco, *The Name of the Rose Including the Author's Postscript*, trans. William Weaver (New York: Harvest Books, 1994), pp. 530–31.

6. Eco, ibid., pp. 511–12.

7. Jay Parini, "The Cultural Work of *The Sopranos*," in Barreca, ed., *A Sitdown with the Sopranos*, p. 85.

Select Bibliography

Affron, Mirella. "The Italian-American in American Films, 1918–1971," *Italian Americana* 3 (1977), 232–55.

Albanese, Catherine L., ed. *A Cobbler's Universe: Religion, Poetry, and Performance in the Life of a South Italian Immigrant.* New York: Continuum, 1997.

Baldassare, Angela. *The Great Dictators: Interviews with Filmmakers of Italian Descent.* Toronto: Tuernica, 1999.

Barreca, Regina, ed. *Don't Tell Mama: The Penguin Book of Italian American Writing.* New York: Penguin, 2002.

———. *A Sitdown with the Sopranos: Watching Italian American Culture on T.V.'s Most Talked-About Series.* New York: Palgrave Macmillan, 2002.

Barolini, Helen. *Umbertina.* New York: The Feminist Press of the City University of New York, 1999 (or. ed. 1979).

Bishop, David. *Bright Lights, Baked Ziti: The Sopranos—An Unofficial and Unauthorized Guide.* London: Virgin Books, 2001.

Biskin, Peter. *"The Godfather" Companion: Everything You Ever Wanted to Know about All Three "Godfather" Movies.* New York: HarperCollins, 1990.

Bogle, Donald. *Toms, Coons, Mulattoes, Mammies, and Bucks: An Interpretative History of Blacks in American Films.* 4th rev. ed. New York: Continuum, 2001.

Bona, Mary Jo. *Claiming a Tradition: Italian American Women Writers.* Carbondale: Southern Illinois University Press, 1999.

Bondanella, Peter. "'Christ in Concrete' di Edward Dmytryk e il neorealismo italiano." *Cinema & Cinema* 11 (1984), 9–16.

———. *The Cinema of Federico Fellini.* Princeton: Princeton University Press, 1992.

———. *The Films of Roberto Rossellini.* New York: Cambridge University Press, 1993.

———. "Gli italoamericani e il cinema," in Gian Piero Brunetta, ed., *Storia del cinema mondiale: Gli Stati Uniti.* Volume IIA. Turin: Einaudi, 1999, pp. 911–38.

———. *Italian Cinema: From Neorealism to the Present.* 3rd rev. ed. New York: Continuum, 2001.

Botham, Noel. *Valentino: The First Superstar.* New York: Metro, 2002.

Bower, Eileen, ed. *Biograph Bulletins 1908–1912.* New York: Octagon Books, 1973.

Bret, David. *Valentino: A Dream of Desire.* New York: Robson, 1999.

Browne, Nick, ed. *Francis Ford Coppola's "Godfather" Trilogy.* Cambridge: Cambridge University Press, 2000.

Brownlow, Kevin. *Behind the Mask of Innocence.* Berkeley: University of California Press, 1990.

Brunetta, Gian Piero. "Un popolo di artisti, pugili, mafiosi." *Altreitalie* 6 (1991), 130–39.

Brunette, Peter, ed. *Martin Scorsese: Interviews.* Oxford: University Press of Mississippi, 1999.

Cannistraro, Philip V., ed. *The Italians of New York: Five Centuries of Struggle and Achievement.* New York: The New York Historical Society and the John D. Calandra Italian American Institute, 1999.

Capeci, Jerry. *The Complete Idiot's Guide to the Mafia.* Indianapolis: Alpha, 2002.

Casella, Paola. *Hollywood Italian: Gli italiani nell'America di celluloide.* Milan: Baldini & Castoldi, 1998.

Cavolina, Ellen, and Jane Cavolina Meara. *How to Really Watch "The Godfather": Capos, Cannolis, Consiglieres, and the Truth About the Corleones.* New York: St. Martin's Press, 1991.

Cinema & Cinema. Special issue on "Italianamericans." 11 (1984).

Ciongoli, A. Kenneth, and Jay Parini. *Passage to Liberty: The Story of Italian Immigration and the Rebirth of America.* New York: HarperCollins, 2002.

Ciongoli, A. Kenneth, and Jay Parini, eds. *Beyond "The Godfather": Italian American Writers on the Real Italian American Experience.* Hanover: University Press of New England, 1997.

Clarens, Carlos. *Crime Movies.* New York: DaCapo Press, 1997.

Clarkson, Wesley. *John Travolta: Back in Character.* Woodstock, NY: The Overlook Press, 1997.

———. *Quentin Tarantino: Shooting from the Hip.* Woodstock, NY: The Overlook Press, 1995.

Cohn, Nik. "Saturday Night's Big Bang." *New York* (8 December 1997), 32–36, 96.

———. "Tribal Rites of the New Saturday Night." *New York* 9, #23 (7 June 1976), 31–43.

Colley, Iain. *GoodFellas: Director, Martin Scorsese.* London: York Press, 2001.

Cooper, Stephen, ed. *The John Fante Reader.* New York: Morrow, 2002.

Cowie, Peter. *"The Godfather" Book.* London: Faber and Faber, 1997.

D'Acierno, Pellegrino, ed. *The Italian American Heritage: A Companion to Literature and Film.* New York: Garland, 1999.

De Rosa, Tina. *Paper Fish.* New York: The Feminist Press of the City University of New York, 1996 (or. ed. 1980).

DeSalvo, Louise and Edvige Giunta, eds. *The Milk of Almonds: Italian American Women Writers on Food and Culture.* New York: The Feminist Press of CUNY, 2002.

Dickos, Andrew. *Street with No Name: A History of the Classic American Film Noir.* Lexington: The University Press of Kentucky, 2002.

Di Donato, Pietro. *Christ in Concrete.* New York: Signet, 1993.

———. *Naked Author.* New York: Phaedra, 1970.

Ets, Marie Hall. *Rosa: The Life of an Italian Immigrant.* 2nd ed. Madison: University of Wisconsin Press, 1999 (or. ed. 1970).

Franzina, Emilio. *Dall'Arcadia in America: Attività letteraria ed emigrazione transoceanica in Italia (1850–1940).* Turin: Edizioni della Fondazione Giovanni Agnelli. 1996.

Friedman, Lawrence S. *The Cinema of Martin Scorsese.* New York: Continuum, 1998.

Friedman, Lester D., ed. *Unspeakable Images: Ethnicity and the American Cinema.* Urbana: University of Illinois Press, 1991.

Gambino, Richard. *Blood of My Blood: The Dilemma of the Italian-Americans.* Toronto: Guernica, 1998.

———. *Vendetta: The True Story of the Largest Lynching in U. S. History.* Toronto: Guernica, 2000.

Gardaphé, Fred L. *Italian Signs, American Streets: The Evolution of Italian American Narrative.* Durham: Duke University Press, 1996.

Geduld, Harry. "'Christ in Concrete': dal romanzo al film." *Cinema & Cinema* 11 (1984), 17–25.

Gevinson, Alan, ed. *American Film Institute Catalog—Within Our Gates: Ethnicity in American Feature Films, 1911–1960.* Berkeley: University of California Press, 1997.

Giordano, Paolo A., and Anthony Julian Tamburri, eds. *Beyond the Margin: Readings in Italian Americana.* Madison: Fairleigh Dickinson University Press, 1998.

Hanson, Patricia King, ed. *The American Film Institute Catalog of Motion Pictures Produced in the United States, Feature Films, 1911–1920.* 2 vols. Los Angeles: University of California Press, 1988.

Holden, Stephen, ed. *"The New York Times" on "The Sopranos".* New York: ibooks, 2000.

Hostert, Anna Camaiti, and Anthony Julian Tamburri, eds. *Scene italoamericane: Rappresentazioni cinematografiche degli italiani d'America.* Rome: Luca Sessella Editore, 2002. English ed. *Screening Ethnicity: Cinematic Representations of Italian Americans in the United States.* West Lafayette: Bordighera, 2003.

Kellman, Steven G., ed. *Perspectives on "Raging Bull."* New York: G. K. Hall, 1994.

Kelley, Kitty. *His Way: The Unauthorized Biography of Frank Sinatra.* New York: Bantam, 1987.

Keyser, Les, and Barbara Keyser. *Hollywood and the Catholic Church: The Image of Roman Catholicism in American Movies.* Chicago: Loyola University Press, 1984.

Kuntz, Tom, and Phil Kuntz, ed. *The Sinatra Files: The Secret FBI Dossier.* New York: Three Rivers Press, 2000.

LaGumina, Salvatore J., ed. *Wop!: A Documentary History of Anti-Italian Discrimination in the United States.* San Francisco: Straight Arrow Books, 1973.

Laurino, Maria. *"Were You Always an Italian?": Ancestors and Other Icons of Italian America.* New York: Norton, 2000.

Lavery, David, ed. *This Thing of Ours: Investigating "The Sopranos."* New York: Columbia University Press, 2002.

Lebo, Harlan. *The Godfather Legacy.* New York: Fireside, 1997.

Lee, Spike, with Lisa Jones. *"Do the Right Thing": A Spike Lee Joint.* New York: Simon & Schuster, 1989.

Lees, Gene. *Singers and the Song II.* New York: Oxford University Press, 1999.

Leider, Emily. *Dark Lover: The Life and Death of Rudolph Valentino.* New York: Farrar Straus & Giroux, 2003.

Levy, Emanuel. *All about Oscar: The History and Politics of the Academy Awards.* New York and London: Continuum, 2003.

Levy, Shawn. *Rat Pack Confidential.* New York: Anchor, 1998.

Lourdeaux, Lee. *Italian and Irish Filmmakers in America: Ford, Capra, Coppola, and Scorsese.* Philadelphia: Temple University Press, 1990.

Macks, Jon. *Fuhgeddaboutit: How to Badda Boom, Badda Bing, and Find Your Inner Mobster.* New York: Simon & Schuster, 2001.

Mangione, Jerre. *Mount Allegro: A Memoir of Italian American Life.* Syracuse: Syracuse University Press, 1998 (or. ed. 1989).

Mangione, Jerre, and Ben Morreale. *La Storia: Five Centuries of the Italian American Experience.* New York: HarperCollins, 1993.

Malyszko, William. *"The Godfather": Director Francis Ford Coppola.* London: York Press, 2002.

Messenger, Chris. *"The Godfather" and American Culture: How the Corleones Became "Our Gang."* Albany: State University of New York Press, 2002.

Munden, Kenneth W., ed. *The American Film Institute Catalog of Motion Pictures Produced in the United States, Feature Films, 1921–1930.* 2 vols. New York: R. R. Bowker, 1971.

Munn, Michael. *The Hollywood Connection: The True Story of Organized Crime in Hollywood.* London: Robson Books, 1993.

Mustazza, Leonard. *Ol' Blue Eyes: A Frank Sinatra Encyclopedia.* Westport, CT: Greenwood Press, 1998.

———. *Sinatra, An Annotated Bibliography, 1939–1998.* Westport, CT: Greenwood Press, 1999.

———, ed. *Frank Sinatra and Popular Culture: Essays on an American Icon.* Westport, CT: Greenwood Press, 1998.

———, and Steven Petkov, eds. *The Frank Sinatra Reader.* New York: Oxford University Press, 1995.

Naremore, James. *More than Night: Film Noir in Its Contexts.* Berkeley: University of California Press, 1998.

Niver, Kemp R., ed. *Biograph Bulletins 1896–1908.* Los Angeles: Artisan Press, 1971.

Pacini, M., P. Gastaldo, and D. Arrigotti, eds. *Integrato metropolitano: New York: Chicago, Torino—tre volti dell'emigrazione italiana.* Turin: Edizioni della Fondazione Giovanni Agnelli, 1982.

Peary, Gerald, ed. *Little Caesar.* Madison: University of Wisconsin Press, 1981.

Pileggi, Nicholas. *Wiseguy: Life in a Mafia Family.* New York: Pocket Books, 1985.

Praz, Mario. *The Flaming Heart: Essays on Crashaw, Machiavelli, and Other Studies in the Relations between Italian and English Literature from Chaucer to T. S. Eliot.* New York: Norton, 1973 (or. ed. 1958).

Puzo, Mario. *The Family.* New York: ReganBooks, 2001.

———. *The Fortunate Pilgrim.* New York: Ballantine, 1998.

———. *The Godfather.* New York: Signet, 1978.

———. *The Godfather Papers and Other Confessions.* New York: Putnam's, 1972.

———. *The Last Don.* New York: Random House, 1996.

———. *Omerta.* New York: Random House, 2000.

Quirk, Lawrence J., and William Schoell. *The Rat Pack: Neon Nights and the Kings of Cool.* New York: Avon, 1998. Original ed. Lawrence J. Quirk, *The Rat Pack: The Hey-Hey Days of Frank and the Boys.* Dallas: Taylor Publishing, 1998.

Reid, Martin A., ed. *Spike Lee's "Do the Right Thing."* New York: Cambridge University Press, 1997.

Richards, David A. J. *Italian American: The Racializing of an Ethnic Identity.* New York: New York University Press, 1999.

Rucker, Allen. *The Sopranos: A Family History.* New York: New American Library, 2000.

Schatz, Thomas. *Hollywood Genres: Formulas, Filmmaking, and the Studio System.* New York: Random House, 1981.

Schumacher, Michael. *Francis Ford Coppola: A Filmmaker's Life.* New York: Crown, 1999.

Scorsese, Martin with Nicholas Pileggi. *GoodFellas.* Ed. David Thompson. London: Faber and Faber, 1990.

Seay, Chris. *The Gospel According to Tony Soprano: An Unauthorized Look into the Soul of TV's Top Mob Boss and His Family.* New York: Tarcher Putnam, 2002.

Serra, Ilaria. *Immagini di un immaginario: L'Emigrazione Italiana negli Stati Uniti fra i due secoli (1890–1924).* Treviso: Cierre edizioni, 1998.

Shadoian, Jack. *Dreams and Dead Ends: The American Gangster/Crime Film.* Cambridge: MIT Press, 1977.

Shulman, Irving. *Valentino.* New York: Pocket Books, 1968.

Sifakis, Carl. *The Mafia Encyclopedia.* New York: Facts on File, 1987.

Simon, David. *Tony Soprano's America: The Criminal Side of the American Dream.* Boulder: Westview Press, 2002.

Talese, Gay. *Honor Thy Father.* New York: Ballantine Books, 1992.

Tamburri, Anthony Julian, Paolo A. Giordano, and Fred L. Gardaphé, eds. *From the Margin: Writings in Italian Americana.* W. Lafayette: Purdue University Press, 2000.

Tarantino, Quentin. *Pulp Fiction: A Quentin Tarantino Screenplay.* New York: Hyperion, 1994.

Thomas, Victoria. *Hollywood's Latin Lovers: Latin, Italian and French Men Who Make the Screen Smolder.* Santa Monica: Angel City Press, 1998.

Thompson, David, and Ian Christie. *Scorsese on Scorsese.* London: Faber & Faber, 1996.

Tonelli, Bill, ed. *The Italian American Reader: A Collection of Outstanding Fiction, Memoirs, Journalism, Essays, and Poetry.* Foreword by Nick Tosches. New York: Morrow, 2003.

Torgovnick, Marianna De Marco. *Crossing Ocean Parkway.* Chicago: University of Chicago Press, 1994.

Tosches, Nick. *Dino: Living High in the Dirty Business of Dreams.* New York: Delta, 1992.

Tricarico, Donald. "Guido: Fashioning an Italian-American Youth Style." *Journal of Ethnic Studies* 10 (1991), 41–66.

Walker, Alexander. *Rudolph Valentino.* New York: Penguin, 1977.

Warshow, Robert. *The Immediate Experience: Movies, Comics, Theatre and Other Aspects of Popular Culture.* Cambridge: Harvard University Press, 2001.

Weiss, Marion. *Martin Scorsese: A Guide to References and Resources.* Boston: G. K. Hall, 1987.

Yacowar, Maurice. "*The Sopranos*" on the Couch: Analyzing Television's Greatest Series. 2nd rev. ed. New York: Continuum, 2003.

Yaquinto, Marilyn. *Pump 'em Full of Lead: A Look at Gangsters on Film.* New York: Twayne, 1998.

Zehme, Bill. *The Way You Wear Your Hat: Frank Sinatra and the Lost Art of Livin'.* New York: Harper, 1997.

Index